The Sullivan Families of
Fall River and Bristol Co. MA

From the Beara Peninsula of Ireland
to America
Descendants of Immigrants born 1845 to 1870
Volume VI

By Dr. Edward F. Foley

The Sullivan Families
of Fall River and Bristol Co. MA

From the Beara Peninsula of Ireland
to America
Descendants of Immigrants born 1845 to 1870
Volume VI

Other Books by the author published by Heritage Books, Westminster, Maryland:

The Descendants of Rev. Joseph Rhea of Ireland (1996)
The Descendants of Matthew 'The Rebel' Rhea of Ireland and Scotland (2000)
The Prestons of Walnut Grove Virginia (2006)

http://www.heritagebooks.com

Published 2017 by
Heritage Capital Inc
4790 N. Via De La Granja
Tucson, AZ 85718

ISBN-13:
978-1541359383

ISBN-10:
1541359380

DEDICATION

This book is dedicated to my father whose Irish roots in Fall River, Massachusetts date back to 1848. Although he was among the first of his family to leave Fall River, first in the Navy, then to Notre Dame with the Fighting Irish and later in Government Service, he kept the connections to the Fall River and Corky Row alive through our yearly summer visits to reconnect with our family there. The Irish character of the neighborhoods and the residents' love of their Irish roots have kept many of us longing for the old country as though it was only a short time since our families made the journey. Our research led to dad's eventual attainment of dual U.S.- Irish citizenship.

ACKNOWLEDGMENTS

Execution of the research has many to thank. I especially want to acknowledge the work of Peggy Guinen who spend so many hours at the Fall River Public Library searching the Fall River papers for Sullivan Obituaries. These really helped to apply color to the lives of those families. Researchers Nancy Coray and Jane Sullivan who each contributed not only family connections, but stories and background on the city of Fall River.

Finally, I want to recognize the invaluable work of Riobard O'Dwyer, the Eyeries, Ireland family researcher who has been instrumental in gathering and preserving the records of the families of the Beara Peninsula. Without his work, I would not have found my family in Ireland, nor been able to connect so many families of Fall River back to this area of County Cork.

FOREWORD

The experience of many researchers who have pursued the trail of our Irish ancestors, is a mixture of hope, frustration, confusion and sometimes elation.   The Famine Irish came to the U.S. by the millions and found life far different than home.   Coming primarily from agricultural roots, with the English hand strong over their right to worship, learn, work, etc. the life in boisterous, burgeoning cities of America held both promise and their own hardships.   Although they came in great numbers, their general poverty at the time of immigration meant a paucity of records both in Ireland and in their adopted country.

Two family patterns have conspired to create problems for researchers trying to trace their Irish familes.   The Irish immigrants tended to settle in large numbers in limited geographic areas, like Boston, or New York, or in some special important cases, Butte, MT, Fall River, MA or Houghton Co. MI.   The other pattern - of Irish naming customs repeating the previous generation's names - compounded the challenge of connecting any particular individual in a particular family in the mass of Irish settlers with similar names.

Like many researchers I started with what was known in the family and began to verify what I heard and built the tree from there.   I found it interesting that my father, aunts and uncles, all grandchildren of the original Irish immigrants, knew little about the old country.   As they told the stories, their parents and grandparents were working hard to make a life in America and did not look back.   This left me working backwards in the records of Fall River, and Bristol Co. Massachusetts putting the family tree together leaf by leaf.   Along the way I identified many other Sullivan families who were not direct ancestors.

During my research I became familiar with the work of genealogist Riobard O'Dwyer of Eyeries, Co. Cork Ireland.   Mr. O'Dwyer has meticulously combed through the parish records of the churches of the Beara Peninsula of County Cork and published the records in six volumes over 20 years.   It was on this Beara Peninsula where I found many of my ancestors using Mr. O'Dwyer's work to guide me through those records.

One method of discovering the origin of ancestors from Ireland, it to use the naturalization records.   To that end I spent a number of days at the Massachusetts State Archives in Boston.   The archives house the Final Naturalization Applications which for many years listed the origin of the applicant in their native country.   I was trolling through the 1880's and decided to record every Sullivan I came across.   To my surprise, 88% of the Sullivans who were applying, noted their birthplace as the Beara Peninsula of County Cork Ireland.   This is where my Foley family originated, and where we thought my Sullivan line was from.   The concentration of Sullivans from this part of Ireland, combined with the availability of the Church records through Mr. O'Dwyer inspired me to complete as many Fall River Sullivan family connections as possible, and tie as many immigrants to their ancestral homes as possible.   This became a researcher's guide to the many similar Sullivan names found.

Ed Foley
2017

INTRODUCTION

This work is a collection of the available records concerning the Sullivans of Fall River and Bristol County Massachusetts. The records include the birth, marriage and death vital records of Bristol Co. Massachusetts, the Federal and State census records, the national immigration and naturalization records, newspaper stories and obituaries, personal letters, and in some cases the Catholic parish and Civil records of Ireland.

The individuals associated with the records have been identified and carefully assembled into their family groups. The families have been connected and each line was traced to its earliest ancestor. In many cases, the families were successfully traced to the Parish records of the Catholic Church in Ireland and in some cases multiple generations were found in the Irish records.

Many Sullivan families members living in Fall River shared the same names. This makes finding records of a single individual a special challenge. The sheer number of Sullivan individuals identified in Bristol County MA created issues to organize the 12,258 individuals and 3,369 marriages. The author arranged these family lines in birth order of the earliest ancestor who was identified, and further by those initial ancestors who were born on the Beara Peninsula of County Cork, Ireland and those whose births were elsewhere or not specifically uncovered. Further, due to publishing limitations, each volume of families could not exceed 600 pages. This necessitated producing 3 volumes of research to cover all descendants of initial Sullivan ancestors from 1760 to 1870.

The names have been fully indexed with an index to the full 6 volumes contained in the final Volume VI. In order to identify a specific individual the names are listed with the pages associated with the name. Common names such as John or Mary Sullivan will of course show many pages on which these names appear. The names of associated maternal lines or that of a spouse will allow the reader to more quickly find a particular individual or family group.

In an effort to maintain the focus on the Sullivan family, for the marriages of Sullivan women, their marriage and one generation of children are shown in these works, although many generations may have been uncovered. Some exceptions, i.e. where future generations again marry into the Sullivan clan, have been made.

There are a number of conventions used in the book. For those individual for whom a birth date or christening date had not been found, one was estimated. For those whose names appear with variations of their surname (i.e. O'Sullivan, OSullivan etc), Sullivan is the one used here in the main record, unless a variation is consistently used after the family arrives in America. Many individuals used both their Gaelic clan names and the adopted 'Sullivan' name in Irish records. For instance, the families of the Sullivan clan Uhoni, meaning Green in Gaelic, sometimes used the name Sullivan or sometimes Greene or Green. If they used Green in America, they appear as Green in these volumes. When the Irish clan name is known, it will be shown in parentheses before the surname as with '(Vallig) Sullivan'.

Each chapter initially listed the names of the ancestors born about a particular date, either on the Beara Peninsula or 'Possibly on the Beara'. Each individual bears a record number. The chapter then proceeds to go down the list of individuals outlining their marriages and descendants with each new individual also numbered.

The descendants are numbered using a common genealogical numbering system called the Modified Register System or NGSQ System.

Every effort has been made to be as accurate as possible when assembling the families. Errors in the source records confound the effort, but errors in transcription, or assumptions based on the association of individuals with families may also have led to errors. The author welcomes corrections so that future editions can reflect these changes. Changes should be sent to DrEdFoley@hotmail.com or to the author at 4790 N Via De La Granja, Tucson, AZ 85718.

During the accumulation of information about both life in Fall River Massachusetts, and life of Fall River residents previously led in Ireland, two articles came to the attention of the researcher which poignantly described each. To put these centuries in perspective, these two articles are reprinted here to set the stage.

LIFE IN THE TENEMENT HOUSES IN FALL RIVER
[From the Boston MA Sunday Herald, 1 July 1879.]

The Fall River mill operative earns, or receives for his work, from 60 cents to $1.75 per day, perhaps in a few instances a little more, and, in proportion to all employed, there are but few hands that average much above $1 per day. The greater portion of the workers are of nationalities having ways differing from those peculiar to the Yankee, and, while their home habits and manners and customs in housekeeping are not generally to be classed as expensive, the fact that many of them are well known to indulge in stimulants, in some form, presupposes the existence of outlay, more or less considerable for its supply, and consequently of some recklessness of expenditure. The question naturally suggests itself, upon learning the amount of their income, "How do these people live, and what sort of homes can they furnish and support upon such sums earned?" If these questions were answered in detail, and the truth was fairly understood in our communities, many a New England housewife, who has heretofore fancied her lot one of peculiar drudgery, would offer thanks for her exalted condition in comparison, and find her sympathies fully enlisted in the cause of her less fortunate neighbors.

Not that there are no comfortable homes among the operatives: there are many such; many, also, more than comfortable, having luxuries...flowers and pictures, and with musical instruments and fancy articles at hand. But such are the exception.

TENEMENT HOUSES

Every mill in the Border City has, usually standing near its own structure, a number of tenement houses, grouped in blocks of six, eight or even more apartments. Besides this property of the mills, the enterprise of citizens - in some cases operatives themselves - has provided other blocks or small collections of tenements, and these are scattered about within city limits, wherever eligible sites are to be found, or the wants of operatives may be met. In some instances, as many as twenty apartments are to be found in a block, varying from four to six pieces or rooms each. The operatives marry young, almost invariably, for reasons which will be hereafter given, and begin housekeeping usually upon the arrival of the children, if they do not immediately after the marriage ceremony. Large families are not unusual, if they are not the rule, and as a matter of course the tenement houses are constructed to meet the best known wants of the class. Usually the tenement consists of a kitchen, the most commodious room in the house, which is also a dining room and living room, a sink closet, and from two to four sleeping rooms, generally small and made on an economical principle so far as space is concerned. The houses are of wood, two or two and a half stories if the roof be flat, or, if a pitched roof is used, the attic is fully utilized, and, in the case of a four tenement house of the latter kind, each family would have part of its sleeping rooms in the attic. So much for general construction.

THE FAMILY

Before alluding further to home life in these tenements, a glance at family life in the mills will illustrate the matter. It often happens that a whole family is employed in the mill, the father, the mother, and one, two or even more of their children. In case all the members are thus employed, of course the home is empty during the day or working hours, and whether it is a palace or a hovel becomes a matter of no moment until the steam whistle announces the close of the working day. In the mill the wife works as hard in her way, perhaps, as any member of the family, certainly as steadily, and, when the mill day is over, mark how her duties become terribly onerous! Upon reaching home supper is to be swallowed - there isn't room for much more of regulation or ceremony about it - and then, while the rest of the family recreate in their own way, all there is of housekeeping is performed by the wife, in some matters, however, occasionally assisted by her children if they are old enough. There will be no time the next morning for cooking and preparing breakfast - it must be looked out for overnight. Dinner is to be taken to the mill, and that must consist of materials substantial enough to support the heavy drag of the day; consequently, these must be cooked during the evening. Bread and meat and simple pie are staples, and in some form must be prepared; While the kettle is bubbling, or the fry pan sizzling, or the oven baking, or all together are sending out their heats, the washing of all the bed and personal clothing for the household may be performed; the old man's pants mended, or the younger children's clothes made or repaired by the mother. If one or two of the brood are sick or ailing, they may also receive attention at the time. With aching bones and weary eyelids, night after night, for heavy weeks and months, the wife and mother toils thus for her family, living a life the like of which no southern slave ever dreamed about, so far as its groveling drudgery is concerned.

MEANS AND ENDS

To bed at last, and for the females described, for as short a night as is known to the workers of any class, although the members of the family not required to work evenings can suit their inclinations regarding bedtime. The mill demands an early visit, work is to be prepared for, the house is locked up for the day, and, dinner pail in hand, the family are off to the work rooms to pursue the endless round.

It is to meet the wants of the people thus employed, that these tenement houses are offered and designed as specified. Not always are they built upon swampy lands, and in times before the present beneficial city water works, the drainage and system of wells was fearful to contemplate. But usually the buildings are well placed and the uneven nature of the ground in these parts renders the chances of good building sites favorable to the occupants of the tenement houses.

Besides these houses of the mills, which provide homes for perhaps one-half or a little more of the mill population, the fact that other tenement houses are prepared for these people has been stated above. The tenements thus provided differ little in construction or character from those built by the mills, except, perhaps, more eligible sites are selected, and the worker may be gratified by the opportunity to get further away from the mills. In some places cottage houses are erected by those outside parties, containing two tenements each, precisely alike in all their features, having a little garden back of the house and a bit of a yard in front. Wherever possible, a few fowls are kept by the operatives, occasionally even the cellar being devoted to the purpose; but the mill men look out sharply for any offence against good sanitary regulations in the housekeeping arrangements of the families. No pigs are kept; so one element of an offensive neighborhood is avoided.

RULES AND REGULATIONS

Often the mill men insist upon workers occupying their tenement houses, that is, if sufficient tenements can be afforded, and instances are not wanting where families violating this rule have been discharged to make room for others willing to occupy the company's property. The English workers like to select their tenements; some of the older spinners own little places or occupy homesteads partly paid for by themselves and which they hope to clear by and by. Many of these are nicely furnished, like the average New England mechanic's house, and a piano, cabinet organ, or pretty figured woolen carpets are not infrequently met with in these abodes. Sewing machines are found by the hundreds in these homes, and often, where there are no carpets, home-made braided rugs are neatly arranged on the floors, and genuine comfort is evident in every detail of the housekeeping. But the condition of heavily worked bodies is always and everywhere present. It may here be stated that the mills close at mid-afternoon on Saturday, and housekeeping duties are pursued at a lively rate thereafter until the week closes, and a great deal of work is done on Sunday. The atmosphere of the mills is hot and full of subtle influences from heat and electricity combined. The regulations connected with many forms of the work render rigid application necessary, and, under those of the Fall River mills, it is impossible for a man to leave his post for hours sometimes, for any purpose whatever, however personally important, without censure, and discharge in case of repetition of the offence. The heat, and the absorbing nature of the attention required to the work, is terribly depressing, and it often happens that a man, dragging himself home from his looms, finds himself unable to do anything until a season of rest is allowed. In this condition he throws himself upon his doorstep, and finds he cannot eat, which he must do in order to work. He sends for a pail of beer-ale from the nearest dealer's cellar and stimulates his appetite. The heat influences of the mills referred to act noticeably and powerfully upon the systems of the young people employed, tending to mature them, and to these agencies must be largely attributed the early marriages among the operatives, which prove both a blessing and a heavy yoke upon them.

HERDING TOGETHER

It may be found that a man and wife, their three children, and a married daughter and her husband constitute the family in one of these tenements, where there are, perhaps, only three sleeping rooms beside the living room above described. The poor fellows get about 60 cents a day - the lowest class of workers - and children of all classes from 22 cents to 40 cents. Sometimes a father at 60 cents, the wife mopping the mill floors at indifferent wages, and their son, a "back boy" at 22 cents daily, throw all their earnings together. The rent of these tenements -both those belonging to the mills and otherwise -ranges from $4.50 to $7 or $8 per month, having been largely reduced in recent times. No wonder, perhaps, that the lower classes herd together as they do, and cram these places in every nook and cranny.

Before taking possession of one of these mill tenements the operative is required, by many mills, to sign an agreement that he will vacate the premises within 24 hours in case of differences arising between himself and the managers of the mill; and it is tacitly understood, even if this agreement is not signed, that upon these terms he occupies the house, and thus it will be seen how striking workmen are held at disadvantage by the mill people. But the better class of workers, and those making the best wages, keep aloof, as has been detailed above, from company tenements, and live as far as possible on a more independent basis.

COMPENSATIONS

But, even under these circumstances, it is possible for the operative and his family to forge ahead in worldly condition, and, when all can and do earn, something is often saved in the aggregate. With many families, however, the utmost endeavor will only suffice for the barest existence, especially if sickness occurs. Little can be spared from the present bill of fare of the mill worker. Whatever is left from his dinner, carried to the mill, must inevitably be thrown away. The air of the mill rooms and the confinement of the pails render the food worthless and, sour and often stinking, it is invariably thrown away at the close of the day's work, however fresh and sweet it may have been in the morning. When a man first takes a wife he often hires a room in the family of some relative of the couple, and, while he and his wife continue their mill life, the latter cooks their food at the common kitchen stove. When the baby comes it is put out to nurse, while the father and mother go on earning for their own and the added mouths, When two children or three have arrived, the oldest takes care of the youngest until one or more of the brood becomes old enough to enter the mills, when the youngest are again put out to nurse during the day. The mother stays in the mill until the number of little ones more than counterbalances by the cost of nursing what she can earn for their support, and then she leaves and takes home charge in person. If sickness occurs among the little ones, the mother, of course, remains at home, and that is why female help in the mills is more uncertain than that of the males.

Fall River Herald, August 16, 1933 (Transcribed by Liz Sullivan 1998)
FALL RIVER BOY WRITES OF HIS VISIT TO IRELAND: John D. Hurley Looks Up His Ancestry in the Old Principality of Beara; Experience of Rare Interest to Thousands of Irish Extraction.

Of keen interest to all Fall River people, and especially to the many thousands of Irish extraction, is the accompanying communication of John Doran Hurley, a native Fall River boy whose career started in the field of journalism in this city and switched off to other lofty heights in the city of New York.

The dreams of a lifetime came true when Mr. Hurley was given an opportunity to visit Ireland this summer. He showed good sense and honesty of purpose, when he resolved on "hoofing" it through Ireland as much as possible, and getting into the hearts and homes of the humble, honest people in the rural districts so that he could truthfully depict conditions as they appeared to him. Looking up his ancestry in the old principality of Beara he had interesting experiences which he describes as follows:--

"Although a sincere, a kindly and a hearty welcome has met me every inch of the road I am travelling about Ireland, yet more than anything else, as the Steamer Princess Beara sailed up Bantry Bay to Castletown, Bearhaven, I felt I was coming home. It was the countryside where my father was born and his father's father before him. Deeply across the generations came the half instinctive feeling of recognition, of a place known through some spiritual kinship, even if my corporal eyes had never seen its hills and waters. Yet I came to Bearhaven fully armed with a hundred stories from this man and that, of Allihies and the copper mines, of

Garnish, Bear Island, Dursey and the "Bull, Cow and Calf," of Hungry Hill and Knockora of Dunboy Castle and Brandyhall Bridge. I knew that I should find, as I did, the Irish names that were most familiar to me in Fall River, the Sullivans, the Harringtons, Murphys and Sheas.

We were a small and oddly assorted group on the little steamer coming up from Bantry: two very interesting nuns of the Order of Mercy from Bantry hospital; a stoker from H. M. S. Emerald, a naval sailor, Sullivan, from Bear Island, going home on leave; and myself, the Yankee--the "returned Yankee" to most people for I seemed to know too much about Ireland and to fall to easily into the ways and speech of the country to be a Yankee born.

Sister Benedict and Sister Evangelist were going on retreat at the Mercy convent in Castletown. They were eagerly interested in what I could tell them of Mount Saint Mary's and the Mercy Order in Fall River. That I had an acquaintance with a number of Sisters of Mercy in the Fall River diocese gave us a ready and certain kinship and we became great friends. They stood by the rail with me, flanked by Sullivan the Sailor, as we passed Adrigole Harbor. They pointed out rugged Hungry Hill standing gauntly against the sky, Roancarrig (Seal Rock) lighthouse and Corrig-a-Waddhera or the Dog rock, with the breakers coloring its half hidden bulk with angry white foam.   Soon afterwards we came into the harbor of Beara with Bear Island on our left, the mainland to the right. One by one Sullivan the Sailor picked out the landmarks for the nuns and myself, Lonarth Point at the eastern tip of the island, the peak of Maulin, Hungry Hill, Waterfall, where the Presentation nuns have a house, Filane and Millcove, just before Castletown, Beara.

On Bear Island's hills martellos stood against the sky, romantic towers. Round towers, Sullivan the Sailor called them; but in truth they dated back not to old Pagan times, not even to the years when O'Sullivan Beara ruled Beara and Bantry. Rather they were the signal towers erected to warn of possible French invasion in the latter part of the 18th century and placed on every lofty summit commanding a view of Bantry Bay from Dursey to Bear Islands. Then soon it was that the Princess Beara docked at the Castletown landing at Barracks Point. Our little group parted, the nuns to their retreat convent, and Sullivan to wait for the military boat to take him out to his home on Bear Island.

At Brandyhall Bridge According to the terms of the treaty, England retains naval rights to certain valuable sea defenses on the Saorstat or Free State coast, Bear Island among them.   Every shop front in Castletown bore its message of the Irish at home in Fall River as I walked up the principal street: Sullivan, Harrington; Sullivan Harrington; Sullivan, Harrington, Shea; Sullivan, Cahill, Lowney, McGrath; then another row of alternate Sullivans and Harringtons.   I come unannounced and found lodgings with Mrs. McGrath, the draper, who has two sons priests, one in Auburn, New York, one in Australia.   But I was not long unannounced. I had soon fallen into the kindly Irish habit of giving "good morning" or "good evening" to everyone I passed on the street or the road. And it was a chorus of "good evening, sir's" that followed me down the town.

I had a particular destination on my first walk in the town and I soon found it; the Brandyhall bridge, crossing a salt water inlet, with the old Brandyhall school beside it, the school of many of Fall River's older citizens. A lad was leaning over the bridge as I crossed it, watching the white swans on the water below.   I gave him a "good evening" and asked him the name of the bridge. "'Tis Mill River bridge," said he, "and that's the old Mill River school above." I was a bit taken back, but I had reason to know my Castletown, Beara. "It wouldn't be called the Brandyhall bridge, would it?" I suggested. "Why, it would now," he said in surprise, "'Tis the old name. I came near forgetting that."

My premise was confirmed then by a passerby. John Houlihan, the parish clerk--"Shawn-a-clark" I was to hear him called from then on. He proved a valuable store of information for a stranger, quickly securing and eagerly loaning (although he knew neither my name nor my address in town) a copy of the Ivernian Historical Journal with an excellent article about Donal O'Sullivan Beare and the seige of Dunboy.

Some Familiar Names And in a lone little farm house towards Clougheen, two tiny lassies leap to their feet at their mother's injunction, to sing, in sweet high voices, a tender song about Castletown Beara which, their father proudly said, is the work of our own "Man About Town." From my meeting with Shawn-a-clark it was Fall River all the way. Everyone had a brother or sister, an uncle or an aunt, a son or daughter, or, at the least, cousins, on Broadway, Third street or Highland avenue. When I stopped for postcards at D. D. Harrington's shop and library, Mrs. Harrington asked if I had known her uncle, Cornelius Sullivan, long alderman from Ward Four. And she and her daughter spoke with reminiscent pleasure of many visits paid them by Fall River people. Along the street the names of Fall River men who had visited Castletown or had returned for a visit were mentioned. Since they had come from Bearhaven across the sea, the memory of their coming had been kept, whether it was one year or twenty. So I heard of the visit of the Most Reverend James E. Cassidy, D. D., Apostolic Administrator; of James A. Burke, Jr., James H. Mahoney; Dr. T. P. Sullivan and Dr. Gerald Sullivan. I heard more directly of Dr. T. P. Sullivan the next day when I tramped the road over Knockgour to Allihies. There I met his nephew, Philip O'Sullivan, whose enterprise in the fish industry had given him the title in Beara of "The Mackerel King." At Allihies I saw the abandoned shafts of the copper mines, closed now for the past five or six years. It was the Portsmouth coal mines that brought so many Bearhaveners to Fall River years ago in another closing of the Allihies shafts; although the Portsmouth mines are now but a memory. At Allihies Timothy O'Sullivan, the master, took me into the old church, built in 1845; the church (St. Michael's) in which many of our older citizens of Fall River were baptized and heard Mass. It was the O'Sullivan master, too, who gave me the names, and directions to the homes of the older men of the district from whom I might possibly learn one of the objects of my search, the farm of my grandfather and grandmother Hurley, the place where my father and the father of the mayor, Joseph L. Hurley, were born. Before long it seemed a hopeless task. At Castletown they assured me that there had been no Hurleys at Allihies or Clougheen, the village I sought within any living man's time. Two families in the district, it was agreed, bore my grandmother's name, Toomey; one just outside the town at Cahergariff, the other near "The Crosshouse" where one road goes to Allihies and one to Clougheen. Mr. Toomey at Cahergariff came quickly in from the fields when he heard of my coming, but he was not, himself, old enough to trace a possible connection back in the 1850's. Regretfully he sent me on my way to Toomey the postman at the Crosshouse, but not before he had urged on me (and it took no great urging) some mugs of fresh milk sweet from the "keeler." He had his link with Fall River, a daughter, who is, I believe, housekeeper for Mr. Chavenson, 594 Broadway. Mr. Toomey, the postman, could give me no information, either, although with true Irish eagerness to be of help to the stranger, he offered to go the rounds of the village that night and get word to me in Castletown if he found a clue.

Irish Rain is Pleasant Rain. So I tramped on, in the rain, for the week had been both "soft" and "hearty" in the Irish phrases, meaning wet and windy. But Irish rain is pleasant rain. You don't mind it; and I had been soaking wet every day all day for a week of tramping. But if old John Murphy of Barnis Gap did not know, nor Michael kelly of Bulloughbwee, old Patrick Sullivan on the Clougheen road did, when I finally reached him after seeming miles of travel over wet land and jumping fences and climbing stiles. Going into his ninetieth year, still his memory was clear. After a little thought he recalled a Hurley or Murley, as the name, translated from the Gaelic Ua-Muirtille, was called in Bearhaven; a Dennis Hurley, the name of my grandfather, and where his holdings were. They were not far away as distances go in Ireland, and I soon found the farmhouse now owned by a Michael Denehy, who remembered immediately that his father had bought the house, land, and three separated farm holdings from Dennis Murley. Three cows and a white horse went as part of the farm goods, he added But better still for me, his aged mother at once spoke of my grandmother, Joanna Toomey, bringing confirmation if I had needed more to be certain I was right. But it was with a certain sadness that I heard her tell that she had been part of the convoy when the exiles left on the road for Queenstown and America. It was the custom then for the neighbors (and a mile makes a close neighbor around Knockoara or Knockgour) to assemble and convey the travelers many miles afoot in farewell along the road. For, sadly, even now she remembers that the mother and the children were in tears; and that she herself "cried hard" on the way back from the parting on the road. It was a common Irish scene then, starting with the famine in the late "forties" - the neighbors' convoy, and the gathering the night before the exiles were to depart. It was more of a wake then a gathering, for the scene was literally a house of mourning. But I went back over the wet road to Castletown with an important pilgrimage done, with a host of messages, too, from old Patrick Sullivan to his nephew, Sergeant John Harrington of the Fall River police force, that his uncle was well and active and able. There were remembrances, too, from his niece to her sister on Third Street as well as to Sergeant Harrington. And there were old Patrick's grandnieces who sang the Berehaven song for me. My tramp has taken me as far as Dursey sound through Killough and Garnish. To Guarrawns' I did not get, so I shall hardly be able to meet Officer Dan Sullivan and hold up my head. But I crossed the strand at Ballydonegan Bay, where Dan's mother was born, and I climbed to Blackball head, to the ruined signal tower. I saw the distant, rocky islands, the Bull, Cow, and Calf; also Crow Head and Glenurra.

Fall River may not be the greatest city in the world; there may be others larger, wealthier, and possibly more beautiful. But in the eyes of Bearhaven it stands alone and high; its citizens are citizens of no mean city--in the minds of those who dwell in the Irish Fall River of Beara."

Table of Contents

1. Sullivans born about 1845 possibly on the BEARA

+   2   M   i.   **Dennis SULLIVAN [104205]** was born about 1840 in Ireland.

Dennis married **Ellen wife of Dennis SULLIVAN** [104206] [MRIN: 35058] (b. Abt 1840)

+   3   M   ii.   **Dennis SULLIVAN [105380]** was born about 1840 in Ireland.

Dennis married **Margaret O'NEIL** [105381] [MRIN: 35482] (b. Abt 1840)

+   4   M   iii.   **Mortimer SULLIVAN [94996]** was born about 1844 in Ireland and died on 7 May 1875 in Fall River, Bristol, Massachusetts about age 31.

Mortimer married **Ellen McGUINESS** [94995] [MRIN: 31762] (b. 1844, d. 27 Sep 1895)

+   5   M   iv.   **Timothy T. SULLIVAN [95595]** was born in 1844 in Ireland and died after 1880 in Fall River, Bristol, Massachusetts.

Timothy married **Margaret wife of Timothy SULLIVAN** [95596] [MRIN: 31953] (b. 1842, d. After 1897) in Ireland.

+   6   M   v.   **Cornelius SULLIVAN [105306]** was born about 1845.

Cornelius married **Catherine SULLIVAN** [105307] [MRIN: 35461] (b. Abt 1845)

+   7   M   vi.   **John SULLIVAN [105626]** was born about 1845 in Co. Cork, Ireland and died between 1879 and 1900 in Ireland.

John married **Margaret HARRINGTON** [105627] [MRIN: 35579] (b. Mar 1857, d. 13 Mar 1909) about 1865 in Co. Cork, Ireland.

+   8   M   vii.   **Jeremiah SULLIVAN [105942]** was born about 1845 in Ireland.

Jeremiah married **Margaret SULLIVAN** [105943] [MRIN: 35703] (b. Abt 1845)

+   9   M   viii.   **Daniel SULLIVAN [97460]** was born about 1845 in Ireland.

Daniel married **Mary HANLEY** [97461] [MRIN: 32534] (b. Abt 1845)

+   10   M   ix.   **Patrick J. SULLIVAN [106435]** was born on 14 Mar 1845 in Rossmiguon, Cork, Ireland, died after 1920 in Newport, Newport, Rhode Island, and was buried in St. Columbas Cem., Middletown, Rhode Island.

Patrick married **Bridget WALL** [106436] [MRIN: 35877] (b. 9 Oct 1848, d. After 1940)

+   11   M   x.   **John SULLIVAN [101925]** was born about 1846 in Ireland and died before 1895.

John married **Mary A. HANNIGAN** [101926] [MRIN: 34192] (b. 1846, d. 13 Apr 1910)

+ 12 M xi. **Daniel J. SULLIVAN [106316]** was born in 1846 in Ireland and died before 1900 in Bristol, Bristol, Rhode Island.

Daniel married **Mary A. SHEA** [106317] [MRIN: 35833] (b. Apr 1856, d. 28 Mar 1931)

+ 13 M xii. **Edward E. SULLIVAN [92413]** was born about 1846 in Berehaven, Cork, Ireland and died before 1888.

Edward married **Catherine wife of Edward C. SULLIVAN** [92412] [MRIN: 30935] (b. 1846, d. 26 Aug 1888)

Children

2. **Dennis SULLIVAN [104205]** (*Sullivans born about 1845 possibly*[1]) was born about 1840 in Ireland.

> General Notes: Named in daughter Catherine Sullivan Mahoney's 1890 Fall River MA marriage record.

Dennis married **Ellen wife of Dennis SULLIVAN** [104206] [MRIN: 35058]. Ellen was born about 1840 in Ireland.

The child from this marriage was:

> \+ 14 F i. **Catherine 'Kate' SULLIVAN [104202]** was born in 1868 in Ireland and died after 1930 in Fall River, Bristol, Massachusetts.
>
> Catherine married **Henry MAHONEY** [104201] [MRIN: 35056] (b. 1864, d. After 1910) on 22 Apr 1890 in Fall River, Bristol, Massachusetts.

3. **Dennis SULLIVAN [105380]** (*Sullivans born about 1845 possibly*[1]) was born about 1840 in Ireland.

> General Notes: Named in daughter Hanora's 1896 Fall River MA marriage record.
>
> This is possibly the couple outlined in 'Annals of the Beara - Volume III':
> Denis O'Sullivan & Margaret O'Neill
> (Park)
> Children: Abbey (Feb. 1860), Daniel (Feb. 1862), Julia (June 1863); Margaret (Aug. 1866) married Florence O'Sullivan (son of John O'Sullivan), Crooha East, Adrigole Parish; Honora (Aug. 1869); twins, Patrick and "Mary" (Feb. 1872); *Eddie (or Edward) (Apr. 1874), known as Eddie (Pairc) settled in the home place and married Brigid Power, daughter of Maurice Power and Ellen O'Sullivan Curryglass; James (Apr. 1878).

Dennis married **Margaret O'NEIL** [105381] [MRIN: 35482]. Margaret was born about 1840 in Ireland.

The child from this marriage was:

> \+ 15 F i. **Hanora SULLIVAN [105379]** was born in Aug 1862 in Ireland and died after 1940 in Gilcrest, Weld, Colorado.
>
> Hanora married **Daniel HARRINGTON** [105378] [MRIN: 35481] (b. 1869, d. After 1940) on 21 Jan 1896 in Fall River, Bristol, Massachusetts.

4. **Mortimer SULLIVAN [94996]** (*Sullivans born about 1845 possibly*[1]) was born about 1844 in Ireland and died on 7 May 1875 in Fall River, Bristol, Massachusetts about age 31.

> General Notes: 1865 Massachusetts State census shows only one Murty, Morty or variation in Fall River enumerated with other young people in ward 3, family #612:
> Sullivan, Daniel, 25, b. Ireland, married, Laborer.
> " Margaret, 24, b. Ireland. married, housewife.
> " Murtagh Jr., 23, b. Ireland, Laborer (USA).
>
> Also in Ward 3 in 1865 is an Ellen Sullivan age 23 b. England, a domestic working for the Kidd family, but the State census notes she is single.   There is no Ellen McGuiness, nor a George b. about 1864.

1873 Fall River MA birth record of daughter Julia notes father works as a Loafer (sic), parents b. Ireland and England.

There is only one Mortimer in the vital records of Fall River born about 1835 to 1845. This is likely the husband of Ellen McGuiness.
1875 May 7 Fall River MA deaths Registered notes
  Mortimer Sullivan, married, age 33 years 9 months (about 1841), died of Congestion of Brain, res. 14 Seventh (Prov. RI written above), Laborer, b. Fall River (sic) to Mortimer, Julia, each b. Ireland.

1880 Federal census shows his widow enumerated with their two children in Fall River MA.

Unable to locate any mention of him in census or vital records, except as the father of George and Julia.

Mortimer married **Ellen McGUINESS** [94995] [MRIN: 31762], daughter of **Patrick McGUINESS** [94997] and **Ellen BRADY** [94998]. Ellen was born in 1844 in England and died on 27 Sep 1895 in Fall River, Bristol, Massachusetts at age 51.

Children from this marriage were:

16 M i. **George SULLIVAN** [98935] was born in 1864 in Fall River, Bristol, Massachusetts and died on 16 Jul 1894 in Fall River, Bristol, Massachusetts at age 30.

General Notes: 1894 July 16 Deaths Recorded in Fall River MA notes:
  George Sullivan, single, age 30 years 1 month 8 days, died of Phthisis, b. Fall River, Weaver, b. to Mortimer, Ellen McGuiness, b. Ireland and England.

+ 17 F ii. **Julia A. SULLIVAN** [98936] was born on 28 Oct 1873 in Fall River, Bristol, Massachusetts and died after 1940 in Fall River, Bristol, Massachusetts.

Julia married **Michael D. GALVIN** [98937] [MRIN: 33052] (b. 1875) on 18 Jan 1899 in Fall River, Bristol, Massachusetts.

5. Timothy T. SULLIVAN [95595] (*Sullivans born about 1845 possibly*[1]) was born in 1844 in Ireland and died after 1880 in Fall River, Bristol, Massachusetts.

General Notes: 1871 the family was in Ireland when son John was born.

1880 Federal census of Fall River, Bristol Co. MA shows the family enumerated in dist 89 at 33 Union St. as family #174:
  Sullivan, T. Timothy (sic), 36, laborer, b. Ireland to Irish parents.
  " Margaret, 38, wife, keeps house, can't read, b. Ireland to Irish parents.
  " Dennis, 16, son, works in cotton mill, b. Ireland.
  " Mary, 15, daughter, works in cotton mill, b. Ireland.
  " Patrick, 11, son, goes to school, b. Ireland.
  " John, 7, son, goes to school, b. Ireland.

1880 Fall River City Directory
- Sullivan Timothy laborer, 33 Union.

1894 Fall River City Directory
- Sullivan Timothy laborer house 33 Union.

1895 Fall River City Directory
- Sullivan Margaret widow of Timothy house 33 Union.
- Sullivan Timothy (of 33 Union) died October 16, 1894.

1894 October the Fall River MA vital records does not shows Timothy Sullivan in the death records.

Timothy married **Margaret wife of Timothy SULLIVAN** [95596] [MRIN: 31953] in Ireland. Margaret was born in 1842 in Ireland and died after 1897 in Fall River, Bristol, Massachusetts.

Children from this marriage were:

    18 M   i.   **Dennis SULLIVAN [95597]** was born in 1864 in Ireland.

    19 F   ii.   **Mary SULLIVAN [95598]** was born in 1865 in Ireland.

    20 M   iii.   **Patrick SULLIVAN [95599]** was born in 1869 in Ireland.

+ 21 M   iv.   **John F. SULLIVAN [105602]** was born in 1871 in Ireland, died on 23 Jan 1906 in Fall River, Bristol, Massachusetts at age 35, and was buried in St. Patrick's Cem., Fall River, Massachusetts.

                     John married **Hanora SULLIVAN** [105603] [MRIN: 35568] (b. Apr 1877, d. 22 Jun 1946) on 27 Dec 1899 in Fall River, Bristol, Massachusetts.

6. **Cornelius SULLIVAN [105306]** (*Sullivans born about 1845 possibly* [1]) was born about 1845.

    General Notes: Named in son Patrick's 1896 Fall River MA marriage record.

    Cornelius married **Catherine SULLIVAN** [105307] [MRIN: 35461]. Catherine was born about 1845.

    The child from this marriage was:

+ 22 M   i.   **Patrick F. SULLIVAN [105304]** was born in 1869 in Ireland and died between 1920 and 1930 in Boston, Suffolk, Massachusetts.

                     Patrick married **Elizabeth 'Lizzie' SPELLACY** [105305] [MRIN: 35460] (b. 1869, d. After 1930) on 27 Oct 1896 in Fall River, Bristol, Massachusetts.

7. **John SULLIVAN [105626]** (*Sullivans born about 1845 possibly* [1]) was born about 1845 in Co. Cork, Ireland and died between 1879 and 1900 in Ireland.

    General Notes: Four children of the couple have been identified in the records of Fall River MA. Additionally, they also appear in the records of Co. Cork in the area of Castletownbere, on the Beara Peninsula.

    There are a number of John and Margaret Harrington Sullivan couples mentioned in Riobard O'Dwyer's book 'Annals of the Beara volume III' of Castletownhere Parish, but none have specifically been identified as this couple.

    Ireland Births and Baptisms with John Sullivan and Margaret Harrington appearing as parents, LDS abstracts note these children who appear to be of the same couple by their birth dates:
     John, 1865 January 16, Kilcatherine, Co. Cork IR (on the Beara May be the John who died in Joliet, IL Dec 15, 1947.);
      Cornelius, 1866 June 13, Castletown, Co. Cork IR (on the Beara);
      Honoria, 1867 March 10, Kilcatherine, Co. Cork IR (on the Beara);
      Eugene, 1869 January 5, Kilcatherine, Co. Cork IR (on the Beara);
      Mary, 1869 November 9, Castletown, Co. Cork IR (on the Beara. May be the Mary Sullivan Kelly who died in Shullsburg, WI, widow of Daniel Kelly.);

Michael 1871 September 28, Glengariff, Co. Cork RI (on the Beara, next to Cappyaugha);
Bridget, 1873 February 24, Co. Cork. (Married James Gray in Fall River.);
Margaret, 1877 February 8, Cappyaugha, Co. Cork RI (on the Beara near Glengariff.);
Catherine, 1878 December 22, Co. Cork IR;
Peter, 1880 July 2, Co. Cork, IR.

Based on the records and associations in Fall River MA of widow Margaret and 4 children, Eugene, Patrick, Bridget, and Margaret who were siblings living in Fall River MA researchers concludes they were the children from the Beara Peninsula in the 1860 and 1870 Irish records. The names and ages in the Co. Cork records and the Fall River MA records correspond.

John married **Margaret HARRINGTON** [105627] [MRIN: 35579], daughter of **Patrick HARRINGTON** [105641] and **Joanna DRISCOLL** [105642],   about 1865 in Co. Cork, Ireland. Margaret was born in Mar 1857 in Co. Cork, Ireland and died on 13 Mar 1909 in Fall River, Bristol, Massachusetts at age 52.

Children from this marriage were:

> 23 M   i.   **Cornelius SULLIVAN [105644]** was born on 13 Jun 1866 in Castletownbere, Cork, IR.
>
> General Notes: Ireland Births and Baptisms with John Sullivan and Margaret Harrington appearing as parents, LDS abstracts note:
> Cornelius, 1866 June 13, Castletown, Co. Cork IR (on the Beara)

> 24 F   ii.   **Honoria SULLIVAN [105647]** was born on 10 Mar 1867 in Kilcatherine, Berehaven, Co. Cork. Ir.
>
> General Notes: Ireland Births and Baptisms with John Sullivan and Margaret Harrington appearing as parents, LDS abstracts note:
> Honoria, 1867 March 10, Kilcatherine, Co. Cork IR (on the Beara)

> 25 M   iii. **Eugene SULLIVAN [105639]** was born on 5 Jan 1869 in Kilcatherine, Berehaven, Co. Cork. Ir and died after 1920 in Fall River, Bristol, Massachusetts.
>
> General Notes: Ireland Births and Baptisms with John Sullivan and Margaret Harrington appearing as parents, LDS abstracts note:
> Eugene, 1869 January 5, Kilcatherine, Co. Cork IR (on the Beara).
>
> 1909 his mother died at 32 Wooley St. in Fall River MA.
>
> 1910 Federal census of Fall River, Bristol Co. MA shows the siblings at 32 Wooley St.,:
> Sullivan, Eugene, head, 40, b. Ireland, to Irish parents. Immigrated 1889, naturalized. Laborer, Water works (This is where brother Patrick works as well)
> " Margaret T., sister, 28, b. Ireland to Irish parents. Immigrated 1892. Weaver, Cotton mill.
> Gray, Bridget, sister, 34, married 7 years, 2 children, 2 living, b. Ireland to Irish parents. Immigrated 1891.
> " Margaret A., niece, 5, b. NY (sic) to English and Irish parents.
> " William J., son, 3, b. MA.
>
> 1916 Fall River City Directory
> - Sullivan Eugene, Water Works repair shop house 32 Wooley.
> - Sullivan Margaret T. weaver boards 32 Wooley.
>
> 1917 and 1918 Fall River City Directory
> - Sullivan Eugene, Water Works repair shop, house 541 Broadway.
> - Sullivan Margaret T. weaver, boards 541 Broadway.

1919 and 1920 Fall River City Directory
- Sullivan Margaret T. weaver, boards 640 Third.
- Sullivan Eugene, Water Works repair shop, house 640 Third.

1920 Federal census of Fall River, Bristol Co. MA shows the extended family at 25 Ford St., as family #267:
 Gray, Bridgett (sic), head, 42, immigrated 1892, Naturalized 1895, b. Ireland to Irish parents. Weaver, Cotton mill.
 " Margaret, daughter, 15, b. NY to English and Irish parents.
 " William J., son, 13, b. MA to English and Irish parents.
 Sullivan, Eugene, brother, 55, single, immigrated 1889, naturalized 1894, b. Ireland, to Irish parents. Waterworks, City.

1921 Fall River City Directory
- Sullivan Eugene repairman FR WW house 25 Ford.
(No Margaret T. weaver listed.)

26 F iv. **Mary SULLIVAN [105648]** was born on 9 Nov 1869 in Castletownbere, Cork, IR.

  General Notes: Ireland Births and Baptisms with John Sullivan and Margaret Harrington appearing as parents, LDS abstracts note:
   Mary, 1869 November 9, Castletown, Co. Cork IR (on the Beara. May be the Mary Sullivan Kelly who died in Shullsburg, WI, widow of Daniel Kelly.)

27 M v. **Michael SULLIVAN [105646]** was born on 28 Sep 1871 in Glengariff, Cork, Munster, Ireland.

  General Notes: Ireland Births and Baptisms with John Sullivan and Margaret Harrington appearing as parents, LDS abstracts note:
   Michael 1871 September 28, Glengariff, Co. Cork IR (on the Beara, next to Cappyaugha).

+ 28 M vi. **Patrick J. SULLIVAN [105624]** was born in 1872 in Ireland and died on 24 Jan 1950 in Fall River, Bristol, Massachusetts at age 78.

  Patrick married **Mary SHEA** [105625] [MRIN: 35578] (b. 1874, d. After 1940) on 26 Oct 1898 in Fall River, Bristol, Massachusetts.

29 F vii. **Margaret T. SULLIVAN [105640]** was born on 8 Feb 1877 in Cappyaugha, Cork, Ireland and died about 1920 in Fall River, Bristol, Massachusetts about age 43.

  General Notes: Ireland Births and Baptisms with John Sullivan and Margaret Harrington appearing as parents, LDS abstracts note:
   Margaret, 1877 February 8, Cappyaugha, Co. Cork IR. (Located on the Beara near Glengariff.)

  1910 Federal census enumerated with her siblings at 32 Wooley.

  1912 Fall River City Directory
  - Sullivan Eugene, Water Works repair shop house 32 Wooley.
  - Sullivan Margaret T. weaver boards 32 Wooley.

  1916 Fall River City Directory
  - Sullivan Eugene, Water Works repair shop house 32 Wooley.
  - Sullivan Margaret T. weaver boards 32 Wooley.

1919 and 1920 Fall River City Directory
- Sullivan Margaret T. weaver, boards 640 Third.
- Sullivan Eugene, Water Worked repair shop, house 640 Third.

1921 Fall River City Directory
- Sullivan Eugene repairman FR WW house 25 Ford.
(No Margaret T. weaver listed.)

+ 30 F viii. **Bridget M. SULLIVAN [105635]** was born in 1878 in Co. Cork, Ireland and died after 1930 in Fall River, Bristol, Massachusetts.

Bridget married **James W. GRAY** [105636] [MRIN: 35581] (b. 1871) on 10 Aug 1902 in Fall River, Bristol, Massachusetts.

31 F ix. **Catherine SULLIVAN [105645]** was born on 22 Dec 1878 in Co. Cork, Ireland.

General Notes: Ireland Births and Baptisms with John Sullivan and Margaret Harrington appearing as parents, LDS abstracts note:
Catherine, 1878 December 22, Co. Cork IR.

32 M x. **Peter P. SULLIVAN [105643]** was born in 1880 in Co. Cork, Ireland and died after 1900 in Fall River, Bristol, Massachusetts.

General Notes: Ireland Births and Baptisms with John Sullivan and Margaret Harrington appearing as parents, LDS abstracts note:
Peter, 1880 July 2, Co. Cork, IR.

1900 Federal census of Fall River MA Peter is enumerated with his mother and siblings showing his birth as June 1880.

1910 Federal census of Fall River MA he is not enumerated with his siblings.

1906 Fall River City Directory
- Sullivan Peter Clerk boards 32 Wooley.
- Sullivan Margaret widow of John house 32 Wooley.

8. Jeremiah SULLIVAN [105942] (*Sullivans born about 1845 possibly* [1]) was born about 1845 in Ireland.

General Notes: Named in daughter Hannah's 1901 Fall River marriage record.

Jeremiah married **Margaret SULLIVAN** [105943] [MRIN: 35703]. Margaret was born about 1845 in Ireland.

The child from this marriage was:

33 F i. **Hannah SULLIVAN [105941]** was born in 1871 in Ireland and died on 10 Jul 1937 in Fall River, Bristol, Massachusetts at age 66.

General Notes: 1885 immigrated to America at about the age of 15 (1920 census).

1901 September 19, Marriages Registered in Fall River MA notes:
James M. (sic) Oxford, 31, first marriage, res. 23 E. Bowery, Newport, RI., laborer, b. Bangor ME, to Robert R., Annie Albro.
Hannah Sullivan, 30, first marriage, res. 176 E. Main, Fall River MA, Domestic, b. Ireland to Jeremiah, Margaret - Sullivan.
Married by M. J. O'Reilly, Priest.

1916 Fall River City Directory
- Oxford Hannah house 124 Hamlet (no other Oxfords in the directory).

1920 Federal census of Fall River, Bristol Co. MA shows the widow enumerated at 44 Hamlet St.:
   Oxford, Hannah, head, rents, 49, widow, immigrated 1885, b. Ireland to Irish parents. No employment.

Hannah married **James W. OXFORD** [105938] [MRIN: 35702], son of **Robert R. OXFORD** [105939] and **Annie ALBRO** [105940], on 19 Sep 1901 in Fall River, Bristol, Massachusetts. James was born in 1870 in Bangor, Penobscot, Maine.

9. **Daniel SULLIVAN [97460]** (*Sullivans born about 1845 possibly*[1]) was born about 1845 in Ireland.

Daniel married **Mary HANLEY** [97461] [MRIN: 32534]. Mary was born about 1845 in Ireland.

The child from this marriage was:

+ 34 F i.   **Annie SULLIVAN [97451]** was born in 1872 in Ireland, died in 1926 in Fall River, Bristol, Massachusetts at age 54, and was buried in St. Patrick's Cem., Fall River, Massachusetts.

              Annie married **Edward J. BARRY** [97450] [MRIN: 32533] (b. 1876, d. 1950) on 22 Jan 1894 in Fall River, Bristol, Massachusetts.

10. **Patrick J. SULLIVAN [106435]** (*Sullivans born about 1845 possibly*[1]) was born on 14 Mar 1845 in Rossmiguon, Cork, Ireland, died after 1920 in Newport, Newport, Rhode Island, and was buried in St. Columbas Cem., Middletown, Rhode Island.

General Notes: 1869 married (1910 census). The couple were from different counties in Ireland and may have married in America although the dates in the census seem to indicate they married the year before they arrived. All their children were born in Rhode Island - as early as 1870.

1870 immigrated to America (1910 census).

1880 Federal census of Newport, RI shows family headed by 'James' the middle name of Patrick at 371 Edward St. as family #486:
   Sullivan, James, 32, Painter, b. Ireland to Irish parents.
   " Delia (sic - common nickname for Bridget), 32, wife, keeps house, b. Ireland to Irish parents.
   " Henry, 10, son, b. RI to Irish parents.
   " James, 7, son, b. RI to Irish parents.
   " William, 4, son, b. RI to Irish parents.
   " John, son, 2, b. RI to Irish parents.
   " Martin, 2/12, b. RI to Irish parent.

1900 Federal census of Newport, Newport Co. RI shows the family enumerated at 678 Thames St. as family #253:
   Sullivan, Patrick J., May 1848, 52, married 31 years, b. Ireland to Irish parents. Immigrated 1866, 34 years prior, Naturalized. House painter.
   " Bridget, wife, April 1846, 54, married 31 years, 6 children, 4 living, b. Ireland to Irish parents. Immigrated 1866, 34 years prior.
   " William F., son, Feb 1876, 24, b. RI to Irish parents. House painter.
   " John J., son, Sept 1877, 22, b. RI to Irish parents. House painter.
   " Mortimer L., son, Feb 1880, 20, b. RI to Irish parents. At school.

1910 Federal census of Newport, Newport Co. RI shows the family enumerated at 678 Thames St. as family #193:

Sullivan, Patrick J., head, 55, married 41 years, b. Ireland to Irish parents. Immigrated 1870, Naturalized. Painter, house. Owns home free of mortgage.

" Bridget, wife, 54, married 41 years, 5 children, 4 living, b. Ireland to Irish parents. Immigrated 1870.

" John J., son, 32, b. RI to Irish parents. Painter, House.

" Mortimer L., son, 30, married 3 years, b. RI to Irish parents. Painter, House.

" Annie A., daughter in law, 19, married 3 years, 1 child, 1 living, b. RI to MA and RI parents.

" Henry M., grand son, 2, b. RI to RI parents.

1920 Federal census of Newport, Newport Co. RI shows the extended family again at 678 Thames St. as family #379:

Sullivan, Patrick J., head, owns home free of mortgage, 68, immigrated 1862, naturalized 1887, b. Ireland. No employment.

" Bridget, wife, 67, immigrated 1867, naturalized 1887, b. Ireland to Irish parents. No employment.

" Henry, grandson, 12, b. RI to RI parents.

" Mary, granddaughter, 9, b. RI to RI parents.

The couple rests at St. Columba Catholic Cemetery, Newport, RI marked without the dates of their deaths:

PAT'K J. O'SULLIVAN
Born March 14, 1845
In Rossmiguon (sic) Co. Cork Ireland
His Wife
BRIDGET WALL
Born Oct 9 1843
In Kilmore, Co. Galway, Ireland.
Their Son
James
Born Dec 7, 1872
Died Oct 9, 1890

Patrick married **Bridget WALL** [106436] [MRIN: 35877]. Bridget was born on 9 Oct 1848 in Kilmore, Galway, Connacht, Ireland and died after 1940 in Newport, Newport, Rhode Island.

Children from this marriage were:

35 M i. **Henry SULLIVAN [106443]** was born in 1870 in Newport, Newport, Rhode Island.

36 M ii. **James SULLIVAN [106442]** was born on 7 Dec 1872, died on 9 Oct 1890 in Newport, Newport, Rhode Island at age 17, and was buried in St. Columbas Cem., Middletown, Rhode Island.

+ 37 M iii. **William F. SULLIVAN [106444]** was born on 14 Feb 1876 in Newport, Newport, Rhode Island and died on 24 Nov 1952 in Newport, Newport, Rhode Island at age 76.

William married **Anna Teresa BULLETT** [106446] [MRIN: 35880] (b. 2 May 1874, d. 23 May 1927) on 12 Jun 1905 in Newport, Newport, Rhode Island.

William next married **Catherine P. BOYLE** [106463] [MRIN: 35887] (b. 2 May 1882, d. 19 May 1968) on 1 Oct 1929 in Johnstown, Cambria, Pennsylvania.

38 M iv. **John SULLIVAN [106441]** was born in 1878 in Newport, Newport, Rhode Island.

39 M v. **Martin SULLIVAN [106445]** was born in 1880 in Newport, Newport, Rhode Island.

+ 40 M vi. **Mortimer L SULLIVAN [106433]** was born in 1881 in Newport, Newport, Rhode Island and died on 4 Dec 1911 in Newport, Newport, Rhode Island at age 30.

Mortimer married **Annie L. ESLECK** [106434] [MRIN: 35876] (b. 1888, d. Bef 1920) on 27 Dec 1906 in Fall River, Bristol, Massachusetts.

11. John SULLIVAN [101925] (*Sullivans born about 1845 possibly* [1]) was born about 1846 in Ireland and died before 1895.

General Notes: The couple John and Mary Hannigan Sullivan are named in the Fall River marriage record of their children William 1898, John 1899, and Catherine in 1894.

The family appears children have immigrated about 1894, his widow appearing in the Fall River City directory in 1895 for the first time. John may have passed away in Wales before the widow and at least 3 adult children came to America.

1914 Fall River MA the detailed obituary of Patrick R. Sullivan, born in Eyeries, Berehaven, Co. Cork Ireland, notes Patrick had nephews in Fall River and other cities. The nephew in Fall River is William R. Sullivan, overseer at Durfee Mill. There is only one supervisor who appears in the Fall River MA City Directory at this time, William the son of this John and Mary.

The implication is this subject, John Sullivan, was a brother of Patrick R. Sullivan, 1818-1914, who immigrated to Massachusetts in 1848. John instead went to Wales, but later he, or at least his widow and children, late immigrated to join Patrick Sullivan in Fall River MA. John would thus be the son of John and Johanna Lynch Sullivan of Eyeries, Ireland.

John married **Mary A. HANNIGAN** [101926] [MRIN: 34192], daughter of **John HANNIGAN** [101964] and **Mary HOLLY** [101963]. Mary was born in 1846 in Ireland and died on 13 Apr 1910 in Fall River, Bristol, Massachusetts at age 64.

Children from this marriage were:

+ 41 M i. **William SULLIVAN [101923]** was born on 13 May 1868 in Wales and died on 9 Nov 1947 in Fall River, Bristol, Massachusetts at age 79.

William married **Catherine HASSEY** [101924] [MRIN: 34191] (b. 15 Dec 1869, d. 20 Aug 1938) on 25 Jan 1898 in Fall River, Bristol, Massachusetts.

42 F ii. **Catherine SULLIVAN [101937]** was born in 1871 in Ireland and died on 26 Jul 1894 in Fall River, Bristol, Massachusetts at age 23.

General Notes: 1894 May 5, Marriages Registered in Fall River MA notes:
 John Aylward, res. Fall River, 21, Weaver, b. Ireland to John, Bridget Slattery, first marriage.
 Catherine Sullivan, res. Fall River, 23, Weaver, b. Wales to John, Mary Hanagan (sic), first marriage.
 Married by C. Hughes, Catholic Priest.

1894 July 26, Deaths Registered in Fall River MA notes:
 Kate (Sullivan) Aylward, married, wife of John Aylward, age 23 years 19 days, died of Heart Disease, res. Fall River, b. Wales, to John, Mary A. - Harrington (sic), each b. Ireland.

Died within a few months of her marriage.

Catherine married **John AYLWARD** [101960] [MRIN: 34206], son of **John AYLWARD** [101961] and **Bridget SLATTERY** [101962],   on 5 May 1894 in Fall River, Bristol, Massachusetts. John was born in 1873 in Ireland and died after 1940 in Fall River, Bristol, Massachusetts.

+   43   M   iii.   **John SULLIVAN [101936]** was born in 1873 in Wales, died on 14 May 1947 in Fall River, Bristol, Massachusetts at age 74, and was buried in St. Patrick's Cem., Fall River, Massachusetts.

John married **Juila DRISCOLL** [101938] [MRIN: 34196] (b. 1877, d. 13 Oct 1929) on 26 Jan 1899 in Fall River, Bristol, Massachusetts.

12.   Daniel J. SULLIVAN [106316] (*Sullivans born about 1845 possibly* [1]) was born in 1846 in Ireland and died before 1900 in Bristol, Bristol, Rhode Island.

General Notes: 1880 Federal census of Bristol, Bristol Co. RI shows a family as dwelling #247:
   Sullivan, Daniel, 34, Reel Works, b. Ireland to Irish parents.
   " Mary, 25, wife, House keeper, b. Ireland to Irish parents.
   " Frank S., 4, son, b. RI.
   " Mary J., 10/12, daughter, b. RI

1900 his widow and children are enumerated in Bristol, Bristol Co., RI

No marriage or death record could be found in the RI vital records for Daniel.

Daniel married **Mary A. SHEA** [106317] [MRIN: 35833], daughter of **Daniel SHEA** [106322]. Mary was born in Apr 1856 in Ireland and died on 28 Mar 1931 in Bristol, Bristol, Rhode Island at age 74.

Children from this marriage were:

44   F   i.   **Mary J. SULLIVAN [106321]** was born in Aug 1879 in Bristol, Bristol, Rhode Island.

45   F   ii.   **Catherine SULLIVAN [106315]** was born in 1881 in Bristol, Bristol, Rhode Island.

General Notes: 1906 February 15, Marriages Registered in Fall River MA notes:
   Joseph Turcotte, 25, first marriage, res. 70 Water, East Providence, RI, Blacksmith, b. Canada to Fabien, Celia Dechesne.
   Catherine Sullivan, 22, first marriage, res. 60 Richmond, Bristol, RI, At home, b. Bristol, RI to Daniel J., Mary A. Shea.
   A. B. Grolleau, Priest.

Catherine married **Joseph TURCOTTE** [106312] [MRIN: 35832], son of **Fabie TURCOTTE** [106313] and **Celia DECHESNE** [106314],   on 15 Feb 1906 in Fall River, Bristol, Massachusetts. Joseph was born in 1881 in Canada.

46   M   iii.   **John Patrick SULLIVAN [106318]** was born on 19 Mar 1882.

47   M   iv.   **Daniel Joseph SULLIVAN [106320]** was born on 22 Jun 1886 in Bristol, Bristol, Rhode Island.

General Notes: 1942 mentioned by brother John P in his draft registration card as the person who 'will know your address'
- Daniel J. Sullivan, Mt. St. Rita Convent, Cumberland, RI.   Employer - State of RI, State Prison, Cranston RI.

48 M   v.   **Edward Eugene SULLIVAN [106319]** was born on 14 Jan 1889 in Bristol, Bristol, Rhode Island and died after 1940 in RI.

General Notes: 1940 Federal census of Cranston RI shows him enumerated at the State Prison:
    Sullivan, Edward E., Deputy Warden, 51, single, 1 year of high school, b. RI.

1942 WWII Draft Registration Card notes:
    Edward Eugene Sullivan, res. 328 Pine St., Providence RI. Age 53. B. Bristol RI, January 14, 1889. Person who will know your address - Daniel J. Sullivan, Mt. St. Rita Convent, Cumberland, RI. Employer - State of RI, State Prison, Cranston RI.
    Height 5'10", weight 185, eyes - blue, hair - brown, bald, complexion - ruddy. Deputy Warden, State Reformatory, 52 week salary $1140.

13. Edward E. SULLIVAN [92413] (*Sullivans born about 1845 possibly*[1]) was born about 1846 in Berehaven, Cork, Ireland and died before 1888.

General Notes: Named in wife Catherine's 1888 Fall River MA death record.

There are a number of individuals born in Ireland, living in Cambridge, MA in the 1870's who marry, noting their parents are Edward and Catherine.

1881 there is a Daniel who died in Boston, MA at the age of 27 (b. 1854) of a compound fracture of the arm, whose parents were Edward and Catherine.

1888 a Margaret died age 28 (b. 1860) in Boston noting her parents were Edward and Catherine.

Edward married **Catherine wife of Edward C. SULLIVAN [92412]** [MRIN: 30935]. Catherine was born in 1846 in Ireland and died on 26 Aug 1888 in Fall River, Bristol, Massachusetts at age 42.

Children from this marriage were:

49 M   i.   **Jeremiah SULLIVAN [107520]** was born in 1849 and died on 25 Mar 1884 in MA at age 35.

General Notes: 1884 March 25, Deaths Registered in Massachusetts LDS abstract notes:
    Jeremiah Sullivan, age 35, b. to Edward, Catherine. (No location given.)

This may be the Jeremiah who married Hannah Haley in Cambridge, Plymouth Co. MA 3 March 1874, also naming parents Edward and Catherine.

50 M   ii.   **Daniel C. SULLIVAN [92414]** was born on 20 May 1854 in Berehaven, Cork, Ireland.

General Notes: Appears in Fall River MA directory with widow Catherine at 12 Tecumseh, who died in 1888.

Grandchildren

14. Catherine 'Kate' SULLIVAN [104202] (*Dennis*[2]*, Sullivans born about 1845 possibly*[1]) was born in 1868 in Ireland and died after 1930 in Fall River, Bristol, Massachusetts.

General Notes: 1880 immigrated to America (1900 census).

1890 April 22, Marriages Registered in Fall River MA notes:
   Henry Mahoney, 26, Teamster, b. Fall River to Dennis, Mary, first marriage.
   Kate Sullivan, 22, Speeder tender, b. Ireland to Dennis, Ellen, first marriage.
   Married by Michael Cassidy, Priest.

Catherine married **Henry MAHONEY** [104201] [MRIN: 35056], son of **Dennis MAHONEY** [104203] and **Mary wife of Dennis MAHONEY** [104204], on 22 Apr 1890 in Fall River, Bristol, Massachusetts. Henry was born in 1864 in Fall River, Bristol, Massachusetts and died after 1910 in Fall River, Bristol, Massachusetts.

Children from this marriage were:

   51 F   i.   **Mary A. MAHONEY [104211]** was born on 16 Feb 1891 in Fall River, Bristol, Massachusetts.

      Mary married **John BUTLER** [104213] [MRIN: 35059] in 1908 in Fall River, Bristol, Massachusetts. John was born in 1886 in MA.

   52 F   ii.   **Katie A. MAHONEY [104210]** was born on 20 Nov 1893 in Fall River, Bristol, Massachusetts and died on 19 Jun 1895 in Fall River, Bristol, Massachusetts at age 1.

      General Notes: 1895 January 19, Deaths Registered in Fall River MA notes:
         Katie A. Mahoney, age 1 years 5 months, died of Scarlatina, b. Fall River to Henry, Catherine - Sullivan, b. Fall River, Ireland.

   53 M   iii.   **James Edward MAHONEY [104209]** was born on 18 Oct 1896 in Fall River, Bristol, Massachusetts.

      General Notes: 1918 June 5, WWI draft registration card notes:
         James Edward Mahoney, res. 10 Cedar St., Fall River, b. Oct 18, 1896, Fall River MA. Father b. Fall River MA. Employer Blair Sign & Advertising Co., 154 Union St., New Bedford, MA. Nearest relative, Henry Mahoney, 10 Cedar St., Fall River MA. Medium height, medium build, brown eyes, black hair.

   54 M   iv.   **Patrick B. MAHONEY [104212]** was born on 17 Feb 1899 in Fall River, Bristol, Massachusetts.

   55 M   v.   **Henry C. MAHONEY [104208]** was born on 17 Dec 1901 in Fall River, Bristol, Massachusetts and died on 7 Feb 1903 in Fall River, Bristol, Massachusetts at age 1.

      General Notes: 1903 February 7, Deaths Registered in Fall River notes:
         Henry C. Mahoney, single, age 1 year 1 month, died of Laryngeal Diphtheria, res. 3 Camden, b. Fall River to Henry, Catherine Sullivan, each b. Fall River, Ireland.

   56 M   vi.   **John J. MAHONEY [104207]** was born on 21 Sep 1904 in Fall River, Bristol, Massachusetts.

15. Hanora SULLIVAN [105379] (*Dennis[3], Sullivans born about 1845 possibly[1]*) was born in Aug 1862 in Ireland and died after 1940 in Gilcrest, Weld, Colorado.

General Notes: 1870 she immigrated to America (1900 census) when she would have been only about 8 years old.   Daniel Harrington immigrated 1890.

1880 unable to confirm a Hanora in the Federal census. No other child of a Dennis and Margaret ONeil Sullivan could be located in the MA vital records.

There are a number of births registered in Kilcatherine, Co. Cork of children to a Dennis Sullivan and Margaret ONeil, including a Hanora in August 1869.

Possibly this subject:
1880 Federal census of Fall River, Bristol Co. MA shows Hanora boarding at 76 South Main in family #493:
   Hacket, Richard, 36, Coachman, b. Ireland.
   " Johanna, 33, wife, Keeping house, b. Ireland.
   Sullivan, Hanora, 15, boarder, In Cotton Mill, b. MA (sic) to Irish parents.
   Harrington, Hannah, 45, boarder, In Cotton mill, b. Ireland.

1896 June 21, Marriages Registered in Fall River MA notes:
   Daniel Harrington, res. Fall River, 27, Carpenter, b. Ireland to James, Hanora - Murphy, first marriage.
   Hanora Sullivan, res. Fall River, 25 (sic), Domestic, b. Ireland to Dennis, Margaret - ONeil, first marriage.
   Married by Edward Colgan, Catholic Priest.

Hanora married **Daniel HARRINGTON** [105378] [MRIN: 35481], son of **James HARRINGTON** [105382] and **Margaret ONEIL** [105383],   on 21 Jan 1896 in Fall River, Bristol, Massachusetts. Daniel was born in 1869 in Ireland and died after 1940 in Gilcrest, Weld, Colorado.

Children from this marriage were:

   57 M i.   **William J. HARRINGTON [105384]** was born on 19 Mar 1989 in Fall River, Bristol, Massachusetts.

   58 M ii.   **James E. HARRINGTON [105385]** was born on 11 Oct 1896 in Fall River, Bristol, Massachusetts and died on 7 Aug 1899 in Fall River, Bristol, Massachusetts at age 2.

        General Notes: 1899 August 7, Deaths Registered in Fall River MA notes:
        James E. Harrington, 2 years 9 months 27 days old, died of Diabetes Mellitius, res. 63 Third, b. Fall River to Daniel, Hanora - Sullivan, parents b. Ireland.

   59 F iii.   **Abbie I. HARRINGTON [105386]** was born on 8 Jun 1900 in Fall River, Bristol, Massachusetts.

   60 F iv.   **Julia J. HARRINGTON [105387]** was born on 19 Jul 1902 in Fall River, Bristol, Massachusetts.

17. Julia A. SULLIVAN [98936] (*Mortimer[4], Sullivans born about 1845 possibly[1]*) was born on 28 Oct 1873 in Fall River, Bristol, Massachusetts and died after 1940 in Fall River, Bristol, Massachusetts.

General Notes: 1899 January 18, Marriages Registered in Fall River MA notes:
   Michael D. Galvin,   237 County, Fall River, 24, Carpenter, b. Fall River to John J., Margaret - Henabury, first marriage.

Julia A. Sullivan, 69 Cornean (?), Fall River, 24, Weaver, b. Fall River to Morty, Ellen-McGinner (sic).
  Married by M. J. Owens, Priest.

1940 Federal census of Fall River, Bristol Co. MA shows the widow at 55 Arthur St.:
  Galvin, Julia, head, owns home, value $500, age 66, widow, school 8 years, b. MA.

Julia married **Michael D. GALVIN** [98937] [MRIN: 33052], son of **John J. GALVIN** [92907] and **Margaret HENABERRY** [92908], on 18 Jan 1899 in Fall River, Bristol, Massachusetts. Michael was born in 1875 in Fall River, Bristol, Massachusetts.

Children from this marriage were:

61 M i. **Ella M. GALVIN [98938]** was born on 9 May 1900 in Fall River, Bristol, Massachusetts and died on 11 Nov 1918 in New London, New London, Connecticut at age 18.

General Notes: 1918 Officers and elisted men of the US Navy who lost their lives...
Galvin, Ella M., yeoman, (F), second class, United States Naval Reserve Force.
Enlisted Newport RI July 23, 1918.
Died Naval Hospital, New London Conn., November 11, 1918.
Cause - Multiple injuries.
Next of kin - Mother, Julia Galvin, 103 Covel St., Fall River MA.

62 M ii. **Edwin GALVIN [98939]** was born on 11 Feb 1903 in Fall River, Bristol, Massachusetts.

General Notes: 1903 February 11, Births Registered in Fall River MA notes:
  Galvin Edwin, b. to Michael D., Julia E. (sic) Sullivan, 183 County, father Laborer, parents b. Fall River.

21. John F. SULLIVAN [105602] (*Timothy T.[5], Sullivans born about 1845 possibly[1]*) was born in 1871 in Ireland, died on 23 Jan 1906 in Fall River, Bristol, Massachusetts at age 35, and was buried in St. Patrick's Cem., Fall River, Massachusetts.

General Notes: 1899 December 27, Marriages Register in Fall River MA notes:
  John F. Sullivan, res. 3 Bank, Fall River, 28, Lineman, b. Ireland to Timothy T., Margaret - Sullivan, first marriage.
  Hanora Sullivan, res. 10 Durfee, Fall River, 22, Weaver, b. Ireland to Patrick, Mary ---, first marriage.
  Married by Matthias McCabe, Priest.

1900 unable to locate the young couple in the Bristol Co. MA Federal census.

1901 Fall River City Directory
- Sullivan John, laborer, house 3 Bank.

1902 Fall River City Directory
- Sullivan Edward F. engineer, house 3 Bank.
- Sullivan John F. lineman, house 3 Bank.

1905 the family was living at 3 Bank St. when daughter Fannie was born.

1906, January 23, Massachusetts Death Certificate notes:

John F. Sullivan, res. 3 Bank St., Fall River, MA died at same, age 33. Married. B. Ireland to Timothy Sullivan, b. Ireland, and Margaret Sullivan, b. Ireland. Laborer. Informant Hanora Sullivan.
Died of Hemorrhage from carotid artery. Burial St. Patrick's Cemetery.

John married **Hanora SULLIVAN** [105603] [MRIN: 35568], daughter of **Patrick D. SULLIVAN** [106099] and **Mary A. SULLIVAN** [106100], on 27 Dec 1899 in Fall River, Bristol, Massachusetts. Hanora was born in Apr 1877 in Cloghane, Allihies Parish, Co. Cork, Ireland and died on 22 Jun 1946 in Fall River, Bristol, Massachusetts at age 69.

Children from this marriage were:

> 63 F   i.   **Margaret J. SULLIVAN [105606]** was born on 26 Feb 1900 in Fall River, Bristol, Massachusetts and died on 23 Aug 1900 in Fall River, Bristol, Massachusetts.
>
> > General Notes: 1900 August 23, Deaths Registered in Fall River MA notes:
> > Margaret Sullivan, age 6 months 5 days, died of Marasmus, res. 3 Bank St., b. Fall River to John F., Hanora - Sullivan, parents b. Fall River, Ireland.
>
> 64 F   ii.   **Lillian C. SULLIVAN [105607]** was born on 24 May 1902 in Fall River, Bristol, Massachusetts, died in 1970 at age 68, and was buried in St. Patrick's Cem., Fall River, Massachusetts.
>
> > General Notes: Two girls named Lillian Sullivan were born May 24, 1902, recorded in the Fall River, Bristol Co. MA vital records - one to John F. and Nora Sullivan and one to George H. and Rose Sullivan.
> >
> > 1902 May 24, Births Registered in Fall River MA:
> > Lillian C., b. to John F., Nora - Sullivan, res. 3 Bank, father Lineman, parents b. Ireland.
>
> Lillian married **Frank William SHEA** [105616] [MRIN: 35573]. Frank was born on 13 Feb 1897 in MA.
>
> 65 F   iii.   **Irene F. SULLIVAN [105604]** was born on 4 Apr 1904 in Fall River, Bristol, Massachusetts and died on 17 May 1984 in Fall River, Bristol, Massachusetts at age 80.
>
> Irene married **Louis CURT** [105617] [MRIN: 35574]. Louis was born in 1905 in Rhode Island and died after 1951.
>
> 66 F   iv.   **Fannie SULLIVAN [105605]** was born on 26 Apr 1905 in Fall River, Bristol, Massachusetts.

22. Patrick F. SULLIVAN [105304] (*Cornelius*[6], *Sullivans born about 1845 possibly*[1]) was born in 1869 in Ireland and died between 1920 and 1930 in Boston, Suffolk, Massachusetts.

> General Notes: 1896 October 27, Marriages Registered in Fall River MA notes:
> Patrick T., Sullivan, res. Boston, MA, 27, Motorman, b. Ireland to Cornelius, Catherine - Sullivan, first marriage.
> Lizzie Spellacy, res. Fall River, 27, Weaver, b. Fall River to Timothy, Margaret - O'Callahan, first marriage.
> Married by M. J. Owens, minister.
>
> 1900 Federal census of Boston, Suffolk Co. MA shows the family enumerated in ward 23, dist 1506 at 13 Anson St.:
> Sullivan, Patrick T. (sic), head, Nov 1870, 30, married 4 years, b. Ireland to Irish parents. Immigrated 1881, 19 years prior. RR Motorman.

" Elizabeth J., wife, Feb 1871, 29, married 4 years, 3 children, 3 living, b. MA to Irish parents.
" Catherine, daughter, July 1897, 2, b. MA.
" Margaret, Oct 1898, 1, b. MA.
" John F., son, Feb 1900 3/12, b. MA.

1906 the family was living at 13 Anson St., Boston, MA when son William died of Marasmus.

1910 Federal census of Boston, Suffolk Co., MA shows the family enumerated in ward 23, dist 1612, at 3640 Washington St. as family #204:
    Sullivan, Patrick F., head, 41, married 13 yeras, b. Ireland.
    " Elizabeth J., wife, 39, married 13 years, 7 children, 4 living, b. MA.
    " Katheryn (sic), daughter, 12, b. MA.
    " Margaret, daughter, 11, b. MA.
    " John F., son, 10, b. MA.
    " George P., son, 7, b. MA.
    Spellacy, Mary J., sister in law, age unknown, b. MA.

1920 Federal census of Boston, Suffolk Co. MA shows the family in ward 23, dist 543 at 33 Sycamore St., as family #4:
    Sullivan, Patrick F., head, owns home with mortgage, 49, immigrated 1881, naturalized 1891, b. Ireland to Irish parents.   Special Police, Railroad.
    " Elizabeth J., wife, 46, b. MA.
    " Catherine, daughter, 22, b. MA.   Stenographer, Office.
    " Margaret, daughter, 21, b. MA.   Stenographer, Office.
    " John F., son, 19, b. MA.   Electrician, Jobbers.
    " George P., son, 17, b. MA.
    Spellacy, Mary J., boarder, 44, b. MA. Weaver, factory.

Patrick married **Elizabeth 'Lizzie' SPELLACY** [105305] [MRIN: 35460], daughter of **Tmothy SPELLACY** [105308] and **Margaret O'CALLAHAN** [105309],   on 27 Oct 1896 in Fall River, Bristol, Massachusetts. Elizabeth was born in 1869 in Fall River, Bristol, Massachusetts and died after 1930 in Boston, Suffolk, Massachusetts.

Children from this marriage were:

> 67   F   i.   **Catherine SULLIVAN [105315]** was born in 1897 in MA.

> 68   F   ii.   **Margaret SULLIVAN [105316]** was born in Oct 1898 in MA.

+ > 69   M   iii.   **John Francis SULLIVAN [105313]** was born on 25 Feb 1900 in Boston, Suffolk, Massachusetts.
>
> > John married **Mary Agnes STARRS** [105317] [MRIN: 35463] (b. 4 Dec 1901, d. 26 Nov 1989)

> 70   F   iv.   **Hannah SULLIVAN [105312]** was born on 28 Oct 1901 in Boston, Suffolk, Massachusetts and died on 7 Dec 1903 in Boston, Suffolk, Massachusetts at age 2.

> 71   M   v.   **George P. SULLIVAN [105314]** was born in 1903 in Boston, Suffolk, Massachusetts.

> 72   F   vi.   **Lizzie SULLIVAN [105310]** was born in 1905 and died on 14 Aug 1905 in MA.

> 73   M   vii.   **William Andrew SULLIVAN [105311]** was born on 17 Sep 1906 in Boston, Suffolk, Massachusetts, died on 25 Oct 1906 in Boston, Suffolk, Massachusetts, and was buried in Calvary Cemetery, Boston, Massachusetts.

General Notes: 1906 October 25, Massachusetts Death Certificate notes:
William A. Sullivan, died 13 Anson St., Boston, MA. Age 1 month 8 days. B. Boston. Father Patrick F., Sullivan, b. Ireland, mother Lizzie Spellacy, b. Ireland (sic). Died of Marasmus. Burial Calvary.

28. Patrick J. SULLIVAN [105624] (*John*[7], *Sullivans born about 1845 possibly*[1]) was born in 1872 in Ireland and died on 24 Jan 1950 in Fall River, Bristol, Massachusetts at age 78.

General Notes: 1870 December 10, Irish Baptisms LDS abstract shows a:
Patrick Sullivan, b. Kilcatherine, Co. Cork, IR (on the Beara Peninsula) to John Sullivan, Margaret Harrington.

1890 immigrated to America (1900 census).

1898 October 26, Marriages Registered in Fall River MA notes:
Patrick Sullivan, res. 51 Oak, Fall River, 26, Laborer, b. Ireland, to John, Margaret Harrington, first marriage.
Mary Shea, res. 51 Oak, Fall River, 24, Domestic, b. Ireland to Michael, Ellen - Driscoll, first marriage.
Married by M. J. Owens, Priest.

1900 Federal census of Fall River, Bristol Co. MA shows the family in Ward 7, dist 150, at 43 Dale St., as family #109:
Sullivan, Patrick, head, Mar 1872, 28, married 1 year, b. Ireland to Irish parents. Immigrated 1890, 10 years prior, naturalized. Laborer.
" Mary, wife, Sept 1873, 26, married 1 year, 1 child, 1 living, b. Ireland to Irish parents. Immigrated 1893, 7 years prior.
" John, son, Oct 1899, 7/12, b. MA to Irish parents.

1910 Federal census of Fall River, Bristol Co. MA shows the family in Ward 8, dist 167, at 634 Prospect St., as family #181:
Sullivan, Patrick J., head, 37, married 11 years, b. Ireland, Immigrated 1890, Naturalized. Laborer, Water Works.
" Mary, wife, 36, married 11 years, 4 children, 4 living, b. Ireland. Immigrated 1893.
" John, son, 10, b. MA.
" Mary, daughter, 8, b. MA.
" Margaret, daughter, 6, b. MA.
" Eugene, son, 5, b. MA.

1920 Federal census of Fall River, Bristol Co. MA shows the family in Ward 8, dist 87, at 634 Prospect St., as family #132:
Sullivan, Patrick J., head, owns home with mortgage, 47, immigrated 1889, naturalized 1900, b. Ireland. Foreman, Water Dept.
" Mary, wife, 45, immigrated 1894, b. Ireland.
" John H., son, 20, b. MA. (Student Wentworth Institued - crossed out and None written).
" Mary V., daughter, 18, b. MA. Bookkeeper, Wholesale grocer.
" Margaret E., daughter, 16, b. MA. Braider, Rope factory.
" Eugene J., son, 15, b. MA. Bobbin assorter, Rope factory.
" Paul P., son, 6, b. MA.

1930 Federal census of Fall River, Bristol Co. MA shows the family at 634 Prospect St as family #254:
Sullivan, Patrick J., head, owns $300, 58, married at 27, b. Ireland. Immigrated 1891. Inspector, Water Works.
" Mary, wife, 56, married at 25, b. Ireland. Immigrated 1893.
" Peter P. son, 16, b. MA.
Lambert, Margaret, Immigrated, 10, b. MA to MA and Irish parents.

1940 Federal census of Fall River, Bristol Co. MA shows the family at 634 Prospect St as family:
   Sullivan, Patrick J., owns $4000, 68, 8 years of school, b. Ireland.
   " Mary, wife, 66, 8 years of school, b. Ireland.
   " John H., son, 40, 4 years of high school, b. MA. Checker, Steamboat Co.
   " Eugene J., son, 35, 1 year of high school, b. MA, previously lived in NY.   Store clerk, Firestone
Co.   32 week salary $450.
   " Peter P., son, 26, b. MA.   Sealer (?) Deputy, City of Fall River.
   Lambert, Margaret F., Immigrated, 20, 4 years of high school, b. MA.   Cutter, Tape factory.   10
week salary $40.

1950 Fall River City Directory
- Sullivan Eugene J. res. 634 Prospect.
- Sullivan John H. res. 634 Prospect.
- Sullivan Patrick J. (Mary A.) house 634 Prospect.

1950 Fall River City Directory
- Sullivan Eugene J., clerk res. 634 Prospect.
- Sullivan John H. res. 634 Prospect.
- Sullivan Mary widow Patrick J. house 634 Prospect.
- Sullivan Patrick J. (Mary A) died Jan 24, 1950.

Patrick married **Mary SHEA** [105625] [MRIN: 35578], daughter of **Michael SHEA** [105628] and **Ellen DRISCOLL** [105629],   on 26 Oct 1898 in Fall River, Bristol, Massachusetts. Mary was born in 1874 in Kilkinnihan, Allihies Parish, Cork, Ireland and died after 1940 in Fall River, Bristol, Massachusetts.

Children from this marriage were:

   74   M   i.   **John H. SULLIVAN [105632]** was born on 16 Oct 1899 in Fall River, Bristol, Massachusetts.

   75   F   ii.   **Mary SULLIVAN [105631]** was born on 3 Aug 1901 in Fall River, Bristol, Massachusetts.

   76   F   iii.   **Margaret SULLIVAN [105634]** was born on 28 Sep 1903 in Fall River, Bristol, Massachusetts.

   77   M   iv.   **Eugene J. SULLIVAN [105630]** was born on 20 Nov 1904 in Fall River, Bristol, Massachusetts.

   78   M   v.   **Peter Paul SULLIVAN [105633]** was born on 7 Nov 1913 in Fall River, Bristol, Massachusetts and died before 2004.

         Peter married **Catherine Marie SHEA** [108543] [MRIN: 33513], daughter of **John SHEA** [108548] and **Margaret KILEY** [108549]. Catherine was born on 18 Mar 1913 in Fall River, Bristol, Massachusetts and died on 11 Feb 2004 in Little Compton, Newport, Rhode Island at age 90.

30.   Bridget M. SULLIVAN [105635] (*John [7], Sullivans born about 1845 possibly [1]*) was born in 1878 in Co. Cork, Ireland and died after 1930 in Fall River, Bristol, Massachusetts.

General Notes: Ireland Births and Baptisms with John Sullivan and Margaret Harrington appearing as parents, LDS abstracts note:
   Bridget, 1873 February 24, Co. Cork.

1902 August 10, Marriages Registered in Fall River MA notes:

James W. Gray, 31, b. to William, Mary O'Neil.
Bridget B. Sullivan, 24, b. to John, Margaret J. Harrington.

1910 Federal census of Fall River, Bristol Co. MA shows the siblings at 32 Wooley St.,:
 Sullivan, Eugene, head, 40, b. Ireland, to Irish parents.   Immigrated 1889, naturalized.   Laborer,
Water works (This is where brother Patrick works as well)
 " Margaret T., sister, 28, b. Ireland to Irish parents.   Immigrated 1892.   Weaver, Cotton mill.
 Gray, Bridget, sister, 34, married 7 years, 2 children, 2 living, b. Ireland to Irish parents.
Immigrated 1891.
 " Margaret A., niece, 5, b. NY (sic) to English and Irish parents.
 " William J., son, 3, b. MA.

1920 Federal census of Fall River, Bristol Co. MA shows the extended family at 25 Ford St., as family
#267:
 Gray, Bridgett (sic), head, 42, immigrated 1892, Naturalized 1895, b. Ireland to Irish parents.
Weaver, Cotton mill.
 " Margaret, daughter, 15, b. NY to English and Irish parents.
 " William J., son, 13, b. MA to English and Irish parents.
 Sullivan, Eugene, brother, 55, single, immigrated 1889, naturalized 1894, b. Ireland, to Irish parents.
Waterworks, City.

1930 Federal census of Fall River, Bristol Co. MA shows the widow at 411 Third St. as family #147:
 Gray, Bridget, head, rents $12, 55, widow, b. Ireland.   Immigrated 1889 (sic), Weaver Cotton mill.
 " William, son, 24, b. MA to Irish parents.   Clerk, Grocery store.

1931 Fall River City Directory
- Bridget widow James house 411 Fourth. (There is only one Bridget in the directory).
- William J. Clerk, 602 Third, res. 411 Fourth.

1934 Fall River City Directory
- Gray Bridget M Mrs. house 616 3rd.

1949 Fall River City Directory
- Gray Bridget M Mrs. house 616 3rd.
- Gray William J. (Lillian C) laborer house 517 4th.

1952 and 1956 Fall River City Directory
- Gray Bridget widow James res 75 Oak.
- Gray William J. (Lillian C) laborer house 517 4th.

1957 Bridget does not appear in the City Directory.

Bridget married **James W. GRAY** [105636] [MRIN: 35581], son of **William GRAY** [105637] and **Mary O'NEIL** [105649],   on 10 Aug 1902 in Fall River, Bristol, Massachusetts. James was born in 1871 in England.

Children from this marriage were:

79 F i. **Margaret A. GRAY [105650]** was born in 1905 in New York.

80 M ii. **William J. GRAY [105638]** was born on 9 Jul 1906 in Fall River, Bristol, Massachusetts.

34.   Annie SULLIVAN [97451] (*Daniel*[9], *Sullivans born about 1845 possibly*[1]) was born in 1872 in Ireland, died in 1926 in Fall River, Bristol, Massachusetts at age 54, and was buried in St. Patrick's Cem., Fall River, Massachusetts.

General Notes: 1889 she immigrated to America (1900 census) when she would have been about 17 years old.

1894 January 22, Marriages Registered in Fall River notes:
Edward J. Barry, res. Fall River, 18, Teamer, b. Fall River, to john, Rosanna Giles, first marriage.
Annie Sullivan, res. Fall River, 22, Warper Tender, b. Ireland, Daniel, Mary Hanley, first marriage.
Married by Mathias McCabe, Catholic Priest.

1900 Federal census shows the young family enumerated at 309 County Road renting from a Mary Sullivan.   This does not appear to be Annie's mother because she immigrated 16 years prior to Annie and notes she has no living children:
Sullivan, Mary, head, March 1832, 68, widow, 0 children, b. Ireland. Immigrated 1873, 27 years prior, Property Owner.   Owns with mortgage.

Annie married **Edward J. BARRY** [97450] [MRIN: 32533], son of **John BARRY** [94991] and **Rosanna GILES** [94992],   on 22 Jan 1894 in Fall River, Bristol, Massachusetts. Edward was born in 1876 in Fall River, Bristol, Massachusetts, died in 1950 in Fall River, Bristol, Massachusetts at age 74, and was buried in St. Patrick's Cem., Fall River, Massachusetts.

Children from this marriage were:

81   M   i.   **John BARRY** [97452] was born on 22 Jun 1894 in Fall River, Bristol, Massachusetts.

82   F   ii.   **Mary BARRY** [97454] was born on 10 Feb 1896 in Fall River, Bristol, Massachusetts and died on 14 Dec 1896 in Fall River, Bristol, Massachusetts.

General Notes: 1896 December 14, Deaths registered in Fall River notes;
Mary Barry, single, age 10m 4d, died Menengitis, b. Fall River to Edward, Annie-Sullivan, b. Fall River and Ireland.

83   F   iii.   **Catherine BARRY** [97462] was born in Feb 1897 in Fall River, Bristol, Massachusetts, died in 1977 at age 80, and was buried in St. Patrick's Cem., Fall River, Massachusetts.

Catherine married **Thomas F. HARTNETT** [97463] [MRIN: 32535]. Thomas was born in 1897 and died in 1970 at age 73.

84   M   iv.   **Edward A. BARRY** [97455] was born on 7 Jun 1900 in Fall River, Bristol, Massachusetts, died on 15 Oct 1921 in Fall River, Bristol, Massachusetts at age 21, and was buried in St. Patrick's Cem., Fall River, Massachusetts.

85   F   v.   **Rosanna BARRY** [97453] was born on 8 Jul 1903 in Fall River, Bristol, Massachusetts and died on 3 Oct 1907 in Fall River, Bristol, Massachusetts at age 4.

General Notes: 1907 October 3, Masachusetts Deaths Certificate of Fall River notes:
Rose A. Barry, res. 577 E. Main St., age 4y 2m, single.   B. Fall River to Edward Barry, b. Fall River, mother Annie Sullivan, b. Ireland.   Informant Edward Barry.   Died of Menengitis.   Burial St. Patricks Cemetery.

37.   William F. SULLIVAN [106444] (*Patrick J.* [10] *, Sullivans born about 1845 possibly* [1]) was born on 14 Feb 1876 in Newport, Newport, Rhode Island and died on 24 Nov 1952 in Newport, Newport, Rhode Island at age 76.

General Notes: 1910 Federal census of Newport, Newport Co. RI shows the young family at 58 Levin St.

Sullivan, William F., head, 35, married 5 family, b. RI to Irish parents.   Painter & Decorator.
Rents.
    " Annie T., wife, 37, married 5 years, 4 children, 4 living, b. NY to parents from England and
Ireland.
    " William P., son, 3, b. RI.
    " Helena F., daughter, 1, b. RI.
    " Harry V., twin son, 2/12, b. RI.
    " Edwin (sic) E., twin son, 2/12, b. RI.

1918 September 12, WWI Draft Registration card notes:
    William Francis Sullivan, res 58 Levin, Newport, RI. 42, b. February 14, 1876. Decorator, George
E. Vernon Co. 91 John, Newport.   Nearest relative - Anna Teresa Sullivan.
Height medium, build medium, eyes gray.

1920 Federal census of Newport, Newport Co. RI shows the family at 58 Levin Street as family #184:
    Sullivan, William F., 43, b. RI. No employment.
    " Annie T., wife, 46, b. NY to English parents.
    " William P., son, 13, b. RI.
    " Helena F., daughter, 11, b. RI.
    " Harry V., son, 9, b. RI.
    " Edmund E., son, 9, b. RI.
    " Mary E., daughter, 7, b. RI.

1929 October 1, married Catherine Boyle at St. John Gaulbert's Church, Johnstown, PA.

1930 Federal census of Newport, Newport Co. RI shows the family at 5 Berkeley Terrace, as family
#42:
    Sullivan, William F., head, rents $40, 54, married first at 29, b. RI to Irish parents. Interior
Decorator, Interior Decorator Shop.
    " Catherine P., wife, 47, married at 47, b. PA to Irish and PA parents.
    " Harry, son, 20, b. RI to RI and NY parents. Clerk, Dry good store.
    " Edmund, son, 20, b. RI to RI and NY parents. Artist, Portrait.

William married **Anna Teresa BULLETT** [106446] [MRIN: 35880], daughter of **Alfred John BULLETT**
[106447] and **Margaret wife of Alfred BULLETT** [106448], on 12 Jun 1905 in Newport, Newport,
Rhode Island. Anna was born on 2 May 1874 in New York, New York, New York and died on 23 May 1927
in Newport, Newport, Rhode Island at age 53.

Children from this marriage were:

   86 M   i.   **William Francis SULLIVAN [106449]** was born on 6 Oct 1906 in Newport, Newport,
            Rhode Island and died on 20 Jun 1968 in Tulsa, Tulsa, Oklahoma at age 61.

            General Notes: 1935 June 14, Ordained at St. Dominic's Church, Washington DC.

            1944 May 5, married Frances Elizabeth Juregenson, Los Angeles, CA.

            William married **Frances Elizabeth JURGENSEN** [106450] [MRIN: 35882], daughter of **Emil B.
            JURGENSEN** [106451] and **Katherien A. VAUGHN** [106452],   on 5 May 1944 in Los Angeles
            Co., CA. Frances was born on 5 Dec 1921 in Hartford, Hartford, Connecticut and died on 11 Mar
            1964 in Tulsa, Tulsa, Oklahoma at age 42.

   87 F   ii.   **Helena F. SULLIVAN [106453]** was born on 7 Aug 1908 in Newport, Newport, Rhode
            Island and died on 19 Jun 1946 in Providence, Providence, Rhode Island at age 37.

Helena married **James L GRIFFIN** [106457] [MRIN: 35884], son of **James L. GRIFFIN** [106458] and **Annie M. wife of James GRIFFIN** [106459], in 1937 in RI. James was born on 15 Aug 1908 in Providence, Providence, Rhode Island, died in May 1986 in Bristol, Bristol, Rhode Island at age 77, and was buried in St. Ann Cemetery, Cranston, RI.

+ 88 M iii. **Edmund Edwards SULLIVAN [106454]** was born on 10 Feb 1910 in Newport, Newport, Rhode Island and died on 14 Aug 1961 in Newport, Newport, Rhode Island at age 51.

Edmund married **Madeline Barbara PEDRO** [106460] [MRIN: 35886] (b. 27 Jan 1916, d. 29 Apr 2008) on 7 Aug 1933 in Newport, Newport, Rhode Island.

89 M iv. **Harry V. SULLIVAN [106455]** was born on 10 Feb 1910 in Newport, Newport, Rhode Island and died on 6 Aug 1947 in Newport, Newport, Rhode Island at age 37.

90 F v. **Mary E. SULLIVAN [106456]** was born in 1913 in Newport, Newport, Rhode Island and died on 13 Aug 1928 in Newport, Newport, Rhode Island at age 15.

William next married **Catherine P. BOYLE** [106463] [MRIN: 35887], daughter of **Patrick J. BOYLE** [106464] and **Catherine wife of Patrick BOYLE** [106465], on 1 Oct 1929 in Johnstown, Cambria, Pennsylvania. Catherine was born on 2 May 1882 in Johnstown, Cambria, Pennsylvania and died on 19 May 1968 in Newport, Newport, Rhode Island at age 86.

40. Mortimer L SULLIVAN [106433] (*Patrick J.*[10], *Sullivans born about 1845 possibly*[1]) was born in 1881 in Newport, Newport, Rhode Island and died on 4 Dec 1911 in Newport, Newport, Rhode Island at age 30.

General Notes: 1906 December 27, Marriages Registered in Fall River MA notes:
   Mortimer L. Sullivan, 25, first marriages, res. 678 Thames, Newport RI, Painter, b. Newport RI to Patrick J., Bridget Wall.
   Annie A. Esleeck, 18, first marriage, res. 40 Green, Newport, RI, At home, b. Newport RI to Charles S., Louise J. Lowe.
   Married by Arthur Brayton, J. P.

1910 Federal census the young couple and son are enumerated in Newport RI with Mortimer's parents at 678 Thames St.

1911 December 4, Rhode Island Deaths LDS abstracts notes:
   Mortimer L. Sullivan, b. 1881, died age 30. Parents Patrick J., Bridget Sullivan.

1920 Federal census the two children of Mortimer and Annie was enumerated with their grandparents again at 678 Thames St. in Newport RI.

Mortimer married **Annie L. ESLECK** [106434] [MRIN: 35876], daughter of **Charles Summer ESLECK** [106437] and **Louise J. LOWE** [106438], on 27 Dec 1906 in Fall River, Bristol, Massachusetts. Annie was born in 1888 in Newport, Newport, Rhode Island and died before 1920.

Children from this marriage were:

91 M i. **Henry M. SULLIVAN [106439]** was born in 1909 in Newport, Newport, Rhode Island.

General Notes: 1910 and 1920 Federal census enumerated at the home of his Sullivan grandparents. In 1920 his parents are no longer shown.

1930 Federal census curiously shows him in Rutherford, Bergen Co. NJ at 158 Vreland Ave:
   Finely, Charles H. head, owns home $14000, 45, married at 20, b. PA. Experimental engineer, Office equipment.

" Helen V., wife, 38, marred at 14 (sic), b. PA.

" Evelyn H., daughter, 10, b. PA.

" Charles A., son, 7, b. PA.

Seltz, Helen, sister in law, 40, widow, married at 25, b. PA.   Head waitress, Hotel

Sullivan, Henry M., nephew, 22, b. RI to RI parents. Painter, Construction (Like his father and grandfather)

Seltz, Thomas, nephew, 19, b. PA. Military, US Army.

92 F   ii.   **Mary SULLIVAN [106440]** was born in 1911 in Newport, Newport, Rhode Island.

41. William SULLIVAN [101923] (*John*[11], *Sullivans born about 1845 possibly*[1]) was born on 13 May 1868 in Wales and died on 9 Nov 1947 in Fall River, Bristol, Massachusetts at age 79.

General Notes: 1894 immigrated to America.

1896 Fall River City Directory
- Sullivan John operative boards 340 Fifth.
- Sullivan Mary A., widow of John, house 340 Fifth.
- Sullivan William, carder, boards 340 Fifth.

1898 January 25, Marriages Registered in Fall River MA notes:
   William Sullivan, 340 Fifth St. Fall River, age 29, Laborer, b. So. Wales, to John, Mary A. - Hannigan, first marriage.
   Catherine Ahassey (written clearly), 400 Fourth St., Fall River, 27, Weaver, b. Ireland to Thomas, Hanora - Brett, first marriage.
   Married by Michael J. McCabe, Priest.

1900 Federal census of Fall River, Bristol Co. MA shows the young family in Ward 4, dist 127 at 340 Fifth St as family #225:
   Sullivan, William, head, May 1871, 28, married 3 years, b. England to English (sic), immigrated 1894, 6 years prior, Alien, Day laborer.
   " Catherine, wife, Dec 1872. 27, married 3 years, 1 child, 1 living, b. MA (sic) to Irish parents.
   " Edmond, son, Dec 1899, 5/12, b. MA to parents from England and MA.
(These two families 224 and 225 were in the same dwelling.   William Sullivan is the son of John and Mary Hannigan Sullivan with no known relation to Catherine Sullivan Burns daughter of a John and Catherine.   They are neighbors again in the 1910 and 1920 census.)

1901 birth record of daughter Gertrude shows father William as a yard man.

1906 September 25, Immigration and Naturalization Service, Fall River Second District Court, Certificate No. 3708 Vol 1902-1906 Year 1906, William Sullivan, 340 Fifth St., Fall River, b. Wales, May 13, 1868.

1908 Fall River City Directory
- Sullivan William yard foreman Laural Lake house 340 Fifth.

1910 Federal census of Fall River, Bristol Co. MA shows the widow in Ward 4, dist 139 again at 340 Fifth St. as family #253:
   Sullivan, William, head, 42, married 12 years, b. Wales, to Irish parents. Immigrated 1894, naturalized. Yard master, Cotton mill.
   " Catherine, wife, 35, married 12 years, 6 children, 4 living, b. Ireland to Irish parents. Immigrated 1892.
   " Edmund, son, 10, b. MA to parents from Wales, Ireland.
   " Gertrude, daughter, 9, b. MA.
   " Mary, daughter, 4, b. MA.
   " William C., son, 3, b. MA.

1920 Federal census of Fall River, Bristol Co. MA show the family still at 340 Fifth St.:
  Sullivan, William, rents, 50, head, b. Wales, immigrated 1895, naturalized 1909 (sic). Foreman,
Cotton Mill.
   " Katherine (sic), wife, 45, immigrated 1883, b. Ireland.
   " Edmund, son, 20, b. MA. Foreman, Cotton mill.
   " Gertrude, daughter, 18, b. MA.   Telephone operator, Telephone Co.
   " Mary, daughter, 14, b. MA.
   " William, son, 13, b. MA.
   " Katherine, daughter, 9, b. MA.
   " Helen (sic), daughter, 9, b. MA.

1930 Federal census of Fall River, Bristol Co. MA shows the family at 580 Second St. as family #354:
   Sullivan, William, head, owns home $12,000, 60, married at 28, b. Wales to Irish parents.
Immigrated 1896 (sic), naturalized.   Foreman, cotton mill.
   " Catherine, wife, 58, married at 26, b. Ireland to Irish parents.   Immigrated 1892, naturalized.
   " Edmund, son, 28, b. MA. Painter, Paint shop.
   " Gertrude, son (sic), 26, b. MA. Operator, Telephone Co.
   " William, son, 22, b. MA,   Printer, shop.
   " Catherine, daughter, 19, b. MA. Student - nurse, Hospital.
   " Ilean (sic) daughter, 17, b. MA.
(There are two other families in the dwelling renting presumably from William, at $30 and $18 rent
respectively.

1931 and 1932 Fall River City Directory
- Sullivan William (Catherine) Yard foreman, Laurel Lakes Mill, house 580 Second.

1936 Fall River City Directory
- Sullivan Eileen housekeeper res. 580 2d.
- Sullivan Gertrude A. phone operator 171 Bank res. 580 2d.
- Sullivan Wm (Catherine) Yard foreman house 580 2d.
- Sullivan Wm C. painter res. 580 2d.

1939 and 1940 Fall River City Directory
- Sullivan Eileen A. bookkeeper 69 Alden, res 580 2d
- Sullivan Gertrude A supervisor NET&T res 580 2d.
- Sullivan Wm. house 580 2d. (No Catherine)
- Sullivan Wm C. painter res. 580 2d.

1947 Fall River City Directory
- Sullivan, Wm house 580 2d.

1949 Fall River City Directory
- Sullivan Eileen A. bookkeeper, house 580 2d.

- Sullivan Gertrude A supervisor NET&T res 580 2d.
- Sullivan Wm died Nov 9, 1947.
- Sullivan Wm C (Kathleen) painter house 522 S. Almond.

William married **Catherine HASSEY** [101924] [MRIN: 34191], daughter of **Thomas HASSEY** [101927]
and **Hanora 'Ann' BRITT** [101928], on 25 Jan 1898 in Fall River, Bristol, Massachusetts. Catherine was
born on 15 Dec 1869 in Portlaw, Waterford, Munster, Ireland and died on 20 Aug 1938 in Fall River,
Bristol, Massachusetts at age 68.

Children from this marriage were:

93 M i. **Edmund Joseph SULLIVAN [101929]** was born on 10 Dec 1899 in Fall River, Bristol, Massachusetts and died on 7 Nov 1944 at age 44.

General Notes: 1899 December 10, Births Registered in Fall River MA notes:
Sullivan, Edmund J., b. to William, Catherine - Hassey, res. 340 Fifth, father Operative, parents b. Wales, Ireland.

94 F ii. **Gertrude A. SULLIVAN [101930]** was born on 22 Jan 1901 in Fall River, Bristol, Massachusetts and died on 18 Jun 1983 in Fall River, Bristol, Massachusetts at age 82.

General Notes: 1901 January 22, Births Registered in Fall River MA notes:
Sullivan, Gertrude A, b. to William, Catherine - Hassey, res. 340 Fifth, father Yard man, parents b. Wales, Ireland.

1918 BMC Durfee High School "Tech Record":
Gertrude Agnes Sullivan
Gertrude is in the Commercial Department and specialized in housekeeping. Her chief characteristic is the fact that she is always quiet. Really we should not forget that she were in our class if one of the teachers did not remind us of the fact now and then by calling on her for a recitation. She doesn't know yet what she will do after graduation, but from the nature of her course we expect that she will do some sort of clerical work.

1949 Fall River City Directory
- Sullivan Eileen A. bookkeeper, house 580 2nd.
- Sullivan Gertrude A supervisor NET&T res 580 2nd.
- Sullivan Wm died Nov 9, 1947.
- Sullivan Wm C (Kathleen) painter house 522 S. Almond.

1983 June social security death index shows Gertrude Sullivan, born 22 January 1901 died last residence Fall River MA.

95 F iii. **Mary A. SULLIVAN [101931]** was born on 18 May 1905 in Fall River, Bristol, Massachusetts and died on 23 Jul 1920 in Fall River, Bristol, Massachusetts at age 15.

General Notes: 1905 May 18, Births Registered in Fall River MA notes:
Sullivan, Mary H., b. to William, Catherine - Hassey (typed), res. 340 Fifth, father Laborer, parents b. Wales, Ireland.

1920 July 23, Massachusetts Death Certificate notes:
Mary H. (sic) Sullivan, died St. Ann's Hospital, res. 340 Fifth St., Fall River MA. Single. Born May 18, 1905. Age 15 years 1 month 5 days. Occupation - At school. Born Fall River to William, b. Wales, mother Catherine Hassey, b. Ireland. Informant William Sullivan 340 Fifth.
Died of Acute Appendicitis, duration 10 days, contributing Peritonitis. Burial St. Patrick's cemetery.

96 M iv. **William C. SULLIVAN [101932]** was born on 19 Sep 1906 in Fall River, Bristol, Massachusetts, died on 24 Oct 1964 in Fall River, Bristol, Massachusetts at age 58, and was buried in St. Patrick's Cem., Fall River, Massachusetts.

General Notes: 1906 September 19, Births Registered in Fall River MA notes:
Sullivan, William C., b. to William, Katherine (sic) - Ahaesay (typed), res. 340 Fifth, father Yard master, parents b. Wales, Ireland.

1939 and 1940
- Sullivan Eileen A. bookkeeper 69 Alden, res 580 2d.

- Sullivan Gertrude A supervisor NET&T res 580 2d.
- Sullivan Wm. house 580 2d. (No Catherine.)
- Sullivan Wm C. painter res. 580 2d.

1945 Fall River City Directory shows   a William C. again after not appearing in 1944:
- Sullivan Wm C. (Kathleen) house 522 S. Almond.

The couple rests at St. Patrick's Cemetery marked with flush stone:
    William C. Sullivan 1906 - 1964
    Kathleen, his Wife 1912 - 1999

William married **Kathleen GRANFIELD** [101935] [MRIN: 34195], daughter of **Michael T. GRANFIELD** [109695] and **Mary OLAUGHLIN** [109696]. Kathleen was born on 26 Mar 1912 in Fall River, Bristol, Massachusetts, died on 17 Jul 1999 in Fall River, Bristol, Massachusetts at age 87, and was buried in St. Patrick's Cem., Fall River, Massachusetts.

97 F   v.   **Catherine Veronica 'Kay' SULLIVAN [101933]** was born on 31 May 1910 in Fall River, Bristol, Massachusetts and died on 31 Dec 2005 in Chelmsford, Middlesex, Massachusetts at age 95.

General Notes: 1910 May 10, Births Registered in Fall River MA notes:
    Sullivan, Catherine., b. to William, Catherine - Hassey, res. 340 Fifth, father Yard foreman, parents b. Wales, Ireland.

2005 December 31, Obituary, Watertown Tab, Watertown, MA
Katherine Cody, Registered nurse
Katherine Veronica "Kay" (Sullivan) Cody of Watertown died Saturday, Dec. 31, 2005, at Sunny Acres Nursing Home in Chelmsford. She was 95.
Mrs. Cody was born in Fall River, a daughter of the late William C. and Catherine G. (Hassey) Sullivan. She was a graduate of St. Mary Cathedral Grammar School and the BMC Durfee High School in Fall River. She was a resident of Watertown for more than 60 years.
Mrs. Cody was a registered nurse and received her nursing education at Chelsea Memorial Hospital School of Nursing and Boston City Hospital School of Nursing with a specialty in pediatrics. She had been on the nursing staff of Kennedy Memorial Hospital in Brighton for 20 years, retiring in 1976.
Wife of the late John Christopher Cody, who died in 1988, she leaves two children, John H. Cody of Chelmsford and Judith C. Vacca of Rochester, N. H.; 10 grandchildren; and 15 great - grandchildren.
She was the sister of the late Eileen A. Sullivan, Gertrude Sullivan, Edmund Sullivan, William Sullivan, Mary Sullivan, Mildred Sullivan and John Sullivan.
Her funeral Mass was celebrated Wednesday, Jan. 4, at the Church of St. Patrick, Watertown.

Catherine married **John Christopher CODY** [107749] [MRIN: 36394], son of **Michael F. CODY** [109901] and **Delia A. KELLY** [109902]. John was born on 10 Mar 1910 in Ballinakilla, Tuam, Gallway, Ireland and died on 30 Sep 1988 in Watertown, Middlesex, MA at age 78.

98 F   vi.   **Eileen A. SULLIVAN [101934]** was born on 25 May 1912 in Fall River, Bristol, Massachusetts and died on 2 Jun 2000 in Fall River, Bristol, Massachusetts at age 88.

General Notes: 1912 May 25, Births Registered in Fall River MA notes:
    Sullivan, Eileen., b. to William, Catherine - Hassey, res. 340 Fifth, father Yardman, parents b. Wales, Ireland.

1949 Fall River City Directory
- Sullivan Eileen A. bookkeeper, house 580 2d.
- Sullivan Gertrude A supervisor NET&T res 580 2d.

- Sullivan Wm died Nov 9, 1947.
- Sullivan Wm C (Kathleen) painter house 522 S. Almond.

43.   John SULLIVAN [101936] (*John[11], Sullivans born about 1845 possibly[1]*) was born in 1873 in Wales, died on 14 May 1947 in Fall River, Bristol, Massachusetts at age 74, and was buried in St. Patrick's Cem., Fall River, Massachusetts.

General Notes: 1896 Fall River City Directory
- Sullivan John operative boards 340 Fifth.
- Sullivan Mary A., widow of John, house 340 Fifth.
- Sullivan William, carder, boards 340 Fifth.

1899 January 26, Marriages Registered in Fall River MA notes:
   John Sullivan, 489 Third, Fall River, 26, Laborer, b. Wales to John, Mary Hannigan, first marriage.
   Julia Driscoll, 58 Branch, Fall River, 22, Rope works, b. MI to Cornelius, Julia - Hurley, first marriage.
   Married by D. F. Sheedy, Priest.

1900 the family was living at 57 Lyons, Fall River when son John was born.

1900 Federal census of Fall River, Bristol Co. MA shows the family in Ward 1, dist 109, at 57 Lyon St., as family #120:
   Sullivan, John, head, April 1873, 27, married 1 year, b. Wales to Irish parents.   Cotton weaver. Rents.
   " Julia, wife, Nov 1876, 23, married 1 year, 1 child 1 living, b. MI to Irish parents. Cotton weaver.
   " John H., son, Jan 1900, 11/12, b. MA to parents from Wales and MI.

1906 the family was living at 1076 (sic) Plymouth Ave. when daughter Katherine was born.

1908 the family was living at 1073 (sic) Plymouth Ave. when son Dennis was born.

1910 Federal census of Fall River, Bristol Co. MA shows the family in Ward 4, dist 139 in a 3 family dwelling at 506 Fourth St. as family #406.
   Sullivan, John, head, 37, married 11 years, b. Wales. Immigrated 1895, Naturalized. Salesman, grocery store.
   " Julia, wife, 30, married 11 years, 4 children, 4 living, b. MI.
   " John H., son, 10, b. MA.
   " Mary E., daughter, 7, b. MA.
   " Kathryn (sic), daughter, 4, b. MA.
   " Dennis, son, 2, b. MA.

1920 Federal census of Fall River, Bristol Co. MA shows the family in Ward 7, dist 82, at 203 Fourth St. as family #162:
   Sullivan, John, head, rents, 46, immigrated 1890, Naturalized 1900, b. Wales.   Shipping clerk, Grocery Stores.
   " Julia, wife, 39, b. MI.
   " John H., son, 19, b. MA. Clerk, Grocery store.
   " Ethel, daughter, 17, b. MA.   Clerk, Jewelry factory.
   " Cathleen (sic), daughter, 13, b. MA.
   " Dennis, son, 12, b. MA.
   " Leo, son, 9, b. MA.
   " Ruth, daughter, 5, b. MA.

1930 Federal census of Fall River, Bristol Co. MA shows the widower at 340 Whipple St., as family #80:

Sullivan, John , head, owns home $7,000, 50, widower, b. England (sic) to Northern Irish parents. Immigrated 1895, Naturalized.   Salesman, Department Store.
  " Ethel M., daughter, 27, b. MA to English and MI parents. Stenographer, Law office.
  " Kathleen F., daughter, 23, b. MA.   Telephone operator, Telephone Co.
  " Dennis J., son, 21, b. MA.
  " Leo T., son, 19, b. MA.
  " Ruth T., daughter, 15, b. MA.

1935 Fall River City Directory
- Sullivan Dennis J. student res. 340 Whipple.
- Sullivan John clerk 251 South Main, house 340 Whipple.
- Sullivan Kathryn F. phone operator 171 Bank, res. 340 Whipple.
- Sullivan Leo T. student res. 340 Whipple.
- Sullivan Ruth T. assistant 400 S. Main, room 4, res. 340 Whipple.

1940 Federal census of Fall River, Bristol Co. MA shows the family at 454 (sic) Whipple:
  Sullivan, John, owns home $1450, head, 65, widower, 6 years of school, b. Scotland (sic).
  " Catherine (sic), daughter, 32, 3 years of high school, b. MA.   Telephone operator, Telephone office, salary $987, 47 weeks.
  " Ruth T., daughter, 25, 4 years of high school, b. MA.   Receptionist, Doctors office, salary $832, 52 weeks.
(The family of James Walsh was renting in the dwelling paying $22.)

1940 Fall River City Directory
- Sullivan Dennis J. res. 340 Whipple.
- Sullivan John clerk house 340 Whipple.
- Sullivan Kathryn F. Telephone operator NET&T Co. res. 340 Whipple.
- Sullivan Leo T. helper res. 673 Walnut.
- Sullivan Ruth T. Dental nurse, res. 340 Whipple.

1946 Fall River City Directory
- Sullivan John clerk house 340 Whipple.

1847 Fall River City Directory
- Sullivan John died May 14, 1947.

The family rests at St. Patrick's Cemetery, Robeson St., Fall River MA - stone marked
Sullivan - Smith
  1873 John Sullivan 1947
  1882 (sic) Julia his wife 1929
  1918 Frances J. Sullivan 1919
  1920 Rev. Leo T. Sullivan 1975
  1919 Lynwood E. B. Smith 1996
  1914 Ruth T. his wife 2007
  1948 Leo D. Smith 1948

John married **Juila DRISCOLL** [101938] [MRIN: 34196], daughter of **Cornelius DRISCOLL** [101939] and **Julia HURLEY** [101940],   on 26 Jan 1899 in Fall River, Bristol, Massachusetts. Juila was born in 1877 in Horton, Jackson, Michigan, died on 13 Oct 1929 in Fall River, Bristol, Massachusetts at age 52, and was buried in St. Patrick's Cem., Fall River, Massachusetts.

Children from this marriage were:

   99   M   i.   **John Henry SULLIVAN [101943]** was born on 14 Jan 1900 in Fall River, Bristol, Massachusetts.

General Notes: 1900 January 14, Births Registered in Fall River MA notes:
  Sullivan, John H., John, Julia - Driscoll, res. 57 Lyons, Operative, parents b. England, Michigan.

+ 100 F ii. **Mary Ethel SULLIVAN [101944]** was born on 24 May 1902 in Fall River, Bristol, Massachusetts and died after 1940 in Fall River, Bristol, Massachusetts.

Mary married **Dr. Arthur William LEARY** [101956] [MRIN: 34204] (b. 23 Jul 1902, d. After 1940)

+ 101 F iii. **Kathleen F. SULLIVAN [101945]** was born on 12 Apr 1906 in Fall River, Bristol, Massachusetts and died on 20 Oct 1989 in MA at age 83.

Kathleen married **John Joseph McGRATH** [101948] [MRIN: 34200] (b. 28 Dec 1902) on 11 Apr 1946 in Seabrook, Rockingham, New Hampshire.

102 M iv. **Dennis J. SULLIVAN [101946]** was born on 29 Jan 1908 in Fall River, Bristol, Massachusetts.

General Notes: 1908 January 29, Births Registered in Fall River MA notes:
  Sullivan, Dennis J., b. to John, Julia Driscoll, res. 1073 (sic) Plymouth Ave., father Clerk, parents b. Wales, Horton, MI.

1935 Fall River City Directory
- Sullivan Dennis J. student res. 340 Whipple.
- Sullivan John clerk 251 South Main, house 340 Whipple.
- Sullivan Kathryn F. phone operator 171 Bank, res. 340 Whipple.
- Sullivan Leo T. student res. 340 Whipple.
- Sullivan Ruth T. assistant 400 S. Main, rm 4, res. 340 Whipple.

1940 Fall River City Directory
- Sullivan Dennis J. res. 340 Whipple.
- Sullivan John clerk house 340 Whipple.
- Sullivan Kathryn F. Telephone operator NET&T Co. res. 340 Whipple.
- Sullivan Leo T. helper res. 673 Walnut.
- Sullivan Ruth T. Dental nurse, res. 340 Whipple.

103 M v. **Rev. Leo T. SULLIVAN [101954]** was born on 12 Dec 1910 in Fall River, Bristol, Massachusetts, died in 1975 at age 65, and was buried in St. Patrick's Cem., Fall River, Massachusetts.

General Notes: 1935 Fall River City Directory
- Sullivan Dennis J. student res. 340 Whipple.
- Sullivan John clerk 251 South Main, house 340 Whipple.
- Sullivan Kathryn F. phone operator 171 Bank, res. 340 Whipple.
- Sullivan Leo T. student res. 340 Whipple.
- Sullivan Ruth T. assistant 400 S. Main, rm 4, res. 340 Whipple.

1940 Fall River City Directory
- Sullivan Dennis J. res. 340 Whipple.
- Sullivan John clerk house 340 Whipple.
- Sullivan Kathryn F. Telephone operator NET&T Co. res. 340 Whipple.
- Sullivan Leo T. helper res. 673 Walnut.
- Sullivan Ruth T. Dental nurse, res. 340 Whipple.

+ 104 F vi. **Ruth T. SULLIVAN [101947]** was born on 17 Dec 1914 in Fall River, Bristol, Massachusetts, died on 29 Aug 2007 in Tiverton, Newport, Rhode Island at age 92, and was buried in St. Patrick's Cem., Fall River, Massachusetts.

Ruth married **Lynwood E. B. SMITH** [101955] [MRIN: 34203] (b. 1914, d. 1996)

105 F vii. **Frances J. SULLIVAN [107893]** was born on 28 Sep 1918 in Fall River, Bristol, Massachusetts, died on 12 Nov 1919 in Fall River, Bristol, Massachusetts at age 1, and was buried in St. Patrick's Cem., Fall River, Massachusetts.

General Notes: Died age 1 year 1 month of Broncho Pneumonia, contributing, Measles. Family was living at 203 Fourth St. Fall River MA.

Great-Grandchildren

69.   John Francis SULLIVAN [105313] (*Patrick F.* [22]*, Cornelius* [6]*, Sullivans born about 1845 possibly* [1]) was born on 25 Feb 1900 in Boston, Suffolk, Massachusetts.

John married **Mary Agnes STARRS** [105317] [MRIN: 35463]. Mary was born on 4 Dec 1901 in Little Falls, Herkimer, New York and died on 26 Nov 1989 in Brighton, Suffolk, Massachusetts at age 87.

The child from this marriage was:

106   M   i.   **John Francis SULLIVAN Jr. [105318]** was born on 16 Jun 1930 in Roslindale, Suffolk, Massachusetts and died on 27 Jan 2003 in Norwood, Norfolk, Massachusetts at age 72.

88.   Edmund Edwards SULLIVAN [106454] (*William F.* [37]*, Patrick J.* [10]*, Sullivans born about 1845 possibly* [1]) was born on 10 Feb 1910 in Newport, Newport, Rhode Island and died on 14 Aug 1961 in Newport, Newport, Rhode Island at age 51.

> General Notes: 1940 Federal census of Newport, Newport Co. RI shows the family at 68 Third St.:
>   Sullivan, Edmund E., head, 30, 8 years of school, b. RI. Painter, Painting Contractor. 40 week salary $1000.
>   " Madeline B., wife, 23, 8 years of school, b. RI.
>   " William E., son, 4, b. RI.
>   " Patricia A., daughter, 2, b. RI.

Edmund married **Madeline Barbara PEDRO** [106460] [MRIN: 35886] on 7 Aug 1933 in Newport, Newport, Rhode Island. Madeline was born on 27 Jan 1916 in Newport, Newport, Rhode Island and died on 29 Apr 2008 in Newport, Newport, Rhode Island at age 92.

Children from this marriage were:

107   M   i.   **William Edmund SULLIVAN [106461]** was born on 6 Sep 1935 in Newport, Newport, Rhode Island and died on 10 Mar 2013 in Tulsa, Tulsa, Oklahoma at age 77.

> General Notes: 2013 March 10 - Cremation Society of Oklahoma Obituaries - William Edmund Sullivan
> William Edmund Sullivan was born September 6, 1935, in Newport, Rhode Island. He died March 10, 2013, in Tulsa, Oklahoma, at the age of 77.
>
> William was a preacher and a resident of Creek county, Oklahoma.

108   M   ii.   **Edmund Edwards SULLIVAN [106462]** was born on 8 Jan 1942 in Newport, Newport, Rhode Island and died on 6 May 1994 in Portsmouth, Newport, Rhode Island at age 52.

100.   Mary Ethel SULLIVAN [101944] (*John* [43]*, John* [11]*, Sullivans born about 1845 possibly* [1]) was born on 24 May 1902 in Fall River, Bristol, Massachusetts and died after 1940 in Fall River, Bristol, Massachusetts.

> General Notes: Birth record notes Mary E. 1920 census shows 'Ethel'.
>
> 1923 Fall River City Directory
> - Sullivan Ethel M clerk 139 South Main house 340 Whipple.

Mary married **Dr. Arthur William LEARY** [101956] [MRIN: 34204]. Arthur was born on 23 Jul 1902 in Fall River, Bristol, Massachusetts and died after 1940 in Fall River, Bristol, Massachusetts.

Children from this marriage were:

   109   F   i.   **Ruth M. LEARY [107941]** was born in 1934 in Fall River, Bristol, Massachusetts.

   110   F   ii.   **SheilaC. LEARY [101958]** was born in 1935 in Fall River, Bristol, Massachusetts.

              General Notes: 2007 she is mentioned as a survivor of aunt Ruth T. Smith. Shelia and husband Michael Craig lived in Annandale VA at that time the Fall River Herald obituary notes.

              SheilaC. married **Michael CRAIG** [101959] [MRIN: 34205]. Michael was born about 1935.

   111   M   iii.   **Francis LEARY C.S.C. [101957]** was born about 1945 in Fall River, Bristol, Massachusetts.

              General Notes: BROTHER FRANCIS LEARY, C.S.C.
Guidance Counselor, Holy Cross High School, Flushing, N.Y.
Brother Francis has served as an educator with the Brothers of Holy Cross for more than 50 years. His career has included serving as a teacher of French, as well a principal. Since 1989, he has worked with teens as a guidance counselor at Holy Cross High School in Flushing, N.Y.

              "As a student at Monsignor Coyle High School in Massachusetts, I looked up to the Brothers of Holy Cross. They were excellent teachers and they inspired me. I'm now in my 54th year as a Brother and I have always taught and worked with young people in our schools.

              Through the years, the students and the culture have changed so much. You have to know how to relate to students today because they're so much more aware of everything. I think they respect me as a Brother, but they also trust me because of who I am as a person.

              The Brothers have given me so many opportunities to grow spiritually over the years. I am fortunate to spend this summer in France at the Holy Cross Legacy Institute, which allows us to explore the history of the congregation and visit the place where it was founded. I've also been enriched by the many students I've met through the years. I'm honored that so many have kept in touch! Hopefully, I've helped them to be better persons."
http://www.holycrossbrothers.org/ourstories.php Feb 2012

101. Kathleen F. SULLIVAN [101945] (*John*[43], *John*[11], *Sullivans born about 1845 possibly*[1]) was born on 12 Apr 1906 in Fall River, Bristol, Massachusetts and died on 20 Oct 1989 in MA at age 83.

     General Notes: 1906 April 12, Births Registered in Fall River MA notes:
      Sullivan, Katherine, b. to John, Julia Driscoll, res. 1076 Plymouth Ave, father Clerk, parents b. Wales, Michigan.

     1989 October 20, Massachusetts Death Index notes Kathleen F. McGrath death in Middleborough, b. MA 1906 April 12.

     1946 April 11, New Hampshire Marriage Records, Seabrook NH notes:
      John Joseph McGrath, 43, son of John E. McGrath, Mary D. Marble.
      Kathleen Francis Sullivan, age 39, daughter of John Sullivan, Julia Driscoll.

Kathleen married **John Joseph McGRATH** [101948] [MRIN: 34200], son of **John E. McGRATH** [101949] and **Mary D. MARBLE** [101950], on 11 Apr 1946 in Seabrook, Rockingham, New Hampshire. John was born on 28 Dec 1902 in NH.

Children from this marriage were:

112 F i. **Kathleen Julia McGRATH [101951]** was born on 30 Jul 1945 in Waltham, Middlesex, Massachusetts, died on 5 Feb 2012 in Florida at age 66, and was buried in St. Mary's Cemetery, Middleboro, Massachusetts.

General Notes: The Enterprise, February 8, 2012 - Kathleen Perkins
  Kathleen (McGrath) Perkins, age 66 years, of Berkley died unexpectedly Sunday, Feb. 5, 2012, while vacationing in Florida. She was the wife of the late John F. Perkins. Born Monday, July 30, 1945, in Waltham, she was the daughter of the late John J. and Kathleen (Sullivan) McGrath.
  Kathleen was a 1963 graduate of Middleboro High School and graduated as a licensed practical nurse from Cape Cod Hospital School of Nursing. She had lived in Middleboro, Lakeville and for the past eight years in Berkley and attended Christ Community Church in East Taunton. She enjoyed vacationing in Florida and golfing but most of all enjoyed spending time with her family.
  She is survived by her five sons, Joseph Perkins and his wife Terri of Middleboro, Gregory Perkins of Taunton, Kevin Perkins and his wife Kristin of Lakeville, Matthew Perkins and his wife Kerrie of Lakeville and Dennis Perkins of Taunton; 11 grandchildren; two brothers, Joseph McGrath of Hingham and Dennis McGrath of Walpole; her fiance, Steven Cambra of Berkley; and many nieces and nephews.
  A funeral service will be held Friday, Feb. 10, 2012, at 10 a.m. in Christ Community Church, 41 Stevens St., East Taunton. Interment will follow in St. Marys Cemetery in Middleboro. Visitation will take place Thursday, Feb. 9, 2012, from 4-8 p.m. in the Dahlborg-MacNevin Funeral Home, 280 Bedford St., Lakeville.

Kathleen married **John F. PERKINS** [101952] [MRIN: 34202]. John was born about 1945.

113 M ii. **Dennis McGRATH [101953]** was born about 1947.

104. Ruth T. SULLIVAN [101947] (*John*[43], *John*[11], *Sullivans born about 1845 possibly*[1]) was born on 17 Dec 1914 in Fall River, Bristol, Massachusetts, died on 29 Aug 2007 in Tiverton, Newport, Rhode Island at age 92, and was buried in St. Patrick's Cem., Fall River, Massachusetts.

General Notes: 1914 December 17, Births Registered in Fall River MA notes:
  Sullivan, Ruth, b. to John, Julia Driscoll, res. 506 Fourth, father Clerk, parents b. Wales, Michigan.

2007 August 29, Fall River MA Herald News,
Ruth T. (Sullivan) Smith, 92, of Tiverton, died, Tuesday, August 28, 2007 at home. She was the wife of the late Lynwood E. B. Smith. Born in Fall River, she was a daughter of the late John and Julia (Driscoll) Sullivan. She had been a resident of Fall River before moving to Tiverton in 1958. Mrs. Smith was a 1934 graduate of B.M.C. Durfee High School. She was a Dental Assistant for her brother-in-law the late Dr. W. Arthur Leary for many years. She was a member of the Sakonnet Club of Tiverton, the Tiverton Senior Citizens Club, and the Tiverton Senior Center. She and her late husband were active members of the Knights of Columbus Father J. Boehr Council #4753 in Tiverton. She is survived by several nieces and nephews including Brother Francis Leary C.S.C. of Flushing, NY., Sheila Leary Craig and her husband Michael of Annandale, VA., Judith Duval and her husband Paul of Fall River, Patricia Kayajan of Middleboro, Sylvia Quinn and her husband Lawrence of Somerset, Phyllis Robb and her husband George of Somerset, Joan Thompson and her husband Russell of Minchin Viejo, CA., and Sandra Goerlitz of Yorba Linda, CA.
She was sister of the late Rev. Leo T. Sullivan, Brother Daniel Sullivan O.F.M., Henry Sullivan, Ethel Leary, and Kathleen McGrath. Her Mass of Christian Burial will be held Thursday, August 30, 2007 at

10:00AM in Holy Ghost Church 316 Judson St. Tiverton, RI. Memorial contributions may be made to Hospice Outreach 502 Bedford St. Fall River, MA Burial in St. Patrick's Cemetery immediately following the Mass.

Ruth married **Lynwood E. B. SMITH** [101955] [MRIN: 34203]. Lynwood was born in 1914, died in 1996 in MA at age 82, and was buried in St. Patrick's Cem., Fall River, Massachusetts.

The child from this marriage was:

   114 M   i.   **Leo D. SMITH [107940]** was born in 1948, died in 1948 in Fall River, Bristol, Massachusetts, and was buried in St. Patrick's Cem., Fall River, Massachusetts.

115.   Sullivans born about 1850 on the Beara

+ 116 M   i.   **Peter (Bachelor) SULLIVAN [99693]** was born about 1850 in Trafask, Adrigole, Cork, IR.

Peter married **Hanora (Capy) HARRINGTON** [99694] [MRIN: 33333] (b. Abt 1850)

+ 117 M   ii.   **Jeremiah (Darb) SULLIVAN [105567]** was born about 1850 in Coulagh, Eyeries Parish, Cork, IR.

Jeremiah married **Ellen 'Helena' DOYLE** [105568] [MRIN: 35554] (b. Abt 1850) in Brooklyn, Kings, New York.

+ 118 M   iii.   **Jeremiah J. SULLIVAN [105989]** was born about 1850 in Lackavane, Adrigole Parish, Cork, IR.

Jeremiah married **Ellen OBRIEN** [105990] [MRIN: 35725] (b. Abt 1850)

Sullivans next married someone.

Children

116.   Peter (Bachelor) SULLIVAN [99693] (*Sullivans born about 1850 on* [115]) was born about 1850 in Trafask, Adrigole, Cork, IR.

General Notes: Named in daughter Mary's 1903 Fall River Marriage Record.

No other marriages or deaths in Fall River MA have been found to correspond to children of this couple.

There were several marriages of a Peter Sullivan and Hanora Harrington recorded in the Allihies parish records, but only one for a couple bearing children at the correct time to be the parents of Mary.   This outline in 'The Annals of the Beara - Volume I' is likely the subject family:
PETER O'SULLIVAN (Bachelor) & HONORA HARRINGTON (Capy)
(Trafrask East)
Children:- 1) Mary (Nov. 1875); 2) Ellen (Sept. 1878); 3) Tim (Dec. 1881); 4) Patrick (Feb. 1885); 5) Honora (Mar. 1888); 6) Denis (Aug. 1891); 7) Margaret (Apr. 1894) married Jeremiah O'Shea, son of Timothy O'Shea & Julia O'Shea, Kildromalive; 8) *Michael (Aug. 1897) settled in the home place and married Catherine (or Kate) O'Sullivan, daughter of Con (Sean) O'Sullivan & Nora Blake, Crooha.

Peter married **Hanora (Capy) HARRINGTON** [99694] [MRIN: 33333]. Hanora was born about 1850.

The child from this marriage was:

+ 119   F   i.   **Mary SULLIVAN [83880]** was born in 1875 in Trafask, Adrigole, Cork, IR and died on 4 Nov 1949 in Fall River, Bristol, Massachusetts at age 74.

Mary married **Stephen FOLEY** [83760] [MRIN: 28143] (b. 1876, d. 22 Jun 1942) on 2 Feb 1903 in Fall River, Bristol, Massachusetts.

117.   Jeremiah (Darb) SULLIVAN [105567] (*Sullivans born about 1850 on* [115]) was born about 1850 in Coulagh, Eyeries Parish, Cork, IR.

General Notes: The family is outlined in 'Annals of the Beara - Volume II' by Riobard O'Dwyer:
Jer (Darb) O'Sullivan & Ellen Doyle
(Coulagh)
Jer and Ellen had 7 children: - (1) Maggie, born in New York, went to Butte, Montana and married Jim Sheehan, Dursey Sound - uncle of Dave Sheehan; (2) Mary (May 23rd 1880) went first to Boston, Mass., and then to Butte, Montana, where she married Michael Sheehan, Dursey Sound - a brother of Maggie's husband; (3) Annie (Dec. 24th 1882) went to Boston, Mass., and married Patsy O'Sullivan (Bawn), Ahabeg, Rosmacowen; (4) * Johnny (Sept. 1885) went first to Butte, Montana, where he married Hannah Downey from Cahirmilebo, Allihies. Hannah was daughter of Jeremiah Downey and Honora (Den D.) Murphy. Honora Murphy was a daughter of Den D. Mor Murphy of Barness. Another of Honora's sisters, Jude Den D. was grandmother of John Kelly, ganger, Pullincha, and a third sister, Mary, was mother of Den Mick O'Sullivan N.T., Cahirmore; (5) Dan (June 1888) went to Butte, Montana and from there to Iowa; (6) Nora (Sept. 1891) married Mike Harrington, Inches, son of Dan (Norr) Harrington & Johanna McCarthy, Milleens; (7) Lena (July 15th 1894) went to Boston, Mass., and married a brother of Standish Barry of Derrimihan, Castletownbere.

His father:
JEREMIAH (OR DARB) O'SULLIVAN (COULAGH)
Darb had 3 sons: Jack, Daniel and Jer. Daniel went to Butte, Montana. *Jer married in Brooklyn, New York, to Ellen Doyle, Boher East, Rosmacowen, and a few years later returned to settle down in the home farm.

LDS digital marriage records shows the marriage records of 5 of the couple's children in MA and MT.

Two Sullivan daughters married Sheehan brothers.

The Butte MT marriage record of daughter Minnie Sullivan notes she was from Eyeries, Co. Cork, Ireland.

Jeremiah married **Ellen 'Helena' DOYLE** [105568] [MRIN: 35554] in Brooklyn, Kings, New York. Ellen was born about 1850 in Rossmacomen, Castletownbere Parish, Cork, Ireland.

Children from this marriage were:

> 120 F i. **Margaret SULLIVAN [109413]** was born in 1880 in Brooklyn, Kings, New York and died after 1913 in MT.
>
> General Notes: 1913 May 31, Marriages registered in Butte, MT shows:
> James Sheehan, age 33, b. Ireland, resides Butte, not previously married. Son of Dennis Sheehan, Lena Sheehan, m. n. Lena Broderick.
> Margaret Sullivan, age 30, b. State of Massachusetts (sic), resides Butte. Daughter Jeremiah Sullivan, Ellen Sullivan m. n. Ellen Doyle.
>
> Margaret married **James SHEEHAN** [109414] [MRIN: 36220] on 31 May 1913 in Butte, Silver Bow, Montana. James was born in 1880 in Castletownbere, Cork, IR.

> 121 F ii. **Annie Josephine SULLIVAN [109405]** was born in 1884 in Brooklyn, Kings, New York and died after 1909 in Malden, Middlesex, Massachusetts.
>
> General Notes: 1909 July 12, Marriages registered in Malden MA notes:
> Sullivan, Patrick J., 32, first marriage, res. Boston, Marine Fireman, b. Ireland to William, Anne Barry.
> Sullivan, Annie J., 25, first marriage, res. Medford, Domestic, b. Ireland to Jeremiah Sullivan, Helena Doyle.
> Married by R. Neagle, Clergy, Malden.
>
> Additional detail appears in the marriage record also recorded in Medford MA:
> 1909 July 12, Marriages registered in Medford MA notes:
> Sullivan, Patrick Joseph, 32, first marriage, res. Roxbury, Boston, Marine Fireman, b. Co. Ireland to William, Anne Barry.
> Sullivan, Annie Josephine, 25, first marriage, res. Medford, Domestic, b. Co. Cork Ireland to Jeremiah Sullivan, Helena Doyle.
> Married by Richardjerem Neagle, Clergy, Malden.
>
> Annie married **Patrick Joseph (Bawn) SULLIVAN** [109406] [MRIN: 35903] on 12 Jul 1909 in Malden, Middlesex, Massachusetts. Patrick was born in 1875 in Ahabeg, Castletownbere, Cork, IR.

> 122 M iii. **John J. SULLIVAN [109407]** was born in 1884 in Brooklyn, Kings, New York and died after 1912 in MT.
>
> General Notes: 1912 August 15, Marriages Registered in Silver Bow, MT:
> John J. Sullivan, age 26, b. Co. Cork, Ireland, resides Butte (MT), not previously married, son of Jeremiah Sullivan and Ellen Sullivan, maiden name Ellen Doyle,
> Anna Downing, age 23, born Co. Cork, Ireland, resides Butte, not previously married.
> Daughter of Jeremiah Downing and Anna Downing maiden name Nora Murphy.
> Witness John J. Foley, Clerk.

The family is outlined in 'Annals of the Beara - Volume II' by Riobard O'Dwyer:
Jer (Darb) O'Sullivan & Ellen Doyle
(Coulagh)
Jer and Ellen had 7 children: - (4) * Johnny (Sept. 1885) went first to Butte, Montana, where he married Hannah Downey from Cahirmilebo, Allihies. Hannah was daughter of Jeremiah Downey and Honora (Den D.) Murphy. Honora Murphy was a daughter of Den D. Mor Murphy of Barness. Another of Honora's sisters, Jude Den D. was grandmother of John Kelly, ganger, Pullincha, and a third sister, Mary, was mother of Den Mick O'Sullivan N.T., Cahirmore.

John married **Hannah 'Anna' DOWNING** [109408] [MRIN: 35963], daughter of **Jeremiah DOWNING** [109409] and **Honora 'Anna' MURPHY** [109410], on 15 Aug 1912 in Silver Bow, Silver Bow, Montana. Hannah was born in 1889 in Cahirmilebo, Allihies Parish, Cork, IR.

123 F iv. **Minnie SULLIVAN [109411]** was born in 1885 in Brooklyn, Kings, New York and died after 1909 in MT.

General Notes: 1909 November 13, Marriages Registered in Butte MT notes:
Michael Sheehan, age 25, b. Castletown, Cork, Ireland, resides Butte. Son of Dennis Sheehan, and Helen Sheehan, m. n. Broderick.
Minnie Sullivan, age 24, born Eyeries, Co. Cork, Ireland, resides Butte. Daughter of Jeremiah Sullivan, Ellen Sullivan, m. n. Ellen Doyle.

Minnie married **Michael SHEEHAN** [109412] [MRIN: 36198] on 13 Nov 1909 in Butte, Silver Bow, Montana. Michael was born in 1884 in Castletownbere, Cork, IR.

+ 124 F v. **Helena T. SULLIVAN [105566]** was born on 15 Jul 1894 in Brooklyn, Kings, New York and died after 1958 in Newport, Newport, Rhode Island.

Helena married **Jeremiah J. BARRY** [105565] [MRIN: 35553] (b. 1883, d. 12 Nov 1958) on 11 Sep 1915 in Brookline, Norfolk, Massachusetts.

118. Jeremiah J. SULLIVAN [105989] (*Sullivans born about 1850 on*[115]) was born about 1850 in Lackavane, Adrigole Parish, Cork, IR.

General Notes: Named in daughter Ellen's 1902 Fall River Marriage record.

There are a number of children born to a Jeremiah and Ellen 'Brien' Sullivan on the Beara in the 1870's. The births are separated at regular intervals indicating the births are to the same parents during this period.

The family is outlined in 'Annals of the Beara - Volume I':
JER O'SULLIVAN (Ukera) & ELLEN O'BRIEN
(Lackavane)
Children:- 1) Mary (July 1871) died aged 53 years; 2) Ellen (Dec. 1873); 3) *Con (Jer) settled in the home farm and married Margaret Downing, daughter of James Downing & Ellen O'Sullivan, Currugh; 4) & 5) Margaret (Feb. 1879) & Patrick (Dec. 1881) both went to the States. Patrick died soon after emigrating; 6) Julia (Feb. 1890) married Patrick O'Sullivan (Keach), son of John O'Sullivan (Keach) & Mary Harrington (Capy), Crooha Lower.

Daughter Margaret's birth record notes Lackavane, a townland in Adrigole Parish on the Beara Peninsula.

1894 daughter Ellen immigrated to America (1910 census) and married in Fall River, moving to Providence about 1906.

1906 son Patrick resided in Fall River MA with sister Margaret's family when he died in Providence RI of Typhoid Fever.

Jeremiah married **Ellen OBRIEN** [105990] [MRIN: 35725]. Ellen was born about 1850 in Ireland.

Children from this marriage were:

125 F i. **Mary SULLIVAN [105999]** was born on 1 Jul 1871 in Lackavane, Adrigole Parish, Cork, IR.

General Notes: 1871 July 1, LDS abstract,
Mary Sullivan, b. Castletown, Co. Cork IR, parents Jeremiah, Ellen Bryan (sic).

+ 126 F ii. **Ellen M. 'Nellie' SULLIVAN [105986]** was born in Dec 1873 in Lackavane, Adrigole Parish, Cork, IR and died after 1930 in Providence, Providence, Rhode Island.

Ellen married **Patrick J. LEAHY** [105985] [MRIN: 35723] (b. 1875, d. After 1930) on 29 Jul 1902 in Fall River, Bristol, Massachusetts.

127 M iii. **Cornelius SULLIVAN [106002]** was born on 20 Nov 1876 in Lackavane, Adrigole Parish, Cork, IR.

General Notes: 1876 November 20, Ireland Births and Baptisms LDS abstracts:
Cornelius Sullivan, b. 20 November 1876, b. Co. Cork, Ireland. Parents Jeremiah Sullivan, Ellen Brien (sic).

+ 128 F iv. **Margaret J. SULLIVAN [104670]** was born on 1 Jul 1879 in Lackavane, Adrigole Parish, Cork, IR and died after 1920 in Fall River, Bristol, Massachusetts.

Margaret married **John D. SULLIVAN** [104659] [MRIN: 35222] (b. 1871, d. Between 1930 and 1940) on 17 Aug 1904 in Fall River, Bristol, Massachusetts.

129 M v. **Patrick SULLIVAN [106000]** was born in Dec 1881 in Lackavane, Adrigole Parish, Cork, IR and died on 5 Oct 1906 in Providence, Providence, Rhode Island at age 24.

General Notes: 1906 October 5, Massachusetts Death Certificate notes:
Patrick Sullivan, died Providence, RI, res. 247 Dover, Fall River MA. Age 22, Single. B. Ireland to Jeremiah Sullivan, b. Ireland; Ellen O'Brien, b. Ireland. Laborer. Informant, sister.
Died of Typhoid fever. Burial St. Patricks Cemetery.
(Sister Ellen Sullivan Leahy lived in Providence RI and sister Margaret in Fall River MA.)

The address shown as his residence in his death certificate.
1906 Fall River City Directory
- Sullivan John D. Hose man Cascade No 8, house 247 Dover. (This is Patrick's brother in law, husband of Margaret Sullivan.)

130 F vi. **Julia SULLIVAN [110229]** was born in Feb 1890 in Lackavane, Adrigole Parish, Cork, IR.

Grandchildren

119.   Mary SULLIVAN [83880] (*Peter (Bachelor)* [116], *Sullivans born about 1850 on* [115]) was born in 1875 in Trafask, Adrigole, Cork, IR and died on 4 Nov 1949 in Fall River, Bristol, Massachusetts at age 74.

General Notes: 1894 she came to America at about the age 19.

1903 February 2, Marriages Registered in Fall River MA notes:
   Stephen Foley, 26, first marriage, 109 Mulberry, Laborer, b. Fall River (sic) to John, Mary Murphy.
   Mary Sullivan, 26, first marriage, 142 Central, Weaver, b. Ireland to Peter, Hanora Harrington. Married by David Jutten, M. G.

1911 Fall River vital records notes the death of her daughter Ellen and shows the mother's maiden name as Mary Sullivan.

1920 Federal census of Bristol Co., MA shows the family enumerated at 381 Fourth St, Fall River, MA.   Mary is a widow?:   There is a married Stephen living with his mother with no wife enumerated on Division St.
   Foley, Mary, head, Rents, 40, married 14 years, immigrated 1894, naturalized 1902, b. Ireland to Irish parents, weaver at cotton mill.
   " John, son, 15, b. MA to parents from MA and Ireland, sweeper, cotton mill.
   " Edward, son, 14, b. MA to parents from MA and Ireland, sweeper, cotton mill.
   " Timothy, son, 12, b. MA to parents from MA and Ireland.

1930 Federal census of Bristol Co., MA shows the family of widow Mary enumerated at 451 Warren St., Fall River: This is the address the cemetery records show for Stephen's last address when he died in 1942.   It appears they may have separated before 1920.
   Foley, Mary, head, owns home, value $4700, has radio, 50, married 23 years, b. Ireland to Irish parents; immigrated 1895, weaver at cotton mill.
   " John, son, 25, b. MA, freight trucker, river boats.
   " Edward, son, 24, b. MA, musician.
   " Timothy, son, 23, b. MA, chofer (sic), lumber.

1949 Nov. 4, St. Patrick Cemetery Fall River records show the death of Mary Foley, age 74, of myocariditis, last address 451 Warren St.

Mary married **Stephen FOLEY** [83760] [MRIN: 28143], son of **John FOLEY** [83758] and **Mary MURPHY** [83759],   on 2 Feb 1903 in Fall River, Bristol, Massachusetts. Stephen was born in 1876 in Wales and died on 22 Jun 1942 in Fall River, Bristol, Massachusetts at age 66.

Children from this marriage were:

   131   M   i.   **John J. FOLEY** [83796] was born on 3 Sep 1904 in Fall River, Bristol, Massachusetts, died on 12 Feb 1971 in Fall River, Bristol, Massachusetts at age 66, and was buried in St. Patrick's Cem., Fall River, Massachusetts.

      General Notes: 1971 St. Patrick cemetery record probably notes his death at age 66, of cerebral hemorrage, last address 108 Warren St., Fall River, on the street his mother lived for many years.

   132   M   ii.   **Edward F. FOLEY** [83797] was born on 27 Dec 1905 in Fall River, Bristol, Massachusetts and died after 1940 in Fall River, Bristol, Massachusetts.

General Notes: 1930 Federal census of Fall River, Bristol Co. MA shows him enumerated with his mother at 451 Warren St.
  " Edward, son, 24, single, b. MA, musician

1940 Federal census of Fall River, Bristol Co. MA shows him enumerated with his parents at 451 Warren St.
  " Edward, son, 34, married (sic), 5 years of school, b. MA. Laborer, cotton mill. Income 40 weeks $600.
  " Anne M., granddaughter, 12, 5 years of school, b. MA.

+ 133 M iii. **Timothy Peter FOLEY [99691]** was born in 1907 in MA and died on 3 Oct 1962 in Fall River, Bristol, Massachusetts at age 55.

Timothy married **Mary A. SULLIVAN** [96540] [MRIN: 33331] (b. 14 Aug 1913, d. 15 Nov 2004) on 18 Mar 1944 in Fall River, Bristol, Massachusetts.

134 M iv. **Patrick FOLEY [72875]** was born on 1 Oct 1908 in Fall River, Bristol, Massachusetts and died on 14 Aug 1909 in Fall River, Bristol, Massachusetts.

General Notes: 1909 Fall River vital records notes the death of Patrick age 10 months of entritis, 142 Columbia Fall River parents Stephen (England) and Mary Sullivan (Ireland).

135 F v. **Mary FOLEY [83881]** was born on 1 Dec 1909 in Fall River, Bristol, Massachusetts and died on 3 Nov 1911 in Fall River, Bristol, Massachusetts at age 1.

136 F vi. **Ellen FOLEY [83879]** was born on 18 Jun 1911 in Fall River, Bristol, Massachusetts and died on 23 Jul 1911 in Fall River, Bristol, Massachusetts.

General Notes: 1912 Fall River vital records notes the death of Ellen, single, gastroenteritis, 1 month 6 days old, 161 Spring Street, parents Stephen (England) and Mary Sullivan (Ireland.)

137 M vii. **Peter FOLEY [83882]** was born in 1912 in Fall River, Bristol, Massachusetts and died on 30 Sep 1912 in Fall River, Bristol, Massachusetts.

General Notes: 1912 Fall River vital records notes the death of Peter Foley, age 2 months, aspyxia, 207 John St., Fall River, father Stephen (Ireland (sic)) mother Mary Sullivan (Ireland).   St. Patrick cemetery records note his death Sept. 30.

124. Helena T. SULLIVAN [105566] (*Jeremiah (Darb)* [117], *Sullivans born about 1850 on* [115]) was born on 15 Jul 1894 in Brooklyn, Kings, New York and died after 1958 in Newport, Newport, Rhode Island.

General Notes: 1910 Federal census unable to locate this subject in Massachusetts.

1915 September 11, Marriages Registered in Brookline MA notes:
  Jeremiah J. Barry, 32, first marriage, US Navy, Fireman, b. Ireland to Daniel, Julia Sullivan.
  Helena J., Sullivan, 21, first marriage, res. Brookline, Domestic, b. Ireland to Jeremiah, Ellen Doyle.
  Married by James J. Farrelly, Catholic Priest.

1957 Newport city directory
- Barry Jeremiah (Helena T.) house 40 Eastnor Rd.

1958 Newport city directory
- Barry Helena widow Jeremiah J. house 40 Eastnor Rd.
- Barry Jeremiah J. died Nov 12 1958.
- Barry Jeremiah J. Jr. Janitor Newport School Dept res. 40 Eastnor Rd.

1959 Newport city directory
- Barry Helena widow Jeremiah J. house 40 Eastnor Rd.

Possible death:
1985 May Social Security Death index notes:
   Helena Barry, b. 1 Sept 1894, New York (sic), died, last residence Newport, RI.

Helena married **Jeremiah J. BARRY** [105565] [MRIN: 35553], son of **Daniel BARRY** [105545] and **Julia SULLIVAN** [105546], on 11 Sep 1915 in Brookline, Norfolk, Massachusetts. Jeremiah was born in 1883 in Derrimihan, Castletownbere Parish, Cork, IR and died on 12 Nov 1958 in Newport, Newport, Rhode Island at age 75.

Children from this marriage were:

   138 F   i.   **Mary E. BARRY** [105569] was born in 1918 in Newport, Newport, Rhode Island.

   139 M   ii.   **Daniel F. BARRY** [105570] was born in 1919 in Newport, Newport, Rhode Island.

   140 F   iii.   **Helena T. BARRY** [105571] was born in 1921 in Newport, Newport, Rhode Island.

   141 F   iv.   **Sheila B. BARRY** [105572] was born in 1924 in Newport, Newport, Rhode Island.

   142 M   v.   **Jeremiah J. BARRY Jr.** [105573] was born in 1926 in Newport, Newport, Rhode Island.

126. Ellen M. 'Nellie' SULLIVAN [105986] (*Jeremiah J.*[118]*, Sullivans born about 1850 on*[115]) was born in Dec 1873 in Lackavane, Adrigole Parish, Cork, IR and died after 1930 in Providence, Providence, Rhode Island.

General Notes: 1874 January 28, Ireland Births and Baptisms LDS abstracts:
   Ellen Sullivan, christened Castletown, Co. Cork, IR. Parents Jeremiah Sullivan, Ellen Brien (sic).

1894 immigrated to America (1910 census).

1902 July 29, Marriages Registered in Fall River, MA notes:
   Patrick J. Leahy, 27, first marriage, res. 125 John St., Laborer, b. Ireland to Jeremiah, Margaret - Harrington.
   Nellie M. Sullivan, 26, first marriage, res. 411 Hunter, Domestic, b. Ireland to Jeremiah, Ellen - OBrien.
   Married by George Maguire, Priest.

Ellen married **Patrick J. LEAHY** [105985] [MRIN: 35723], son of **Jeremiah LEAHY** [105987] and **Margaret HARRINGTON** [105988], on 29 Jul 1902 in Fall River, Bristol, Massachusetts. Patrick was born in 1875 in Ireland and died after 1930 in Providence, Providence, Rhode Island.

Children from this marriage were:

   143 M   i.   **James F. LEAHY** [105992] was born on 28 Oct 1903 in Fall River, Bristol, Massachusetts.

   144 F   ii.   **Ellen Genevieve LEAHY** [105991] was born on 11 Feb 1905 in Fall River, Bristol, Massachusetts.

   145 F   iii.   **Mary A. LEAHY** [105993] was born in 1909 in Providence, Providence, Rhode Island and died in Dec 1983 in Santa Barbara, Santa Barbara, California at age 74.

Mary married **Antonio ANDRADE** [105998] [MRIN: 35726]. Antonio was born in 1910 and died in 1996 at age 86.

146 M iv. **John E. LEAHY [105994]** was born in 1912 in Providence, Providence, Rhode Island.

147 F v. **Julia V. LEAHY [105995]** was born in 1915 in Providence, Providence, Rhode Island.

148 M vi. **Francis LEAHY [105996]** was born in 1917 in Providence, Providence, Rhode Island.

149 M vii. **Joseph A. LEAHY [105997]** was born in 1920 in Providence, Providence, Rhode Island.

128. Margaret J. SULLIVAN [104670] (*Jeremiah J.*[118]*, Sullivans born about 1850 on*[115]) was born on 1 Jul 1879 in Lackavane, Adrigole Parish, Cork, IR and died after 1920 in Fall River, Bristol, Massachusetts.

General Notes: 1879 July 1, Ireland Births and Baptisms, LDS abstract notes:
Margaret Sullivan, b. Lackavane, (Adrigold Parish), Co. Cork, Ireland. Parents Jeremiah Sullivan, Ellen Brien (sic).

1906 she is probably the informant on her brother Patrick's death record shown as 'Sister'. Patrick's residence address on that record is that of his brother in law John D. Sullivan.

1920 Federal census of Fall River, Bristol Co. MA shows John without his family but with the family of his brother Jeremiah D. Sullivan at 50 Tremont, as family #65:
Sullivan John D., brother 49, married, immigrated 1889, Naturalized 1905, b. Ireland to Irish parents. Fireman, Fire dept.

1920 wife and daughter are still enumerated at 507 Fourth St. this year as family #106:
Sullivan, Margaret, head, 40, married, immigrated 1904 (sic), naturalized 1904, b. Ireland. Laundress, private family.
" Margaret, daughter, 12, b. MA.

1930 Federal census of Fall River, Bristol Co. MA shows the mother and daughter at 358 Robeson St. as family #116:
Sullivan, Margaret J., head, rents $16, 49, married at 23, b. Ireland. Immigrated 1900, naturalized. No employment.
" Margaret M., daughter, 22, b. MA. Teacher, Public School.

1940 Federal census of Fall River, Bristol Co. MA shows them at 358 Robeson:
Sullivan, Margaret J., head, 58, widow, 8 years of school, b. Ireland.
" Margaret M., daughter, 32, single, 4 years of college, b. MA. Teacher, Public School. 40 weeks of salary $1000.

Margaret married **John D. SULLIVAN** [104659] [MRIN: 35222], son of **Dennis D. SULLIVAN** [104649] and **Hanora 'Nora' SULLIVAN** [104650], on 17 Aug 1904 in Fall River, Bristol, Massachusetts. John was born in 1871 in Ireland and died between 1930 and 1940 in Fall River, Bristol, Massachusetts.

Children from this marriage were:

150 M i. **Jeremiah J. SULLIVAN [104672]** was born on 31 Aug 1905 in Fall River, Bristol, Massachusetts and died on 16 Mar 1908 in Fall River, Bristol, Massachusetts at age 2.

General Notes: 1908 March 16, Massachusetts Death Certificate notes:
Jeremiah J. Sullivan, res. 507 Fourth St., age 2 years, 8 months 10 days. B. Fall River to John D. Sullivan, b. Ireland, Margaret Sullivan, b. Ireland. Informant Father. Died of Scarlet Fever, contributing Tonsillitis. Burial St. Patrick's Cemetery.

151 F   ii.   **Margaret M. SULLIVAN [104671]** was born on 24 May 1907 in Fall River, Bristol, Massachusetts.

152 M   iii.   **John V. SULLIVAN [104673]** was born on 4 Jan 1909 in Fall River, Bristol, Massachusetts and died on 3 Feb 1909 in Fall River, Bristol, Massachusetts.

General Notes: 1909 February 3, Massachusetts Death Certificate notes:
John V. Sullivan, res. 507 Fourth St., age 29 days. B. Fall River. Father John D. Sullivan, b. Ireland; Margaret Sullivan, b. Ireland. Informant mother. Died of acute gastritis. Burial St. Patrick Cemetery.

Great-Grandchildren

133.   Timothy Peter FOLEY [99691] (*Mary SULLIVAN*[119]*, Peter (Bachelor)*[116]*, Sullivans born about 1850 on*[115]) was born in 1907 in MA and died on 3 Oct 1962 in Fall River, Bristol, Massachusetts at age 55.

General Notes: 1942 November 13, US WWII Army Enlistment records note:
Enlisted in Boston MA.   Timothy P. Foley, b. 1907, res. Bristol Co. MA.   Grade Private.   1 year of high school.   Semiskilled chauffer/driver.   Height 69, weight 165.

Herald News -Fall River, MA Oct 3, 2012
1942, Timothy P. Foley, unmarried, became the first city police officer drafted into military service. The start of his Army tenure came eight months after he joined the full-time police force in the summer of 1941, and Foley would not return and resume his career until Oct. 28, 1945, after World War II ended and he was back home safe.
As she stood braced by a metal crutch on a sunny afternoon this week beside the tall bronze memorial dedicated to her father at lower Kennedy Park, adjacent to the fountain and the wading pool that children once enjoyed, Angela Foley recalled his proud police career cut short.
Fifty years ago today, with 21 years as an officer and three more with the police reserves, Sgt. Timothy Peter Foley died after suffering his second heart attack in 11 days. He was admitted to Charlton Memorial Hospital after his first heart attack, but never left, recalled his only child.
Like it was yesterday, Angela Foley recounted how, after his day shift as acting commander of the southern division, her father awoke suddenly in the early morning hours sweating and stricken with pain.
Police officers came swiftly to their South End home on Snell Street and at 3 a.m. rushed Foley to Charlton, not waiting for an ambulance.
The damage to his heart was severe. Several days later, doctors told Foley his police career was over.
"When he was told by his doctors you'll never work again, he cried," his daughter said.
On Oct. 3, 1962, a second heart attack in the hospital claimed his life.
A headline in The Herald News announced his death: "One of Fall River's best known police officers dies at 55."
"Sgt. Timothy Foley joined the Fall River Police Department in 1938, and served most honorably until his untimely death in 1962. Sgt. Foley was called up by the United States Army to serve his country in World War II, returning to the FRPD in 1945," the city's current Police Chief Daniel Racine wrote in a statement this week.
Eleven years before his death, Foley had been promoted to police sergeant.
"Sgt. Foley was a decorated public servant, and we are honored his family shared him with us for 24 years," Racine wrote (Norman Bowers was chief in Foley's time).
Angela, a retired city elementary school teacher, shared a cherished old photograph of her father leading the police division during the St. Patrick's Day Parade down Main Street in the late 1950s.
  father loved St. Patrick's Day. Look how proud he was with the green flower in his lapel," his daughter said, her memory still able to pick sharp colors from the black and white photo.
The framed image also hangs in the foyer at police headquarters.
Foley was a cop who walked the beat with distinction during his 21 full-time years, someone respected and well known in his home city.
"He didn't want a cruiser. He just wanted to get around," Angela said. "He was a roving sergeant."
She said he'd jump on a bus on Pleasant or Bedford Street — or hop a ride in someone's car — to hustle to wherever police work required his presence.
Eleven months after he died, on Sept. 8, 1963, the 4-foot monument was erected at Kennedy Park, under then-Mayor John M. Arruda. Contributions from nearly 20 businesses helped build the nearby pool and fountain, dedicated in Foley's name, "in loving memory by the children of Fall River."
The shallow and vast concrete pool had been important to her father, Angela said.
"He wanted something here for the children; to have a pool for the (young) children to come to."

Angela told how her father and mother, the former Mary Sullivan, married late: he at 36, she at 30, while he was on leave from the service. The date was March 18, 1944 — the day after St. Paddy's Day, so the Irish Catholic family could have meat at the wedding.
The next year they had their only child.

They lived in a 20th century triple-decker Sullivan's grandfather, Michael Franey, a stone mason, had built at 325 Snell St. It's where Angela still lives.
This policeman's daughter lost her father at the tender age of 17. She was a recent High School graduate, fresh from the halls of the former St. Mary's Academy on Second Street.
After college she followed in his footsteps, dedicating her life to city children. She spent most of her 31-year career as a second grade teacher. Her last nine years were spent teaching at Susan Wixon Elementary School, after 18 years at Coughlin and a couple of years each at Lincoln and Belisle — all older schools no longer in use.
Six years ago Angela suffered a serious infection after breaking her leg in two places and requiring a hip replacement. It took six operations in 12 months, and her mobility is limited. She now gets around with the aid of two crutches.

After she walked slowly from her car to her father's monument, she sat on a bench and was asked what she'd tell him today.
"I'd say, 'Well, Dad, things have changed. The Police Department isn't as big as when you were there. A lot of the laws have changed.'"
Angela said she'd tell her father how respect seems harder to earn these days, for both police officers and teachers.
Then she remembered how her father got around his city. She recalled how hard he worked to earn his citywide reputation.
"He gave it his all," she said.

US Headstone Application notes:
Foley, Timothy Peter, service #31232K5, pension #xc6638039. Enlisted 27 Nov 1942, discharged 30 Sep 1945, honorable. Grade CPL. Regiment - SQE 592nd AAF Base Unit. A.U.S. WWII. Born 12 Feb 07, died 3 Oct 1962. Applicant Mary A. Foley, Widow, 325 Snell St., Fall River, Oct 29, 1962. Cemetery St. Patricks, Fall River MA.

Timothy married **Mary A. SULLIVAN** [96540] [MRIN: 33331], daughter of **William H. SULLIVAN** [96533] and **Margaret G. FRANEY** [96534],   on 18 Mar 1944 in Fall River, Bristol, Massachusetts. Mary was born on 14 Aug 1913 in Fall River, Bristol, Massachusetts, died on 15 Nov 2004 in Fall River, Bristol, Massachusetts at age 91, and was buried in St. Patrick's Cem., Fall River, Massachusetts.

The child from this marriage was:

   153   F   i.   **Angela FOLEY [99692]** was born about 1945 in Fall River, Bristol, Massachusetts.

154. Sullivans born about 1850 possibly on the Beara

+ 155 M i. **Jeremiah SULLIVAN [107195]** was born about 1850 in Ireland.

Jeremiah married **Mary HAMPSTON** [107196] [MRIN: 36169] (b. Abt 1850)

+ 156 M ii. **Jeremiah SULLIVAN [106092]** was born about 1850 in Ireland.

Jeremiah married **Norah HARRINGTON** [106093] [MRIN: 35761] (b. Abt 1850)

+ 157 M iii. **John SULLIVAN [99161]** was born about 1850 in Ireland.

John married **Mary T. SULLIVAN** [99162] [MRIN: 33130] (b. Abt 1850)

+ 158 M iv. **James SULLIVAN [104713]** was born about 1850.

James married **Lena OBRIEN** [104714] [MRIN: 35239] (b. Abt 1850)

+ 159 M v. **Mortimer SULLIVAN [105393]** was born about 1850 in Ireland.

Mortimer married **Hanora CURRAN** [105394] [MRIN: 35488] (b. Abt 1850)

+ 160 M vi. **Timothy T. SULLIVAN [105595]** was born about 1850 in Ireland.

Timothy married **Mary SULLIVAN** [105596] [MRIN: 35565] (b. Abt 1840)

+ 161 M vii. **Richard SULLIVAN [105925]** was born about 1850 in Sneem, Kerry, Munster, Ireland.

Richard married **Johanna FITZGERALD** [105926] [MRIN: 35699] (b. Abt 1850)

+ 162 M viii. **John SULLIVAN [106521]** was born about 1850 in Ireland.

John married **Catherine WALSH** [106520] [MRIN: 35908] (b. Abt 1850)

+ 163 M ix. **Michael SULLIVAN [106059]** was born about 1850 in Ireland.

Michael married **Johanna KANE** [106060] [MRIN: 35745] (b. Abt 1850)

+ 164 M x. **John SULLIVAN [106323]** was born about 1850 in Ireland and died before 1897 in Danielson, Windham, Connecticut.

John married **Catherine HANLEY** [106324] [MRIN: 35836] (b. Aug 1863, d. After 1930)

+ 165 M xi. **Daniel SULLIVAN [105254]** was born about 1850 in Dublin, Dublin, Leinster, Ireland and died after 1914.

Daniel married **Martha CROSSLAND** [105255] [MRIN: 35442] (b. 1844, d. Bef 1914) in England.

+ 166 M xii. **Jeremiah J. SULLIVAN [106493]** was born in Mar 1852 in Ireland and died on 1 Apr 1910 in Pawtucket, Providence, Rhode Island at age 58.

Jeremiah married **Margaret McQUILLEN** [106494] [MRIN: 35896] (b. May 1856, d. Between 1900 and 1905)

+ 167 M xiii. **Thomas SULLIVAN [92395]** was born on 9 Oct 1852 in Co. Cork, Ireland and died after 1905 in Fall River, Bristol, Massachusetts.

Thomas married **Catherine SHEEHAN** [92396] [MRIN: 30929] (b. 1845, d. Bef 1900)

+ 168 M xiv. **Jeremiah P. SULLIVAN [106774]** was born in May 1856 in Ireland and died after 1915 in Newport, Newport, Rhode Island.

Jeremiah married **Julia M. SHEA** [106775] [MRIN: 36006] (b. Sep 1848, d. After 1915) in 1877 in England.

+ 169 M xv. **Eugene SULLIVAN [94305]** was born in Mar 1858 in Ireland and died on 11 Jan 1938 in Fall River, Bristol, Massachusetts at age 79.

Eugene married **Margaret E. HEALY** [94306] [MRIN: 31559] (b. Dec 1858, d. 4 Jun 1936) about 1878 in Fall River, Bristol, Massachusetts.

Children

155.   Jeremiah SULLIVAN [107195] (*Sullivans born about 1850 possibly* [154]) was born about 1850 in Ireland.

General Notes: Named in daughter Mary's 1916 Fall River MA marriage record.

Jeremiah married **Mary HAMPSTON** [107196] [MRIN: 36169]. Mary was born about 1850 in Ireland.

The child from this marriage was:

> 170   F   i.   **Mary SULLIVAN [107194]** was born in 1877 in Ireland and died after 1920 in Fall River, Bristol, Massachusetts.

> General Notes: 1897 immigrated to America (1920 census).

> 1916 July 3, Marriages Registered in Fall River MA notes:
>   James McDonald, 45, second marriage, widower, res. 1026 Slade, Taxi driver, b. England to Patrick, Mary Blake.
>   Mary Sullivan, 39, first marriage, res. 17 Colfax, Housekeeper, b. Ireland to Jeremiah, Mary Hampston.
>   Married by John McCarthy, Priest.

> Mary married **James McDONALD** [107193] [MRIN: 36168], son of **Patrick McDONALD** [107197] and **Mary BLAKE** [107198],   on 3 Jul 1916 in Fall River, Bristol, Massachusetts. James was born in 1871 in England and died after 1920 in Fall River, Bristol, Massachusetts.

156.   Jeremiah SULLIVAN [106092] (*Sullivans born about 1850 possibly* [154]) was born about 1850 in Ireland.

General Notes: Named in son Patrick's 1903 Fall River MA marriage record.

Jeremiah married **Norah HARRINGTON** [106093] [MRIN: 35761]. Norah was born about 1850 in Ireland.

The child from this marriage was:

> 171   M   i.   **Patrick SULLIVAN [106094]** was born in 1877 in Ireland.

> General Notes: 1903 September 3, Marriages Registered in Fall River MA notes:
>   Patrick Sullivan, 28, first marriage, res. 332 Spring, Fireman, b. Ireland, to Jeremiah, Norah Harrington.
>   Julia Driscoll, 28, first marriage, 116 Branch, Domestic, b. Ireland to Jeremiah, Margaret Harrington.
>   Married by M. J. O'Reilly, Priest.

> 1903 nor 1904 Fall River City directories show a Patrick as fireman nor one on Spring St.

> No children of the couple could be identified in the Bristol Co. MA vital records.

> 1910 unable to identify a couple Patrick and Julia in the Federal census.

Patrick married **Julia DRISCOLL** [106095] [MRIN: 35762], daughter of **Jeremiah DRISCOLL** [106096] and **Margaret HARRINGTON** [106097],   on 3 Sep 1903 in Fall River, Bristol, Massachusetts. Julia was born in 1877 in Ireland.

157.   John SULLIVAN [99161] (*Sullivans born about 1850 possibly*[154]) was born about 1850 in Ireland.

General Notes: Named in son's 1898 Fall River MA marriage record.

John married **Mary T. SULLIVAN** [99162] [MRIN: 33130]. Mary was born about 1850 in Ireland.

The child from this marriage was:

+ 172   M   i.   **Timothy J. SULLIVAN [99159]** was born in 1877 in Ireland and died before 1920 in Fall River, Bristol, Massachusetts.

Timothy married **Laura W. WILSON** [99160] [MRIN: 33129] (b. 1878, d. After 1930) on 2 Jun 1898 in Fall River, Bristol, Massachusetts.

158.   James SULLIVAN [104713] (*Sullivans born about 1850 possibly*[154]) was born about 1850.

General Notes: Named in daughter Lena Sullivan Gotham's 1893 Fall River MA marriage record.

James married **Lena OBRIEN** [104714] [MRIN: 35239]. Lena was born about 1850.

The child from this marriage was:

+ 173   F   i.   **Lena SULLIVAN [104712]** was born on 20 Nov 1873 in Providence, Providence, Rhode Island and died on 20 Sep 1949 in Middleboro, Plymouth, Massachusetts at age 75.

Lena married **James E. GOTHAM** [104711] [MRIN: 35238] (b. Jul 1873, d. 8 Jun 1926) on 21 Nov 1893 in Fall River, Bristol, Massachusetts.

159.   Mortimer SULLIVAN [105393] (*Sullivans born about 1850 possibly*[154]) was born about 1850 in Ireland.

General Notes: Named in daughter Annie's 1896 Fall River MA marriage record.

Mortimer married **Hanora CURRAN** [105394] [MRIN: 35488]. Hanora was born about 1850 in Ireland.

The child from this marriage was:

+ 174   F   i.   **Annie SULLIVAN [105389]** was born in May 1874 in Ireland and died after 1940 in Fall River, Bristol, Massachusetts.

Annie married **Thomas F. DONNELLY** [105390] [MRIN: 35486] (b. May 1874, d. After 1940) on 28 Jul 1896 in Fall River, Bristol, Massachusetts.

160.   Timothy T. SULLIVAN [105595] (*Sullivans born about 1850 possibly*[154]) was born about 1850 in Ireland.

General Notes: Named in the 1897 marriage record of son Patrick.

There are two Sullivan boys John F. and Patrick H. Sullivan who married within two years of each other in Fall River.   The names of the mothers in their marriage records are Mary Sullivan and

Margaret Sullivan.   However, the widow of John F. Sullivan is living in the same dwelling as the family of Patrick Sullivan in 1920.   It is reasonable to speculate these two may have been brothers.

Timothy married **Mary SULLIVAN** [105596] [MRIN: 35565]. Mary was born about 1840 in Ireland.

The child from this marriage was:

+ 175 M   i.   **Patrick H. SULLIVAN [105593]** was born in Mar 1869 in Ireland and died after 1930 in Fall River, Bristol, Massachusetts.

         Patrick married **Hanora ONEIL** [105594] [MRIN: 35564] (b. Sep 1862, d. Between 1920 and 1930) on 5 Oct 1897 in Fall River, Bristol, Massachusetts.

161.   Richard SULLIVAN [105925] (*Sullivans born about 1850 possibly* [154]) was born about 1850 in Sneem, Kerry, Munster, Ireland.

     General Notes: There are a number of births reported in the LDS abstracts for Sneem, Co. Kerry, Ireland.

     Only daughter Catherine Sullivan has been found in Fall River, MA, although Catherine indicated she came to America about 1871 at age 7 years old.

Richard married **Johanna FITZGERALD** [105926] [MRIN: 35699]. Johanna was born about 1850 in Ireland.

Children from this marriage were:

176 M   i.   **Daniel SULLIVAN [105935]** was born on 10 Feb 1871 in Sneem, Kerry, Munster, Ireland.

177 M   ii.   **James SULLIVAN [105933]** was born on 18 Oct 1872 in Sneem, Kerry, Munster, Ireland.

178 M   iii.   **Dennis SULLIVAN [105936]** was born on 29 Dec 1874 in Sneem, Kerry, Munster, Ireland.

179 M   iv.   **John SULLIVAN [105937]** was born on 23 Jul 1876 in Sneem, Kerry, Munster, Ireland.

+ 180 F   v.   **Catherine G. SULLIVAN [105924]** was born on 1 Jul 1878 in Co. Kerry, Ireland and died in 1940 in Newport, Newport, Rhode Island at age 62.

         Catherine married **Edward C. FITZGERALD** [105921] [MRIN: 35698] (b. 1878, d. After 1940) on 28 Aug 1901 in Fall River, Bristol, Massachusetts.

181 M   vi.   **Richard SULLIVAN [105934]** was born on 26 May 1880 in Sneem, Kerry, Munster, Ireland.

162.   John SULLIVAN [106521] (*Sullivans born about 1850 possibly* [154]) was born about 1850 in Ireland.

     General Notes: Named in daughter Katherine's 1907 Fall River MA marriage record.   No other children of the couple could be found in the Bristol Co. MA vital records.

John married **Catherine WALSH** [106520] [MRIN: 35908]. Catherine was born about 1850.

The child from this marriage was:

+ 182 F i. **Catherine 'Kate' SULLIVAN [106519]** was born in 1877 in Ireland and died on 4 Nov 1929 in New Bedford, Bristol, Massachusetts at age 52.

Catherine married **George F. GUILD** [106518] [MRIN: 35907] (b. 20 Apr 1866, d. After 1930) on 15 Dec 1907 in Fall River, Bristol, Massachusetts.

163. Michael SULLIVAN [106059] (*Sullivans born about 1850 possibly* [154]) was born about 1850 in Ireland.

Michael married **Johanna KANE** [106060] [MRIN: 35745]. Johanna was born about 1850 in Ireland.

The child from this marriage was:

+ 183 F i. **Julia V. SULLIVAN [106058]** was born in 1879 in Ireland, died in 1939 in Fall River, Bristol, Massachusetts at age 60, and was buried in St. Patrick's Cem., Fall River, Massachusetts.

Julia married **Joseph KEELEY** [106055] [MRIN: 35744] (b. 1878, d. 1939) on 11 Dec 1902 in Fall River, Bristol, Massachusetts.

164. John SULLIVAN [106323] (*Sullivans born about 1850 possibly* [154]) was born about 1850 in Ireland and died before 1897 in Danielson, Windham, Connecticut.

General Notes: Named in son Thomas' 1906 Fall River MA marriage record.

John married **Catherine HANLEY** [106324] [MRIN: 35836]. Catherine was born in Aug 1863 in CT and died after 1930 in Hartford, Hartford, Connecticut.

The child from this marriage was:

+ 184 M i. **Thomas F. SULLIVAN [106325]** was born in 1885 in Danielson, Windham, Connecticut and died after 1930 in Taunton, Bristol, Massachusetts.

Thomas married **Alice M. WESTGATE** [106326] [MRIN: 35837] (b. 1883, d. After 1930) on 6 Apr 1906 in Fall River, Bristol, Massachusetts.

165. Daniel SULLIVAN [105254] (*Sullivans born about 1850 possibly* [154]) was born about 1850 in Dublin, Dublin, Leinster, Ireland and died after 1914.

General Notes: 1891 Census of Saddleworth, Yorkshire, West Riding, England, shows the family enumerated on Horsforth Road:
Daniel Sullivan, head, 47, married, Cotton Carder, b. Dublin Ireland.
Martha Sullivan, wife, married, age 47, b. Saddleworth, Yorkshire, England.
Hannah Sullivan, daughter, 26, Reeler of Cotton, b. Mossley, Lancashire, England.
Albert Sullivan, son, 20, Operative of Cotton, b. Mossley, Lancashire, England.
William Sullivan, son, 17, Cotton Card Grinder, b. Mossley, Lancashire, England.
Robert Sullivan, son, 15, Reeler of Cotton, b. Mossley, Lancashire, England.
George Sullivan, son, 13, Cotton Warehouseman, b. Mossley, Lancashire, England.
Sarah Sullivan, daughter, 11, Reeler of Cotton, b. Saddleworth, Yorkshire, England.
Ethel Sullivan, daughter, 6, Scholar, b. Saddleworth, Yorkshire, England.
Harry Sullivan, son, 4, Scholar, b. Saddleworth, Yorkshire, England.

At least two members of the family immigrated, sons Daniel and Albert; Albert about 1892 (son Albert's enumeration in 1900 and 1910 census).

The obituary of son Daniel in Fall River MA in 1914 notes he leaves living his Father, and four surviving brothers Robert, George, Henry and William of England.

Daniel married **Martha CROSSLAND** [105255] [MRIN: 35442] in England. Martha was born in 1844 in Saddleworth, , Yorkshire, England and died before 1914.

Children from this marriage were:

185   F   i.   **Hannah SULLIVAN [105267]** was born in 1865 in Mossley, , Lancashire, England.

186   M   ii.   **Daniel SULLIVAN [105259]** was born in 1869 in Mossley, , Lancashire, England, died on 2 Jun 1914 in Fall River, Bristol, Massachusetts at age 45, and was buried in St. Patrick's Cem., Fall River, Massachusetts.

General Notes: 1889 April 18, Marriages Registered in Friezland, Manchester, Lancashire, England LDS abstract notes:
  Daniel Sullivan, single, son of Daniel Sullivan
  Eliza Hawkyard, single, daughter of Charles Hawkyard.

1900 Federal census of Fall River, Bristol Co. MA shows the couple in ward 4, dist 127 at 253 Fifth St. as family #95:
  Sullivan, Daniel, head, April 1866, 34, married 11 years, b. England to English parents. Immigrated 1890, 10 years, alien.   Web Drawer In, Cotton Mill.
  " Eliza, wife, Oct 1861, 38, married 11 years 0 children, b. England to English parents. Immigrated 1890, 10 years prior.   Weaver.

1914 June 2, Massachusetts Death Certificate notes:
  Daniel Sullivan, res. 122 John St., Fall River, MA.   Married.   B. 1869, age 45. Spinner. B. England.   Father Daniel Sullivan, b. Ireland, mother Martha Crossland, b. England. Informant Eliza Sullivan,122 John St.
  Died Myelitis of Spinal Cord ascending type, duration 2 months.
  Burial St. Patrick's Cemetery.

1914 June 3, Fall River Daily Globe
Daniel Sullivan
Daniel Sullivan, a well known resident of the city passed away yesterday afternoon at his home 122 John Street.   Deceased was born in England and came to this country when a small boy.   About 25 years ago he came to this city.   He was a member of the Spinners union and was president for two terms.   Deceased was very well known and leaves a wide circle of friends to mourn his loss.   Besides his wife, who was Miss Eliza Hawkyard before her marriage, he leaves his father.
He also leaves six brothers, Albert of this city, James of Connecticut and Robert, George, Henry and William of England.   He also leaves three sisters, Sarah E. Sullivan, Mrs. Ethel Smith and Mrs. Anna Schofield.   He was a member of Good Samaritan court No. 2, F. of A. and held every office in the court at different times.   The funeral will be held Friday morning and a high mass of requiem for the repose of his morning will be celebrated at St. Mary's Cathedral at 9 o'clock.

Daniel married **Eliza HAWKYARD** [105260] [MRIN: 35445], daughter of **Charles HAWKYARD** [105261],   on 18 Apr 1889 in Manchester, , Lancashire, England. Eliza was born about 1868 in England and died after 1914 in Fall River, Bristol, Massachusetts.

187   M   iii.   **James SULLIVAN [105262]** was born about 1870 in Mossley, , Lancashire, England and died after 1914 in CT.

188 M iv. **Albert SULLIVAN [105253]** was born in 1871 in Mossley, , Lancashire, England and died after 1920 in Fall River, Bristol, Massachusetts.

General Notes: 1895 Fall River City Directory (for the first time)
- Sullivan Albert, spinner, boards 40 Morgan.

1900 Federal census of Fall River, Bristol Co. MA shows him at 95 Stone St.,:
Sullivan, Albert, boarder, Nov. 1862, 27, b. England, immigrated 1892, 8 years prior. Alien. Spinner, Cotton mill.

1908 August 25, Marriages Registered in Fall River MA notes:
Albert E. E. (sic) Sullivan, 35, first marriage, res. 129 John St., Spinner, b. England to Daniel, Martha Crosslynd (sic).
May (sic) C. Robinson, 33, first marriage, 296 Tremont, Dress maker, b. England, to Wyndham O., Genevieve Vane, first marriage.
Married by J. T. O'Grady, Priest.

1910 Federal census of Fall River, Bristol Co. MA shows the couple at Mary's old address 296 Tremont as family #198:
Sullivan, Albert, head, 35 (sic), married 1 years, b. England to English parents. Immigrated 1892, naturalized. Mule spinner, Cotton mill.
" Mary C., wife, 34, married 1 year, 0 children, b. England to English parents. Immigrated 1880. Dress maker, At home.
Brown, Catherine M., Aunt, 80, widow, 2 children, 0 living, b. Ireland to Irish parents. Immigrated 1881.

1920 Federal census of Fall River, Bristol Co. MA shows the couple in ward 4, dist 57 at 983 Rodman St., as family #316:
Sullivan, Albert, head, rents, 46, immigrated 1894, alien, b. England to English parents. Operative, Cotton mill.
" Mary, wife, 43, immigrated 1893, alien, b. England to English parents.
Peabody, Elaine, immigrated, 2 6/12, b. MA to MA parents.

Albert married **Mary C. ROBINSON** [105256] [MRIN: 35443], daughter of **Wyndham O. ROBINSON** [105257] and **Genevieve VANE** [105258], on 25 Aug 1908 in Fall River, Bristol, Massachusetts. Mary was born in 1877 in England.

189 M v. **Robert SULLIVAN [105263]** was born about 1872 in England.

190 M vi. **George SULLIVAN [105264]** was born about 1873 in England.

191 M vii. **William SULLIVAN [105265]** was born in 1873 in Mossley, , Lancashire, England.

192 F viii. **Ethel SULLIVAN [105266]** was born in 1885 in Saddleworth, , Yorkshire, England.

193 M ix. **Harry SULLIVAN [109910]** was born in 1887 in Saddleworth, , Yorkshire, England.

166. Jeremiah J. SULLIVAN [106493] (*Sullivans born about 1850 possibly* [154]) was born in Mar 1852 in Ireland and died on 1 Apr 1910 in Pawtucket, Providence, Rhode Island at age 58.

General Notes: 1862 immigrated to America at about the age 10 (1900 census).

1900 Federal census of Cumberland, Providence Co. RI show the family enumerated at 313 Titus St. as family #435:
Sullivan, Jeremiah J., head, Mar 1852, 48, married 23 years, b. Ireland to Irish parents. Immigrated 1862, 38 years prior. Day laborer.

" Margaret A., wife, May 1859, 41, married 23 years, 2 children,1 living, b. Ireland to Irish parents. Immigrated 1876, 24 years prior.

" John J., son, April 1881, b. RI to Irish parents.   Day laborer.

1905 Rhode Island Census of Cumberland shows:
Sullivan, Jeremiah, 11 Maple, head, age 48, b. Ireland.   Married. Number in family 3. Immigrated 1867, 38 *(sic) years in US, 38 years in Rhode Island.   Parents b. Ireland. Naturalized.   Laborer, Day. Roman Catholic.   Can't read or write.
Sullivan, John J., res. 11 Maple, son, age 24, b. April 1881, Providence, RI.   Parents b. Ireland. Occupation Motorman.   Catholic.

1906 Pawtucket City Directory
- Sullivan Jeremiah J. house furnishing goods 88 Lawn.
- Sullivan John J. variety Mineral Springs Ave. boards 88 Lawn.

1907 Pawtucket City Directory
- Sullivan Jeremiah J. house furnishing goods 88 Lawn.
- Sullivan John J. boards 88 Lawn.
- Sullivan John laborer boards 47 Railroad Ave.
- Sullivan John J. laborer boards 47 Railroad Ave.

1908 Pawtucket City Directory
- Sullivan John J. Motorman house 440 Dexter Central Falls.

1909 and 1913 Pawtucket City Directory
- Sullivan Jeremiah J. house furnishing goods 88 Lawn Ave house 88 Lawn.
- Sullivan John J. boards 88 Lawn.
- Sullivan John J. motorman house 14 Richardson Central Falls.

Probably death:
1910 April 1, Deaths Registered in Pawtucket, RI LDS abstract:
Jeremiah Joseph Sullivan, age 60, father John Sullivan, mother Julia.

Jeremiah married **Margaret McQUILLEN** [106494] [MRIN: 35896]. Margaret was born in May 1856 in Ireland and died between 1900 and 1905 in Cumberland, Providence, Rhode Island.

The child from this marriage was:

+ 194 M   i.   **John Joseph SULLIVAN [106492]** was born in 1881 in Cranston, Providence, Rhode Island and died on 22 Apr 1929 in Pawtucket, Providence, Rhode Island at age 48.

John married **Agnes M. FLYNN** [106495] [MRIN: 35897] (b. 26 Sep 1880, d. 9 Aug 1921) on 8 May 1907 in Fall River, Bristol, Massachusetts.

John next married **Madeline Mary RICE** [106501] [MRIN: 35900] (b. Abt 1881)

167.   Thomas SULLIVAN [92395] (*Sullivans born about 1850 possibly*[154]) was born on 9 Oct 1852 in Co. Cork, Ireland and died after 1905 in Fall River, Bristol, Massachusetts.

General Notes: 1872 the couple was living in Rhode Island when their son Thomas was born.

There is another couple Thomas and Catherine Sheehan Sullivan in Fall River about this time.   That Thomas was a seaman, born in Lowell MA.

1876 this subject couple was living in New York when their daughter Elizabeth was born.

1880 Federal census shows the family enumerated in Fall River, Bristol, MA as family 156:
   Sullivan, Thomas, 35, cotton mill, b. Ireland .to Irish parents.
   " Catherine, 35, wife, keeping house, b. Ireland to Irish parents.
   " Thomas, 8, son, b. Rhode Island to Irish parents.
   " Elizabeth, daughter, b. New York to Irish parents.
(In the same household.)
   Sheehan, Abby, 36, sister in law, single,cotton mill, b. Ireland to Irish parents.   (Married in 1889.)

1888 2nd District Court Fall River final naturalization application shows:
   Sullivan, Thomas, b. Kantusk (?) Co. Cork, Ireland Oct 9, 1852. Now 35.   Arrived NY Apr 12, 1868 (he would have been 16).   Resides 14 Seabury Fall River.   Witness William Carroll 29 Third St., John Haly 101 Eight St.

1889 Fall River Directory
- Sullivan Thomas card grinder, 14 Seabury.
Sullivans also at 14 Seabury Patrick a laborer, Margaret a widow, Eugene a laborer.

1896 Fall River Directory shows the same group from 1889 now at 36 Seabury.

1900 Fall River Directory shows only Thomas and now a Thomas Jr. at 36 Seabury.

1900 Federal census shows one Thomas and Thomas Sullivan Jr. in Fall River, enumerated at 36 Seabury, a triple decker with French Canadians in the other two units:
   Sullivan, Thomas, head, b. Mar 1851, 49, widowed, b. Ireland to Irish parents.   Immigrated 1865, 35 years prior.   Naturalized.   Cotton grinder. Rents.
   " Thomas, son, Feb 1872, 27, single, b. Rhode Island to Irish parents.   Hostler.

The Thomas and Thomas Jr. on Albion cannot be the same as the 1900 pair if the 1910 census for the family at 223 Albion is true.   This shows Thomas F. Sullivan married 36 years to Susan M. with 5 children.

1901   Fall River City Directory
- Sullivan Thomas card grinder 36 Seabury.
(There are a Thomas F Jr. and Sr. at 223 Albion. Thomas F. died 1912 at Albion b. 1846.)

1902 Fall River City Directory
- Sullivan Thomas house 36 Seabury.
- Sullivan Thomas Jr. mule spinner boards 36 Seabury.

1903 Fall River City Directory - No Thomas on Seabury, nor Thomas as a mule spinner.

1904 Fall River City Directory
- Sullivan Thomas, coachman, 19 highland Ave. boards 36 Seabury.
- Sullivan Thomas, Jr. mule spinner, boards 36 Seabury.

1905 Fall River City Directory
- Sullivan Thomas coachman, 19 Highland Ave, boards 306 Tremont.
No other Thomas as mule spinner.   No other on Tremont.

1906 Fall River City Directory shows two drivers at Tremont addresses.   No continuity with these previous Thomas Sullivans.

Thomas married **Catherine SHEEHAN** [92396] [MRIN: 30929], daughter of **Florence SHEEHAN** [107517] and **Joanna wife of Florence SHEEHAN** [107518]. Catherine was born in 1845 in Ireland and died before 1900 in Fall River, Bristol, Massachusetts.

Children from this marriage were:

195 M i. **Thomas F. SULLIVAN [92397]** was born in 1872 in Albion, Providence, Rhode Island.

General Notes: 1873 Feb 27, in Civil, Smithfield Township RI a Thomas Sullivan is born and registered, parents Thomas Sullivan and Catherine.

1906 Sept 6 Marriages registered in Fall River shows:
  Thomas F. Sullivan, 33, res. 3030 Whipple, Teamster, b. Albion, RI, parents Thomas, Catherine Sheehan.
  Mary L. Drogue, 30, res. 46 Wanton, Weaver, b. Fall River, parents John A., Bridget Chasity.
  Married by W. J. OReilly Pr. 1598 South Main.

Thomas married **Mary L DROUGE** [92399] [MRIN: 30930], daughter of **John R. DROUGE** [92400] and **Bridget CHASITY** [92401], on 24 Sep 1906 in Fall River, Bristol, Massachusetts. Mary was born about 1873 in Fall River, Bristol, Massachusetts.

+ 196 F ii. **Elizabeth Katherine SULLIVAN [92398]** was born on 1 Feb 1876 in New York and died after 1930 in Fall River, Bristol, Massachusetts.

Elizabeth married **Jeremiah McCARTHY** [92402] [MRIN: 30932] (b. 1877, d. After 1930) on 27 Jul 1898 in Fall River, Bristol, Massachusetts.

168. Jeremiah P. SULLIVAN [106774] (*Sullivans born about 1850 possibly* [154]) was born in May 1856 in Ireland and died after 1915 in Newport, Newport, Rhode Island.

General Notes: 1880 the family was in Wales when daughter Mary M. was born.

1881 Census of England and Wales shows the family enumerated on Castle Street, Merthyr Tydfil, Glamorganshire, Wales:
  Jeremiah Sullivan, head, 24, b. Ireland.
  Julia ", wife, 22, b. Wales.
  Patrick ", son, 3, b. Wales.
  Mary ", daughter, 1, b. Wales.
  Stephen Dealey, lodger, 20, b. Ireland.
  Bath Brennan, lodger, 24, b. Ireland.
  Con Harrington, lodger, 25, b. Ireland.

1883 the couple and daughter Mary immigrated to America (1900 census).

1900 Federal census of Newport, Newport Co. RI show the family at 23 Cannon St., as family #43:
  Sullivan, Jerey (sic) P., head, May 1856, 44, married 23 years, b. Ireland to Irish parents. Immigrated 1883, 17 years prior, Naturalized. Day laborer. Rents.
  " Julia, wife, Sept 1858, 41, married 23 years, 13 children, 6 living, b. England to Irish parents. Immigrated 1883, 17 years prior.
  " Mary M., daughter, March 1880, 20, b. England to Irish and English parents. Immigrated 1883, 17 years prior. Apprentice dress maker.
  " Timothy F., son, Marc 1886, 14, b. RI to Irish and English parents. At school.
  " Julia, daughter, March 1890, 10, b. RI to Irish and English parents.
  " Jerry, son, Oct 1891, 8, b. RI to Irish and English parents. At school.
  " Annie, daughter, August 1895, 4, b. RI to Irish and English parents. At school.
(Jerry 27 b. England and Mary65 b. Ireland Shea are enumerated in the next house at 25 Cannon St. They immigrated in 1890.)

1910 Federal census of Newport, Newport Co. RI shows the family enumerated at 23 Cannon St. as family #212:

Sullivan, Jeremiah P., head, 55, married 33 years, b. Ireland to Irish parents. Immigrated 1880, Naturalized. Contractor, Teaming & Foundations. Rents.

" Julia M., wife, 51, married 33 years, 13 children, 6 living, b. Wales to Irish parents. Immigrated 1880.

" Patrick J., son, 31, widower, 2 children (sic), b. Wales, to Irish and Wales parents. Immigrated 1880. Bar Tender, Cafe.

" Timothy F., son, 24, b. RI to Irish and Wales parents. Restaurant, Eating house.

" Jeremiah J., son, 18, b. RI. Apprentice, Machinist.

" Mary F., daughter, 20, b. Wales. Immigrated 1880. Dress maker, Department Store.

" Julia M. Jr., daughter, 20, b. RI. Bookkeeper, Retail merchant.

" Annie C., daughter, 14, b. RI.

" Jerry (sic), Grand son, 7, b. RI to Wales parents.

" Catherine, Grand daughter, 6, b. RI to Wales parents.

" Patrick J., nephew, 24, b. RI to Irish and Welch parents. Teamer for Coal dealer.

" Michael, nephew, 22, b. RI to Irish and Welch parents. Teamer for Quarry.

" Timothy, nephew, 18, b. RI to Irish and Welch parents. Teamer for Quarry.

(The next house at 27 Cannon has a Mary Shea age 75 - Julia's mother?)

Jeremiah married **Julia M. SHEA** [106775] [MRIN: 36006], daughter of **Mary wife of SHEA** [106781], in 1877 in England. Julia was born in Sep 1848 in Wales and died after 1915 in Newport, Newport, Rhode Island.

Children from this marriage were:

+ 197 M i. **Patrick Joseph SULLIVAN [106794]** was born on 10 Jun 1877 in Merthyr Tydfil, Glamorganshire, Wales and died on 19 Feb 1923 in Newport, Newport, Rhode Island at age 45.

Patrick married **First wife of Patrick SULLIVAN** [106796] [MRIN: 36011] (d. Abt 1904) about 1900.

Patrick next married **Nellie HOULIHAN** [106798] [MRIN: 36012] (b. Abt 1880) after 1910 in Newport, Newport, Rhode Island.

198 F ii. **Mary M. SULLIVAN [106783]** was born in Mar 1880 in Merthyr Tydfil, Glamorganshire, Wales and died after 1900 in Newport, Newport, Rhode Island.

+ 199 M iii. **Timothy Francis SULLIVAN [106776]** was born in 1886 in Newport, Newport, Rhode Island and died on 8 Apr 1954 in Newport, Newport, Rhode Island at age 68.

Timothy married **Mary A. McGUIRE** [106777] [MRIN: 36007] (b. 1886, d. 3 Oct 1952) on 24 Oct 1910 in Fall River, Bristol, Massachusetts.

+ 200 F iv. **Julia Monica SULLIVAN [106784]** was born in Mar 1890 in Newport, Newport, Rhode Island and died on 16 May 1949 in Newport, Newport, Rhode Island at age 59.

Julia married **Jeremiah S. SULLIVAN** [106799] [MRIN: 36013] (b. 1889, d. After 1940) about 1912 in Newport, Newport, Rhode Island.

201 M v. **Jeremiah SULLIVAN [106785]** was born in Oct 1891 in Newport, Newport, Rhode Island.

202 F vi. **Annie SULLIVAN [106786]** was born in Aug 1895 in Newport, Newport, Rhode Island.

169.   Eugene SULLIVAN [94305] (*Sullivans born about 1850 possibly*[154]) was born in Mar 1858 in Ireland and died on 11 Jan 1938 in Fall River, Bristol, Massachusetts at age 79.

> General Notes: 1864 to 1867 he immigrated per the 1910 or 1920 census.   He would have been only 8 or 10.

> 1872 he was naturalized per his 1920 census statement.

> 1878 or so the couple would have been married.   Margaret was born in WI so the couple likely married in MA or WI.

> 1880 Federal census of Fall River shows the family at 46 John St. as family 102:
> Sullivan, Eugene, 25, works in Cotton mill, b. Ireland.
> " Margaret, 21, wife, keeping house, b. Wisconsin.
> " Matilda, 11/12, June, daughter, at home, b. Mass.

> 1891 daughter Catherine was born in Fall River.   Father noted as Weaver.   Mother born in New Diggings (This is in Wisconsin.)

> 1898 daughter Sullivan, Julia, was born showing family at 125 Wade St., - father Insurance Agent, parents b. Ireland and Wisconsin.

> 1900 Federal census shows the family enumerated in Fall River, Bristol Co. MA at 53 Hambly, as family 169:
> Sullivan, Eugene, head, Mar 1858, 42, married 21 years, b. Ireland to Irish parents.   Immigrated 1880 (sic - daughter born in 1879 in MA), 20 years prior. Naturalized.   Insurance agent.   Owns home with mortgage.
> " Margaret, wife, Dec 1858, 41, married 21 years, 7 children, 7 living, b. Wisconsin (sic) to parents from Ireland.
> " Matilda, daughter, June 1879, b. MA to parents from Ireland and WI.
> " Mary J., daughter, Nov 1880, 19, b. MA.
> " Mortimer, son, Apr 1883, 17, b. MA.
> " Margaret, daughter, Aug 1885, 14, b. MA.
> " Catherine A., daughter, Jan 1889, 11, b. MA.
> " Louisa, daughter Aug 1891, 8, b. MA.
> " Julia, daughter, Apr 1898, 2, b. MA.

> 1910 Federal census shows the family enumerated in Fall River, Bristol Co. MA at 55 (clearly not 53) Hambly, as family 169 (again):
> Sullivan, Eugene, head 54, married 32 years, b. Ireland.   Immigrated 1864 (sic) Naturalized. Agent, Insurance.
> " Margaret, wife, 51, married 32 years, b. Wisconsin, to Irish parents.
> " Mary J., daughter, 28, b. MA.   Weaver, cotton mill.
> " Mortimer, 27, b. MA.   Conductor, Street Car.
> " Margaret, daughter, 24, b. MA.   Weaver, cotton mill.
> " Catherine A., daughter, 20, b. MA.   Sewer, bleachery
> " Louise (sic), 17, b. MA. Operator, telephone.

> 1920 Federal census of Fall River shows the family enumerated in Ward 1, dist 28 at 55 Hambly St.:
> Sullivan, Eugene, head, owns home free of mortgage, 58, immigrated 1867, Naturalized 1872. b. Ireland.   Insurance Agent. Insurance Of.
> " Margaret E., wife, 61, b. Illinois (sic) to parents from Ireland.
> " Mary J., 39, b. MA.   Weaver, cotton mill.
> " Mortimer, son, 37, b. MA.   Mechanic, Garage.
> " Margaret E., daughter, 33, b. MA.   Weaver, cotton mill.

1930 Federal census of Fall River, Bristol MA shows the family enumerated at 53 (sic) Hambly St.:
  Sullivan, Eugene, head, owns home $2000,   72, married at 21, b. Ireland.
  " Margaret, wife, 71, married at 70, b. Wisconsin.
  " Mertimer (sic), son, 46, single, b. MA.   Trucking salesman.
  " Margaret E., daughter, 44, b. MA.   Trimmer, cloth room.
  Cote, Mary J., daughter, 48, married at 40, b. MA.
(Daughter Louisa's family is enumerated at 71 Hambly.)

There is another family renting in the dwelling, for $27/month.

1933 and 1935 Fall River Directory
- Sullivan Eugene (Margaret E.) 91 S. Main room 3 h 55 Hambly.

1936 Fall River Directory Sullivans - oddly -
- Sullivan Eugene (Margaret E.) 91 S. Main room 3 h 55 Hambly
- Sullivan Eugene (Eliz M A) pres home Circle Stores 405 Pleasant h 55 Hambly
- Sullivan Eugene (Eliz M A) gro 221 John h. 366 Whipple.

1937 Fall River Directory oddly
- Sullivan Eugene pres Home Circle Stores 405 Pleasant h 55 Hambly. (No spouse shown.)
- Sullivan Margaret E. (Mrs Eugene) died June 4 1936.

1939 Fall River Directory
- Sullivan Eugene (55 Hambly) died Jan 11, 1938.

Eugene married **Margaret E. HEALY** [94306] [MRIN: 31559], daughter of **John HEALY** [94320] and **Margaret wife of John HEALY** [94321],   about 1878 in Fall River, Bristol, Massachusetts. Margaret was born in Dec 1858 in New Diggings, Lafayette, Wisconsin and died on 4 Jun 1936 in Fall River, Bristol, Massachusetts at age 77.

Children from this marriage were:

203   F   i.   **Matilda SULLIVAN [94307]** was born in Jun 1879 in Fall River, Bristol, Massachusetts and died on 2 Aug 1901 in Fall River, Bristol, Massachusetts at age 22.

General Notes: 1901 Aug 2, Deaths Registered in Fall River, MA shows:
  Matilda Sullivan, single, 22 years, 1 month, 23 days, Nephritis, res. 55 Hambly St., b. Fall River, to Eugene, Margaret E. - Healy, b. Ireland and Wisconsin.

204   F   ii.   **Mary J. SULLIVAN [94308]** was born on 4 Nov 1880 in Fall River, Bristol, Massachusetts.

General Notes: 1930 Federal census of Fall River MA shows her enumerated with her parents as Mary J. Cote, 48, married at 40.

Mary married **Mr. COTE** [94322] [MRIN: 31565]. Mr. was born in 1840.

205   M   iii.   **Mortimer 'Murtie' SULLIVAN [94309]** was born in Apr 1883 in Fall River, Bristol, Massachusetts.

General Notes: 1883 April 10 Births Registered in Fall River notes:
  Sullivan Murtee (sic) b. Fall River to Eugene, Margaret, res. Fall River.   Father Weaver. Parents b. Ireland and Illinois (sic).

206 F iv. **Margaret SULLIVAN [94310]** was born on 11 Aug 1885 in Fall River, Bristol, Massachusetts.

General Notes: 1885 August 11, Births Registered in Fall River notes;
Sullivan, Margaret b. to Eugene, Margaret, father weaver. Father b. Ireland, mother Wisconsin.

+ 207 F v. **Catherine Agnes SULLIVAN [94311]** was born on 25 Jan 1889 in Fall River, Bristol, Massachusetts and died on 4 Jun 1941 in Providence, Providence, Rhode Island at age 52.

Catherine married **Edgar F. ONEIL** [94317] [MRIN: 31562] (b. 1 Oct 1890, d. After 1930) on 17 Jun 1914 in Fall River, Bristol, Massachusetts.

+ 208 F vi. **Louisa M. SULLIVAN [94312]** was born in Aug 1891 in Fall River, Bristol, Massachusetts.

Louisa married **Bernard A. FLYNN** [94314] [MRIN: 31560] (b. 1890) on 5 Jun 1912 in Fall River, Bristol, Massachusetts.

209 F vii. **Julia SULLIVAN [94313]** was born in Apr 1898 in Fall River, Bristol, Massachusetts and died on 17 Apr 1898 in Fall River, Bristol, Massachusetts.

General Notes: 1898 April 19 Births Registered in Fall River notes:
Sullivan, Julia, b. Fall River to Eugene, Margaret - Healy, res 125 Wade St., father Insurance Agent, parents b. Ireland and Wisconsin.

Grandchildren

172.   Timothy J. SULLIVAN [99159] (*John*[157]*, Sullivans born about 1850 possibly*[154]) was born in 1877 in Ireland and died before 1920 in Fall River, Bristol, Massachusetts.

General Notes: 1898 June 2, Marriages Registered in Fall River notes:
   Timothy J. Sullivan, res 7 Camden, Fall River, 21, Weaver, b. Fall River to John, Mary T. - Sullivan, first marriage.
   Laura W. Wilson, 85 John St., Fall River, 20, Weaver, b. Fall River to Thomas W., Sarah - Robinson, first marriage.
   Married by Cornelius W. Smith, Clergyman.

1898 August daughter Florence is born.   Family is living at 85 John St., father working as Third Hand.

1899 birth of son Arthur shows the couple as Timothy J. and Laura A. Wilson, res. 44 Brow St., father b. Ireland, works as Third Hand.   (Brow St. is around the corner from John St. just a block from Tecumseh Mill.)

1900, 1910 and 1920 Federal census shows his wife and children enumerated at 44 Brow St., but without Timothy.   His wife indicates she is married in 1900 and 1910, a widow in 1920.

Timothy married **Laura W. WILSON** [99160] [MRIN: 33129], daughter of **Thomas W. WILSON** [99163] and **Sarah ROBINSON** [99164], on 2 Jun 1898 in Fall River, Bristol, Massachusetts. Laura was born in 1878 in England and died after 1930 in Fall River, Bristol, Massachusetts.

Children from this marriage were:

+   210   F   i.   **Florence SULLIVAN [99165]** was born on 14 Aug 1898 in Fall River, Bristol, Massachusetts and died on 8 Nov 1981 in Fall River, Bristol, Massachusetts at age 83.

Florence married **Paul GROSS** [99167] [MRIN: 33132] (b. 1899, d. Between 1920 and 1930)

Florence next married **Harold CONBOY** [99172] [MRIN: 33133] (b. 24 May 1900)

+   211   M   ii.   **Arthur Warren SULLIVAN [99166]** was born on 7 Nov 1899 in Fall River, Bristol, Massachusetts and died after 1952.

Arthur married **Margaretta L. M. wife of Arthur SULLIVAN** [99177] [MRIN: 33138] (b. 1907, d. After 1952) in Fall River, Bristol, Massachusetts.

   212   F   iii.   **Hilda SULLIVAN [99171]** was born on 30 Jul 1910 in Fall River, Bristol, Massachusetts and died on 28 Jul 2002 in Fall River, Bristol, Massachusetts at age 91.

General Notes: The Fall River vital records shows her father as James F. Sullivan, mother Laura Wilson.   She appears with Laura in the 1900, 1910, 1920 and 1930 Federal census.

1910 July 30, Births Registered in Fall River, MA notes:
   Sullivan, Hilda, b. Fall River to James F., Laura Wilson, 44 Brow St., father Sergeant, USA, b. Ireland , mother b. England.

2002 July 28, Fall River MA Herald News
Hilda M. (Sullivan) Hanson, 91, of 100 Amity St., Fall River, formerly of 181 South Main St., died Friday at South Pointe Rehabilitation & Skilled Nursing Center, Fall River. She was the

wife of the late William F. Hanson. Born in Fall River, daughter of the late Laura Sullivan, she had lived in Fall River for all of her life and was educated in local schools. She was a communicant of Holy Cross Church of Sts. Peter and Paul Parish. Mrs. Hanson was employed at the former Lamport Manufacturing Co. in Fall River. She later worked in the Fall River School Department's Foster Grandparent Program. She was a member of the Borden West Adult Day Care. She leaves sic grandchildren, several great - grandchildren, several nieces and nephews, and a grand-niece. She also was the mother of the late Kenneth E. Hanson, and step-mother of the late Lorraine Forgette and William Hanson.

213 F iv. **Margaret W. SULLIVAN [99170]** was born in 1917 in Fall River, Bristol, Massachusetts.

173. Lena SULLIVAN [104712] (*James* [158]*, Sullivans born about 1850 possibly* [154]) was born on 20 Nov 1873 in Providence, Providence, Rhode Island and died on 20 Sep 1949 in Middleboro, Plymouth, Massachusetts at age 75.

General Notes: Unable to find Lena with her parents in the 1880 Federal census or RI or MA.

1893 November 21, Marriages Registered in Fall River MA notes:
James E. Gotham, 21, Teamster, b. Blackstone, MA to James M., Eliza Keenan, first marriage.
Lena Sullivan, 20, Cloth Trimmer, b. Providence, RI, to James, Lina O'Brien, first marriage.
Married by M. J. Cook, Catholic Priest.

Lena married **James E. GOTHAM** [104711] [MRIN: 35238], son of **James M. GOTHAM** [104715] and **Eliza KEENAN** [104716], on 21 Nov 1893 in Fall River, Bristol, Massachusetts. James was born in Jul 1873 in Blackstone, Worcester, Massachusetts and died on 8 Jun 1926 in Taunton, Bristol, Massachusetts at age 52.

Children from this marriage were:

214 M i. **Stephen Edward GOTHAM [104717]** was born on 11 Feb 1896 in Fall River, Bristol, Massachusetts and died on 9 Oct 1966 in Taunton, Bristol, Massachusetts at age 70.

Stephen married **Anna M. wife of Stephen GOTHAM** [104719] [MRIN: 35241]. Anna was born on 25 Oct 1896 in MA and died on 4 Jan 1968 in Taunton, Bristol, Massachusetts at age 71.

215 F ii. **Annie Marie GOTHAM [104718]** was born on 16 Jun 1898 in Fall River, Bristol, Massachusetts and died on 20 Jul 1983 in Taunton, Bristol, Massachusetts at age 85.

Annie married **James Henry McCAFFREY** [104720] [MRIN: 35242]. James was born in 1890 and died in 1949 at age 59.

216 M iii. **James Edward GOTHAM [104721]** was born on 3 Oct 1906 in Fall River, Bristol, Massachusetts and died on 27 Dec 1969 in Middleboro, Plymouth, Massachusetts at age 63.

James married **Julia McGUINESS** [104722] [MRIN: 35243]. Julia was born in 1902 and died in 1987 at age 85.

174. Annie SULLIVAN [105389] (*Mortimer* [159]*, Sullivans born about 1850 possibly* [154]) was born in May 1874 in Ireland and died after 1940 in Fall River, Bristol, Massachusetts.

General Notes: 1881 immigrated to America (1900 census).

1896 July 28, Marriages Registered in Fall River MA notes:

Thomas Donnelly, res. Fall River, 21, Coachman, b. Fall River, Thomas, Jane - McNamara, first marriage.

Annie Sullivan, res. Fall River, 23, Weaver, Ireland, Mortimer, Hanora - Corran (sic), first marriage. Married by James A. Gleason, Catholic Priest.

Annie married **Thomas F. DONNELLY** [105390] [MRIN: 35486], son of **Thomas DONNELLY** [105391] and **Jane McNAMARA** [105392], on 28 Jul 1896 in Fall River, Bristol, Massachusetts. Thomas was born in May 1874 in Fall River, Bristol, Massachusetts and died after 1940 in Fall River, Bristol, Massachusetts.

Children from this marriage were:

217 M i. **Child DONNELLY** [105399] was born on 24 Nov 1897 in Fall River, Bristol, Massachusetts and died on 24 Nov 1897 in Fall River, Bristol, Massachusetts.

General Notes: Still born child.

218 M ii. **Raymond DONNELLY** [105400] was born in Apr 1899 in Fall River, Bristol, Massachusetts.

219 M iii. **Thomas H. DONNELLY** [105396] was born on 15 Aug 1901 in Fall River, Bristol, Massachusetts and died on 23 Aug 1905 in Fall River, Bristol, Massachusetts at age 4.

General Notes: 1905 August 23, Massachusetts Death Certificate notes:
Thomas H. Donnelley, died 206 Jones, Fall River, age 4 years. B. Fall River. Father Thomas T. (?) Donnelley, b. Fall River; mother Annie Sullivan, b. Ireland. Informant, mother.
Died of Diphtheria, duration 3 weeks.
Burial St. Patricks Cemetery.

220 F iv. **Mary DONNELLY** [105397] was born on 29 Nov 1903 in Fall River, Bristol, Massachusetts.

221 F v. **Annie DONNELLY** [105398] was born on 17 Mar 1908 in Fall River, Bristol, Massachusetts.

222 M vi. **William DONNELLY** [105395] was born on 12 Mar 1911 in Fall River, Bristol, Massachusetts.

175. Patrick H. SULLIVAN [105593] (*Timothy T.*[160], *Sullivans born about 1850 possibly*[154]) was born in Mar 1869 in Ireland and died after 1930 in Fall River, Bristol, Massachusetts.

General Notes: 1890 immigrated to America. (1900 census).

1897 October 5, Marriages Registered in Fall River MA notes:
Patrick H. Sullivan, 29, Freight Handler, b. Ireland to Timothy, Mary (sic) - Sullivan, first marriage.
Hanora O'Neil, 34, Domestic, b. Ireland, Patrick, Mary - Sughrue, first marriage.
M. J. Owens, Priest.

1900 Federal census of Fall River, Bristol Co. MA shows the young couple in a 4 family dwelling at 30 Hunter St. as family #39:
Sullivan, Patrick, head, March 1869, 31, married 3 years, b. Ireland to Irish parents. Immigrated 1890, 10 years prior. Freight Handler. Rents.
" Hannah, wife, Sept 1862, 37, married 3 yeras, 1 child, 1 living, b. Ireland to Irish parents. Immigrated 1885, 15 Ireland prior.
" Francis, son Oct 1898, 1, b. MA.

1910 Federal census of Fall River, Bristol CO. MA shows the family in ward 7, dist 164, at 40 Danforth St. as family #387:

   Sullivan, Patrick F. (sic), head, 41, married 12 years, b. Ireland.   Immigrated 1895 (sic), alien, Freight Handler, Boat. Rents.

   " Hannah, wife, 40 (sic), married 12 years, 2 children, 2 living, b. Ireland.   Immigrated 1890 (sic).

   " Francis, son, 11, b. MA.

   " Mary E., daughter, 9, b. MA.

1920 Federal census of Fall River, Bristol Co. MA shows the family at 85 Van Buren St. as family #33:

   Sullivan, Patrick, head, rents, 54, immigrated 1895, b. Ireland.   Freight handler, Dock.

   " Hannah, wife, 54 (sic), immigrated 1882, b. Ireland.

   " Francis, son, 21, b. MA.   Clerk, Drug Store.

   " Mary, daughter, 18, b. MA.   Operative, Laundry.

(In the same dwelling as family #32 may be the family of his late brother)

   Price, John H., head, 35, b. MA to Irish parents. Fireman, Mill.

   " Hanora, wife, 43, b. MA (sic) to Irish parents.

   Sullivan, Lillian, step daughter, 17, b. MA. Operative, Print Works.

   " Irene, step daughter, 15, b. MA.   Operative, Print Works.

   Price, Margaret, daughter, 6, b. MA.

   " John, son, 4 8/12, b. MA.

   " Francis, son, 3 4/12, b. MA.

1930 Federal census of Fall River, Bristol Co. MA shows the family at 203 Durfee St. as family #254:

   Sullivan, Patrick, head, owns $500, 60, married at 25, b. Ireland. Immigrated 1890 (sic), naturalized.

   " Anna (sic), wife, 60 (sic), married at 24, b. Ireland.   Immigrated 1890 (sic).

   " Mary, daughter, 28, b. MA. Sorter, Laundry.

   " Francis, son, 32, b. MA.   Salesman, Retail Drugs.

Patrick married **Hanora ONEIL** [105594] [MRIN: 35564], daughter of **Patrick ONEIL** [105597] and **Mary SUGHRUE** [105598],   on 5 Oct 1897 in Fall River, Bristol, Massachusetts. Hanora was born in Sep 1862 in Ireland and died between 1920 and 1930 in Fall River, Bristol, Massachusetts.

Children from this marriage were:

   223   M   i.   **Francis SULLIVAN [105599]** was born in Oct 1898 in Fall River, Bristol, Massachusetts.

   224   F   ii.   **Mary E. SULLIVAN [105600]** was born in 1901 in Fall River, Bristol, Massachusetts.

180.   Catherine G. SULLIVAN [105924] (*Richard*[161], *Sullivans born about 1850 possibly*[154]) was born on 1 Jul 1878 in Co. Kerry, Ireland and died in 1940 in Newport, Newport, Rhode Island at age 62.

   General Notes: 1878 July 1, Ireland Births and Baptism LDS abstracts

   Catherine Sullivan, b. Co. Kerry, IR, parents Richard, Johanna Fitzgerald.

   1887 immigrated to America at about age 9 (1930 census).

   1900 Federal census unable to locate Catherine in the Newport RI enumeration.

   1901 August 28, Marriages Registered in Fall River MA notes:

   Edward C. Fitzgerald, 23, first marriage, res. 42 Mott, Fall River, Lineman, b. Ireland to Daniel, Mary - Riley.

   Catherine G., Sullivan, 22, first marriage, 34 Hammond, Newport, RI, Domestic, b. Ireland to Richard, Johanna Fitzgerald.

Catherine married **Edward C. FITZGERALD** [105921] [MRIN: 35698], son of **Daniel FITZGERALD** [105922] and **Mary RILEY** [105923],   on 28 Aug 1901 in Fall River, Bristol, Massachusetts. Edward was born in 1878 in Ireland and died after 1940 in Newport, Newport, Rhode Island.

Children from this marriage were:

    225 F   i.   **Mary FITZGERALD [105927]** was born in 1903 in Newport, Newport, Rhode Island.

    226 M   ii.   **Daniel FITZGERALD [105928]** was born in 1905 in MA.

    227 M   iii.   **Henry FITZGERALD [105929]** was born in 1907 in Newport, Newport, Rhode Island.

    228 M   iv.   **Edward FITZGERALD [105930]** was born in 1908 in NY.

    229 F   v.   **Anna FITZGERALD [105931]** was born in 1911 in Newport, Newport, Rhode Island.

    230 F   vi.   **Catherine FITZGERALD [105932]** was born in 1914 in MA.

182.   Catherine 'Kate' SULLIVAN [106519] (*John* [162], *Sullivans born about 1850 possibly* [154]) was born in 1877 in Ireland and died on 4 Nov 1929 in New Bedford, Bristol, Massachusetts at age 52.

    General Notes: 1895 immigrated to America at about the age 18 (1910 census).

    1907 December 15, Marriages Registered in Taunton, MA shows a marriage that took place in Fall River MA:
      George F. Guild, 41, second marriage, widower, res. Taunton, MA, Shipper, b. Seekonk MA to George W. Guild, Annie Phillips.
      Kate Sullivan, 30, first marriage, res. Taunton, MA, Housework, b. Ireland to John Sullivan, Kate Walsh.
      Married by David B. Jutten, Minister of the Gospel, Fall River MA.

    1929 Massachusetts Death Index notes:
      Guild, Katherine M. (Sullivan) died New Bedford, 1929, vol. 53 page 349.

    1930 New Bedford City Directory
    - Guild Katherine M. (Mrs. George F.) died Nov 4, 1929.   (George is not listed separately in the directory this year.)

Catherine married **George F. GUILD** [106518] [MRIN: 35907], son of **George Whitfield GUILD** [106531] and **Annie PHILIPS** [106523],   on 15 Dec 1907 in Fall River, Bristol, Massachusetts. George was born on 20 Apr 1866 in Seekonk, Bristol, Massachusetts and died after 1930.

Children from this marriage were:

    231 M   i.   **George F. GUILD Jr. [106522]** was born on 20 Apr 1910 in New Bedford, Bristol, Massachusetts.

    232 F   ii.   **Louisa C. GUILD [106524]** was born on 10 Dec 1908 in Taunton, Bristol, Massachusetts.

        General Notes: 1908 December 10, Births Registered in Taunton MA:
        Louisa C. Guild, b. to George F. Guild, Catherine M. Sullivan, father Shipper, parents b. Seekonk MA., Ireland.

    233 M   iii.   **Charles H. GUILD [106533]** was born in 1914 in MA.

234 M iv.   **Raymond E. GUILD [106534]** was born on 13 Oct 1914 in Taunton, Bristol, Massachusetts and died on 21 Nov 1981 in San Antonio, Bexar, Texas at age 67.

Raymond married **Carmen Valdez WONG** [106536] [MRIN: 35911]. Carmen was born on 17 Sep 1926 and died on 2 Apr 1978 in Del Rio, Val Verde, Texas at age 51.

235 F v.   **Elizabeth J. GUILD [106535]** was born in 1917 in MA.

183. Julia V. SULLIVAN [106058] (*Michael*[163], *Sullivans born about 1850 possibly*[154]) was born in 1879 in Ireland, died in 1939 in Fall River, Bristol, Massachusetts at age 60, and was buried in St. Patrick's Cem., Fall River, Massachusetts.

> General Notes: 1902 December 11, Marriages Registered in Fall River MA notes:
> Joseph Keeley, 24, first marriage, res. 17 Palmer, Card Grinder, b. Fall River, to John, Eliza - (not named).
> Julia V. Sullivan, 23, first marriage, res. 144 Tuttle, Speeder tender, b. Ireland to Michael, Johanna - Kane.
> Married by M. J. Cooke, Priest.
>
> 1902 or 1903 no Sullivan listed in the Fall River City Directory at 144 Tuttle.

Julia married **Joseph KEELEY** [106055] [MRIN: 35744], son of **John KEELEY** [106056] and **Eliza wife of John KEELEY** [106057], on 11 Dec 1902 in Fall River, Bristol, Massachusetts. Joseph was born in 1878 in Fall River, Bristol, Massachusetts, died in 1939 in Fall River, Bristol, Massachusetts at age 61, and was buried in St. Patrick's Cem., Fall River, Massachusetts.

Children from this marriage were:

236 M i.   **Edward J. KEELEY [106062]** was born on 8 Mar 1903 in Fall River, Bristol, Massachusetts and died on 20 Aug 1903 in Fall River, Bristol, Massachusetts.

> General Notes: 1903 August 20, Massachusetts Death Certificate notes:
> Edward J. Keeley, res. 121 Freedom, Fall River, MA. Died age 5 months, 12 days. B. Fall River. Father Joseph b. Fall River, mother Julia Sullivan, b. Ireland.
> Died of Cholera Infantum.
> Burial St. Patricks Cemetery.

237 F ii.   **Elizabeth KEELEY [106063]** was born on 19 Jun 1904 in Fall River, Bristol, Massachusetts.

238 M iii.   **William P. KEELEY [106064]** was born on 13 Mar 1906 in Fall River, Bristol, Massachusetts.

239 F iv.   **Lillian KEELEY [106061]** was born on 21 Aug 1910 in Fall River, Bristol, Massachusetts.

240 M v.   **John K. KEELEY [106066]** was born on 5 May 1913 in Fall River, Bristol, Massachusetts.

241 M vi.   **Joseph KEELEY [106065]** was born on 11 Mar 1915 in Fall River, Bristol, Massachusetts.

184. Thomas F. SULLIVAN [106325] (*John*[164], *Sullivans born about 1850 possibly*[154]) was born in 1885 in Danielson, Windham, Connecticut and died after 1930 in Taunton, Bristol, Massachusetts.

General Notes: 1900 Federal census he is enumerated in Killingsly, Windham Co. CT with his mother and step father, age 12 (sic).

1906 April 6, Marriages Registered in Fall River MA notes:
   Thomas F. Sullivan, 21, first marriage, res. 123 Ingell, Taunton MA, Bookkeeper, b. Danielson, CT, to John, Catherine Hanley.
   Alice M. Westgate, 23, first marriage, res. 961 North Main, At home, b. New Bedford, MA to John, Laura Adams.
   Married by Rennetts C. Miller, Cl. (sic)

1908 the family was living at 961 North Main St., Fall River MA when son Edward was born.

1910 his family is enumerated without him in Taunton, MA.

1920 Federal census of Taunton, Bristol Co. MA in January shows the family at 41 East Walnut St., as family #202:
   Sullivan Thomas F., head, rents, 33, b. CT to CT parents. Molder, Stove Co.
   " Alice M., wife, 35, b. MA to MA parents.
   " Catherine F., daughter, 13, b. MA.
   " Edward W., son, 11, b. MA.
   " Marion L., daughter, 1 4/12, b. MA.
   " Alice M., daughter, 6/12, b. MA.
(Also in the dwelling as family #203 may be Thomas' mother)
   Sullivan, Catherine L., head, 50, rents, widow, b. MA to Irish parents.
   " James S., son, 20, b. MA to MA parents. Machinist, Machine shop.
   " Christine L., daughter, 16, b. RI to MA parents. Plater, wire factory.
   Soden, Catherine E., niece, 17, b. MA to MA and Irish parents. Plater, wire factory. (Children of Eugene Soden and Mary A. Jones)
   " Thomas E., nephew, 13, b. MA to MA and Irish parents.
   " Mary E., niece, 12, b. MA. MA to MA and Irish parents.
(The 10 year gap in the births of children Catherine and Alice makes the later children appear to be from a second wife, but the 'second wife' appears to be the same Alice Westlake Thomas married in 1906.)

1930 Federal census of Taunton, Bristol Co. MA shows the family at 11 Pratt St.:
   Sullivan, Thomas F., head, rents, 43, married at 18, b. CT. Molder, Stove foundry.
   " Alice M., wife, 46, married at 22, b. MA.
   " Catherine F., daughter, 23, b. MA. Trimmer, Rubber Hose Co.
   " Edward W., son, 22, b. MA. Molder, Stove foundry.
   " Marion L., daughter, 12, b. MA.
   " Alice M., daughter, 10, b. MA.
   " Thomas F., son, 9, b. MA.
   " John L., son, 2 7/12, b. MA.

Thomas married **Alice M. WESTGATE** [106326] [MRIN: 35837], daughter of **John WESTGATE** [106327] and **Laura ADAMS** [106328], on 6 Apr 1906 in Fall River, Bristol, Massachusetts. Alice was born in 1883 in Marion, Plymouth, Massachusetts and died after 1930 in Taunton, Bristol, Massachusetts.

Children from this marriage were:

242   M   i.   **Edward W. SULLIVAN [106329]** was born on 13 Feb 1908 in Fall River, Bristol, Massachusetts.

          General Notes: 1908 February 13, Births Registered in Fall River MA notes:
            Sullivan, Edward W., b. to Thomas F., Alice W. Westgate, res. 961 North Main, father Foundry man, parents b. CT, Marion, MA.

243 F   ii.   **Catherine SULLIVAN [106330]** was born on 4 Jul 1906 in Taunton, Bristol, Massachusetts.

> General Notes: 1906 July 4, Births Registered in   Taunton, MA notes
> Catherine Sullivan, b. Taunton, to Thomas F. Sullivan, Alice M. Westgate, res. Taunton, MA, father RR Clerk, parents b. Danielson, CT, Marion MA.

244 F   iii.   **Alice M. SULLIVAN [106331]** was born on 14 Dec 1919 in Fall River, Bristol, Massachusetts and died on 13 Mar 1994 in Middletown, Newport, Rhode Island at age 74.

> Alice married **John Okill RICHARDSON** [106332] [MRIN: 35839]. John was born on 13 May 1926 in Providence, Providence, Rhode Island and died on 28 Jan 1990 in Middletown, Newport, Rhode Island at age 63.

245 F   iv.   **Marion L. SULLIVAN [106336]** was born in 1917 in MA.

246 M   v.   **Thomas F. SULLIVAN Jr. [106467]** was born in 1921 in Taunton, Bristol, Massachusetts.

247 M   vi.   **John L. SULLIVAN [106468]** was born in 1927 in Taunton, Bristol, Massachusetts.

194.   John Joseph SULLIVAN [106492] (*Jeremiah J.*[166], *Sullivans born about 1850 possibly*[154]) was born in 1881 in Cranston, Providence, Rhode Island and died on 22 Apr 1929 in Pawtucket, Providence, Rhode Island at age 48.

> General Notes: 1905 Rhode Island Census of Cumberland shows:
> Sullivan, Jeremiah, 11 Maple, head, age 48, b. Ireland.   Married. Number in family 3. Immigrated 1867, 38 years in US, 38 years in Rhode Island.   Parents b. Ireland. Naturalized.   Laborer, Day.   Roman Catholic.   Can't read or write.
> Sullivan, John J., res. 11 Maple, son, age 24, b. April 1881, Providence, RI.   Parents b. Ireland.   Occupation Motorman.   Catholic.
>
> 1907 May 8, Marriages Registered in Fall River MA notes:
> John J. Sullivan, 26, first marriage, res. Broad, Valley Falls, RI, Motorman, b. Cranston RI., to Jeremiah, Margaret McQuillam.
> Agnes M. Flynn, 26, first marriage, res. 43 John, Speeder tender, b. Fall River, to John, Margaret Laney.
> Married by John McKeon, Priest.
>
> 1908 Pawtucket City Directory
> - Sullivan John J. Motorman house 440 Dexter Central Falls.
>
> 1909 and 1913 Pawtucket City Directory
> - Sullivan Jeremiah J. house furnishing goods 88 Lawn Ave house 88 Lawn.
> - Sullivan John J. boards 88 Lawn.
> - Sullivan John J. motorman house 14 Richardson Central Falls.
>
> 1910 Federal census of Central Falls, Providence Co. RI, shows the couple enumerated with Agnes' mother at 14 Richardson St., as family #6:
> Flynn, Margaret, head, 65, widow, 8 children, 2 living, b. Ireland to Irish parents.   Immigrated 1860. Housekeeper, House.
> Sullivan, Agnes, daughter, 28, married 3 years, 2 children, 1 living, b. MA to Irish parents.   Doffer, Cotton mill.
> " John J., son in law, 28, married 3 years, b. RI to Irish parents.   Motorman, Street   Rry (sic).

" John, grand son, 15/12, b. RI to RI and MA parents.

1920 Federal census of Central Falls, Providence Co. RI shows the family at 438 Dexter St. as family #139:
   Sullivan, John J., head, 38, b. RI to Irish parents.   Motorman, Street Railway.
   " Agnes, wife, 39, b. MA to Irish parents.
   " John E., son, 10, b. MA to Irish parents.

1925 Rhode Island State census shows the widower at 432 (sic) Dexter St as family #127:
   Sullivan, John J., head, 44, b. RI.
   " John E., son, 15, b. RI.

1929 April 22, Rhode Island deaths registered in Pawtucket, RI LDS abstract notes:
   John Joseph Sullivan, 48, b. 1881, son of Jeremiah, Margaret McQuillen (sic).   Spouse Madeline Mary Rice.

John married **Agnes M. FLYNN** [106495] [MRIN: 35897], daughter of **John FLYNN** [106496] and **Margaret DELANEY** [106497], on 8 May 1907 in Fall River, Bristol, Massachusetts. Agnes was born on 26 Sep 1880 in Fall River, Bristol, Massachusetts and died on 9 Aug 1921 in Central Falls, Providence, Rhode Island at age 40.

Children from this marriage were:

  248 M   i.   **Jeremiah Edmond SULLIVAN [106498]** was born on 1 Mar 1908 in Cranston, Providence, Rhode Island.

  249 M   ii.   **John Edwin SULLIVAN [106499]** was born on 13 May 1909 in Cranston, Providence, Rhode Island.

John next married **Madeline Mary RICE** [106501] [MRIN: 35900]. Madeline was born about 1881.

196. **Elizabeth Katherine SULLIVAN [92398]** (*Thomas*[167]*, Sullivans born about 1850 possibly*[154]) was born on 1 Feb 1876 in New York and died after 1930 in Fall River, Bristol, Massachusetts.

   General Notes: 1898 July 27 Marriages registered in Fall River
    Jeremiah F. McCarthy, 115 Orange, 21, weaver, b Fall River, parents Jeremiah, Sophia Monahan.
    Elizabeth K. Sullivan, 36 Seabury, 21, speeder tender, b. NY, NY, parents Thomas, Catherine Sheehan.
    Married by Mathias McCabe, 78 Linden (he was a priest at St. Mary's).

Elizabeth married **Jeremiah McCARTHY** [92402] [MRIN: 30932], son of **Jeremiah McCARTHY** [92403] and **Sophia MONAHAN** [92404], on 27 Jul 1898 in Fall River, Bristol, Massachusetts. Jeremiah was born in 1877 in Fall River, Bristol, Massachusetts and died after 1930 in Fall River, Bristol, Massachusetts.

Children from this marriage were:

  250 M   i.   **Daniel McCARTHY [105658]** was born on 12 Aug 1900 in Fall River, Bristol, Massachusetts.

  251 M   ii.   **Thomas McCARTHY [92405]** was born on 3 Oct 1902 in Fall River, Bristol, Massachusetts.

  252 M   iii. **William McCARTHY [105657]** was born on 30 Aug 1904 in Fall River, Bristol, Massachusetts.

253 F iv. **Mary McCARTHY [92406]** was born on 21 Dec 1906 in Fall River, Bristol, Massachusetts, died on 14 Jul 2004 in Fall River, Bristol, Massachusetts at age 97, and was buried in St. Patrick's Cem., Fall River, Massachusetts.

General Notes: 2004 July 17, Fall River MA Herald News - Funeral Shannon -- (McCarthy) Mary V., age 97, July 14, 2004 of Fall River. Wife of the late Charles J. Shannon. Sister of Catherine (McCarthy) Coelho, Elizabeth Cottrell, Jeremiah McCarthy & the late Helen Fortin, Daniel, William & Thomas McCarthy. Funeral mass Monday, July 19, 2004 9:00 AM in Sacred Heart Church Linden St. Fall River. Relatives and friends invited. Arrangements in the care of Waring-Sullivan Home of Memorial Tribute at Cherry Place, 178 Winter St. Fall River. Burial in St. Patrick's Cemetery Fall River. [Providence RI Journal, Saturday 17 July 2004] Fall River - Mary V. (McCarthy) Shannon, 97, of Whipple Street, a retired textile worker, died Wednesday at the Crawford Nursing Home. She was the wife of the late Charles J. Shannon. A lifelong Fall River resident, she was a daughter of the late Jeremiah and Elizabeth (Sullivan) McCarthy. She was educated in Fall River schools. Mrs. Shannon had worked for the Small Brothers Rope Works for 37 years, and later for Chace Curtain, until retiring in 1971. She was a lifelong parishioner of Sacred Heart Church, where she was a member of the senior citizens' and sewing groups. She leaves two sisters, Catherine (McCarthy) Coelho of Fall River and Elizabeth Cottrell of Cranston; a brother, Jeremiah McCarthy in California; and several nieces and nephews. She was a sister of the late Daniel, William and Thomas McCarthy and Helen Fortin. A funeral Mass will be celebrated Monday at 9 a.m. in Sacred Heart Church, Linden Street. Burial will be in St. Patrick's Cemetery.

Mary married **Charles J. SHANNON** [108484] [MRIN: 22409]. Charles was born about 1906.

254 M v. **Jeremiah McCARTHY [92409]** was born on 13 Feb 1909 in Fall River, Bristol, Massachusetts.

255 F vi. **Margaret McCARTHY [92408]** was born on 5 Mar 1912 in Fall River, Bristol, Massachusetts.

256 F vii. **Ellen McCARTHY [92407]** was born on 11 Dec 1913 in Fall River, Bristol, Massachusetts.

General Notes: 2004 she is called the late Helen Fortin in her sister Mary Shannon's obituary.

257 F viii. **Catherine McCARTHY [105659]** was born in 1914 in Fall River, Bristol, Massachusetts.

Catherine married **Mr. COELHO** [108485] [MRIN: 26850].

197. Patrick Joseph SULLIVAN [106794] (*Jeremiah P.*[168]*, Sullivans born about 1850 possibly*[154]) was born on 10 Jun 1877 in Merthyr Tydfil, Glamorganshire, Wales and died on 19 Feb 1923 in Newport, Newport, Rhode Island at age 45.

General Notes: 1880 Merthyr Tydfil, Glamorganshire, Wales census shows him with his parents, age 3.

1882 immigrated to America at age 18 (1900 census).

1900 Federal census of Brooklyn, Kings Co. NY shows him enumerated at the US Naval Hospital and Laboratory, US Marine Corps Barracks in June:
   Sullivan, Patrick J., rank - Hospital App(rentice?), 1st Class, res. Newport RI, 23 Cannon St., b. June 1877, age 22, b. Wales, parents from Ireland, Wales. Immigrated 1882, at age 18, alien.

1902 September the couple was in New York when son Jeremiah was born.

1904 March daughter Catherine was born.   By the 1905 State census Patrick was a widower.

1905 Rhode Island State census of Newport RI card notes family #166:
   Sullivan, Patrick J. res. 23 Cannon, Newport, son, b. Wales, age 27, foreign born, widower, immigrated 1883, age 22 (sic).   Years in Rhode Island, 22.   Father b. Ireland, Mother, Wales. Naturalization P. A. Occupation Clerk, Wine.   Soldier during Civil or Spanish war - No.   Catholic.

1910 Federal census of Newport, RI shows him a widower with two children, living in the household of his father Jeremiah Sullivan.

1918 September 12, WWI Draft Registration Card notes:
   Patrick Joseph Sullivan, res. 20 Mill Newport, RI, 40 years old.   Born June 10, 1878 (sic). Naturalized Citizen.   Contractor, Employer J. P. Sullivan & Sons, Lee Hwy, Newport, RI.   Nearest Relative - Julia Sullivan, 32 (sic) Cannon, Newport, RI.
Height medium, build stout, eyes brown, hair gray brown.

1920 Federal census of Newport, RI shows Patrick enumerated as a lodger with the family of E. Richstalt at 181 Thames St.:
   Sullivan, Patrick J., boarder, 41, widower, immigrated 1883, PA, b. Wales to parents from Ireland, Wales.   Contractor, Mason.

1928 February 19, Rhode Island Deaths LDS abstract notes:
   Patrick J. Sullivan, died age 45 (born about 1878), married (sic) to Nellis Houlehan (sic), parents Jeremiah C. (sic) Sullivan, Julea (sic) M. Shea.

Patrick married **First wife of Patrick SULLIVAN** [106796] [MRIN: 36011] about 1900. First was born in Ireland and died about 1904 in Newport, Newport, Rhode Island.

Children from this marriage were:

   258   M   i.   **Jeremiah SULLIVAN [106795]** was born on 23 Sep 1903 in Brooklyn, Kings, New York.

   General Notes: 1905 Rhode Island State census card of Newport RI shows him listed with the family of his grandfather Jeremiah Sullivan in family 166:
      Sullivan, Jeremiah, res. 23 Cannon, Newport RI., grand son, age 2, b. September 23, 1902 (written over 1903), in New York (sic). Parents b. Wales, Ireland.   Religion Protestant (sic).

   Possible death:
   1968 May social security death index notes:
      Jeremiah Sullivan, b. 21 (sic) September 1902, last residence Newport, RI, age 66.

   259   F   ii.   **Catherine SULLIVAN [106797]** was born on 2 Mar 1904 in Newport, Newport, Rhode Island.

   General Notes: 1905 Newport Rhode Island State census of family 166, person 8:
      Sullivan, Catherine, res. 23 Cannon, Newport, grand daughter, age 1, born March 2, 1904, Newport RI. Father b. Wales, mother b. Ireland.

Patrick next married **Nellie HOULIHAN** [106798] [MRIN: 36012] after 1910 in Newport, Newport, Rhode Island. Nellie was born about 1880.

199.   Timothy Francis SULLIVAN [106776] (*Jeremiah P.* [168], *Sullivans born about 1850 possibly* [154]) was born in 1886 in Newport, Newport, Rhode Island and died on 8 Apr 1954 in Newport, Newport, Rhode Island at age 68.

General Notes: 1910 October 24, Marriages Registered in Fall River MA notes:

Timothy F. Sullivan, 24, first marriage, res. 23 Cannon, Newport, RI, Restaurant keeper, b. Newport RI to Jeremiah P., Julia Shea.

Mary A. McGuire, 24, first marriage, res. 1459 Plymouth Ave., Speeder tender, b. England to James, Helen Benson.

Married by Joseph W. Griffin, Priest.

1920 Federal census of Newport, RI shows the young family at 30 Berkley Avenue.

1930 Federal census of Newport RI in April shows the family enumerated at 137 Hay Street Blvd. as family #340:

Sullivan, Timothy F., head, owns home $9000, age 44, married at 24, b. RI to Irish parents.   General Contractory, Landscape, Grade.

" Mary A., wife, 44, married at 24, b. England to Irish parents.   Immigrated 1885.

" Francis X., son, 18, b. RI to RI and English parents.

" William T., son, 16, b. RI to RI and English parents.

" Joseph T., son, 14, b. RI to RI and English parents.

" Paul, son, 5 10/12, b. RI to RI and English parents.

" Henry, son, 3 11/12, b. RI to RI and English parents.

" Mary, daughter, 1 6/12, b. RI to RI and English parents.

1940 Federal census of Newport, Newport Co. RI shows the family at 84 Eustes Ave.:

Sullivan, Timothy F., head, owns home $6800, 54, 2 years of high school, b. RI.   General contracting, Own Business.   52 weeks salary 0.

" Mary A., wife, 54, 1 year of high school, b. England.

" Francis X., son, 28, 1 year of college, b. RI.   General Superintenant, PWA. 52 week salary $1500.

" William T., son, 26, 4 years of high school, b. RI.   General Constructoin, Own Business.   52 weeks salary 0.

" Paul, son, 15, 8 years of school, b. RI.

" Henry, son, 13, 6 years of school, b. RI.

" Mary, daughter, 11, 5 years of school, b. RI.

1943 June 23, WWII Draft Registration Card notes:

Timothy Francis Sullivan, res 84 Eustis Ave. Newport, RI. Age 57. B. Newport RI March 1, 1886. Person who will know your address - Mary A. Sullivan, 84 Eustis Ave. (No employer shown.) Height 5' 8 1/2", weight 178, eyes hazel, hair gray, complexion light.

Timothy married **Mary A. McGUIRE** [106777] [MRIN: 36007], daughter of **James McGUIRE** [106778] and **Helen BENSON** [106779], on 24 Oct 1910 in Fall River, Bristol, Massachusetts. Mary was born in 1886 in England and died on 3 Oct 1952 in Newport, Newport, Rhode Island at age 66.

Children from this marriage were:

260   M   i.   **Francis X. SULLIVAN [106787]** was born in 1912 in Newport, Newport, Rhode Island and died after 1940.

261   M   ii.   **William T. SULLIVAN [106788]** was born in 1914 in Newport, Newport, Rhode Island.

262   M   iii.   **Henry T. SULLIVAN [106791]** was born on 17 Oct 1916 in Newport, Newport, Rhode Island and died on 23 Jan 2001 in Middletown, Newport, Rhode Island at age 84.

General Notes: 2001 January 23 he died.   Rests in WWII veterans' gravesite at St. Columba Cemetery, Browns Lane, Middletown, RI.

263 M iv. **John SULLIVAN [106780]** was born in 1922 and died on 26 Nov 1922.

264 M v. **Paul SULLIVAN [106790]** was born in 1924 in Newport, Newport, Rhode Island.

265 M vi. **Joseph T. SULLIVAN [106789]** was born in 1928 in Newport, Newport, Rhode Island.

266 F vii. **Mary SULLIVAN [106792]** was born in 1928 in Newport, Newport, Rhode Island.

200. Julia Monica SULLIVAN [106784] (*Jeremiah P.*[168], *Sullivans born about 1850 possibly*[154]) was born in Mar 1890 in Newport, Newport, Rhode Island and died on 16 May 1949 in Newport, Newport, Rhode Island at age 59.

General Notes: 1949 Rhode Island Deaths, LDS abstract notes:
Julia M. Sullivan, died age 59, b. 1890 in Newport, RI. Married. Husband Jeremiah S. Sullivan. Parents Jeremiah P. Sullivan, Julia Shea.

Julia married **Jeremiah S. SULLIVAN** [106799] [MRIN: 36013], son of **Patrick C. SULLIVAN** [106805] and **Ellen F. MURPHY** [106806], about 1912 in Newport, Newport, Rhode Island. Jeremiah was born in 1889 in Rhode Island and died after 1940 in Newport, Newport, Rhode Island.

Children from this marriage were:

267 F i. **Mary Margaret SULLIVAN [106800]** was born in 1913 in Newport, Newport, Rhode Island and died on 3 Jul 1925 in RI at age 12.

General Notes: 1915 July 13, Rhode Island deaths LDS abstract:
Mary Margaret Sullivan, age 12, father Jeremiah S. Sullivan, mother Julia Monica Sullivan.

268 M ii. **Joseph A. SULLIVAN [106801]** was born in 1915 in Newport, Newport, Rhode Island.

269 F iii. **Monica J. SULLIVAN [106802]** was born in 1917 in Newport, Newport, Rhode Island.

270 F iv. **Margaret L. SULLIVAN [106803]** was born in 1923 in Newport, Newport, Rhode Island.

271 M v. **Henry F. SULLIVAN [106804]** was born in 1926 in Newport, Newport, Rhode Island.

207. Catherine Agnes SULLIVAN [94311] (*Eugene*[169], *Sullivans born about 1850 possibly*[154]) was born on 25 Jan 1889 in Fall River, Bristol, Massachusetts and died on 4 Jun 1941 in Providence, Providence, Rhode Island at age 52.

General Notes: 1889 January 25 Births Registered in Fall River notes:
Sullivan, Catherine A., b. Fall River to Eugene, Margaret, b. Ireland and Wisconsin.

1914 June 17, Marriages Registered in Fall River notes:
Edgar F. O'Neil, 23, res. 83 Walnut, Boston, MA, Piano polisher, b. Fall River, to James, Agnes Martin,
Catherine A. Sullivan, 55 Hambly, at home, b. Fall River, to Eugene, Margaret Haley (sic).
Married by John F. McKeoe, Pr. 42 Chicago.

Catherine married **Edgar F. ONEIL** [94317] [MRIN: 31562], son of **James ONEIL** [94318] and **Agnes MARTIN** [94319], on 17 Jun 1914 in Fall River, Bristol, Massachusetts. Edgar was born on 1 Oct 1890 in Fall River, Bristol, Massachusetts and died after 1930.

Children from this marriage were:

272   F   i.   **Doris ONEIL [107163]** was born on 26 Jun 1916 in Rhode Island.

273   M   ii.   **Edgar ONEIL [107164]** was born on 2 Apr 1923 in Rhode Island.

274   F   iii.   **Ruth Patricia ONEIL [107165]** was born on 2 Mar 1915 in Boston, Suffolk, Massachusetts.

> General Notes: 1915 March 3, Births Registered in Boston MA notes:
> Ruth Patricia O'Neil, b. to Edgar F., Catherine A. Sullivan, res. 114 King St., father Piano Polisher, parents b. Fall River.

208. Louisa M. SULLIVAN [94312] (*Eugene*[169]*, Sullivans born about 1850 possibly*[154]) was born in Aug 1891 in Fall River, Bristol, Massachusetts.

> General Notes: 1891 Births Registered in Fall River
>
> 1912 June 5, Marriages Registered in Fall River notes:
> Bernard A. Flynn, 22, 168 Tecumseh, Collector, b Fall River to John F. Annie O. Connell.
> Louise M. Sullivan, 19, res. 55 Hambly, Telephone Operator, b. Fall River, to Eugene, Margaret Healy
> Married by H J Noon, Pr. 42 Chicago.

Louisa married **Bernard A. FLYNN** [94314] [MRIN: 31560], son of **John F. FLYNN** [94315] and **Annie O. CONNELL** [94316], on 5 Jun 1912 in Fall River, Bristol, Massachusetts. Bernard was born in 1890 in Fall River, Bristol, Massachusetts.

The child from this marriage was:

275   F   i.   **Anna M. FLYNN [97356]** was born on 12 Mar 1913 in Fall River, Bristol, Massachusetts.

Great-Grandchildren

210. Florence SULLIVAN [99165] (*Timothy J.*[172]*, John*[157]*, Sullivans born about 1850 possibly*[154]) was born on 14 Aug 1898 in Fall River, Bristol, Massachusetts and died on 8 Nov 1981 in Fall River, Bristol, Massachusetts at age 83.

General Notes: 1920 and 1930 she is enumerated with her mother at 44 Brow St. Fall River MA.

1930 Federal census she is a widow with 4 children at 44 Brow, enumerated as family #8:
   Gross, Florence, head, rents $15, 31, married at 20, b. MA to New York (sic) and English parents. Machine worker, blouse factory.
   " Helen L., daughter, 10, b. MA to parents from PA and MA.
   " Pauline M., daughter, 7, b. MA.
   " Margaret F., daughter, 5, b. MA.
   " Warren, son, 3 6/12, b. MA.
(Her mother is enumerated at the same address as family #9)

1939 Fall River City Directory
- Conboy Harold (Florence W.) rigger house 242 5th.

Florence married **Paul GROSS** [99167] [MRIN: 33132]. Paul was born in 1899 in PA and died between 1920 and 1930 in Fall River, Bristol, Massachusetts.

Children from this marriage were:

276   F   i.   **Pauline M. 'Penny' GROSS [99168]** was born in 1922 in Fall River, Bristol, Massachusetts and died on 6 Jun 2011 in Salisbury, Wicomico, Maryland at age 89.

General Notes: Salisbury- Pauline "Penny" Matthews 89, of Salisbury and formerly of Kingston, died Monday, June 6, 2011 at the Wicomico Nursing Home in Salisbury. Born May 30, 1922 in Fall River, Massachusetts she was the daughter of the late Florence and Harold Conboy.
"Penny" was a 1939 graduate of Durfee High School in Fall River, Mass. She was a charter member of the ladies Auxiliary of the Crisfield Elks Lodge 1044, Past President of the Princess Anne Lioness Club, Past President of the Senior Board of Mc Cready Memorial Hospital. Past president of the Cancer Society of Somerset Co., and a member of the Happy Timers of Salisbury. Her numerous hobbies included bowling, bridge, traveling and especially fishing.
Her Survivors include five children, Stanley Matthews, Jr. and his wife Kathy of Salisbury, Ronald F. Matthews of Onancock, Va., Sandra Marshall and her husband Larry, of Crisfield, Bonnie Clayton and her husband Paul of Wilmington, N.C., Robin Matthews and his wife Pam of Salisbury, Md. Seven grandchildren, Ronald F. Matthews, Jr. and his wife Tammy, Scott Matthews and his wife Beth, Todd Matthews and his wife Andie, Lori Mrohs and her husband Mike, Jeffery Marshall, and David and Michelle Clayton. Nine great-grandchildren, Ashleigh Miller and husband Matt, Justin Matthews, Victoria Kelly, Taylor Clayton, Coby Clayton, Abby and Caroline Matthews, Amanda and Connor Mrohs. One sister Ellen Mockas and her husband Paul, One brother Ted Gross and several nieces and nephews.
She was preceded in death by her husband of 55 years, Stanley M. Matthews, Sr., a sister Margaret "Peggy" Baker, a daughter in-law Rochelle Matthews and a great granddaughter, Caroline Mrohs.
A funeral service will be held Thursday at 2:00 Pm. at the Hinman Funeral Home in Princess Anne, where friends may call one hour prior to the service. Interment will follow in the Beechwood Cemetery. In Princess Anne.
A special thanks to all the staff m

embers at the Wicomico Nursing Home for their exceptional care over the past 2 1/2 years. In lieu of flowers contributions may be made to the American Cancer Society at PO. Box 163, Salisbury Md. 21801 or to the Special Activities Fund at the Wicomico Nursing Home at 900 Booth St., Salisbury Md. 21802.

Pauline married **Stanley M. MATTHEWS** [99175] [MRIN: 33135]. Stanley was born about 1922.

277 F ii. **Margaret GROSS [99169]** was born on 4 Apr 1925 in Fall River, Bristol, Massachusetts and died on 30 Apr 2002 in Fall River, Bristol, Massachusetts at age 77.

General Notes: Mentioned in her sister's 2011 Obituary as predeceasing her.

Margaret married **Mr. BAKER** [99176] [MRIN: 33136]. Mr. was born about 1925.

Florence next married **Harold CONBOY** [99172] [MRIN: 33133], son of **John W. CONBOY** [99173] and **Elizabeth WALKER** [99174]. Harold was born on 24 May 1900 in Fall River, Bristol, Massachusetts.

211. Arthur Warren SULLIVAN [99166] (*Timothy J.*[172]*, John*[157]*, Sullivans born about 1850 possibly*[154]) was born on 7 Nov 1899 in Fall River, Bristol, Massachusetts and died after 1952.

General Notes: 1917 WWI draft registration card notes:
Arthur Warren Sullivan, res. 44 Brow Fall River Mass, age 18, b. Nov. 7, 1899. Occupation - in Laundry, 237 Hartwell, Fall River. Nearest relative, Mrs. Laura Sullivan, 44 Brow St. Height - medium. Build - slender. Eyes - hazel. Hair - brown.

1940 Federal census of Fall River, Bristol Co. MA shows the young family around the corner from where Arthur grew up, at 222 John St.:
Sullivan, Arthur W., head, 40, 8 years of school, b. MA. Rents, $13. General helper, US Naval Torpedo Station, income $1456.
" Margaretta L M, wife, 33, 6 years of school, b. No. Ireland, Naturalized.
" Margaret M., daughter, 1, b. MA.

1946 Fall River Directory - Sullivan Arth (sic) W. (Margaretta L M) Torpedo sta (Newport, RI) h. 175 Snell.

1950, 1952 Fall River Directory - Sullivan Arth (sic) W (Margaretta L M) mach h 175 Snell.

Arthur married **Margaretta L. M. wife of Arthur SULLIVAN** [99177] [MRIN: 33138] in Fall River, Bristol, Massachusetts. Margaretta was born in 1907 in Ireland and died after 1952.

The child from this marriage was:

278 F i. **Margaret M. SULLIVAN [99178]** was born in 1939 in Fall River, Bristol, Massachusetts.

279. Sullivans born about 1860 possibly on the Beara

+ 280 M i. **Daniel J. SULLIVAN [96917]** was born about 1857 and died before 1900.

Daniel married **Mary HOLLAND** [96916] [MRIN: 32351] (b. May 1855, d. 3 Sep 1900)

+ 281 M ii. **Mark SULLIVAN [106215]** was born about 1860 in Ireland and died before 1910.

Mark married **Catherine 'Kate' SHEA** [106216] [MRIN: 35796] (b. Abt 1850, d. Between 1910 and 1920)

+ 282 M iii. **Eugene S. SULLIVAN [104846]** was born in Apr 1867 in Ireland and died after 1940 in Fall River, Bristol, Massachusetts.

Eugene married **Bridget OBRIEN** [104847] [MRIN: 35286] (b. Dec 1867, d. Between 1930 and 1940) on 19 Jul 1887 in Calumet, Houghton, Michigan.

Children

280. Daniel J. SULLIVAN [96917] (*Sullivans born about 1860 possibly*[279]) was born about 1857 and died before 1900.

Daniel married **Mary HOLLAND** [96916] [MRIN: 32351], daughter of **Cain HOLLAND** [96918]. Mary was born in May 1855 in Ireland and died on 3 Sep 1900 in Fall River, Bristol, Massachusetts at age 45.

Children from this marriage were:

+ 283   M   i.   **Jeremiah Joseph SULLIVAN [96928]** was born on 4 Feb 1878 in Co. Cork, Ireland, died on 22 Aug 1908 in Fall River, Bristol, Massachusetts at age 30, and was buried in St. Patrick's Cem., Fall River, Massachusetts.

Jeremiah married **Florence May BULGER** [100025] [MRIN: 33465] (b. Oct 1885, d. After 1940) on 24 Nov 1904 in Providence, Providence, Rhode Island.

284   M   ii.   **Daniel SULLIVAN [96919]** was born in 1885 in Ireland and died on 22 Feb 1904 in Fall River, Bristol, Massachusetts at age 19.

General Notes: 1904 February 22, Massachusetts Death certificate notes:
    Daniel Sullivan, 170 John St., died age 19.   Single.   B. Ireland to Daniel J. Sullivan, b. Ireland and Mary Holland, b. Ireland.   Informant Jeremiah J. Sullivan.   Died of Phthisis, duration 5 months.   Burial St. Patrick's Cemetery.

285   F   iii.   **Agnes SULLIVAN [96929]** was born in Feb 1887 in Ireland and died after 1900 in Fall River, Bristol, Massachusetts.

281. Mark SULLIVAN [106215] (*Sullivans born about 1860 possibly*[279]) was born about 1860 in Ireland and died before 1910.

General Notes: 1910 his widow was enumerated in the Federal census of Fall River MA with their married daughter Ellen.   The widow does not appear with her daughter's family in 1920.

This may be the family outlined in 'Annals of the Beara - Volume II':
Marcus O'Sullivan & Catherine O'Shea
(Pallace)
After Denis O'Shea, the next tenant in the original O'Connor (Martin) farm was Marcus O'Sullivan, son of Mark O'Sullivan and Mary Leahy, Derriveggil. Marcus had returned from Butte, Montana, and he married Catherine O'Shea (or Cait as she was known) - aunt of Tady O'Shea - daughter of Curley O'Shea and Mary O'Shea, Claondaire. Marcus and Catherine had a family of 5: - (1) & (2) were twins, John and *Con. John went to Boston, Mass., where he worked on the railroad and married a girl named White who came from the Black Shop (Westcove) district between Sneem and Waterville, Co. Kerry. Con known as Con Marcus, settled in the Pallace farm and married Brigid Lowney, daughter of Simon Lowney and Mary Harrington, Bunskellig; (3), (4) & (5), Ellen (Dec. 22nd 1878), Patrick (Mar. 17th 1882) and Julia (Sept. 21st 1883) all went to Boston, Mass.

Mark married **Catherine 'Kate' SHEA** [106216] [MRIN: 35796]. Catherine was born about 1850 in Ireland and died between 1910 and 1920 in Fall River, Bristol, Massachusetts.

The child from this marriage was:

+ 286   F   i.   **Nellie A. SULLIVAN [106214]** was born in 1883 in Ireland and died after 1930 in Swansea, Bristol, Massachusetts.

Nellie married **Merton S. SMITH** [106213] [MRIN: 35795] (b. 1875, d. After 1930) on 1 Feb 1905 in Fall River, Bristol, Massachusetts.

282. Eugene S. SULLIVAN [104846] (*Sullivans born about 1860 possibly* [279]) was born in Apr 1867 in Ireland and died after 1940 in Fall River, Bristol, Massachusetts.

General Notes: 1885 immigrated to America (1900 census 1878 in 1910 census).

1880 Federal census of Franklin, Houghton Co. MI shows a Eugene who could be the subject in family #275:
Sullivan, John, 25, miner, b. Ireland.
" Johanna, 26, wife, keeping house, b. Ireland. (May be Johanna Shea, who married a John Sullivan in Houghton MI in 1874.)
" Eugene, 19, Brother, miner, b. Ireland.

1886 daughter Mary was born.

1887 July 19, Marriages Registered in Calumet, Houghton, Michigan, notes:
Eugene Sullivan, res. Osceola, 23, b. Ireland.   Laborer.
Brigett (sic) O'Bryan (sic), res. Osceola, 21, b. Ireland.
Married by M. Faust, Minister.
Witnesses Michael Howard, Osceola, Mary Harrington, Osceola.

1900 Federal census of Fall River, Bristol Co. MA shows the family enumerated in Ward 5, dist 141 at 49 North Eighth St., as family #164:
Sullivan, Eugene, head, April 1867, 33, married 16 years, b. Ireland to Irish parents.   Immigrated 1885, 15 years prior, naturalized.   Highway laborer. Rents.
" Bridget, wife, Dec 1867, 32, married 16 years, 7 children, 5 living, b. Ireland to Irish parents. Immigrated 1883, 17 years prior.
"Mary, daughter, May 1886, 14, b. MI to Irish parents.   Shoe maker.
(note the 6 year gap in children's births)
" Bella E., daughter, July 1892, 7, b. MI. At school.
" Anne, daughter, June 1895, 4, b. MA.
" Lucy, daughter, June 1899, 11/12, b. MA.
" Sadie, daughter, June 1899, 11/12, b. MA.
(There are also three other Sullivan heads of household enumerated in the dwelling at 49 North Eighth St.)

1910 Federal census of Fall River, Bristol Co. MA shows the family in Ward 5, dist 151, at 453 Bank St., as family #236:
Sullivan, Eugene S., head, 39, married 21 years, b. Ireland to Irish parents.   Immigrated 1878 (sic), naturalized.   Constable, City.
" Bridget E., wife, 38, married 21 years, 7 children, 6 living, b. Ireland to Irish parents.   Immigrated 1888 (sic).
" Mary E., daughter, 21, b. MI to Irish parents.   Apprentice, nurse.
" Mabel L. E., daughter, 18, b. MI to Irish parents.   Speeder Tender, Cotton Mill.
" Annie, daughter 14, b. MA.   Apprentice, millinery.
" Lucy, daughter, 10, b. MA.
" Sadie, daughter, 10, b. MA.
" Margaret, daughter, 6, b. MA.

1920 Federal census of Fall River, Bristol Co. MA shows the family in Ward 1, dist 36, 763 Plymouth Avenue as family #38:
Sullivan, Eugene S., head, rents. 54 (sic), immigrated 1883 (sic), naturalized 1899, b. Ireland.
Sheriff, Deputy.

" Bridget, wife, 54, immigrated unk, naturalized 1888 (sic), b. Ireland.
" Mary A., daughter, 30, b. MI.   Nurse, Graduate.
" Mable I. (sic), 25, b. MI.   Nurse, Graduate.
" Annie V., daughter, 23, b. MA.   Hair Dresser, Hair Parlor.
" Sadie C., daughter, 20, b. MA.
" Lucy A., daughter, 20, b. MA.   Cuff Button maker, Jewelry Factory.
" Margaret L., daughter, 16, b. MA.

1930 Federal census of Fall River, Bristol Co. MA shows the extended family at 23 Covel St.:
  Sullivan, Eugene S., head, owns $4000, 63, married at 21, b. Ireland.   Deputy Sheriff, Own
Account.
  " Bridget, wife, 64, married at 22, b. Ireland.
  " Mary A., daughter, 41, b. MI.   Private family.
  " Lucy, daughter, 29, b. MA.   Nurse,
  " Margaret, daughter, 25, b. MA.   Stenographer, Mill Office.
(In the same household is the family of daughter Sadie)
  Southworth, James, head, rents $20, 25, married at 21, b. England. Chauffeur, Transit Company.
  " Sadie, wife, 29, married at 25, b. MA to Irish parents.
  " Gene, son, 1 11/12, b. MA.

1940 Federal census of Fall River, Bristol Co. MA shows the widower at 21 Covel St.:
  Sullivan, Eugene, head, 73, widower, 5 years of school, b. Ireland.
  " Lucy, daughter, 40, 8 years of school, b. MA.   Speeder tender, textile.   52 week salary $980.
  " Margaret, daughter, 36, 4 years of high school, b. MA.   Telephone operator, Hospital.   52 week
salary $1800.

Eugene married **Bridget OBRIEN** [104847] [MRIN: 35286] on 19 Jul 1887 in Calumet, Houghton, Michigan. Bridget was born in Dec 1867 in Ireland and died between 1930 and 1940 in Fall River, Bristol, Massachusetts.

Children from this marriage were:

  287   F   i.   **Mary A. SULLIVAN [104848]** was born in May 1886 in MI.

  288   F   ii.   **Mabel E. 'Bella' SULLIVAN [104849]** was born in Jul 1892 in MI.

  289   F   iii.   **Anne V. SULLIVAN [104850]** was born in Jun 1894 in Fall River, Bristol,
                     Massachusetts.

  290   F   iv.   **Lucy A. SULLIVAN [104851]** was born in Jun 1899 in Fall River, Bristol,
                     Massachusetts.

+ 291   F   v.   **Sarah C. 'Sadie' SULLIVAN [104852]** was born on 9 Jun 1899 in Fall River, Bristol,
                     Massachusetts and died after 1930 in Fall River, Bristol, Massachusetts.

                     Sarah married **James SOUTHWORTH** [104854] [MRIN: 35288] (b. 1905) in 1926 in
                     Fall River, Bristol, Massachusetts.

  292   F   vi.   **Margaret L SULLIVAN [104853]** was born in 1906 in Fall River, Bristol,
                     Massachusetts.

Grandchildren

283. **Jeremiah Joseph SULLIVAN [96928]** (*Daniel J.*[280], *Sullivans born about 1860 possibly*[279]) was born on 4 Feb 1878 in Co. Cork, Ireland, died on 22 Aug 1908 in Fall River, Bristol, Massachusetts at age 30, and was buried in St. Patrick's Cem., Fall River, Massachusetts.

> General Notes: 1878 February 4, Births Registered in Co. Cork Ireland LDS abstracts:
>   Jeremiah Sullivan, b. to Daniel Sullivan, Mary Whoilhan (aka Holland).
>
> 1904 Jeremiah J. Sullivan was the Informant on the Fall River death record of his brother Daniel.
>
> 1904 November 24, Marriages Registered in Fall River MA notes a marriage performed in Providence RI:
>   Jeremiah J. Sullivan, 26, first marriage, res. Fall River, Cotton weaver, b. Ireland to Daniel, Mary Holland.
>   Florence W. Bolger (sic), first marriage, res. Providence RI, b. Fall River to Joseph, Bridget Sullivan.
>   Married by Edward Seagrave, Priest, Providence RI.
>
> 1904 November 24, marriages registered in Rhode Island LDS abstract shows marriage in Fall River MA (?):
>   Jeremiah Joseph Sullivan, 26, son of Daniel, Mary.
>   Florence May Bolger (sic), daughter of Joseph, Bridget.
>
> 1910 wife and son Florence and William are enumerated with Florence's father in Fall River.
>
> Probable death:
> 1908 August 22, Massachusetts Death Certificate notes:
>   Jeremiah J. Sullivan, died age 30, married, b. Ireland.   Father Daniel Sullivan, b. Ireland; mother Margaret (sic) Sullivan, b. Ireland.   Mill Hand.   Informant 'wife'.   Died of Nephritis.   Burial St. Patrick's Cemetery.

Jeremiah married **Florence May BULGER** [100025] [MRIN: 33465], daughter of **Joseph W. BULGER** [100013] and **Bridget SULLIVAN** [100014],   on 24 Nov 1904 in Providence, Providence, Rhode Island. Florence was born in Oct 1885 in Fall River, Bristol, Massachusetts and died after 1940 in NY.

The child from this marriage was:

> 293   M   i.   **William F. SULLIVAN [100026]** was born on 19 Jun 1906 in Fall River, Bristol, Massachusetts.

286. **Nellie A. SULLIVAN [106214]** (*Mark*[281], *Sullivans born about 1860 possibly*[279]) was born in 1883 in Ireland and died after 1930 in Swansea, Bristol, Massachusetts.

> General Notes: Possible birth:
> 1878 December 22, LDS Birth abstracts notes:
>   Ellen Sullivan, born Cork Ireland to Mark Sullivan, Kate Shea.
>
> The family with daughter Ellen born in 1878 is outlined in 'Annals of the Beara - Volume II':
> Marcus O'Sullivan & Catherine O'Shea
> (Pallace)
>
> 1900 she immigrated to America (1910 census).

1905 February 1, Marriages Registered in Fall River MA notes:

   Merton S. Smith, 30, Second marriage, Divorced, 347 High St., Coachman, b. Colchester VT, to Frank P., Ellen M. Severance.

   Nellie A. Sullivan, 22 (sic - about 1883), First marriage, 673 Walnut, Domestic, b. Fall River (sic), to Mark, Kate Shay.

   Married by Payson Lyman, M. G.

(The family is living at 674 Walnut St. in 1910.)

Nellie married **Merton S. SMITH** [106213] [MRIN: 35795], son of **Franklin Pierce SMITH** [106217] and **Ellen Marie SEVERANCE** [106218],   on 1 Feb 1905 in Fall River, Bristol, Massachusetts. Merton was born in 1875 in Colchester, Chittenden, Vermont and died after 1930 in Swansea, Bristol, Massachusetts.

Children from this marriage were:

   294 F   i.   **Ruth SMITH [106219]** was born in 1908 in Fall River, Bristol, Massachusetts.

   295 M ii.   **Franklin SMITH [106220]** was born in 1910 in Fall River, Bristol, Massachusetts.

291.   Sarah C. 'Sadie' SULLIVAN [104852] (*Eugene S.*[282]*, Sullivans born about 1860 possibly*[279]) was born on 9 Jun 1899 in Fall River, Bristol, Massachusetts and died after 1930 in Fall River, Bristol, Massachusetts.

   General Notes: 1899 June 9, Births Registered in Fall River MA notes:

     Sullivan, Sarah, b. to Eugene E., Bridget - O'Brien, res. 436 Bank St., father laborer, parents b. Ireland.

Sarah married **James SOUTHWORTH** [104854] [MRIN: 35288] in 1926 in Fall River, Bristol, Massachusetts. James was born in 1905 in England.

The child from this marriage was:

   296 M   i.   **Eugene SOUTHWORTH [104855]** was born in 1927 in Fall River, Bristol, Massachusetts.

297.   Sullivans born about 1870 on the BEARA

+ 298 M   i.   **Dennis SULLIVAN [108504]** was born about 1870 in Kilmichael, Cork, Munster, Ireland.

Dennis married **Mary (Causkey) 'Minnie' HARRINGTON** [108505] [MRIN: 30912] (b. Abt 1870)

Children

298. Dennis SULLIVAN [108504] (*Sullivans born about 1870 on* [297]) was born about 1870 in Kilmichael, Cork, Munster, Ireland.

> General Notes: Named Dennis Sullivan and Mary Harringgton in daughter Nora Quigley's Rhode Island obituary, but the family is likely the on outlined in 'The Annals of the Beara - Volume 1' by Riobard O'Dwyer:
> Denny (Paddy "Malachy") O'Sullivan & Minnie Harrington (Causkey) (Kilmichael)
> Children: Patrick (Apr. 1907) died fairly young; Nora (Mar. 1909) became Mrs. Quigley in Providence; twins, Michael and Denis (Sept. 1910) died young; *Mary (born in 1911, and died on Oct. 12th 1946 aged 35) settled in the home place and married her 2nd and 3rd cousin John (Batt "West") Harrington (Causkey), son of Batt "West" Harrington (Causkey) and Minnie Dennehy, Tillickafinne; Kate (Apr. 1915) was the 1st wife of Jack (Batt Con) Murphy, son of Batt (Con) Murphy and Catherine O'Leary, Kilkinnihan.

Dennis married **Mary (Causkey) 'Minnie' HARRINGTON** [108505] [MRIN: 30912]. Mary was born about 1870 in Kilmichael, Cork, Munster, Ireland.

Children from this marriage were:

> 299 M i. **Michael SULLIVAN [108508]** was born about 1904.

> 300 M ii. **Patrick SULLIVAN [108507]** was born in Jun 1907 in Kilmichael, Cork, Munster, Ireland.

> + 301 F iii. **Nora SULLIVAN [108503]** was born in Mar 1909 in Dursey Island, Allihies Parish, Co. Cork, Ireland, died on 11 Feb 2004 in Providence, Providence, Rhode Island at age 94, and was buried in Gate of Heaven Cemetery, East Providence, RI.
>
> Nora married **Michael QUIGLEY** [108502] [MRIN: 30069] (b. Abt 1900)

> 302 M iv. **Dennis SULLIVAN [108509]** was born in Sep 1910 in Kilmichael, Cork, Munster, Ireland.

> 303 M v. **Michael SULLIVAN [93967]** was born in Sep 1910 in Kilmichael, Cork, Munster, Ireland.

> 304 F vi. **Mary SULLIVAN [108510]** was born in 1911 in Kilmichael, Cork, Munster, Ireland.

> 305 F vii. **Catherine SULLIVAN [108511]** was born in Apr 1915 in Kilmichael, Cork, Munster, Ireland.

Grandchildren

301.   Nora SULLIVAN [108503] (*Dennis*[298]*, Sullivans born about 1870 on*[297]) was born in Mar 1909 in Dursey Island, Allihies Parish, Co. Cork, Ireland, died on 11 Feb 2004 in Providence, Providence, Rhode Island at age 94, and was buried in Gate of Heaven Cemetery, East Providence, RI.

General Notes: 1926 she immigrated to America.

2004 February 12, Providence RI Journal, Thursday
Providence - Nora Quigley, 94, of Sawyer Street, a homemaker, died yesterday at the Morgan Health Center, Johnston. She was the wife of the late Michael Quigley. Born in Dursey Island, Castletownbere, County Cork, Ireland, a daughter of the late Denis and Mary (Harrington) Sullivan, she came to this country in 1926, settling in Providence. Mrs. Quigley was a communicant of St. Matthew Church, Cranston. She was a member of the Irish Ceilidhe Club of Rhode Island. She leaves a son, James M. Quigley of Bonita Springs, Fla.; a granddaughter, Suzanne L. Amon of Warren, VT; a grandson, Paul J. Quigley of Harrisburg, Pa.; and three great-grandchildren. She was the sister of the late Patrick, Michael and Denis O'Sullivan, Mary Harrington and Kate Murphy. The funeral will be held Saturday at 8:45 a.m. from Frank P. Trainor & Sons Funeral Home, 982 Warwick Ave., Warwick, with a Mass of Christian Burial at 10 in St. Matthew Church, Elmwood Avenue, Cranston. Burial will be in Gate of Heaven Cemetery, East Providence.

Nora married **Michael QUIGLEY** [108502] [MRIN: 30069]. Michael was born about 1900.

The child from this marriage was:

306   M   i.   **James M. QUIGLEY [108506]** was born about 1930 in Providence, Providence, Rhode Island.

General Notes: 2004 he was living in Bonita Springs FL

307.   Sullivans born about 1870 possibly on the BEARA

+ 308   M   i.   **James SULLIVAN [108564]** was born in 1868 in Ireland and died between 1900 and 1910 in Fall River, Bristol, Massachusetts.

James married **Julia SULLIVAN** [108565] [MRIN: 34180] (b. May 1871, d. 19 Dec 1921)

+ 309   M   ii.   **Daniel J. SULLIVAN [108533]** was born in 1872 in Ireland, died in 1952 in Newport, Newport, Rhode Island at age 80, and was buried in St. Columbas Cem., Middletown, Rhode Island.

Daniel married **Ellen LEARY** [108534] [MRIN: 33301] (b. 1868, d. 1919) in 1895.

+ 310   M   iii.   **Patrick D. SULLIVAN [106736]** was born in 1882 in Ireland and died on 28 Apr 1956 in Fall River, Bristol, Massachusetts at age 74.

Patrick married **Nora CLIFFORD** [106737] [MRIN: 35994] (b. 1884, d. 3 Jun 1949) in 1908 in Massachusetts.

Children

308. James SULLIVAN [108564] (*Sullivans born about 1870 possibly*[307]) was born in 1868 in Ireland and died between 1900 and 1910 in Fall River, Bristol, Massachusetts.

General Notes: 1891 immigrated to America (1900 census).

1892 married in America.

1900 Federal census of Fall River, Bristol Co. MA shows the family enumerated in a multifamily dwelling at 126 Hamlet St. as family #101:
   Sullivan, James head, Mar 1868, 32, married 8 years, b. Ireland to Irish parents.   Immigrated 1891, 9 years prior, naturalized.   Hat finisher.
   " Julia, wife, May 1871, 29, married 8 years, 1 child, 1 living, b. Ireland to Irish parents. Immigrated 1891, 9 years prior.
   " James, son, April 1894, 6, b. New York to Irish parents.   At school.

1904 Fall River City Directory
- Sullivan James, hatter, house 126 Hamlet.

1905 Fall River City Directory
- Sullivan Henry Clerk boards 126 Hamlet.
- Sullivan James Mrs. house 126 Hamlet. (No James at 126 Hamlet and no death noted in the directory.)

No death record for James has been located in the Bristol Co. MA vital records 1900 to 1906.

1920 his widow and son are enumerated in the Federal census at 126 Hamlet St. Fall River MA.

James married **Julia SULLIVAN** [108565] [MRIN: 34180]. Julia was born in May 1871 in Ireland and died on 19 Dec 1921 in Fall River, Bristol, Massachusetts at age 50.

The child from this marriage was:

+ 311 M   i.   **James S. SULLIVAN [108558]** was born on 24 Apr 1894 in New York, New York, New York and died after 1940 in Fall River, Bristol, Massachusetts.

James married **Helena M. ARSNOW** [108559] [MRIN: 34076] (b. 20 Oct 1899, d. After 1940)

309. Daniel J. SULLIVAN [108533] (*Sullivans born about 1870 possibly*[307]) was born in 1872 in Ireland, died in 1952 in Newport, Newport, Rhode Island at age 80, and was buried in St. Columbas Cem., Middletown, Rhode Island.

General Notes: 1882 immigrated to America (1905 State census).

1900 Federal census of Newport, Newport Co. RI shows the family enumerated at 83 Tilden St. as family #108:
   Sullivan, Daniel J., head, (no birth date) 29, married 6 years, b. Ireland to Irish parents.   Immigrated 1885 (sic), 15 years prior.   Blacksmith. Rents.
   " Ellen, wife, (no birth date), 33, married 6 years, 3 children, 3 living, b. Ireland to Irish parents.
   " Timothy (sic) J., son, March 1895, 5, b. RI.
   " Daniel F., son, Jan 1897, 3, b. RI.
   " Jeremiah, son, Dec 1898, 1, b. RI.

1905 Rhode Island state census of Newport RI shows:
   Sullivan, Daniel J., res. 3 Vicksburg Place, head of house, 33, b. 1872, Ireland.   Married.
Immigrated 1882, 18 years prior.   18 years in Rhode Island.   Naturalized.   Blacksmith.   Catholic.

1910 Federal census of Newport, Newport Co. RI shows the family enumerated at 30 Edgar Court, as
family #222:
   Sullivan, Daniel J., head, 38, married 15 years, b. Ireland to Irish parents. Immigrated 1870 (sic),
naturalized.   Blacksmith, Blacksmith shop.   Owns home with mortgage.
   " Ellen E., wife, 42, married 15 years, 4 children, 4 living, b. Ireland to Irish parents.   Immigrated
1890.
   " Joseph T. (sic), son, 15, b. RI to Irish parents.
   " Daniel, daughter (sic), 13, b. RI to Irish parents.
   " Jeremiah, son, 11, b. RI to Irish parents.
   " Catherine, daughter, 8, b. RI to Irish parents.

1915 Rhode Island state census of Newport, RI shows the family enumerated at 30 Edgar Court as
family #81:
   Sullivan, Daniel J., head, 45, b. Ireland to Irish parents. Naturalized. Blacksmith, Horseshoes.
   " Ellen, wife, 47, b. Ireland to Irish parents.
   " Timothy (sic), J., son, 19, b. US. Farmer.
   " Daniel J., son, 17, b. US. Machinist, Apprentice.
   " Jeremiah, son, 15, b. US.
   " Catherine, daughter, 13, b. US.

1920 Federal census of Newport, RI shows the family at 30 Edgar Court as family #136:
   Sullivan, Daniel J., head, owns home, 54, married, (Ellen is not listed) immigrated 1883, naturalized
1887, b. Ireland to Irish parents.   Helper, Torpedo Station.
   " Timothy J., son, 25, b. RI to Irish parents.   Mariner, Passenger boat.
   " Daniel F., son, 23, b. RI to Irish parents.   Chauffeur, Torpedo Station.
   " Jeremiah J., son, 21, b. RI to Irish parents.   Mariner, Freight board.
   " Catherine L., daughter, 18, b. RI to Irish parents.   Stenographer, Farm bureau.

1930 Federal census of Newport, RI possibly shows the subject enumerated at the RI Henderson House
for Aged Men at 14 Clark St.:
   Sullivan, Dan J., inmate, 59, widower, b. Ireland to Irish parents.   Immigrated 1890.

The couple rests at St. Columba Cemetery, Middletown, RI marked with an upright granite stone:
   Sullivan
   Daniel J. Sullivan
   1868 - 1952
   His wife
   Ellen Leary
   1865 - 1919
   Both Born In County Kerry Ireland.

Daniel married **Ellen LEARY** [108534] [MRIN: 33301] in 1895. Ellen was born in 1868 in Ireland, died in
1919 in Newport, Newport, Rhode Island at age 51, and was buried in St. Columbas Cem., Middletown,
Rhode Island.

Children from this marriage were:

+ 312 M   i.   **Joseph James SULLIVAN [108530]** was born on 6 Mar 1895 in Newport, Newport,
                   Rhode Island and died after 1940 in Swansea, Bristol, Massachusetts.

                   Joseph married **Elizabeth BRIGGS** [108531] [MRIN: 33155] (b. 1900) in 1925.

313 F ii. **Daniel F. SULLIVAN [108535]** was born on 9 Jan 1897 in Newport, Newport, Rhode Island.

314 M iii. **Jeremiah J. SULLIVAN [108536]** was born on 20 Dec 1898 in Newport, Newport, Rhode Island and died on 27 Jul 1939 in Burrillville, RI at age 40.

> General Notes: 1939 July 27 Rhode Island deaths LDS abstracts notes:
> Jeremiah John Sullivan, died age 39, parents Daniel J. Sullivan, Ellen Leary.

315 F iv. **Catherine L. SULLIVAN [108537]** was born in 1902 in Newport, Newport, Rhode Island and died after 1920.

310. Patrick D. SULLIVAN [106736] (*Sullivans born about 1870 possibly*[307]) was born in 1882 in Ireland and died on 28 Apr 1956 in Fall River, Bristol, Massachusetts at age 74.

> General Notes: 1898 or 1899 immigrated to America (1910 and 1920 census). Nora Clifford notes she immigrated about 1906
>
> 1900 Federal census shows one Patrick Sullivan in the area of Fall River, who matches this subject. He is enumerated in nearby Newport, RI at 673 Thomas St. with the family of Thomas and Annie Harrington Winters:
> Sullivan, Patrick, boarder, b. March 1882, 18, b. Ireland to Irish parents. Immigrated 1900, 0 years prior. Day laborer.
>
> 1908 the couple married per the 1910 census. No marriage record for the couple was found from 1900 to 1910 in Massachusetts nor in Rhode Island. There is coincidently a Patrick Sullivan and Nora Clifford who were married and living in Newport RI before 1900. That Nora passed away in 1937 and should not be confused with this subject.
>
> 1909 February son John F. Sullivan is born in Fall River MA.
>
> 1909 naturalized per 1920 census but later census shows him as an alien.
>
> 1910 Federal census of Fall River, Bristol Co. MA shows the young couple at 304 Second St.:
> Sullivan, Patrick, head, 27, married 1 time, 2 years, b. Ireland to Irish parents. Immigrated 1899, Alien, Fireman, steamboat. Rents.
> " Nora, wife, 26, married 1 time 2 years, 2 children, 2 living, b. Ireland to Irish parents. Immigrated 1905.
> " John F., son, 0/12, (sic) b. MA.
> " Eugene, son, 0/12, b. MA.
> (The birth of John F. is shown in the Fall River MA vital records in Feb 1909.)
>
> 1920 Federal census of Fall River, Bristol Co. MA shows the family at 351 John St. as family #101:
> Sullivan, Patrick, head, rents, 35, immigrated 1889 (sic), naturalized 1909, b. Ireland. Laborer, Street work.
> " Nora, wife, 35, immigrated date unknown, b. Ireland. Housework, Private family.
> " John, son, 11, b. MA.
> " Eugene, son, 9, b. MA.
> " Margaret, daughter, 5, b. MA.
> " William, son, 3, b. MA.
> " Dennis, son, 11/12, b. MA.
> Malloy, Katherine, housekeeper, 38, married, immigrated 1888, b. England, Housekeeper, Private family.
>
> 1930 Federal census of Fall River, Bristol Co. MA shows the family at 411 Fifth Street as family #478:

Sullivan, Patrick, head, rents $18, 48, married at 26, b. Ireland. Immigrated 1898, Alien (sic), Fireman, NYNHH Railroad.

" Nora, wife, 46, married at 24, b. Ireland.   Immigrated 1904.

" Helen, daughter, 4, b. MA.

" Eugene, son, 19, b. MA.   Stencilor, American Print Works.

" Margaret, daughter, 15, b. MA.

" William, son, 13, b. MA.

" Dennis, son, 11, b. MA.

" Rita, daughter, 8, b. MA.

" Catherine, daughter, 6, b. MA.

1940 Federal census of Fall River, Bristol Co. MA shows the family at 147 Branch St.:

Sullivan, Patrick, head, 58, 5 years of school, b. Eire.   Fireman, Industrial Building, 17 week salary, $255.

" Nora, wife, 56, 8 years of school, b. Eire.

" John, son, 31, 6 years of school, b. MA. Laborer, W. P. A. Rifle Range Payer (?). 36 week salary $486.

" Eugene, son, 29, 4 years of high school, b. MA.   Attendant, Amusement.   52 weeks salary $624.

" Margaret, daughter, 25, 2 years of high school, b. MA.   Housekeeper, Private family.   39 week salary $442.

" William, son, 24, 4 years of high school, b. MA.   Machinist Helper, Bathrots (?) Mfg.   26 week salary $312.

" Dennis, son, 21, 1 year of high school, b. MA. Rope Hoister, Thread mill. 10 week salary $140.

" Rita, daughter, 18, 4 years of high school, b. MA. Saleslady, Department Store.   1 week salary $12.

" Kathleen, daughter, 16, 1 year of high school, b. MA.

" Helen, daughter, 14, 7 years of school, b. MA.

Clifford, Patrick, Lodger, 52, single, 8 years of school, b. Eire.   Previous res. New London CT.

1947 Fall River City Directory

- Sullivan Dennis B. laborer res 117 Branch.
- Sullivan Eleanor R. telephone operator NET&T Co. res 117 Branch.
- Sullivan Helen T. telephone operator res 117 Branch.
- Sullivan John F. laborer res 117 Branch.
- Sullivan Patrick D. (Nora) laborer house 117 Branch.

1950 Fall River City Directory

- Sullivan Nora (Mrs. Patrick D.) died June 3, 1949.
- Sullivan Patrick D. laborer house 117 Branch.

1957 Fall River City Directory

- Sullivan Dennis B. laborer res 117 Branch.
- Sullivan Eleanor T (sic) telephone operator NET&T Co. res 117 Branch.
- Sullivan John F. laborer res 117 Branch.
- Sullivan Patrick D. died April 28, 1956.

Patrick married **Nora CLIFFORD** [106737] [MRIN: 35994] in 1908 in Massachusetts. Nora was born in 1884 in Ireland and died on 3 Jun 1949 in Fall River, Bristol, Massachusetts at age 65.

Children from this marriage were:

316   M   i.   **John F SULLIVAN [106738]** was born on 10 Feb 1909 in Fall River, Bristol, Massachusetts.

General Notes: 1909 February 10, Births Registered in Fall River, MA notes:

Sullivan John F. b. to Patrick, Nora Clifford, res. 304 Second St., father Boat Hand, parents b. Ireland.

317 M ii. **Eugene SULLIVAN [106739]** was born on 21 Apr 1910 in Fall River, Bristol, Massachusetts.

General Notes: 1910 April 24, Births Registered in Fall River MA notes:
Sullivan, Eugene, b. to Patrick, Nora Clifford, res. 616 Third, father Fireman, parents b. Ireland.

318 M iii. **James J. SULLIVAN [106747]** was born on 19 Mar 1912 in Fall River, Bristol, Massachusetts, died on 14 Aug 1912 in Fall River, Bristol, Massachusetts, and was buried in St. Patrick's Cem., Fall River, Massachusetts.

General Notes: Died at age 25 days of Gastro Enteritis. Burial St. Patrick's. The family was living at 462 Second St. Fall River MA.

319 F iv. **Mary M. SULLIVAN [106746]** was born on 12 Aug 1913 in Fall River, Bristol, Massachusetts and died on 31 Aug 1913 in Fall River, Bristol, Massachusetts.

General Notes: Died of valvular disease of the heart, age 19 days. Burial St. Patrick's Cemetery.

320 F v. **Margaret SULLIVAN [106740]** was born on 6 Nov 1914 in Fall River, Bristol, Massachusetts.

General Notes: 2004 called the late Margaret Bagnall in her sister Kathleen's Fall River MA obituary.

Margaret married **Mr. BAGNALL** [108553] [MRIN: 33908]. Mr. was born about 1914.

321 M vi. **William SULLIVAN [106741]** was born in 1916 in Fall River, Bristol, Massachusetts.

322 M vii. **Joseph SULLIVAN [106748]** was born on 6 Aug 1916 in Fall River, Bristol, Massachusetts.

General Notes: 1916 August 6, Births Registered in Fall River MA notes:
Sullivan, William, b. to Patrick, Nora Clifford, res. 724 Plymouth Ave. father Laborer, parents b. Ireland.

323 M viii. **Dennis B. SULLIVAN [106742]** was born in 1919 in Fall River, Bristol, Massachusetts, died on 26 Dec 2007 in Fall River, Bristol, Massachusetts at age 88, and was buried in St. Patrick's Cem., Fall River, Massachusetts.

General Notes: SULLIVAN - Fall River MA Herald News, Thursday 27 Dec 2007
Dennis B. Sullivan, "Dinny," age 88, of Fall River, passed away, Wednesday, December 26, 2007 in Sarah S. Brayton Nursing Care Center in Fall River. Born in Fall River, he was a son of the late Patrick and Nora (Clifford) Sullivan. He had been a lifelong resident of Fall River. He worked at Weyerhaeuser Company for 34 years as a General Laborer and retired in 1981 as Night Watchman. He was a Veteran of the United States Army serving during World War II in Northern France, Rhineland, and Central Europe. He was the recipient of numerous medals. Mr. Sullivan was a lifetime member of the Corky Row Club and a member of the V.F.W. post 486. He loved to travel especially Australia and was an avid walker. He is survived by one sister Eleanor T. "Helen" Terceiro of Fall River and several nieces and nephews and great nieces and nephews. He was brother of the late Margaret Bagnall, Rita Robertson, and Kathleen, Mary, James, Eugene, John, and William Sullivan. His Funeral

will be held Saturday, December 29, 2007 at 8:00 AM from the Waring - Sullivan Home of Memorial Tribute at Cherry Place, 178 Winter St., Fall River (at Cherry, Locust, and High Sts.) followed by a Funeral Mass at 9:00 AM in St. Mary's Cathedral, Spring St., Fall River. Burial in St. Patrick's Cemetery.

324 F   ix.   **Rita SULLIVAN [106743]** was born in 1922 in Fall River, Bristol, Massachusetts.

General Notes: 2004 called the late Rita Robertson in her sister Kathleen's Fall River MA obituary.

Rita married **Mr. ROBERTSON** [108554] [MRIN: 33999]. Mr. was born about 1922.

325 F   x.   **Kathleen P. SULLIVAN [106744]** was born in 1924 in Fall River, Bristol, Massachusetts, died on 7 Jul 2004 in Fall River, Bristol, Massachusetts at age 80, and was buried in St. Patrick's Cem., Fall River, Massachusetts.

General Notes: 2004 July 8, Fall River MA Herald News, Thursday
Sullivan - Kay Kathleen P., age 80, in Fall River Wednesday, July 7, 2004, sister of Eleanor T. Sully Terceiro and Dennis B. Sullivan. Her funeral will be held Saturday, July 10, 2004 at 8 AM from the Waring - Sullivan Home of Memorial Tribute at Cherry Place 178 Winter St., followed by a funeral Mass at 9:00 in St Mary's Cathedral, Spring St. Fall River. Relatives and friends invited. Visiting hours Friday 4 - 8 PM. Burial will be in St. Patrick's Cemetery Fall River.

2004 July 8, Providence RI Journal, Thursday
Fall River - Kathleen P. "Kay" Sullivan, 80, of 4901 North Main St., a retired clerk and secretary, died yesterday at the Sarah S. Brayton Nursing Home after an illness. Born in Fall River, a daughter of the late Patrick and Nora (Clifford) Sullivan, she had been a lifelong resident of the area. Ms. Sullivan was a clerk and secretary at the former American Optical, now affiliated with Warner-Lambert, retiring in the late 1970's. She was a graduate of BMC Durfee High School, Class of 1943. Ms. Sullivan loved dancing. She leaves a sister, Eleanor T. "Sully" Terceiro, and a brother, Dennis Sullivan, both of Fall River; and several nieces and nephews, and great-nieces and great-nephews. She was the sister of the late James, Eugene, William, John and Mary Sullivan, Margaret Bagnall and Rita Robertson. The funeral service will held Saturday at 8 a.m. from the Waring-Sullivan Home of Memorial Tribute at Cherry Place, 178 Winter St., with a funeral Mass at 9 in St. Mary's Cathedral, Spring Street. Burial will be in St. Patrick's Cemetery.

326 F   xi.   **Eleanor T. SULLIVAN [106745]** was born in 1926 in Fall River, Bristol, Massachusetts.

General Notes: 2004 called Eleanor T. 'Sully' Terciero, a survivor, in her sister Kathleen's Fall River MA obituary.

Eleanor married **Mr. TERCEIRO** [108555] [MRIN: 34006]. Mr. was born about 1926.

Grandchildren

311. James S. SULLIVAN [108558] (*James* [308], *Sullivans born about 1870 possibly* [307]) was born on 24 Apr 1894 in New York, New York, New York and died after 1940 in Fall River, Bristol, Massachusetts.

General Notes: 1894 April 24 Births Registered in Fall River MA (sic) notes:
  Sullivan, James, b. New York, NY (sic) to James, Julia - Sullivan, father salesman, parents b. Ireland.

1894 April 24, New York Births LDS abstracts notes:
  James Sullivan, b. Manhattan, NY to James Sullivan, Julia Sullivan.

1900 Federal census James is enumerated with his parents in Fall River MA, age 6, birth noted as April 1894.

1919 Fall River City Directory
- Sullivan James carder rooms 123 Fourth. (Only one carder, no James S.)

1920 Fall River City Directory
- Sullivan James carder rooms 123 Fourth.
- Sullivan Julia widow James house 12 Barrett.

1920 Federal census of Fall River, Bristol Co. MA shows James with his widowed mother enumerated at 12 Barrett St.
  Sullivan, Julia, head, rents, widow, 52, immigrated 1890, naturalized, b. Ireland to Irish parents.
  " James S., son, 24, b. NY to Irish parents.   Machinist, Cotton mill.

1921 Fall River City Directory
- Sullivan James S. (Helena M.) carder house 91 Pelham.

1922 Fall River City Directory
- Sullivan James S. (Helena M.) overseer carding 230 Pocasset house 91 Pelham.
- Sullivan Julia widow James house 12 Barrett.

1923 Fall River City Directory
- Sullivan Julia widow James died Dec 19 1921.

1930 Federal census of Fall River, Bristol Co. MA shows the family enumerated 81 (sic) Pelham St. as family #413:
  Sullivan, James S., rents, $24, 34, married at 24, b. MA to NY parents (sic). O(Overseer) Carding, Cotton mill.
  " Dorles (sic), daughter, 5, b. MA to MA parents.
  " Helena, wife, 30, married at 20, b. NY to NY parents.
  " James, son, 3, b. NY to MA and NY parents.
(Helena's Arsnow family is enumerated in the same building).

1940 Federal census of Fall River, Bristol Co. MA shows the family enumerated at 64 Bowers St.:
  Sullivan, James S. head, 44, 8 years of school, b. MA.   Machinist, Torpedo Station, 50 week salary $1250.
  " Helena M., wife, 40, 8 years of school, b. MA.
  " Dolores L., daughter, 17, 3 years of high school, b. MA.
  " James, son, 13, 7 years of school, b. MA.
  " Doland E., son, 9, 4 years of school, b. MA.
  " Rose Marie, daughter, 1, b. MA.

1941 Fall River City Directory
- Sullivan James S. (Helen M.) foreman house 64 Bowers.

1955 Fall River City Directory
- Sullivan Donald E. res. 2 Osborn.
- Sullivan James S. (Helena M.) engineer house 2 Osborn.

1956 Fall River City Directory does not list James S. nor Helena.

James married **Helena M. ARSNOW** [108559] [MRIN: 34076], daughter of **George ARSEAULT** [108566] and **Helena OBRIEN** [108567]. Helena was born on 20 Oct 1899 in Fall River, Bristol, Massachusetts and died after 1940.

Children from this marriage were:

   327 F   i.   **Dolores L. SULLIVAN [108562]** was born in 1925 in Fall River, Bristol, Massachusetts and died after 2010.

                  General Notes: 2004 called a survivor, Dolores Carreiro of Tiverton, RI in her brother James' Fall River MA obituary.

                  Dolores married **Edward J. CARREIRO Sr.** [108563] [MRIN: 34149], son of **Joseph CARREIRO** [93699] and **Mary FREITAS** [93700]. Edward was born on 14 Jul 1923 in Tiverton, Newport, Rhode Island, died on 15 Mar 2010 in Tiverton, Newport, Rhode Island at age 86, and was buried in Hillside Cemetery, Tiverton, RI.

+ 328 M   ii.   **James F. 'Sully' SULLIVAN [108560]** was born on 11 Feb 1927 in Fall River, Bristol, Massachusetts and died on 14 Oct 2004 in Fall River, Bristol, Massachusetts at age 77.

                  James married **Claire M. DANIS** [108561] [MRIN: 34126] (b. 1929, d. 6 Feb 2015)

   329 M   iii. **Donald SULLIVAN [109203]** was born about 1931 in Fall River, Bristol, Massachusetts.

   330 F   iv. **Rosemary Bridgid SULLIVAN [109202]** was born on 8 Dec 1938 in Fall River, Bristol, Massachusetts, died on 24 Dec 2004 at age 66, and was buried in Gate of Heaven Cemetery, East Providence, RI.

                  General Notes: 2004 she was named a surviving sister of James Sullivan, Rosemary Murphy, in James' obituary.

                  2004 December 24 Social Security records shows Rosemary B. Sullivan Murphy, daughter of James, Helena Arsnow, born 8 December 1938, Fall River MA.   July 1957 name Rosemary B. Sullivan, Jan 1963 Rosemary Murphy, 19 Sept 1979 name Rosemary B. Murphy, 24 March 1989 name Rosemary Briget Murphy.

                  She and husband James rest at Gate of Heaven Cemetery, East Providence, RI marked with an upright granite stone:
1908 Dr. James E. Murphy 1981
1908 wife Gertrude M. Leary 1987
1935 Sister Eileen Murphy 1963
1938 James E. Murphy 1979
(Murph)
1938 Rosemary B. Murphy 2004
(Sullivan)

Rosemary married **James E. MURPHY** [109204] [MRIN: 36905], son of **James E. MURPHY** [103592] and **Gertrude M. LEARY** [110122]. James was born in 1938, died in 1979 at age 41, and was buried in Gate of Heaven Cemetery, East Providence, RI.

312.   Joseph James SULLIVAN [108530] (*Daniel J.*[309], *Sullivans born about 1870 possibly*[307]) was born on 6 Mar 1895 in Newport, Newport, Rhode Island and died after 1940 in Swansea, Bristol, Massachusetts.

General Notes: He appears in the Rhode Island records alternately as Timothy J. and Joseph J.

1910 Federal census of Newport, Newport Co. RI shows him enumerated at 30 Edgar Court with his parents and siblings:
   Joseph T. (sic), age 15, b. RI to Irish parents.   No employment.

1917 June 4, WWI draft registration card notes:
   Joseph James Sullivan, age 22, res. 30 Edgar Court, Newport, RI.   Born March 6, 1895, Natural born, Newport, RI.   Quarter Master, N. E. Steamship Co., where employed - Steamer New Haven, Single.
Short, Medium build, eyes gray, hair brown.

1930 Federal census of Fall River, Bristol Co. MA shows the family enumerated in at 57 Arizona St. as family #266:
   Sullivan, Joseph J., head, rents, $26.00, 35, married at 30, b. RI to Irish parents.   Pilot, Steamship Co.
   " Elizabeth, wife, 30, married at 25, b. MA to parents from England.
   " Joseph, son, 1 7/12, b. MA to RI and MA.

1940 Federal census of Swansea, Bristol Co. MA shows the family enumerated at 187 Gardner Neck Road:
   Sullivan, Joseph, head, owns home $3150, 44, 8 years of school, b. RI.   Pilot, Boat.   52 week salary $1700.
   " Elizabeth A., wife, 40, 7 years of school, b. MA.
   " Joseph J., son, 11, b. MA.
   " Mary E., daughter, 8, b. MA.
   " Helen M., daughter, 4, b. MA.

Joseph married **Elizabeth BRIGGS** [108531] [MRIN: 33155] in 1925. Elizabeth was born in 1900 in MA.

Children from this marriage were:

+   331   M   i.   **Joseph J. SULLIVAN Jr. [108532]** was born in 1928 in Fall River, Bristol, Massachusetts, died on 9 Aug 2003 in Wareham, Plymouth, Massachusetts at age 75, and was buried in st. Anthony Cemetery, Wareham, MA.

         Joseph married **Beryl M. DECOSTA** [108538] [MRIN: 33369] (b. Abt 1928, d. After 2003)

    332   F   ii.   **Helen M. SULLIVAN [108540]** was born about 1930.

    333   F   iii.   **Mary V. SULLIVAN [108541]** was born about 1932.

         Mary married **Mr. HORNBOSTEL** [108542] [MRIN: 33420]. Mr. was born about 1932.

Great-Grandchildren

328.   James F. 'Sully' SULLIVAN [108560] (*James S.*[311], *James*[308], *Sullivans born about 1870 possibly*[307]) was born on 11 Feb 1927 in Fall River, Bristol, Massachusetts and died on 14 Oct 2004 in Fall River, Bristol, Massachusetts at age 77.

General Notes: 2004 October 1, Fall River MA Herald News, Saturday
James F. "Sully." Husband of Fifty three years to Claire M. (Danis) Sullivan, son of the late James S. and Helena (Arsnow) Sullivan, father of Betsi E. Oliveira, Brian J. Sullivan, Barry M. Sullivan and the late Brad P. Sullivan, brother of Dolores Carreiro, Rosemary Murphy, and Donald Sullivan, loving grandfather of Elizabeth, Justin, Jessica, Brady, and Benjamin. His funeral will be held on Monday at 8:45 AM from the Hathaway Community Home for Funerals, 900 Buffington St., Somerset followed by a Mass of Christian burial at 10 AM in Saint Patrick Church, 306 South St., Somerset. Relatives are invited to attend, burial to follow Saint Patrick Cemetery Somerset. Memorial donations in his memory to the Coach James F. Sullivan Scholarship Fund. C/O Somerset Federal Credit Union, 740 County St., Somerset, MA 2726. Calling hours Sunday 4-8 PM.

2004 October 16, New Bedford MA Standard Times, Saturday
Fall River -- James F. "Sully" Sullivan, 77, of Somerset died Thursday, Oct. 14, 2004, at St. Anne's Hospital. He was the husband of Claire M. (Danis) Sullivan; they were married 53 years. Born in Fall River, the son of the late James S. and Helena (Arsnow) Sullivan, he resided in Somerset 50 years. He graduated from Monsignor Coyle High School in 1945. He graduated from Providence College in 1950 with a political science degree, and was the starting shortstop for the college. He received a master's degree in education in 1957 from Bridgewater State College. He served in the Navy during World War II. Mr. Sullivan was a biology teacher and then head of the Science Department at Somerset High School; he retired in 1990. At the high school, he was a football coach for nine years and baseball coach for more than 30 years. He was an assistant coach at U Mass Dartmouth for 14 years, and was director of the Bay State Baseball camp held there. He was a Southeastern Massachusetts football official. Survivors include a daughter, Betsi E. Oliveira of Somerset; two sons, Brian J. Sullivan of Somerset and Barry M. Sullivan of Cranston, R.I.; two sisters, Dolores Carreiro of Tiverton, R.I., and Rosemary Murphy of Florida; a brother, Donald Sullivan of Somerset; five grandchildren; and several nieces and nephews. He was the father of the late Brad P. Sullivan. His funeral will be at 8:45 a.m. Monday at Hathaway Community Home for Funerals, 900 Buffington St., Somerset, with a Mass at 10 at St. Patrick's Church. Burial will follow in St. Patrick's Cemetery, Somerset.

2004 October 16, Providence RI Journal, Saturday
Somerset -- James F. "Sully" Sullivan, 77, of Lewis Avenue, a local baseball coaching legend and retired science teacher, died Thursday St. Anne's Hospital, Fall River. As head baseball coach at Somerset High School for 30 years , his teams compiled a record of 442-199, and his 1979 team won the state Division 2 championship. Two of his former players, Jerry Remy, Class of 1970, and Greg Gagne, Class of 1979, played major league baseball and recalled his influence. Former Red Sox infielder Remy, now an analyst for New England Sports Network, said of his former coach, "For me, he was like a member of the family. He's been part of my life since high school. He's the guy who taught me how to do things right -- [in] baseball and personally." Remy was an American League All-Star and played on the 1978 Red Sox team that lost to the Yankees in a playoff. Gagne credits Mr. Sullivan and his father, Elmer Gagne, with righting his ship when he was a rebellious teenager with a talent for baseball. "He had a belief in my talent. He had a big influence with what I did after high school," Gagne said. "I had the talent and ability, but he said I'd waste it if I didn't straighten out." The Minnesota Twins won two World Series titles with Gagne as their starting shortstop, with Gagne knocking in the winning run in Game 7 of the 1987 World Series against the Cardinals. Mr. Sullivan started the Bay State Camps at U-Mass-Dartmouth, then SMU, in the 1980's, and Remy, then with the Sox, would come down to the camp, in full uniform, and give tips to the youngsters. The camp has been run every summer for 23 years. Mr. Sullivan's primary job at Somerset High School had been as a

biology teacher, and later, head of the science department for many years before retiring in 1990. He had been an assistant coach at U-Mass-Dartmouth for 14 years under coach Bruce Wheeler, and had also been a Southeastern Massachusetts football official. He was the husband of Claire M. (Danis) Sullivan. They had been married for 53 years. Born in Fall River on Feb. 11, 1927, a son of the late James S. and Helena (Arsnow) Sullivan, he had lived in Somerset for 50 years. He was a Navy veteran of World War II. A graduate of Monsignor Coyle High School, Class of 1945, he graduated from Providence College in 1950 with a degree in political science, and was the baseball team's starting shortstop. He earned his master's degree in education from Bridgewater State College in 1951. Besides his wife, he leaves a daughter, Betsi E. Oliveira of Somerset; two sons, Brian J. Sullivan of Somerset and Barry M. Sullivan of Cranston; two sisters, Dolores Carreiro of Tiverton and Rosemary Murphy in Florida; a brother, Donald Sullivan of Somerset; five grandchildren; and several nieces and nephews. He was the father of the late Brad P. Sullivan. The funeral will be held Monday at 8:45 a.m. from Hathaway Community Home for Funerals, 900 Buffington St., with a Mass of Christian Burial at 10 in St. Patrick's Church, 306 South St. Burial will follow in St. Patrick's Cemetery.

James married **Claire M. DANIS** [108561] [MRIN: 34126], daughter of **Alfred DANIS Jr.** [109949] and **Irene M. L. CLEMENT** [109950]. Claire was born in 1929 in Fall River, Bristol, Massachusetts and died on 6 Feb 2015 in Fall River, Bristol, Massachusetts at age 86.

Children from this marriage were:

    334   F   i.   **Betsi SULLIVAN [109952]** was born about 1950.

    335   M   ii.   **Brian SULLIVAN [109953]** was born about 1952.

    336   M iii.   **Barry SULLIVAN [109954]** was born about 1954.

331.   **Joseph J. SULLIVAN Jr.** [108532] (*Joseph James*[312], *Daniel J.*[309], *Sullivans born about 1870 possibly*[307]) was born in 1928 in Fall River, Bristol, Massachusetts, died on 9 Aug 2003 in Wareham, Plymouth, Massachusetts at age 75, and was buried in st. Anthony Cemetery, Wareham, MA.

General Notes: 2003 August 9,
Sullivan - New Bedford MA Standard Times, Wareham - Joseph J. Sullivan, 74, of Mattapoisett died Wednesday, Aug. 6, 2003, at Tobey Hospital after a long illness. He was the husband of Beryl M. (DeCosta) Sullivan. Born in Fall River, the son of the late Joseph J. and Elizabeth A. (Briggs) Sullivan, he lived in Mattapoisett most of his life where he was a communicant of St. Anthony Church. Mr. Sullivan was a firefighter at Otis Air National Guard Base for more than 30 years until retiring. He also served with the Mattapoisett Volunteer Fire Department. He was an assistant building inspector for the town of Mattapoisett and maintenance supervisor for Village Court Housing Development. He served in the Navy during the end of World War II and was the past commander of the Florence Eastman American Legion Post 280, Mattapoisett. Survivors include his widow; three sons, Timothy Sullivan and his wife, Kelle, of Tampa, Fla., Daniel Sullivan and his wife, Maryann, of Rochester, and Joseph J. Sullivan Jr. of Mattapoisett; a daughter, Mary Ellen Stanley of Petersborough, N. H.; and 12 grandchildren, Patricia Stanley, Nichole Sullivan, Rebecca Stanley, Matthew Stanley, Daniel Sullivan, Katelyn Sullivan, Jessica Sullivan, Timothy Sullivan, Vanessa Sullivan, Samantha Sullivan, Molly Sullivan and Jillian Sullivan. He was the brother of the late Helen M. Sullivan and Mary V. Hornbostel. His funeral Mass will be at 10 a.m. Tuesday in St. Anthony Church with burial to follow in St. Anthony Cemetery. Arrangements are by the Saunders-Dwyer Mattapoisett Home for Funerals, 50 County Road, Mattapoisett.

Joseph married **Beryl M. DECOSTA** [108538] [MRIN: 33369], daughter of **Anthony DECOSTA** [106193] and **Grace NAPIER** [106194]. Beryl was born about 1928 and died after 2003.

Children from this marriage were:

337 M   i.   **Timothy SULLIVAN [108539]** was born about 1950.

338 M   ii.   **Daniel SULLIVAN [108544]** was born about 1952.

339 M   iii. **Joseph J. SULLIVAN [108545]** was born about 1954.

340 F   iv. **Mary Ellen SULLIVAN [108546]** was born about 1958.

General Notes: 2003 called Mary Ellen Stanley of Petersborough NH in her father's obituary.

Mary married **Mr. STANLEY** [108547] [MRIN: 33541].

Volume VI
Descendants of Immigrants born 1845 – 1870
Name Index

Peter [83882], 43
Stephen [83760], 38, 42
Timothy Peter [99691], 43, 47
FRANEY
Margaret G. [96534], 48
FREITAS
Mary [93700], 97
GALVIN
Edwin [98939], 16
Ella M. [98938], 16
John J. [92907], 16
Michael D. [98937], 4, 16
GILES
Rosanna [94992], 22
GOTHAM
Anna M. wife of Stephen
[104719], 65
Annie Marie [104718], 65
James E. [104711], 52, 65
James Edward [104721], 65
James M. [104715], 65
Stephen Edward [104717], 65
GRANFIELD
Kathleen [101935], 28
Michael T. [109695], 28
GRAY
James W. [105636], 8, 21
Margaret A. [105650], 21
William [105637], 21
William J. [105638], 21
GRIFFIN
Annie M. wife of James
[106459], 24
James L [106457], 24
James L. [106458], 24
GROSS
Margaret [99169], 79
Paul [99167], 64, 78
Pauline M. 'Penny' [99168],
78
GUILD
Charles H. [106533], 68
Elizabeth J. [106535], 69
George F. [106518], 54, 68
George F. Jr. [106522], 68
George Whitfield [106531], 68
Louisa C. [106524], 68
Raymond E. [106534], 69
HAMPSTON
Mary [107196], 49, 51
HANLEY
Catherine [106324], 49, 54
Mary [97461], 1, 9
HANNIGAN
John [101964], 11
Mary A. [101926], 1, 11
HARRINGTON

Abbie I. [105386], 15
Daniel [105378], 3, 15
Hanora (Capy) [99694], 37,
38
James [105382], 15
James E. [105385], 15
Julia J. [105387], 15
Margaret [105627], 1, 6
Margaret [105988], 44
Margaret [106097], 52
Mary (Causkey) 'Minnie'
[108505], 86, 87
Norah [106093], 49, 51
Patrick [105641], 6
William J. [105384], 15
HARTNETT
Thomas F. [97463], 22
HASSEY
Catherine [101924], 11, 26
Thomas [101927], 26
HAWKYARD
Charles [105261], 55
Eliza [105260], 55
HEALY
John [94320], 62
Margaret E. [94306], 50, 62
Margaret wife of John
[94321], 62
HENABERRY
Margaret [92908], 16
HOLLAND
Cain [96918], 81
Mary [96916], 80, 81
HOLLY
Mary [101963], 11
HORNBOSTEL
Mr. [108542], 98
HOULIHAN
Nellie [106798], 60, 74
HURLEY
Julia [101940], 30
JURGENSEN
Emil B. [106451], 23
Frances Elizabeth [106450],
23
KANE
Johanna [106060], 49, 54
KEELEY
Edward J. [106062], 69
Eliza wife of John [106057],
69
Elizabeth [106063], 69
John [106056], 69
John K. [106066], 69
Joseph [106055], 54, 69
Joseph [106065], 69
Lillian [106061], 69

William P. [106064], 69
KEENAN
Eliza [104716], 65
KELLY
Delia A. [109902], 28
KILEY
Margaret [108549], 20
LEAHY
Ellen Genevieve [105991], 44
Francis [105996], 45
James F. [105992], 44
Jeremiah [105987], 44
John E. [105994], 45
Joseph A. [105997], 45
Julia V. [105995], 45
Mary A. [105993], 44
Patrick J. [105985], 41, 44
LEARY
Arthur William (Dr.) [101956],
31, 34
Ellen [108534], 89, 91
Francis C.S.C. [101957], 34
Gertrude M. [110122], 98
Ruth M. [107941], 34
SheilaC. [101958], 34
LOWE
Louise J. [106438], 24
MAHONEY
Dennis [104203], 14
Henry [104201], 3, 14
Henry C. [104208], 14
James Edward [104209], 14
John J. [104207], 14
Katie A. [104210], 14
Mary A. [104211], 14
Mary wife of Dennis [104204],
14
Patrick B. [104212], 14
MARBLE
Mary D. [101950], 35
MARTIN
Agnes [94319], 76
MATTHEWS
Stanley M. [99175], 79
MCCAFFREY
James Henry [104720], 65
MCCARTHY
Catherine [105659], 73
Daniel [105658], 72
Ellen [92407], 73
Jeremiah [92402], 59, 72
Jeremiah [92403], 72
Jeremiah [92409], 73
Margaret [92408], 73
Mary [92406], 73
Thomas [92405], 72
William [105657], 72

MCDONALD
James [107193], 51
Patrick [107197], 51
MCGRATH
Dennis [101953], 35
John E. [101949], 35
John Joseph [101948], 31, 35
Kathleen Julia [101951], 35
MCGUINESS
Ellen [94995], 1, 4
Julia [104722], 65
Patrick [94997], 4
MCGUIRE
James [106778], 75
Mary A. [106777], 60, 75
MCNAMARA
Jane [105392], 66
MCQUILLEN
Margaret [106494], 50, 57
MONAHAN
Sophia [92404], 72
MURPHY
Ellen F. [106806], 76
Honora 'Anna' [109410], 40
James E. [103592], 98
James E. [109204], 98
Mary [83759], 42
NAPIER
Grace [106194], 100
OBRIEN
Bridget [104847], 80, 83
Ellen [105990], 37, 41
Helena [108567], 97
Lena [104714], 49, 52
O'CALLAHAN
Margaret [105309], 18
OLAUGHLIN
Mary [109696], 28
ONEIL
Doris [107163], 77
Edgar [107164], 77
Edgar F. [94317], 63, 76
Hanora [105594], 53, 67
James [94318], 76
Margaret [105383], 15
Patrick [105597], 67
Ruth Patricia [107165], 77
O'NEIL
Margaret [105381], 1, 3
Mary [105649], 21
OXFORD
James W. [105938], 9
Robert R. [105939], 9
PEDRO
Madeline Barbara [106460],
24, 33
PERKINS

John F. [101952], 35
PHILIPS
Annie [106523], 68
QUIGLEY
James M. [108506], 88
Michael [108502], 87, 88
RICE
Madeline Mary [106501], 57,
72
RICHARDSON
John Okill [106332], 71
RILEY
Mary [105923], 68
ROBERTSON
Mr. [108554], 95
ROBINSON
Mary C. [105256], 56
Sarah [99164], 64
Wyndham O. [105257], 56
SEVERANCE
Ellen Marie [106218], 85
SHANNON
Charles J. [108484], 73
SHEA
Catherine 'Kate' [106216], 80,
81
Catherine Marie [108543], 20
Daniel [106322], 12
Frank William [105616], 17
John [108548], 20
Julia M. [106775], 50, 60
Mary [105625], 7, 20
Mary A. [106317], 2, 12
Mary wife of [106781], 60
Michael [105628], 20
SHEEHAN
Catherine [92396], 50, 58
Florence [107517], 58
James [109414], 39
Joanna wife of Florence
[107518], 58
Michael [109412], 40
SLATTERY
Bridget [101962], 12
SMITH
Franklin [106220], 85
Franklin Pierce [106217], 85
Leo D. [107940], 36
Lynwood E. B. [101955], 32,
36
Merton S. [106213], 82, 85
Ruth [106219], 85
SOUTHWORTH
Eugene [104855], 85
James [104854], 83, 85
SPELLACY

Elizabeth 'Lizzie' [105305], 5,
18
Tmothy [105308], 18
STANLEY
Mr. [108547], 101
STARRS
Mary Agnes [105317], 18, 33
SUGHRUE
Mary [105598], 67
SULLIVAN
Agnes [96929], 81
Albert [105253], 56
Alice M. [106331], 71
Anne V. [104850], 83
Annie [105389], 52, 65
Annie [106786], 60
Annie [97451], 9, 21
Annie Josephine [109405], 39
Arthur Warren [99166], 64, 79
Barry [109954], 100
Betsi [109952], 100
Brian [109953], 100
Bridget [100014], 84
Bridget M. [105635], 8, 20
Catherine [101937], 11
Catherine [105307], 1, 5
Catherine [105315], 18
Catherine [105645], 8
Catherine [106315], 12
Catherine [106330], 71
Catherine [106797], 74
Catherine [108511], 87
Catherine Agnes [94311], 63,
76
Catherine G. [105924], 53, 67
Catherine 'Kate' [104202], 3,
14
Catherine 'Kate' [106519], 54,
68
Catherine L. [108537], 92
Catherine Veronica 'Kay'
[101933], 28
Catherine wife of Edward C.
[92412], 2, 13
Cornelius [105306], 1, 5
Cornelius [105644], 6
Cornelius [106002], 41
Daniel [105254], 49, 54
Daniel [105259], 55
Daniel [105935], 53
Daniel [108544], 101
Daniel [96919], 81
Daniel [97460], 1, 9
Daniel C. [92414], 13
Daniel F. [108535], 92
Daniel J. [106316], 2, 12
Daniel J. [108533], 89, 90

Daniel J. [96917], 80, 81
Daniel Joseph [106320], 12
Dennis [104205], 1, 3
Dennis [105380], 1, 3
Dennis [105936], 53
Dennis [108504], 86, 87
Dennis [108509], 87
Dennis [95597], 5
Dennis B. [106742], 94
Dennis D. [104649], 45
Dennis J. [101946], 31
Dolores L. [108562], 97
Donald [109203], 97
Edmund Edwards [106454], 24, 33
Edmund Edwards [106462], 33
Edmund Joseph [101929], 27
Edward E. [92413], 2, 13
Edward Eugene [106319], 13
Edward W. [106329], 70
Eileen A. [101934], 28
Eleanor T. [106745], 95
Elizabeth Katherine [92398], 59, 72
Ellen M. 'Nellie' [105986], 41, 44
Ellen wife of Dennis [104206], 1, 3
Ethel [105266], 56
Eugene [105639], 6
Eugene [106739], 94
Eugene [94305], 50, 61
Eugene J. [105630], 20
Eugene S. [104846], 80, 82
Fannie [105605], 17
First wife of Patrick [106796], 60, 74
Florence [99165], 64, 78
Frances J. [107893], 32
Francis [105599], 67
Francis X. [106787], 75
George [105264], 56
George [98935], 4
George P. [105314], 18
Gertrude A. [101930], 27
Hannah [105267], 55
Hannah [105312], 18
Hannah [105941], 8
Hanora [105379], 3, 15
Hanora [105603], 5, 17
Hanora 'Nora' [104650], 45
Harry [109910], 56
Harry V. [106455], 24
Helen M. [108540], 98
Helena F. [106453], 23
Helena T. [105566], 40, 43

Henry [106443], 10
Henry F. [106804], 76
Henry M. [106439], 24
Henry T. [106791], 75
Hilda [99171], 64
Honoria [105647], 6
Irene F. [105604], 17
James [104713], 49, 52
James [105262], 55
James [105933], 53
James [106442], 10
James [108564], 89, 90
James F. 'Sully' [108560], 97, 99
James J. [106747], 94
James S. [108558], 90, 96
Jeremiah (Darb) [105567], 37, 38
Jeremiah [105942], 1, 8
Jeremiah [106092], 49, 51
Jeremiah [106785], 60
Jeremiah [106795], 74
Jeremiah [107195], 49, 51
Jeremiah [107520], 13
Jeremiah Edmond [106498], 72
Jeremiah J. [104672], 45
Jeremiah J. [105989], 37, 40
Jeremiah J. [106493], 49, 56
Jeremiah J. [108536], 92
Jeremiah Joseph [96928], 81, 84
Jeremiah P. [106774], 50, 59
Jeremiah S. [106799], 60, 76
John [101925], 1, 11
John [101936], 12, 29
John [105626], 1, 5
John [105937], 53
John [106323], 49, 54
John [106441], 10
John [106521], 49, 53
John [106780], 76
John [99161], 49, 52
John D. [104659], 41, 45
John Edwin [106499], 72
John F [106738], 93
John F. [105602], 5, 16
John Francis [105313], 18, 33
John Francis Jr. [105318], 33
John H. [105632], 20
John Henry [101943], 30
John J. [109407], 39
John Joseph [106492], 57, 71
John L. [106468], 71
John Patrick [106318], 12
John V. [104673], 46
Joseph [106748], 94

Joseph A. [106801], 76
Joseph J. [108545], 101
Joseph J. Jr. [108532], 98, 100
Joseph James [108530], 91, 98
Joseph T. [106789], 76
Julia [105546], 44
Julia [108565], 89, 90
Julia [110229], 41
Julia [94313], 63
Julia A. [98936], 4, 15
Julia Monica [106784], 60, 76
Julia V. [106058], 54, 69
Kathleen F. [101945], 31, 34
Kathleen P. [106744], 95
Lena [104712], 52, 65
Leo T. (Rev.) [101954], 31
Lillian C. [105607], 17
Lizzie [105310], 18
Louisa M. [94312], 63, 77
Lucy A. [104851], 83
Mabel E. 'Bella' [104849], 83
Margaret [105316], 18
Margaret [105634], 20
Margaret [105943], 1, 8
Margaret [106740], 94
Margaret [109413], 39
Margaret [94310], 63
Margaret J. [104670], 41, 45
Margaret J. [105606], 17
Margaret L [104853], 83
Margaret L. [106803], 76
Margaret M. [104671], 46
Margaret M. [99178], 79
Margaret T. [105640], 7
Margaret W. [99170], 65
Margaret wife of Timothy [95596], 1, 5
Margaretta L. M. wife of Arthur [99177], 64, 79
Marion L. [106336], 71
Mark [106215], 80, 81
Martin [106445], 11
Mary [105596], 49, 53
Mary [105631], 20
Mary [105648], 7
Mary [105999], 41
Mary [106440], 25
Mary [106792], 76
Mary [107194], 51
Mary [108510], 87
Mary [83880], 38, 42
Mary [95598], 5
Mary A. [101931], 27
Mary A. [104848], 83
Mary A. [106100], 17

Volume I
Descendants of Immigrants born 1760 – 1790
Name Index

Bartholomew J. [106279], 440

Edward A. [106283], 440

Edward J. [106278], 393, 440

Elizabeth Ann [72508], 46, 79

Mary wife of William [91813], 79

William [91814], 79

CARNEY

Daniel [93867], 329

Katherine 'Kate' [93866], 329

CARR

Charles A. [95447], 233

Charles F. [95442], 194, 232

Ella F. [95446], 233

Henry [95443], 232

Henry C. [95451], 233

John [95449], 233

Margaret V. [95445], 233

Mary [95450], 232

Mary wife of Henry [95444], 232

Patrick William [95448], 233

CARRAGHER

Bridget [94975], 287

CARY

Joanna [94328], 30

CASEY

Bridget [99352], 87

CASSIDY

Rose Veronica [108570], 85

CHASE

Carroll Wilmont [106856], 180

Omar Clarence [106857], 180

CHATTERTON

Lucy Mason [94370], 177

CLARK

Ann [93662], 332

Catherine [101702], 437

Catherine [93622], 402

Cornelius [93043], 411

Eleanor J. [93111], 38, 66

Ellen wife of Cornelius [93044], 411

Richard [100141], 66

Susan J. [93042], 357, 411

CLEARE

Elizabeth Gertrude 'Lizzie J.' [93185], 355, 400

Lawrence [98721], 400

CLEMMEY

Alice [96041], 166

Eleanor V. [96042], 166

Elizabeth [96044], 166

Elizabeth wife of John [96047], 165

Florence [96045], 166

John [96046], 165

John L. [96040], 166

Leonard V. [96043], 166

Louis [96037], 143, 165

Margaret A. [96038], 165, 179

Mary E. [96039], 165

CLYNE

Catherine Mary [91816], 79, 102

Patrick [91820], 102

CLYNER

Margaret [100212], 311, 341

CODY

Bridget wife of Robert [92996], 239

Margaret J. 'Maggie' [92994], 202, 239

Robert [92995], 239

COLEMAN

Catherine [94341], 59

COLLINS

Henrietta 'Hetty' [100885], 112, 135, 317, 368

James [104871], 105, 111, 368

Margaret [104944], 112, 137

Mary [104879], 112

Nora [4439], 45, 76

William E. [5549], 76

CONLEY

Owen   Joseph [102743], 257

Philip [102744], 257

CONNELLY

Dennis [92335], 223

Ellen [92327], 189, 224

John [92333], 223

Margaret T. [92334], 223

Mary [92332], 223

Timothy Joseph [92331], 223

CONNER

Rhoa Ree [98618], 149

CONNOLLY

Annie M. [104885], 136

Daniel [92527], 136

Denis Jr. [92313], 224

Dennis [88995], 189, 223

Ellen Mary [88996], 224, 279

James [110141], 189

James [92311], 223

John [92314], 223

John [92322], 188

Margaret [92325], 189

Mary [92315], 223

Mary [92326], 189

Patrick [92312], 223

Quinlan [92324], 189

Timothy [92319], 183, 188

Timothy Jr. [92323], 188, 222

CONNOR

Mary A. [96510], 91

CONNORS

Mary [99626], 83

CONROY

Dennis [96877], 315, 357

Hannah [96882], 357

Mark [96881], 358

Mary [96880], 358

Michael [96879], 358

COOK

Sarah A. [97758], 238

COSTIGAN

Catherine [107918], 427

Daniel [107894], 426

Daniel [107913], 426

Elizabeth [107916], 427

James [107915], 427

James [96184], 366, 426

John F. [107912], 426

Margaret [107917], 427

Mary Jane 'Jennie' [107914], 427

Michael H. [107911], 426

COUGHLAN

Mary R. [92282], 443

COUGHLIN

Catherine C. [99039], 59

Catherine L. [94343], 26

Daniel [103241], 60

Daniel [94347], 25

Daniel [99228], 25

Elizabeth [94344], 26

Ellen [108586], 25

Ellen wife of Daniel [99229], 25

James [94325], 7, 25

James H. [103240], 59

James H. [94338], 26

Joanna [94342], 25

John [93835], 292
John H. [99038], 26, 58
John H. [99043], 59
Mary [93834], 240, 292
Mary J. [85989], 25
Michael [108587], 26
Thomas [94345], 26
COX
George T. [101202], 157
John [101203], 157
CRAMER
Andrew [95508], 194, 229
Margaret [95511], 230
Margaret wife of Peter [95510], 229
Peter [95509], 229
CRANDLE
Ethelinda [99290], 381
CRAPO
Sarah [106862], 267
CRAWFORD
Thomas J. [101209], 158
CREAMER
Hannah F. [95512], 230
John [95513], 229
Mary 'Mamie' [95514], 229
Matthew [95515], 230
CROSSON
James F. [104045], 436
CROWLEY
John [95455], 193
Julia [94263], 377
Mary (Ceohane) [95439], 184, 193
CUDDY
Catherine [98310], 288
Thomas [109593], 288
CULLIGAN
Catherine 'Kate' [101472], 176
Isabelle F. [101475], 181
Isabelle wife of William [101473], 176, 181
Lois Mae [101474], 181
Patrick [101469], 176
William F. [101468], 153, 176
William Francis [101471], 176, 180
CUMMINGS
Catherine [79192], 454
Mary [93836], 292
CURRAN
Annabel T. [96830], 172
Mary [101450], 152, 171
Mary [96829], 173

Peter Francis [96826], 152, 172
Peter Sr. [96827], 171, 172
CURRY
John T. [104941], 163
CURTIS
Mary [101470], 176
CUSHMAN
Margaret [96066], 167
CUSICK
Flora [93876], 329
Hannah wife of Thomas [93878], 329
Thomas [93877], 329
DACEY
Elizabeth [108988], 197
DAWSON
Emily [104038], 388
DEEGAN
John [94713], 212
Thomas [94712], 212
DEMPSEY
Mary [100176], 396
DENEAL
Hannah [94052], 374
DESMOND
Johanna [93230], 242, 309, 322
John [94867], 322
DIAMOND
Catherine Ann [108167], 454
DIT LALIBERTE
Zoe Colin [101733], 438
DOBBIN
Ellen [97399], 139
DODGE
Clara F. [102909], 261
DOHERTY
John [100183], 407
Mary E. [92271], 357, 407
DONAHUE
Richard A. [108489], 305
DONOVAN
Cornelius [94327], 30
Dennis [104361], 362
Elizabeth 'Betsy' [107713], 227
Ellen wife of Patrick [104363], 362
Hannah wife of Patrick [106925], 235
Jeremiah [106227], 235
Joanna [94337], 30
Michael [108139], 430

Michael Edward [94326], 7, 30
Patrick [104362], 362
Patrick [106924], 235
DORAN
Anne Gertrude [96240], 69, 91
Joseph [96509], 91
DOUCET
Mr. [96336], 92
DOWNING
Edward H. [96493], 30
Elizabeth [96497], 30
George F. [96495], 30
Hannah wife of Thomas [96492], 30
Louisa [96496], 31
Margaret E. [96823], 152, 171
Margaret wife of Michael [96825], 171
Michael [96824], 171
Thomas [96490], 7, 30
Thomas [96491], 30
Thomas A. [96494], 31
DOYLE
Cornelius [96886], 358
Eliza wife of Michael [100299], 342
Frank J. [107167], 244
Jeremiah H. [99040], 59
John [100297], 342
Margaret [94395], 445
Mary [98725], 264
Mary Evelyn [107166], 244
Michael [100298], 342
Thomas [99041], 59
DRISCOLL
Agnes J. [107901], 428
Annie M. [107902], 428
Daniel [107721], 190
Daniel L. [95877], 366, 419, 428
Daniel Louis Jr. [107898], 428
Geroge S. [93647], 170
Henry M. [107899], 428
Herbert [93646], 170
James [107904], 428
James F. [107906], 428
Jane [107900], 428
John [109374], 169
John [97017], 365
John F. [93645], 169
John W. [107903], 428
Margaret [109601], 288

Jeremiah [98293], 203, 245
Jeremiah 'Darb' [104756], 9, 35
Jeremiah 'Jerry' [93377], 338
Joanna [104770], 9
Joanna [97014], 316, 364
Johanna [106579], 357, 410
John [104771], 35
John [93378], 337
John [94271], 377
John [94332], 8, 31
John [98150], 246
John [98342], 32
John [98834], 191, 227
John [99268], 277
John [99273], 277
John E. [72903], 56
John Francis [101725], 453
John P. [109604], 235
John S. [104928], 162
John Sylvester [104868], 137, 162
Joseph [1533], 54
Joseph R. [104939], 163
Julia (Caupey) [98178], 182, 186
Julia [108994], 195
Julia [109961], 258
Julia [72904], 54
Julia [96910], 235
Julia M. [104938], 163
Julia M. [92305], 35, 60
Julia wife of Daniel [105189], 364
Julia wife of Timoty [109683], 387
Leroy [101728], 438
Louise A. [104930], 163
Maggie J. [104039], 436
Margaret (Trokirre) [93514], 42
Margaret [109681], 387
Margaret [110135], 1, 2
Margaret [3629], 15
Margaret [79350], 246
Margaret [93150], 183, 187
Margaret [98345], 32
Margaret wife of Daniel [106658], 54
Margaret wife of Dennis [94334], 31
Margaret wife of Eugene [98851], 191
Mary [104773], 35, 60
Mary [106226], 234

Mary [83630], 15
Mary [93300], 307, 313
Mary [93376], 337
Mary [94875], 307, 312
Mary [98296], 245
Mary [99042], 59
Mary A. [100140], 10, 37
Mary E. [79349], 246
Mary H. [104932], 163
Mary Hazel [101729], 438
Mary Louisa [79256], 56
Mary M. [92193], 19
Mary wife of James [95896], 360
Michael [109607], 235
Michael [98156], 246
Michael [98843], 227
Patrick [83629], 14
Patrick [88993], 223
Patrick H. [93371], 386
Paul [101719], 389, 437
Peter [109602], 235
Peter H. [98837], 228
Philip [103251], 234
Philip [83626], 12
Philip [94262], 377
Philip H. [98311], 199, 234
Rose Elaine [104731], 63, 85
Samuel [93382], 389
Samuel Francis [101723], 438, 452
Stephen F. [93372], 387
Susan 'Sarah' [92417], 57
Thomas M. [104733], 85
Timothy [109682], 387
Timothy [92194], 19
Timothy [99267], 218, 277
William [98344], 31
HARRIS
Albert [91827], 103
Daughter [91823], 103
David Laurence [91822], 102, 103
HART
Charles S. [102908], 261
James D. [108151], 451
Sumner F. [102907], 261
HAYES
Catherine wife of Michael [109211], 60
Gladys E. [109219], 60
Kathleen [109218], 60
Leo E. [109217], 60
Michael [109210], 60
Michael F. [109216], 60

William Henry [109209], 28, 60
HEAFFEY
Delia F. [99785], 448
HEALEY
Annie [94729], 268
Elizabeth [94730], 268
James C. [94727], 267
Mary U. [94731], 268
William F. [94726], 212, 267
HEFFERNAN
James [110115], 236
John [93842], 201, 236
John [93844], 237
Margarert wife of Michael [93846], 237
Michael J. [93843], 237
Patrick [93845], 237
HENNESSEY
Mary [94844], 431
HERLIHY
Dennis J. [106353], 286
Irene Margaret [106355], 286
HICKEY
Annie Teresa [109213], 28
William [109214], 28
HIGGINS
John [98171], 294
Margaret [98173], 294
William E. [98170], 248, 294
HITT
Stuart Borden [106233], 441
HODNETT
Mary [93851], 237
HOLLAND
Annie [94751], 261
Catherine Agnes [94754], 261
Dennis [96914], 128
Ellen [96199], 108, 128
Ellen wife of Dennis [96915], 128
Jeremiah [107710], 227
John [94752], 261
Mary J. [94750], 260
Michael [94749], 261
Nancy 'Annie' [98394], 351
Patrick [94748], 211, 260
Patrick H. [107709], 227
Timothy [98713], 260
William F. [94753], 261
HOLMAN
Doris [101726], 453
HOPKINS

Bridget Beatrice [93384], 389, 437
John [93385], 437
HORAN
Mary [92787], 251
HOWARD
Cornelius [98300], 378
Cornelius [98302], 379
Ellen [94931], 379
Joseph F. [93875], 379
Margaret [98301], 378
Mary [94929], 378
Michael [94930], 378
Mr. [101197], 160
Peter [93874], 327, 378
HURLEY
Ambrose D. [95874], 419, 428
Celeste J. wife of Jospeh [86036], 419, 447
Denis [86026], 419
Francis A. 'Frank' [95875], 419
John E. [86033], 419
John T. [86028], 360, 419, 428
Joseph [86037], 447
Joseph L. [86035], 419, 447
Mary E. [86034], 419
Mr. [96883], 358
IRWIN
Sarah [102731], 158
IVERS
Catherine wife of Michael [97942], 449
Eugene [97950], 449
John E. [97939], 426, 449
John E. [97946], 449
Louise [97949], 449
Michael [97941], 449
Raymond C. [97947], 449
Ruth [97948], 449
KEANY
Isabelle [97900], 334
KEELY
Marie [79450], 78
KEENAN
Anna M. [101188], 135
James [101189], 135
KELLY
Annie J. [95829], 357, 415
Catherine [97710], 9
Cornelius [101738], 389
Cornelius [98191], 206
Daniel [104766], 2, 8
Daniel [93748], 320

Daniel J. [97711], 9
Ellen L. [92843], 9, 35
Hannah [93729], 309, 320
Honora [104757], 9, 34
Honora [104772], 35
Jeremiah [104768], 1, 2
Jeremiah [104769], 9
Joanna [98190], 206
Joanna F. [94215], 9
Julia wife of Patrick [95831], 415
Margaret [93380], 338, 389
Margaret wife of Cornelius [101739], 389
Mary [101192], 105, 110
Mary [97709], 9
Mary wife of Cornelius [98192], 206
Patrick [95830], 415
Rose [107923], 426
KENDRICK
John [94865], 371
Mary [94854], 322, 371
KENNEDY
Charles [98384], 382
KENNEY
Joseph I. [108492], 179
William C. [108491], 179
KENYON
Catherine wife of James [93724], 158
Charles E. [93718], 159
Elizabeth [101199], 159
Herbert [93720], 159
James [101200], 158
James [93723], 158
James H. [93717], 133, 158
Jennie E. [101201], 159
Julia [93721], 159
Margaret L. [93719], 159
Mary [93722], 159
KIERNAN
Corinne Ursula [107130], 297
KIRKWOOD
Harold [96239], 92
Mr. [96237], 69, 92
Virginia [96238], 92
KITTY
Mary [100179], 396
KNECHT
Edward [104931], 163
KNIGHT
James [88998], 280
James B. [88997], 224, 279
KRAFT

Mr. [104933], 163
LACY
Catherine [106224], 290
LAMBERT
Annie V. [94717], 264
Catherine [98728], 265
Elizabeth [98726], 265
Ethel M. [94718], 265
Irene [94719], 265
James [96230], 383
John [98724], 264
John Joseph [94716], 264
Lulu [96224], 383
Mary E. [98727], 264
Thomas C. [94715], 212, 264
LANNAHAN
Mary [96090], 412
LANNON?
Winifred Frances [91826], 103
LAWLOR
Jennie [93116], 148, 168
Robert [93117], 168
LEARY
Charles [106473], 83
Dennis [110036], 24
Dennis [94621], 373
Dorothy [106475], 83
Hannah J. [109671], 452
James [110040], 23
Jeremiah [110038], 23
John J. [110037], 23
John T. [104774], 35, 60
Leo [106474], 83
Leonard, [106471], 83
Margaret [107905], 428
Marion [106477], 83
Mary (Keen) [79168], 318, 369
Mary [94684], 211
Mary wife of Dennis [94622], 373
Mary wife of Michael [110042], 23
Michael [110041], 23
Nellie T. [94620], 373
Patrick [93167], 7, 23
Quinlan [110039], 24
Raymond [106472], 83
Timothy Joseph [99630], 60, 82
Wiliam [108990], 196
William [101575], 196
William [106476], 83
LEE

Johh P. [99564], 57
Kyong Sook [108169], 454
LEES
Augustus Edward [96229], 383
Chester Bernard [96227], 383
Cora Marion [96226], 383
Emma Ceclia [96225], 383
John [98391], 382
John Frederick [96223], 382
Joseph R. Jr. [96228], 383
Joseph Robert [93659], 331, 382
Maria wife of John [98392], 382
LEESON
Elizabeth [92797], 295
LENAGAN
Edward [102582], 221
Margaret A. [95729], 221
Margaret wife of Edward [102583], 221
LEONARD
Mr. [101837], 155
LIBBEY
Maude E. [106858], 180
LONG
Frederic [94720], 265
Katherine M. [100569], 375, 434
Mary [103540], 118, 288
Thomas [104724], 434
LOOMIS
Ellen [92528], 136
LOONEY
Cornelius [92191], 19
Joanna [92190], 19
Mary wife of Cornelius [92192], 19
LOUGHLIN
Mary [93499], 155
LOWNEY
Sylvester F. [93156], 274
LUND
Lilly P. [95938], 69
LYNCH
Ellen [102740], 257
Ellen [98844], 227
Eugene P. [104793], 84
Francis 'Frank' [94737], 269
Henry Benedict [94696], 268
James W. [104792], 61, 83
John [102421], 83
John E. [94736], 268

John J. [94695], 213, 268
Marian [94738], 268, 300
Timothy J. [98632], 268
William Austin [94697], 269
LYONS
Johanna [100887], 161
John [92786], 251
Margaret T. [92785], 251
MAHONEY
Hannah F. [92800], 298, 323, 374
James H. [94051], 374
Joanna [94868], 322
Leonora Philomena 'Margaret Fitzgerald' [76866], 299
MALONE
Elizabet F. [99271], 277
MALONEY
Mary G. [106222], 290
Thomas [106223], 290
MANCHESTER
Almira D. [94050], 324
MANNING
Andrew [99786], 424
Bridget [102661], 150
Cora [108897], 424
Dennis Joseph [108894], 361, 424
Mary [99787], 424
Patrick [108898], 424
MARROW
Catherine [94044], 385
MARTIN
Katherine V. [107077], 161
Manuel [107078], 161
Mary wife of Richard [93726], 132
Nancy 'Ann' [93705], 111, 132
Richard [93725], 132
MATHER
John M. [94721], 265
MCALPINE
Mary [96500], 30
MCARDLE
Mary Ann wife of Peter [98841], 228
Peter [98840], 228
Sarah [98839], 228
MCCARTHY
Catherine L. [96630], 259
Catherine wife of Daniel [93394], 386
Hannah F. [96631], 258
Helen [96633], 259

James [109960], 258
John F. [96632], 259
Julia A. [96627], 259
Margaret G. [96629], 259
Mary F. [96634], 259
Timothy [96624], 209, 258
William S. [96628], 259
MCCARTY
Achibald [98306], 287
Alexander 'Sandy' [98305], 234, 287
Catherine [93370], 338, 386
Child [103256], 304
Daniel [93393], 386
Dora A. [97754], 238, 291
James [103249], 287, 303
Jeremiah [98309], 287
John Vincent [103255], 304
Kate wife of Archibald [98307], 287
Martin [94589], 70
Mary [103258], 304
Mary wife of Martin [94590], 70
Patrick [103257], 304
Patrick L. [109599], 288
Rosanna [94588], 43, 70
Timothy [109598], 288
MCDERMOTT
Andrew [93708], 111, 134
Catherine wife of Francis [101212], 134
Francis [101211], 134
Mary [101210], 134
Mary [96957], 279
MCDONALD
John J. [100886], 161
John J. [105960], 141
Mary A. [100883], 137, 161
Mr. [29246], 46, 80
MCDONOUGH
Elizabeth A. [104796], 84
Joseph [79449], 78
Mary M. [104797], 84
Sarah A. [76977], 78
Thomas [104795], 84
Thomas Joseph [104794], 61, 84
MCGAN
Ellen [93872], 379
MCGAW
Annie [93714], 157
Catherine J. [93713], 157
Catherine wife of Edward [97847], 157
Edward [97846], 157

Elizabeth [101208], 158
George [93711], 132, 157
George Edward Jr. [93716], 158
Mary [93712], 157
Rose E. [93715], 157
MCGOVERN
Charles [94043], 385
Charles [97796], 385
Daniel [94045], 385
John M. [97795], 385
Peter [94042], 336, 385
MCGRADY
Hannah Wife Of James [83670], 57
James [83669], 57
Joseph [79262], 57
MCGRAW
John [93162], 302
John F. [102189], 302
John Jr. [93161], 276, 302
Margaret wife of John F. [102190], 303
Sarah [92419], 81
MCGUINESS
Mary [100556], 418
MCGUIRE
Ann Marie [92300], 454
Ann wife of James [92991], 241
Elizabeth [92989], 202, 241
James [92990], 241
John James [92299], 445, 454
MCGUIRK
William [93285], 340, 392
MCHAN
Catherine [93620], 355, 402
John [93621], 402
MCINTIRE
Bridget [93173], 380
MCKENNEY
Elizabeth wife of Philip [94402], 270
James E. [95880], 419
Marietta C. [95879], 419
Mary E. [94383], 214, 270
Philip [94403], 270
MCKEON
Mary wife of Patrick [101443], 25
Patrick [101442], 25
Patrick [94346], 25
MCLACHLAN
Mary [96498], 30
Phillip [96499], 30

MCLEAN
Helen [92296], 445
MCMAHON
Catherine [99621], 397
John B. [105910], 225, 286
Martha [95583], 394
MCMELLON
John [99013], 359
John [99014], 359
Nancy wife of John [99015], 359
MCNAMARA
Delia [93100], 343, 394
Roger [95582], 394
MCNERNEY
James Daniel [889], 96
John Francis [75639], 96
MCQUEENEY
Mary E. [104863], 137, 164
Michael [104864], 164
MCQUIRK
Lawrence [93287], 392
Margaret [93286], 392
MEANY
Margaret [93171], 328, 380
Patrick [93172], 380
MEEHAN
Annie [102906], 261
MILBY
George [96952], 379
Hugh [93871], 379
John [96949], 379
Robert [93870], 328, 379
Robert Jr. [96950], 379
Samuel [96948], 379
William [96951], 379
MILLER
James [97391], 139
Jane wife of James [97392], 139
Susan [92954], 113, 139, 300
MINEHAN
Daniel Sylvester [93480], 396
MINNEHAN
Daniel [100175], 396
John [93475], 349, 396
MITCHELL
James [79260], 81
James [92418], 81
Robert F. [79259], 57, 81
MOONEY
James B. [104897], 162, 179
Kathleen M. [104898], 179

MORAN
John [98145], 120
Kathleen [11045], 101
Thomas [98146], 120
MORGAN
Ellen F. [93326], 276, 301
Patrick G. [93327], 301
MORIARTY
Jeremiah [97611], 420
Joanna Wife Of Michael [83672], 56
Johanna [97605], 361, 420
John W. [79261], 56
Michael [83671], 56
MORISS
Mary [79452], 78
MORLEY
Elizabeth Anne [108165], 454
Lewis Richard [108166], 454
MORRIS
Bridget [100142], 66
MORRISSEY
Alice [79188], 451
Catherine wife of William [97819], 346
Mary [97817], 346
William [97818], 346
MOSS
Mary A. [104352], 450
MULLANEY
Agnes [109600], 288
Dorothy Bridget [107131], 297
MULLINS
Ellen [93294], 314, 348
Jeremiah [93301], 348
MURPHY
Anna [94864], 431, 452
Anna wife of Daniel [93389], 387
Catherine [96088], 357, 412
Cornelius [104346], 316, 361
Cornelius [96305], 221
Daniel [104354], 362
Daniel [93388], 387
Daniel [96800], 234
Delia [107921], 426
Dennis [108420], 203
Dennis [93278], 391
Dennis [98200], 254
Ellen [104357], 363
Ellen [92957], 185, 201, 375
Ellen T. [93277], 339, 391

Hannah [95920], 11, 40, 273
Hannah [95966], 108, 126
Hannah [97944], 362, 425
Hannah 'Joanna' [77088], 76
Hanora [107704], 227
Hanora [97271], 310, 334
James [104356], 363
Jennie P. [92277], 406, 442
Jeremiah [98184], 206, 254
Jeremiah [98185], 254
Johanna [106581], 410
John [101423], 22
John [104353], 362
John [104359], 308, 316
John [98934], 282
Julia [104901], 162
Julia [96799], 234
Julia [97551], 334
Margaret [93512], 3, 10
Margaret [95852], 312, 344
Margaret [98149], 186, 203
Margaret [98199], 254
Margaret [98379], 310
Margaret wife of Dennis [108421], 203
Martin [104383], 363
Mary [101422], 7, 22
Mary [92012], 299
Mary [96300], 188, 221
Mary A. [104355], 362
Mary E. [101207], 157
Mary E. [106280], 440
Mary wife of Cornelius [96306], 221
Mary wife of Daniel [96908], 234
Mary wife of Michael [93856], 201
Matthew [104358], 363
Michael [104381], 363
Michael [93855], 201
Mr. [93832], 201
Patrick [100566], 442
Peter [104382], 363
Theresa [104384], 362
Theresa [93387], 387
Thomas [107922], 426
Thomas [96089], 412
Timothy [101466], 126, 344
MURRAY
Jeremiah [94101], 274
Lawrence [93153], 217, 274
Margaret [93154], 274
Mary C. [93155], 274

MYLES
Edward [94516], 300
Gertrude A. [94518], 300
James E. [94519], 301
James T. [94515], 270, 300
Jennie A. [94520], 301
Margaret [94522], 301
Raymond [94521], 301
NAVIN
Ellen [95010], 226
Margaret [99778], 421, 448
William P. Sr. [99779], 448
NAWROCKI
Margaret Mary [108571], 86
NEWMAN
Joanna [97390], 105, 113
NEYLAN
Charles P. [93470], 398
NOONAN
John [94348], 26
Michael [94349], 26
NUGENT
Mary A. [97397], 139
Thomas [97398], 139
OBRIEN
Catherine [100562], 447
Ellen [92344], 280
Harriett [93849], 237
James W. [100561], 418, 446
John J. [92343], 224, 280
Margaret [101194], 134
Michael [104949], 280
William [93850], 237
O'BRIEN
Edward [94340], 59
Elizabeth J. [94339], 26, 59
OCONNELL
Catherine [93302], 348
David [98114], 278
David A. [98116], 278
Florence [98122], 279
Joanna [98120], 278
John E. [98118], 279
Mary E. [98119], 278
Michael [98112], 218, 278
Michael [98121], 279
Stephen J. [98117], 279
OCONNOR
Anna B. [99191], 439
Daniel Francis [99185], 391, 439
Daniel Jr. [99188], 439
Ellen J. [99189], 439
John [99186], 439
John Joseph [99190], 439

Margaret L. [99192], 439
Mary [99193], 439
ODONNEL
Stephen E. [29257], 81
O'LEARY
Dennis P. [102738], 209, 257
Elizabeth 'Lizzie' H. [102748], 257
Ellen F. [102746], 257
Hannah M. [102747], 257
Julietta [102742], 257
Mary Elizabeth [102741], 257
Timothy [102739], 257
ONEAL
Ellen Wife Of Jeremiah [4939], 18
Margaret wife of Timothy [93320], 216
Timothy [93319], 216
ONEIL
Catherine [101439], 7, 23
Catherine [79383], 19
Catherine [84014], 5
Catherine [92854], 118
Corneilius [5205], 5, 16
Cornelius [96067], 145
Daniel [91900], 20
Dennis [79378], 2, 5
Dennis [79384], 19
Dennis [84015], 5
Edmund [5228], 19
Genevieve Theresa [11094], 77, 95
Hannah [93658], 306, 310
Hanora 'Annie' [79386], 20, 58
James E. [79385], 19
Jeremiah [83968], 5
Jeremiah H. [79381], 18
Johanna [110116], 236
John [98378], 310
John E. [92188], 18
Josephine [105828], 178
Margaret [93176], 122, 145
Margaret wife of Cornelius [96068], 145
Mary [92189], 19
Mary [92647], 187, 216
Mary [93868], 329
Mary wife of Cornelius [91300], 1, 3
Michael [97899], 334
Mr. [100157], 37
Patrick [84016], 5

Bartholomew [83621], 180
Bartholomew 'Batt'
(Suonish) [98177], 182, 185
Bartholomew 'Battey'
[93175], 122, 144
Benjamin [96031], 143
Bernadette [96335], 91
Bertha [99357], 87
Bridget [103250], 287, 304
Bridget [93374], 311, 336
Bridget [93654], 332
Bridget [94350], 26
Bridget [97612], 420
Bridget Mary [97471], 120
Bridget wife of Daniel
[94059], 306, 309
Bridget wife of Daniel
[94259], 306, 309, 353
Catherine [100152], 37
Catherine [100296], 104,
106, 198
Catherine [104347], 316,
362
Catherine [104947], 138
Catherine [108991], 196
Catherine [109206], 28
Catherine [109597], 288
Catherine [92276], 359, 417
Catherine [92623], 1, 2
Catherine [92968], 7, 28
Catherine [93318], 217
Catherine [93623], 354
Catherine [94249], 327, 377
Catherine [94624], 325
Catherine [94685], 165,
211, 261
Catherine [95441], 194, 232
Catherine [96149], 192
Catherine [96185], 366, 426
Catherine [96304], 222
Catherine [96817], 152, 172
Catherine [97346], 334
Catherine [97472], 121
Catherine [97554], 334
Catherine [99788], 361
Catherine A. [99037], 26, 59
Catherine F. [79348], 204,
245
Catherine F. [93642], 148,
169
Catherine Gertrude 'Katie'
[99629], 60, 83
Catherine 'Kate' [100429],
423
Catherine 'Katie' [96614],
207

Catherine L. [104873], 137,
160
Catherine L. [93652], 332
Catherine L. [96617], 209,
258
Catherine Linus [92293],
444
Catherine M. [106281], 393,
439
Catherine mother of
Hannah [100446], 120
Catherine wife of Charles
[104976], 293, 305
Catherine wife of Daniel
[108442], 1
Catherine wife of Daniel
[99790], 308, 316
Catherine wife of James
[93236], 309, 318
Catherine wife of Jeremiah
[91907], 307, 314
Catherine wife of Joseph
[104882], 136, 308, 317
Catherine wife of Michael
[98161], 248
Charles [107750], 66
Charles [95725], 222
Charles [95940], 69
Charles A. [94571], 42
Charles A. [94910], 71
Charles D. [93829], 240
Charles E. [105290], 168
Charles Henry [105187],
364
Charles M. [106147], 284
Charles R. [104978], 305
Charles Raymond [104972],
292, 304
Child [101198], 134
Child [94994], 282
Child [96069], 145
Child [99359], 88
Clara [100428], 423
Clara G. [104891], 162
Clarence [100431], 423
Clarence Gray [94592], 71
Cornelius [107938], 366
Cornelius [91299], 1, 3
Cornelius [92062], 3
Cornelius [92961], 202
Cornelius [93221], 182, 184
Cornelius [93558], 106, 114
Cornelius [95461], 33
Cornelius [96307], 183, 187
Cornelius [96612], 209
Cornelius [96622], 292

Cornelius [97272], 306, 310
Cornelius [97389], 105, 112
Cornelius [97408], 113
Cornelius [97410], 104, 105
Cornelius [97552], 333
Cornelius [98159], 204, 246
Cornelius A. [98165], 249
Cornelius B. ' Cornie'
[96611], 186, 206
Cornelius D. [95828], 357,
413
Cornelius D. Jr. [95837],
416, 445
Cornelius J. [101476], 153,
176
Cornelius M. [96299], 188,
219
Cornelius M. [96997], 118
Cornelius 'Neil' [101477],
177
Daniel [100217], 306, 311
Daniel [100221], 341
Daniel [103539], 118, 288
Daniel [108441], 1
Daniel [92840], 307, 311
Daniel [93238], 318
Daniel [93269], 311, 334
Daniel [93282], 336
Daniel [93324], 306, 310
Daniel [93610], 125
Daniel [93657], 306, 310
Daniel [94058], 306, 309
Daniel [94096], 307, 315
Daniel [94258], 306, 309,
353
Daniel [94623], 325
Daniel [94971], 231
Daniel [95871], 307, 315
Daniel [96048], 106, 121
Daniel [96059], 145
Daniel [96198], 108, 126
Daniel [96309], 188
Daniel [96747], 192, 228
Daniel [96977], 119
Daniel [97563], 312, 344
Daniel [98148], 186, 202
Daniel [98169], 248
Daniel [99789], 307, 316
Daniel A. [95154], 241
Daniel B. [95965], 108, 125
Daniel C. [100884], 112,
136, 317, 366
Daniel C. [93280], 311, 338
Daniel C. [94385], 270
Daniel C. [96593], 208

Daniel C. Jr. [93274], 339, 389
Daniel D. [93293], 314, 346
Daniel David (Rev.) [92280], 443
Daniel David [92262], 356, 359, 402, 417
Daniel David Jr. [92268], 407
Daniel Dennis [92963], 202, 240
Daniel Dennis [93304], 350
Daniel F. [93317], 218
Daniel F. [94392], 410, 445
Daniel F. Jr. [94399], 445
Daniel H. [100213], 393
Daniel J. [105827], 178
Daniel J. [105832], 179
Daniel K. [93261], 310, 332
Daniel O. [93314], 216
Daniel P. [107700], 190, 227
Daniel R. [92799], 298, 323, 373
Daniel R. [96203], 129
Daniel Robert [94029], 143
Daniel S. [92008], 204, 250, 433
Daniel S. Jr. [92780], 251
Daughter [92857], 36
David [95469], 409
David [96907], 290
Dennis (Shearhig) [107722], 182, 183
Dennis (Vallig) [93840], 182, 185
Dennis [101444], 34
Dennis [104348], 425
Dennis [104945], 112, 137
Dennis [92415], 53
Dennis [93291], 33
Dennis [93298], 349
Dennis [93615], 123, 182, 184
Dennis [94040], 340
Dennis [94247], 326
Dennis [94382], 214, 269
Dennis [95971], 126
Dennis [96733], 67, 90
Dennis [96884], 307, 315
Dennis [99200], 306, 311
Dennis J. [101191], 105, 108
Dennis J. [109670], 452
Dennis V. [94533], 202, 241, 324, 375

Donal (Scan) [110143], 189
Dora [109208], 28
Dora [97654], 7, 27
Dora [97804], 345, 395
Dora F. [94690], 212, 265
Dorothy M. [105700], 180
Edmond Robert [96236], 69, 91
Edmond Robert Jr. [99221], 91
Edward [94874], 307, 312
Edward [95926], 42
Edward A. Jr. [100571], 434
Edward Anthony [94055], 375, 433
Edward E. [106142], 284
Edward F. [94577], 43, 69
Edward F. [95927], 135, 159
Edward F. 'Eddie' [96739], 67, 86
Edward Francis [94366], 178
Edward J. [94908], 70
Edward M. [98168], 249
Eileen [104790], 61
Eliza C. [100422], 361, 422
Elizabeth [100155], 38
Elizabeth [101258], 114
Elizabeth [106229], 289
Elizabeth [79401], 450
Elizabeth [92337], 224
Elizabeth [94708], 263
Elizabeth [98717], 401
Elizabeth [99517], 63
Elizabeth A. wife of Frank [99884], 375
Elizabeth 'Betsy' [97808], 395
Elizabeth F. [99358], 87
Elizabeth G. [93710], 133
Elizabeth 'Lizzie' [93466], 350
Elizabeth 'Lizzie' [94689], 212, 267
Elizabeth T. [96736], 89
Ellen [100974], 344
Ellen [102422], 83
Ellen [108995], 195
Ellen [109941], 313
Ellen [110142], 189
Ellen [92258], 315, 356, 417
Ellen [92970], 8, 31
Ellen [93635], 148
Ellen [93656], 332
Ellen [93873], 327, 378

Ellen [94682], 186, 211
Ellen [96205], 130
Ellen [96310], 228
Ellen [97018], 365
Ellen [97465], 106, 120
Ellen [97470], 120
Ellen [97614], 316, 360
Ellen [99012], 359
Ellen [99197], 339
Ellen [9983], 95
Ellen A. 'Nellie' [95014], 225, 284
Ellen F. 'Lena' [94706], 139, 165, 262, 300
Ellen M. [97945], 426
Ellen 'Nellie' [100430], 423
Ellen 'Nellie' [106311], 350
Ellen Theresa [94988], 225, 285
Ellen V. [93556], 118
Ellen V. [94540], 244
Ellen W. [93605], 125, 149
Ellen wife of Jeremiah [92837], 312, 343
Ellen wife of John [102185], 218
Ellen wife of Michael [107920], 308, 316
Ellen wife of Timothy [101490], 104, 107
Emma F. [100143], 66
Emma G. [92801], 252
Estelle M. [96508], 92
Esther [97406], 139
Ethel Victoria [95934], 69
Eugene (Skilty) [92965], 2, 5
Eugene [101428], 22
Eugene [92254], 61
Eugene [92303], 35, 61
Eugene [93072], 165, 212, 262
Eugene [93290], 33
Eugene [94707], 263
Eugene [95724], 221
Eugene [96751], 228
Eugene [96797], 235, 288
Eugene [97407], 114
Eugene [97655], 27
Eugene [97807], 395
Eunice [105289], 168
Florence [101838], 104, 108
Florence [92646], 187, 214
Florence [97000], 141
Florence Jr. [93148], 218

Frances G. [101724], 438, 452

Frances M. [104892], 162

Francis [93159], 276

Francis A. [94859], 432

Francis A. 'Frank' [98715], 400

Francis 'Frank' [95941], 69

Francis 'Frank' [97653], 7, 26

Francis P. 'Frank' [94925], 380

Francis S. [104895], 161

Francis Timothy [101626], 58

Frank [100432], 424

Frank [93112], 66

Frank [96093], 413

Frank A. [92782], 252

Frank Robert [94054], 374

Franklin [94595], 71

Frederick Thomas [94863], 432

Genevieve [105292], 168

Genevieve [93186], 401

Genevieve [99514], 63

George [93177], 145

George [96036], 143

George F. [92648], 276

George F. [94972], 232

Gerald [97003], 141

Gertrude [94359], 155

Gertrude [94391], 271

Gertrude C. [98718], 401

Gertrude M. [100568], 375

Grace L [94591], 71

Hannah [100219], 341

Hannah [107464], 185, 198

Hannah [92838], 343

Hannah [92959], 201

Hannah [93237], 318

Hannah [93483], 350

Hannah [93634], 148

Hannah [93753], 321

Hannah [94401], 214

Hannah [96151], 192

Hannah [96301], 221, 279

Hannah [96623], 209

Hannah [96816], 152

Hannah [96878], 315, 357

Hannah [96980], 104, 106

Hannah [98578], 316

Hannah 'Anna' [92342], 225

Hannah 'Anna' [95110], 194, 229

Hannah 'Annie' F. [93651], 331, 380

Hannah 'Annie' V. [96998], 119, 140

Hannah E. [92263], 357, 359, 406, 416

Hannah M. 'Annie' [93617], 124, 147, 354, 399

Hannah wife of Cornelius [96308], 183, 188

Hannah wife of Dennis [99201], 306, 311

Hannah wife of James [97469], 106, 120

Hanora [92255], 61

Hanora [94041], 336

Hanora 'Annie' [94686], 212

Hanora wife of Patrick [105191], 308, 316

Helen [106145], 284

Helen [95013], 282

Helen L. [94219], 63, 84

Helen M. [96606], 160

Helen P. 'Ella' [95836], 416

Helena G. 'Lena' [100144], 66

Helena T. 'Lena' [94692], 213, 268

Helena V. [92281], 443

Helene [104889], 164

Henry Aloysious [98167], 249

Henry Francis [107124], 297

Henry Francis [92778], 251, 296

Henry Patrick [93557], 117

Hetty E. [104888], 164

Humphrey [97336], 307, 313

Isabella [100225], 342

Isabella 'Bella' [94852], 371, 431

Isabelle E. 'Bella' [94858], 432

Isabelle T. 'Belle' [93831], 240, 293

James [100425], 423

James [106143], 284

James [93235], 309, 318

James [94260], 307, 314, 325

James [96221], 331

James [96780], 192

James [97466], 104, 106

James [97473], 120

James A. [94857], 431, 451

James Buffington [94535], 243

James D. [92259], 357, 410

James E. [101445], 33

James E. [93045], 411

James E. [94352], 409

James E. [94987], 225, 283

James E. [96741], 90

James Edward [92264], 406, 441

James Edward [92278], 442

James Edward [92784], 251, 294

James Eugene [96594], 159, 393

James F. [100511], 395

James F. [94389], 270

James F. [97464], 106, 119

James Francis [101478], 177

James Lester [97610], 421

James M. [105829], 161, 178

James M. [107672], 153

James M. [95923], 40

James P. [93924], 361, 422

James W. [93160], 276, 301

Jane [94057], 323

Jeffery E. [108572], 85

Jeffery E. [92846], 36, 61

Jeffery E. Jr. [94218], 63

Jeffrey (Shearhig) [94386], 67, 187, 213

Jeffrey E. [96734], 67

Jeffrey 'Jefferson' [94384], 270

Jennie E. [105291], 168, 180

Jennie V. [92779], 252

Jeremiah [100224], 342

Jeremiah [101449], 171

Jeremiah [101480], 176

Jeremiah [104971], 292

Jeremiah [108443], 4

Jeremiah [91906], 307, 314

Jeremiah [92644], 217, 274

Jeremiah [92802], 250

Jeremiah [92844], 9, 36

Jeremiah [93149], 183, 187

Jeremiah [93479], 307, 313

Jeremiah [93611], 124, 146, 354, 399

Jeremiah [93633], 148

Jeremiah [93879], 328

Jeremiah [95226], 348

Jeremiah [96206], 129
Jeremiah [96815], 152, 170
Jeremiah [96981], 116
Jeremiah [97608], 421
Jeremiah [97712], 36
Jeremiah [98393], 351
Jeremiah B. [92962], 202, 238
Jeremiah B. [93168], 310, 327
Jeremiah B. [93830], 240, 291
Jeremiah C. [92777], 250
Jeremiah C. [92836], 312, 342
Jeremiah C. 'Jerry' [92853], 118
Jeremiah 'Jerry' [95968], 126
Joanna [101429], 22
Joanna [109207], 28
Joanna [93292], 33
Joanna [98152], 204, 248
JoAnna 'Hannah' [94047], 323
Joannah C. [96616], 209, 256
Joannah K. [97553], 333
Johanna [93166], 7, 23
Johanna [93232], 356
Johanna [93869], 328, 379
Johanna [94363], 130
Johanna Josephine [94687], 212, 263
Johanna M. [92009], 204, 250, 433
Johanna wife of Cornelius [97273], 306, 310
Johanna wife of Jeremiah [97713], 36
Johannah wife of Timothy [98849], 182, 183
John (Suonish) [95453], 182, 184
John [100156], 38
John [100443], 422
John [100447], 120
John [101196], 104
John [101421], 7, 20
John [101427], 22
John [102184], 218
John [103252], 182, 185
John [104894], 137
John [104946], 138
John [107463], 185, 199
John [109678], 306, 311

John [110134], 1
John [93174], 409
John [93316], 217
John [93727], 320
John [94094], 354
John [94387], 182, 186
John [94464], 194
John [94576], 43
John [94625], 326
John [94683], 211
John [94688], 213
John [94850], 372, 431
John [94970], 231
John [95967], 126
John [96202], 128
John [96303], 221
John [96979], 104, 105
John [97474], 121
John [97564], 307, 312
John [99196], 339
John A. [94357], 156, 177
John Aloysius (Rev.) [92267], 406
John B. [96057], 145
John C. [100334], 208
John C. [93099], 343, 393
John C. [94572], 42
John D. [93273], 336
John D. [93496], 129, 154
John D. [93703], 110
John D. [99024], 59
John E. [100426], 422
John E. [101479], 177
John E. [93115], 148, 167
John E. [94855], 431
John E. [97951], 426, 449
John Ed [106582], 410
John F. [96995], 117
John father of Hannah [100445], 120
John Francis [94365], 178
John H. [95157], 241
John H. [98153], 204
John J. [101463], 171
John J. [96814], 152
John J. [97607], 421, 447
John J. [99781], 448
John Joseph [97088], 165, 180
John L. [93329], 302
John L. [94547], 242
John L. [97943], 362, 425
John M. [100139], 10, 36
John M. [95922], 40
John P. [95011], 282
John Philip [109212], 28

John T. [93515], 11, 42
John T. [94046], 322
John W. [92260], 357, 411
John W. [98174], 249
John Walter [109947], 452
Joseph [104881], 136, 308, 317
Joseph [104948], 136
Joseph A. [92270], 407
Joseph H. [104869], 137, 162
Joseph H. [93276], 336
Joseph Lawrence [94361], 155, 177
Joseph William [94860], 432
Julia (Suonish) [98179], 186, 204
Julia [101426], 22
Julia [104950], 280
Julia [106228], 290
Julia [108109], 430
Julia [108996], 195
Julia [92839], 344
Julia [92969], 7, 29
Julia [93147], 218, 276
Julia [93604], 107, 122, 184, 198, 399
Julia [93702], 111, 134
Julia [93709], 133
Julia [94250], 326, 377
Julia [96049], 106, 122
Julia [96987], 106
Julia A. [100223], 341
Julia A. [93227], 322, 372
Julia A. [94691], 212, 266
Julia A. [95878], 366, 419, 427
Julia A. [97475], 121
Julia Ann [101716], 389, 437
Julia E. [93275], 336
Julia L. [100210], 341, 393
Julia M. [104867], 137, 162
Julia wife of Daniel [93325], 306, 310
Julia wife of Dennis [92416], 53
Julia wife of James [97467], 104, 106
Julia wife of John [109606], 182, 185
Julia wife of John [94388], 183, 187
Julia wife of John [97565], 307, 312

Julia wife of Timothy [94324], 1, 2
Kate [94578], 43
Katherine [94216], 62
Katherine A. [92650], 276, 302
Kathryn F. [93330], 302
Kathryn Louise [94367], 178
Kenneth L. [100572], 434
Lawrence J. [94861], 432
Leanore Gertrude [94368], 178
Lena F. [94594], 70
Leo [104973], 293
Leonora [104788], 61, 83
Lillian [94356], 155
Lillian M. [94372], 177
Lillian M. [97002], 141
Loretta M. [104887], 164
Louise C. [98166], 249, 294
Mae R. [108490], 177
Margaret (Cumba) [97806], 313, 344
Margaret (Rocktirre) [110144], 189
Margaret [100153], 38
Margaret [100220], 341
Margaret [101425], 22
Margaret [104872], 105, 111, 368
Margaret [104893], 137
Margaret [106141], 284
Margaret [108440], 1, 3
Margaret [1489], 3, 11
Margaret [92328], 189, 223
Margaret [92341], 224, 280
Margaret [92960], 202, 237
Margaret [93239], 318
Margaret [93272], 336
Margaret [93281], 311, 339
Margaret [93283], 340
Margaret [93303], 349, 397
Margaret [93340], 436
Margaret [93612], 125
Margaret [93628], 354
Margaret [93707], 133, 158
Margaret [94574], 42
Margaret [95972], 126, 153
Margaret [96062], 145
Margaret [96183], 317, 366
Margaret [96201], 128
Margaret [96885], 307, 315
Margaret [97405], 139
Margaret [98151], 246
Margaret [98157], 203, 245
Margaret [98295], 245

Margaret [98579], 316
Margaret [98835], 191, 227
Margaret [99516], 63
Margaret A. [100789], 208, 255
Margaret Ellen [92275], 360, 418, 428
Margaret Ellen [99184], 391, 438
Margaret G. [106503], 118, 140
Margaret J. [94252], 326
Margaret J. [98162], 248, 294
Margaret Jane [94534], 202, 242, 324, 375
Margaret L. [104789], 61, 84
Margaret L. [81208], 252, 298
Margaret M. [107125], 297
Margaret M. [95924], 42
Margaret 'Maggie' [95727], 222
Margaret Marion [95935], 69
Margaret T. J. [93745], 321
Margaret V. [93152], 217, 273
Margaret wife of Dennis [93616], 123, 182, 184
Margaret wife of Humphrey [97337], 307, 313
Margaret wife of Jeremiah [96982], 116
Margaret wife of John D. [93704], 111
Margaret wife of McCann [93511], 1, 2
Margaret wife of Timothy [104878], 104, 105
Margaret wife of Timothy [96779], 228
Marguerite R. [94056], 298
Maria [96204], 130
Marion wife of Arthur [98720], 402
Mark [93509], 2, 9
Mark [94586], 43
Mark [95726], 222
Mark A. 'Marcus' [93110], 38, 63
Martha L. [93101], 394, 440
Mary (Fune) [94061], 58
Mary (Shearhig) [107706], 183, 189

Mary [100218], 341
Mary [103254], 304
Mary [104360], 308, 316
Mary [106146], 284
Mary [108899], 424
Mary [110238], 214
Mary [1511], 13, 53
Mary [91908], 314
Mary [92010], 250
Mary [92436], 334, 383
Mary [92851], 343
Mary [92958], 201, 236
Mary [92967], 7, 24
Mary [93632], 147
Mary [94049], 324
Mary [94217], 62
Mary [94256], 326, 376
Mary [94362], 129
Mary [94693], 211, 259
Mary [95012], 282
Mary [95046], 26
Mary [95456], 193
Mary [95462], 34
Mary [95970], 126
Mary [96055], 122
Mary [96186], 366
Mary [96607], 160
Mary [96637], 22
Mary [96748], 192, 228
Mary [97409], 113
Mary [97555], 334
Mary [98186], 254
Mary [98312], 199, 233
Mary [98845], 192
Mary [99195], 391
Mary A. [100154], 38
Mary A. [104883], 136
Mary A. [106352], 286
Mary A. [93284], 339, 392
Mary A. [93289], 8, 33
Mary A. [93296], 349, 396
Mary A. [93653], 331, 382
Mary A. [94969], 231, 286
Mary A. [95930], 111, 134
Mary A. [96060], 145
Mary A. [96302], 221
Mary Ann [93271], 335, 384
Mary Ann [93602], 124, 149
Mary Ann [93625], 354
Mary Ann [93706], 132, 156
Mary Ann [98113], 218, 278
Mary Catherine [92279], 443
Mary D. [92297], 445, 453
Mary D. [94536], 244
Mary E. [92266], 406

Mary E. [92649], 275
Mary E. [93046], 411
Mary E. [93559], 106, 116
Mary E. [93828], 240
Mary E. [94099], 402
Mary E. [94355], 155
Mary E. [94396], 409
Mary E. [94514], 270, 300
Mary E. [94705], 262
Mary E. [95584], 395
Mary E. [96092], 413
Mary E. [96978], 117
Mary E. [98163], 248
Mary Ellen [109205], 28, 60
Mary Ellen [97609], 421, 448
Mary Etta [101451], 172
Mary F. [94909], 71
Mary F. [96818], 153, 175
Mary Geneveive [95835], 415
Mary H. [92273], 315, 358, 406
Mary J. [102188], 276
Mary J. [79379], 2, 4
Mary J. [97394], 139
Mary J. [99353], 87
Mary Jane [100333], 208, 254
Mary Jane [94573], 42
Mary L. [104974], 293
Mary L. [94856], 431
Mary Louise [105831], 178
Mary Louise [99337], 416
Mary Louise [99339], 446
Mary M. [93516], 11, 42
Mary M. [96731], 40, 66, 214, 273
Mary W. [104977], 305
Mary wife of Cornelius [97411], 104, 105
Mary wife of Daniel [92841], 307, 312
Mary wife of Daniel [94097], 307, 315
Mary wife of Daniel [95872], 307, 315
Mary wife of Dennis [104349], 425
Mary wife of Dennis [107723], 182, 183
Mary wife of Eugene [97656], 27
Mary wife of Florence [101839], 104, 108

Mary wife of James [94261], 307, 314, 325
Mary wife of John [100444], 422
Mary wife of John [109680], 306, 311
Mary wife of Michael [96087], 307, 315
Mary wife of Michael [96813], 126, 152
Mary wife of Timothy [93747], 306, 309
Mary wife of Timothy [94680], 182, 186
Matilda Ellen [93638], 148
Matilda S. [94100], 402
Maurice F. 'Morris' [94989], 225
McCann [93510], 1, 2
Michael [101430], 22
Michael [101446], 34
Michael [107919], 308, 316
Michael [93288], 8, 32
Michael [94027], 122, 141
Michael [95111], 194
Michael [96086], 307, 315
Michael [96200], 128
Michael [97657], 28
Michael [98160], 248
Michael [99625], 83
Michael D. [92256], 315, 355, 417
Michael D. [96812], 126, 151
Michael D. Jr. [92261], 357, 407
Michael E. [104866], 136
Michael F. [93070], 262
Michael F. [95015], 284
Michael F. [96058], 146
Michael Francis [98164], 248
Michael H. [94397], 409
Michael H. [95728], 221
Michael Henry [92265], 406, 443
Michael Henry [92295], 445
Michael James [96732], 67, 88
Michael M. [95921], 11, 38, 273
Michael T. [96182], 317, 365
Mildred [95838], 416
Mildred [99513], 63
Miriam [98723], 401

Mortimer [100209], 341, 392
Mortimer [100211], 311, 340
Mortimer J. [93609], 124
Mortimer 'Murtaugh' [93603], 107, 123, 184, 197, 399
Nancy [94248], 309, 314, 325, 351
Nora 'Annie' [96063], 146, 166
Owen 'Eugene' [95019], 362
Owen Eugene [98842], 184, 191
Owen J. [94221], 63
Patrick (Vallig) [92956], 185, 199, 375
Patrick [101701], 437
Patrick [103253], 304
Patrick [105190], 308, 316
Patrick [107703], 227
Patrick [107892], 284
Patrick [108391], 344
Patrick [92934], 107
Patrick [94694], 213
Patrick [95480], 34
Patrick [95873], 359
Patrick [95969], 126
Patrick [97013], 316, 363
Patrick [97613], 316, 360
Patrick [98158], 203
Patrick [98847], 192
Patrick D. [92736], 128
Patrick D. [93649], 310, 329
Patrick D. [93701], 111, 131
Patrick H. [104884], 136
Patrick K. [93865], 328
Patrick P. [92338], 189, 224
Patrick R. [93184], 355, 399
Patrick R. [93618], 147, 315, 353
Paul Brendan [100573], 435
Pauline G. [94711], 165
Peter [93728], 309, 318
Peter [97604], 361, 419
Peter F. [100882], 137, 161
Philip [92272], 315, 359, 406
Philip [92336], 224
Philip [94993], 282
Philip Fidelis Harrington [106221], 289
Phillip [92340], 224
Ralph Tangney [96737], 89
Regina [96235], 69
Regina M. [99219], 91
Rena J. [98716], 401

Richard [100159], 11
Richard [93299], 349
Richard [99354], 88
Richard James [95925], 40, 68
Robert J. [104862], 137, 163
Robert J. [104886], 164
Robert Vincent [94862], 432
Roseanna [92345], 282
Ruth [104890], 164
Sarah [101452], 172
Sarah Jane [108893], 361, 424
Sarah Jane [97606], 421
Stephen [96743], 214
Susan wife of Philip [106230], 290
Susanah G. [97404], 139
Sylvester [93467], 350
Theresa [94358], 155
Thomas [94853], 322, 371
Thomas [94924], 380
Thomas [97015], 364
Thomas [97658], 27
Thomas F. [92953], 113, 138, 300
Thomas F. [93170], 328, 379
Thomas F. Jr. [97393], 139
Thomas K. [97548], 334
Timothy (Suonish) [93513], 42
Timothy (Suonish) [95438], 184, 192
Timothy [100222], 341
Timothy [101489], 104, 107
Timothy [104791], 61
Timothy [104877], 104, 105
Timothy [109394], 351
Timothy [92850], 344
Timothy [93229], 242, 309, 321
Timothy [93315], 216
Timothy [93339], 436
Timothy [93614], 124
Timothy [93746], 306, 309
Timothy [93864], 328
Timothy [94060], 58
Timothy [94251], 309, 314, 324, 353
Timothy [94323], 1, 2
Timothy [94587], 43
Timothy [94679], 182, 186
Timothy [94681], 186, 209
Timothy [94843], 431

Timothy [94873], 312
Timothy [94965], 194, 230
Timothy [95222], 321
Timothy [96056], 122
Timothy [96778], 228
Timothy [97412], 114
Timothy [97468], 120
Timothy A. [96730], 40, 67, 214, 271
Timothy E. [99355], 88
Timothy F. [94986], 225, 280
Timothy J. [94066], 20, 58
Timothy O. [101570], 324
Timothy O. [94048], 323
Timothy 'Timy' [98848], 182, 183
Walter [97396], 139
Wife of John [95454], 182, 184
wife of Patrick [93598], 107
William [94095], 354
William [96061], 146
William Ambrose [94710], 139, 164, 263, 300
William E. [92795], 295
William E. [94390], 271
William Edward [94030], 143
William F. [106148], 284
William H. [93833], 240
William H. [99356], 87
William James [96742], 89
William Joseph [104732], 85
William S. [94220], 63, 84
William Stephen [107126], 297
Winfred [95939], 69, 92
Winifred [105293], 168
SWEENEY
James L [94523], 301
Joseph F. [94524], 301
SWEET
Mary E. [94928], 380
SYNAN
Catherine F. [92847], 36, 62
William [92848], 62
TABER
Olive [94926], 380
Thomas [94927], 380
TABOR
Sylvia H. [96746], 89
TANGNEY
Ellen V. 'Nellie' [96735], 67, 89
James [99360], 89

Margaret wife of James [99361], 89
TAYLOR
Ellen [107720], 190
Joanna [107702], 190, 226
John [107705], 183, 190
Patrick [107719], 191
William [107718], 190
THURSTON
Albert G. [93606], 125, 150
Vernon [102662], 150
Vernon [93608], 150
TOOLIN
Annie N. [95008], 226
James [95009], 226
TOOMEY
Ellen [93169], 310, 327
Margaret wife of Timothy [94923], 306, 310
Mary [93749], 320
Timothy [94922], 306, 309
TOUHEY
James [102730], 158
Olive [102729], 158
TRIPP
Ellis D. [107925], 427
Frederick S. [97757], 238
George Frederick [107924], 427
William Frederick [97756], 238
TROWBRIDGE
Eliza A. [98381], 382
TSIKNAS
Helen [96738], 89
TURNER
Child [94627], 378
John [94255], 327, 378
John [94628], 378
TWOOMEY
Johanna [86027], 419
TYNON
Sarah A. [94734], 266
UOHNI
James First of [79193], 12
Mother [79166], 12
VANSTONE
William McClintock [93624], 354
WAGNER
John C. [106502], 118, 140
John M. [106504], 140
Mary [106508], 140
WALKER
Ixabelle A. [104927], 162
WALSH

Volume II
Descendants of Immigrants born 1790 – 1800
Name Index

BRITLAND
Charlotte M. 'Lottie' [98495], 356
Ellen [98494], 355
James [98492], 355
Lauretta W. [98496], 356
Lincoln [98491], 308, 355
BRODERICK
Catherine [92538], 447
BROGAN
Francis [102804], 250
Margaret Gertrude [102802], 207, 250
Nancy [108618], 75
BROWN
Amy [98067], 494
Garret [98064], 495
Mr. [105957], 322
William [98063], 495
BROWNELL
Henry F. [106865], 87
Mr. [102761], 553
Rhoda M. [106864], 72, 87
BUCKLEY
Ellen [95743], 469
BURGMYER
Leonard [108632], 92
BURKE
Mary Ellen [93454], 158, 223
Patrick [100516], 223
BYRNE
Julia V. [95169], 60
Luke [95170], 60
Margaret [102161], 386
CAHILL
Anna G. [98817], 556
Daniel O. [98822], 556
Francis [98816], 556
Ilene [98819], 556
Julia [98823], 556
Margaret M. [98818], 556
Mary T. [94013], 283, 341
Michael F. [98810], 500, 556
Ruth [98821], 556
Thomas [94014], 341
Thomas [98811], 556
Thomas [98820], 556
CALLAHAN
Patrick [105338], 366
Winifred T. [105334], 318, 366
CALLIGHAN
Julia [102083], 199
CALVERT
Mary wife of Thomas [102224], 19
Thomas [102223], 19
Thomas P. [102222], 19
CAMPBELL

Susanne [101308], 86
CANANAN
Margaret E. [99550], 443
Patrick [99551], 443
CANNEY
Mary [110210], 240
CANNON
Catherine [108127], 26, 57
Patrick [108823], 57
CAPWELL
Phebe F. [103709], 202
CAREY
Mary J. [92185], 45
CARLIN
Dorothy L. [92619], 341
John A. [92620], 341
CARNEY
Annie [95735], 468
Daniel [93867], 428
Katherine 'Kate' [93866], 428
CARRAGHER
Ann [93495], 237
CARROLL
Annie [93481], 177, 237
Annie Francis [96762], 83
Catherine [96765], 83
Edward [93311], 146
Edward J. [96761], 83
Genevieve [96766], 83
Gertrude V. [96760], 83
Henry [93494], 237
Henry [96764], 83
James [93312], 146
James H. [96755], 59, 82
James H. [96759], 83
John W. [96901], 82
Louisa E. [96763], 82
Margaret [96758], 83
Mary C. [95815], 97, 121
Mary F. wife of James [93313], 146
Patrick [95820], 121
Peter [96756], 82
Peter [96767], 83
CARTER
Mary A. [105005], 78
CASEY
Mary [95259], 99, 131
Mary wife of Timothy [95281], 131
Michael J. [92533], 447
Patrick [92534], 447
Timothy [95280], 131
CASSIDY
Rose Veronica [108570], 245
CAVENEY
Margaret [108621], 88

CAWLEY
Bridget Ann [105353], 319, 368
Patrick [100038], 368
CHRISTMAS
Charles [98219], 434
Charles [98220], 434
Evelyn [98222], 434
Helena [98217], 434
Jane A. [98218], 434
Jennie A. [98216], 434
Thomas [98215], 434
Thomas J. [98214], 411, 434
CLAREY
Catherine [109919], 160
CLARK
Cornelius [93043], 214
Edward J. [101067], 564
Ellen wife of Cornelius [93044], 214
Michael [101068], 564
Susan J. [93042], 152, 214
CLARKSON
Elizabeth Rose [98866], 172
CLEAR
Margaret [98812], 556
CLIFF
Albert Jefferson [96458], 541
CLIFFORD
Margaret [99215], 517
CLINTON
Alice [101073], 564
CLOUTIER
Mary Jane [109900], 243
CODY
James [107179], 378
Margaret M. [107178], 327, 378
COFFEY
Anna [95088], 376
Child [95105], 376
Dennis [95078], 326, 376
Dorothy [95103], 377
Francis J. [95097], 377
Jeremiah F. [95092], 326, 377
John Dennis [95089], 376
John J. [95093], 326, 376
Julia [95098], 377
Margaret 'Maggie' [101119], 230
Martin D. [101122], 189, 244
Martin J. [104968], 244
Mary [95091], 326
Mary [95099], 377
Michael [101118], 230, 244
Michael [108786], 326
Michael [95079], 278, 326
Michael [95090], 326
Michael W. [101120], 230
Patrick [101117], 163, 230

COLBY
Ellen E. [97833], 169
COLE
Emily [96898], 83
COLEMAN
David [98016], 417
Dennis [96725], 189
John [98017], 417
Mary [96724], 130, 189
COLLINS
Anne M. [102175], 405
Elizabeth V. [102176], 405
James Joseph [102172], 404
Joseph M. [102174], 405
Margaret M. [102173], 404
Mary [100180], 177, 241
Michael [100181], 241
Michael [95057], 518
Nora [4439], 582
Patricia [102170], 404
Pauline [108569], 260
Shirley A. [102169], 404
William J. [102171], 404
William J. Sr. [102165], 400, 404
COLYAR
Clifton Lincoln Sr. [103719], 202
CONNELL
Catherine [102690], 306
CONNELLY
Ellen [92327], 275, 315, 569
William H. [99773], 69
CONNITY
Anna [91857], 85
CONNOLLY
Timothy [92319], 315
CONNORS
Catherine F. [92179], 44
Catherine wife of Walter
[99628], 171
Mary [99626], 108, 171
Michael [92180], 44
Walter [99627], 171
CONROY
Bridget [93122], 32
Bridget [96854], 303
Daniel [96853], 303
Daniel [96858], 302
Daniel Joseph [96869], 350
Edward F. [96842], 303, 352
Elizabeth [96867], 350
Ellen [96852], 302
Ellen [96872], 351
Emma [96874], 351
Hannah [96837], 303, 352
Helen [96862], 353
James [96841], 303

Jane [89255], 85
John [96871], 350
Julia [108095], 278, 327
Julia [96847], 303
Margaret [92467], 415, 443
Margaret [93364], 263, 271, 290
Margaret [96754], 303, 351
Mary [96851], 302, 351
Mary J. [96876], 350
Michael [92553], 558
Patrick [96855], 302, 350
Philip [96839], 268, 302
Philip [96873], 351
Phillip [92468], 407, 415
Rosemary [105118], 79
Teresa [106050], 505, 558
William [96875], 350
CONSIDINE
Michael [99751], 85
Thomas [99750], 85
COOKLEY
Margaret [108386], 228
COOPER
Florence [107219], 392
Genevieve [107220], 392
Harold E. [107218], 392
Harold E. [97264], 345, 392
Henry [107216], 392
Ralph [107221], 392
Ruth [109126], 444
CORR
Edward Thomas [101124], 231
Mary [101123], 231
COTE
Amelia J. [106751], 221, 256
Eugene J. [106752], 256
COUGHLAN
Mary R. [92282], 251
COUGHLIN
James [94325], 518
Michael [108587], 518
COYNE
Pauline Etta [96870], 350
CRAIG
Mary L. [92621], 341
CRAWFORD
Mary A. [107257], 537
CROSBY
Margaret [102287], 260
CROSSON
James F. [104045], 346
CROWLEY
Anna Margaret [96144], 206, 249
Bridget [102688], 306
Catherine (Ceohane) [94016], 262, 265, 288

Catherine A. [92859], 423, 504
Daniel (Ceohane) [92869], 23, 504
Daniel [105843], 373
Ellen [96844], 352
John [96145], 249
John A. [107629], 199
Mary (Ceohane) [105406], 277, 323
Mary [105842], 323, 373
Mary [94869], 5, 23
Michael [102689], 306
Patrick (Ceohane) [108723], 323
Phoebe A. [107628], 199
CROWTHER
Sarah [109976], 84
CULLEN
Catherine [97083], 565
Edward M. [108486], 84, 92
Maureen [108487], 92
CULP
Herbert Joseph [98524], 393
CURRY
Catherine [109331], 402
CURTIN
Jeremiah [91854], 33, 65
Katherine Florence [91855], 65
CUSICK
Annie [97780], 225
Catherine [97778], 225
Ellen [97779], 225
Flora [93876], 428
Hannah wife of Thomas
[93878], 428
Henry [97787], 225
Jane [101069], 564
Margaret M. [97788], 225
Mary [97777], 225
Michael [101825], 225
Michael [97775], 159, 225
Michael Thomas [97776], 225
Thomas [93877], 428
DAHILL
Timothy E. [96986], 447
DALEY
Daniel [104588], 220
Hannah L. [97420], 155, 220
DAVIS
Edith May [102599], 229
Everett H. [102600], 229
DAY
Catherine [102791], 247
Gerald [102793], 247
Joseph [102790], 247
Joseph F. [102789], 199, 247
Sheila [102792], 247

DELEHANTY
Bridget wife of John [97200], 540
John [97199], 540
Mary [97198], 467, 540
DENNEHY
Catherine [108084], 396
Patrick [108086], 396
Stephen [108080], 379, 396
Timothy [108085], 396
DERMODY
Catherine [95036], 572
DERRICK
Sarah [99498], 523
DESMOND
Annie [95069], 518
Dennis [95070], 518
Dennis J. [102160], 386
Johanna P. [102154], 331, 386
Mary [95071], 518
DEVITA
Antionette 'Antonia' [92099], 580
DEVITT
Bartholomew [106734], 391
John [106749], 391
Patrick Joseph [93791], 342, 391
Timothy [106750], 391
Wiliam [106733], 391
DIETZ
Annie [109645], 158, 224
John [109646], 224
DILLON
Catherine [103569], 145
DISKIN
James [100502], 290, 345
John [100503], 345
DOHERTY
John [100183], 211
John F. [95072], 517
Mary [101438], 195
Mary E. [92271], 152, 211
DOLAN
William G. [106727], 459
DOMINA
Harry Francis [96896], 83
Louis [96897], 83
DONALDSON
Jay Claude [96487], 231
DONEGAN
Mary [108434], 487
DONLIN
John E. [104057], 590
DONNELLY
Elizabeth [103982], 529
DONOVAN
Annie L. [97049], 562

Daniel [97280], 422
Dennis [104361], 516
Ellen wife of Jeremiah [97046], 562
Ellen wife of Patrick [104363], 516
Hannah [97052], 563
Jeremiah [97044], 509, 562
Jeremiah [97045], 562
Leora [97047], 562
Mary L. [97055], 563
Mary wife of Timothy [97283], 422
Michael H. [97053], 563
Patrick [104362], 516
Rosella [97054], 563
Timothy [97282], 422
DOWNEY
Catherine [94545], 370
Dennis [102078], 142
Mary [102077], 100, 142
DOYLE
James [97269], 384
Margaret [94395], 254
Margaret M. [97262], 331, 384
Mary [108644], 76, 89
Patrick [108645], 89
DRISCOLL
Catherine [108192], 294
Catherine [94559], 371
Mary [97362], 52
Miss [108826], 1, 5
DROGUE
Florence Angela [94698], 380
DROHAN
Catherine [98003], 417, 459
John [98011], 459
DUCHER
Jane [100567], 251
DUDLEY
Ellen [92320], 315
DUNHAM
Lucy L. [109935], 244
DUNN
Anna wife of Dennis [96115], 32
Caroline [101799], 157, 221
Dennis [96114], 32
Julia wife of Patrick [101801], 221
Margaret [95153], 176
Mary E. [93896], 32
Patrick [101800], 221
DUNNE
Nora [79251], 262, 267
DUVILL
Bridget [93249], 175
DWYER

Dorothy Irene [105115], 79
Edward Francis [105117], 79
Grace Madeline [105114], 79
Joanna [102674], 274
Johanna or Margaret [96456], 166
Mary [107972], 394
Mary Jane [99930], 93
Michael [105013], 79
Richard William [105119], 79
Thomas Edward [105012], 46, 79
DYER
Annie F. [89253], 65, 85
James [89254], 85
John 'Jack' T. [29124], 544
Peter [85203], 544
EAGAN
Bridget [93433], 95, 105
Catherine [92849], 192
Thomas [101823], 105
ELBERT
Elizabeth [106758], 256, 261
ELWOOD
Alice S. [93816], 118, 183
Bridget wife of Michael [94836], 183
Michael [94835], 183
ENTWISTLE
Agnes [95538], 444
George [109125], 444
EVANS
Andrew J. Jr. [106904], 367
Andrew Johnson [106897], 319, 367
George E. [106898], 367
Mary [106903], 367
FADDEN
Bridget [106893], 366
FALVEY
Edward F. [105388], 198
FANNING
Francis J. [96625], 571
James Joseph [98068], 494
John H. [95890], 188
Kate F. [95893], 189
Luke [109589], 188
Mary E. [95892], 189
William [95889], 124, 188
William [95891], 188
FARRELL
Ellen [108792], 76, 90
FEENEY
Ann T. [110156], 573
FELLEN
Ann wife of Patrick [100890], 32
FENNELLY

John Francis [104459], 243
William Henry [109899], 243
FIDRYCH
Frank [104457], 243
Stella [104454], 185, 243
FILLION
Josephine [97233], 542
FINN
Michael William [94746], 396, 402
Thomas [94747], 402
FINNEGAN
James [95045], 517
FISH
Elizabeth C. [97365], 52, 81
Frank I. [97366], 81
FITZGERALD
Bridget [106593], 414, 439
Catherine 'Kate' [95832], 152, 218
Frances wife of Patrick [106595], 439
John [105077], 579
John [95543], 524
Mary wife of Patrick [95834], 218
Patrick [106594], 439
Patrick [95833], 218
FITZPATRICK
Michael [98864], 172
FITZSIMMONS
Sarah [94985], 548
FLAHERTY
John [95366], 133
John W. [95349], 133
FLEMMING
Mary [95021], 520
FLYNN
James Leo [108585], 200
Mary E. T. [95034], 520, 572
Patrick [95035], 572
FOGARTY
Andrew [106663], 329, 381
Gerald A. [106664], 381
John [106665], 381
John [106667], 381
Margaret [106668], 381
Margaret wife of John [106666], 381
FOLEY
Bridget [83747], 66
Diana wife of Lawrence [99753], 67, 86
Edward Francis [1], 544, 582
Edward Francis Jr. [44412], 583
Elizabeth [83837], 67
Elizabeth [99755], 86

Genevieve Patricia [22201], 582
Helene L. [33309], 583
James [83639], 65
James F. [89248], 85, 92
James F. Sr. [83746], 65, 85
James Francis [89256], 92
Jeannette [99754], 86
John J. [72877], 65
John T. [83641], 33, 65
Joseph H. [83748], 67
Lawrence H. [83805], 67, 85
Margaret [89250], 85
Margaret G. [83715], 67, 85
Marilyn Ann [89257], 92
Mary J. [83806], 67
Mary Loretta [102805], 250
Michael H. [83749], 67
Patrick Edward [3332], 582
Raymond James [89249], 85
Rose A. [83838], 67
FORD
Bartholomew [101941], 105, 160
Bartholomew [105779], 160
Catherine Louise [99857], 227
Catherine S. [105774], 160
Daniel [109918], 160
Daniel [99855], 160, 227
Ellen [105772], 160
John Daniel [99856], 227
Julia Ann [105773], 160
Maggie [105780], 160
Mary [105776], 160
FORISTEL
John [105508], 222
Margaret [105507], 158, 222
FOSTER
Margaret [95028], 363
FOX
Ellen 'Nellie [108211], 297
James [108212], 297
FRANCIS
Jeffrey Scott [102137], 406
Jennifer Lynn [102136], 406
Ronald R [102135], 403, 406
Stephanie Michelle [102138], 406
FRARER
Bella [96481], 231
FRAWLEY
Bridget [106735], 391
FREEMAN
John J. [105422], 205
Rose A. [105324], 365
FULLER
Agnes wife of John [103979], 527

Esther A. [103976], 461, 527
John [103978], 527
GAFFNEY
Bridget [108213], 297
Ellen [102151], 331, 387
Partrick [102152], 387
GAHAGAN
Mary A. [102973], 145
Mary wife of Patrick [102975], 145
Patrick [102974], 145
GAINES
Mary [99549], 442
GALLAGHER
Arthur [110155], 573
Mary [95068], 569
Rita Ipheginia [107442], 573
GARNEY
Mary A. [109366], 189
Stephen [109365], 126, 189
GARVEY
Andrew [98461], 355
Margaret A. [75650], 582
Thomas [98460], 308, 355
GAUTHIER
Hector [108631], 93
GEDDES
Andrew F. [93199], 313
James [93200], 313
GIBBONS
James [107512], 567
Julia [107511], 511, 567
Margaret wife of James [107513], 567
GILCHRIST
Catherine [106586], 439, 521
GILES
Rosanna [94992], 360
GILL
John [95734], 468
Michael J. [95733], 468
GILLESPIE
Ethel May [103262], 551
GILSDORF
Elizabeth Maria [105959], 323
GIROUARD
Mr. [106478], 234
GLEMSON
Mary [105947], 322
GLINEBURG
Robert (Dr.) [108633], 93
GOLDSMITH
Lillian [97497], 448
GORMAN
Mary [107505], 511
GORTON
Eilene V. [95436], 576

John Barton [95419], 536, 576
John Barton Jr. [95433], 576
Lucius [95434], 576
Thomas [95432], 576
Vernon [95437], 577
GOULET
Cypien F. [96290], 528
Omer L. [96291], 528
GOURD
Alphonsine [106753], 256
GRAHAM
Angela [96349], 575
George [96348], 532, 575
George [96351], 575
George Alfred [96353], 575
GRANDFIELD
Mary [100064], 73
GRANT
Ellen [103732], 203
Henry [103733], 203
John William [103734], 203
Joseph B. [103723], 203
Mary Isabell [103735], 203
Susie F. [103739], 203
William J. [103722], 147, 203
GREEN
Catherine [108115], 57, 82
Catherine [97499], 415, 444
Catherine [97568], 173
Catherine wife of Cornelius
[102610], 161
Cornelius [102609], 161
Cornelius J. (Sullivan) [108111],
26, 57
Daniel [96567], 173
Daniel [96578], 173
Daniel J. [108126], 25, 56
Dennis (Sullivan) [108817], 25
Dennis [108812], 26
Dennis [97500], 444
Edward [108816], 26
Edward [97572], 235
Eugene [97566], 173
James [108815], 26
James [96566], 110, 173
James [97567], 173
James [97570], 173, 234
Joanna T. [96570], 173
John (Uohni) [108113], 5, 25
Joseph [108810], 57
Julia [96569], 173
Julia wife of Daniel [96568], 173
Kizzie wife of James [97571],
173, 234
Margaret wife of John [108818],
25
Mary [108819], 26

Mary A. wife of Charles [94354],
56
Matthew [108814], 26
Michael [108129], 26
Patrick [108813], 26
Rosa [97569], 173
Sarah [102593], 105, 161
GREENE
Catherine C. [96245], 98, 128
Charles E. [108132], 56
Cora [108131], 56
Cornelius (Uohni) [108171], 128
Eileen 'Della' [108130], 55
Harry J. [94353], 56
John [98331], 25, 55
Margaret L. [97195], 467
Mary E. [98336], 55, 81
Matthew Richard [108137], 56
Thomas J. [97196], 467
GRIFFIN
James [107625], 198
Patrick F. [102107], 198
GRONQUIST
Dora [109647], 224
GUILKA
Marguerite Evelyn [55521], 586
William Edward [39970], 586
HACKETT
Catherine [101550], 545
Francis Ann wife of Patrick
[101304], 70
Julia A. [101302], 34, 70
Patrick [101303], 70
HAGERTY
James Francis [11049], 587
HAGGERTY
Kathleen 'Colleen' [778], 587
HALEY
Arthur [98333], 193
Christopher [108811], 193
Esther [93593], 193
John [93596], 136, 193
Mary [98334], 193
HALL
Emma [95094], 326, 377
John [95095], 377
HALLIGAN
Ann wife of Patrick [94150], 546
Annie M. [94148], 480, 546
Patrick [94149], 546
HANLEY
Annie [101269], 529
Annie [95016], 362, 431, 520
Catherine [101270], 530
Daniel [101256], 463, 529
Daniel [97734], 414
Daniel J. [101262], 530

Hannah [110035], 318
Jeremiah [101259], 529
John [108188], 296
John [95020], 520
John [96848], 303
John Gilbert 'Dutch' [101264],
530
Julia [98553], 268, 302
Katherine [97058], 563
Mariah [108187], 296
Mary [100579], 414
Mary [95982], 94, 97
Mary A. [101261], 529
Mary wife of John [101260], 529
Nora [101268], 529
Patrick [109457], 302
Peter [96849], 303
HANNIGAN
Annie M. [95367], 133
HARDING
Esther [104051], 346
HARGRAVES
Charles J. [58545], 583
Joseph W. [109977], 84
Mary T. [96107], 63, 84
William Robert [33310], 583
HARNLEY
David [94004], 438
Jeremiah [94000], 412, 438
Jeremiah [94003], 438
John [94001], 438
John [94005], 438
Margaret wife of John [94002],
438
Mary wife of Michael [94480],
170
HARRINGTON
Anna (Urdil) [108722], 263, 277
Annie [96892], 351
Annie [98425], 357
Bernard E. [105446], 248
Bridget [67744], 471
Bridget [98633], 279, 327
Bridget M. [93740], 15, 48
Catherine (Caupey) [108097],
263, 278
Catherine (Causkey) [102341],
336
Catherine [100947], 140, 196
Catherine [101163], 339
Catherine [95888], 124
Catherine [98308], 551
Catherine [99025], 227
Catherine A. [93819], 118, 185
Catherine 'Kate' (Causky)
[108083], 327, 379
Catherine 'Kate' [102283], 240

Volume II Name Index

Sean Bhain (Trokirre) [102340], 336

Susan 'Sarah' [92417], 474

Thomas [101160], 339

Thomas [108062], 299

Thomas M. [104733], 245

Timothy [102282], 240

Timothy [96889], 351

Timothy [97834], 32

Timothy [98415], 309, 357

William [106915], 388

William [98426], 357

William F. [98431], 395

William H. [101157], 339

HARTFORD

Ellen wife of James [97332], 310

George [93520], 271, 310

George [97335], 310

James [97331], 310

James [97333], 310

Mary J. [97334], 310

HAWKESWORTH

Edward Francis [102290], 260

Edward S. [102286], 260

George Alexander [102285], 240, 260

Irene M. [102289], 260

Margaret M. [102288], 260

HAYES

Elizabeth Eva [102090], 199

James J. [98498], 356

James W. [98497], 356

John [102091], 199

Julia [102079], 142

Nora B. wife of James [98499], 356

HEALEY

Margaret [98732], 327

HEANEY

Thomas F. [96350], 532, 575

Thomas F. Jr. [96355], 575

HERLIHY

Dennis J. [106353], 363

Irene Margaret [106355], 363

HERNON

Viola A. [107437], 520, 573

HERRICK

Ernest P. [107256], 537

Warren C. [107253], 537

HICKEY

Margaret [93597], 347

Mary [98512], 392

Patrick J. [107495], 511

Patrick J. [107506], 511

HIGGINS

Patrick [97660], 113

HIGHLAND

Ann [97111], 566

HIOTELLIS

Katherine [89259], 85

HOAR

Charles P. [96362], 539

Mary E. [96361], 463, 539

Sarah wife of Charles [96363], 539

HOCROFT

Elizabeth [98490], 355

HODGE

Edward [100958], 246

Elizabeth [99762], 68

HOGAN

Bridget [83793], 558

Margaret [97358], 19, 52

Thomas [97361], 52

HOLEN

Emily wife of Thomas [104123], 64

Mary E. [104127], 64

Raymond F. [104126], 64

Thomas G. [104122], 64

William [104120], 33, 64

HOLLAND

Ellen [105526], 422, 497

James [105529], 497

Mary [96850], 303

HOLLIHAN

Mary [98018], 417

HOLMES

Alfred [96287], 528

Ellen wife of Alfred [96288], 528

John W. [96286], 462, 528

Margaret [96293], 528

Mary E. [96289], 528

HOPKINS

Anna M. [104808], 77

Anne M [95574], 77

Patrick [104809], 77

HORAN

Ellen F. [101407], 458

John [101408], 458

HOUGH

Ellen T. [104460], 183, 242

Ellen wife of John [104462], 242

John [104461], 242

HOWARD

Cornelius [98300], 513

Cornelius [98302], 513

Ellen [94931], 513

Joseph F. [93875], 513

Margaret [98301], 513

Mary [94929], 513

Michael [94930], 513

Peter [93874], 427, 513

HUGHES

Ellen [96861], 353

HURLEY

Ann [103857], 222

Catherine wife of Jeremiah [99793], 50

Daniel [102082], 199

Daniel [102787], 199

David [102081], 142, 199

Dennis [99505], 302

Ellen [107305], 198

Ellen [94135], 259

Jeremiah J. [99791], 17, 50

Juila V. [102788], 199, 246

Julia [103589], 1, 4

Margaret [93783], 342

Margaret [93979], 174

Margaret [98525], 268, 302

Mary [102786], 199

Mary [109624], 432

Mary wife of Dennis [99508], 302

Patrick [99792], 50

INIS

Sarah [96352], 575

IVERS

John E. [97939], 568

JACKSON

Patrick J. [100066], 74

Sarah E. [100065], 39, 74

JACOBS

Roy C. [101271], 530

JOHNSON

Harold [105146], 78

JOYCE

Bridget [101824], 105

JUNEAU

Diana [106761], 52, 81

Telesphore 'John' [106762], 81

KANE

Ellen [102012], 566

John [108463], 40

Mary Elizabeth [108462], 10, 40

KEANE

Ellen [100517], 223

KEATING

Dennis [108385], 228

Dennis Joseph [108384], 228

KELLEY

Daniel [106641], 587

Frances Colburn [106640], 550, 587

KELLY

Annie J. [95829], 152, 218

Bridget [93351], 345

Catherine [93246], 112, 175

Catherine wife of Timothy [100495], 344
Daniel [100492], 290, 344
Daniel [100496], 344
Daniel [104766], 134
Daniel [106732], 389
Daniel [109103], 262, 267
Duncan [93785], 389
Duncan T. [93784], 342, 389
Elizabeth M. A. [106509], 344, 391
Ellen L. [92843], 99, 134
Johanna [94899], 41, 267, 297
Julia [98601], 274
Julia wife of Patrick [95831], 218
Mary [102153], 387
Mary F. [100497], 344
Michael [102673], 274
Michael [93248], 175
Patrick [95830], 218
Rose [92659], 335
Samuel [106730], 389
Thomas [92183], 45
Timothy [100494], 344
Timothy [100505], 344
KENNEDY
Bridget [96757], 82
George W. [105006], 78
John [105004], 78
John L. [105008], 78
John R. [105000], 46, 78
Margaret wife of Thomas [102693], 306
Mary [102691], 306
Mary [106044], 558
Mary L. [105007], 78, 90
Thomas [102692], 306
KENNEPHOL
Clara [101220], 532
KENNEY
Bridget wife of Martin [99489], 522
Maria A. [99487], 441, 522
Martin [99488], 522
Mary [99504], 522
KERINS
Bridget wife of Patrick [107133], 389
Gerald R. [93787], 389
Henry J. [107134], 389
James C. [93788], 389
Margaret F. [107135], 389
Patrick [107132], 389
Patrick Henry [93786], 342, 389
William [107136], 389
KEROACK
Albert [95427], 536, 577

Marie [95431], 577
Philip [95428], 577
Rose [95430], 577
KERR
Margaret E. [93789], 342, 390
KERWIN
Edward [93826], 118
Julia [93810], 68, 97, 118
KILBRIGHT
Mr. [96181], 417
KILEY
Daniel Francis [109956], 403
Loretta [102127], 400, 403
KING
Mary [104589], 220
Mr. [108638], 76
KINNANAN
Mary [103714], 202
KIRBY
John [100063], 73
John E. [100062], 73
Margaret I. [100061], 73
Michael Francis [100060], 39, 73
KIRKMAN
Thomas H. [108117], 82
William H. [108116], 57, 82
William Henry [108119], 82
LACHAPELLE
Nancy [102164], 405
Roger N. [102162], 401, 405
Steven T. [102163], 405
LAFFERTY
Henry [81219], 481
John [73853], 481
LAMBERT
Jennie [95821], 121
LANDERYOU
Dorothy [102623], 578
John [95423], 578
John N. [95422], 536, 578
Vernon [102624], 578
LANDRY
Celia [97040], 566
LANNAHAN
Mary [96090], 216
LARRIVEE
Alphonse [100953], 196, 246
Emma F. [100955], 246
Jules [100954], 246
Jules Javier [100956], 246
LAW
Betsy wife of Henry [96342], 531
Henry [96341], 531
Sarah M. [96340], 463, 531
LEARY

Anna J. [92168], 77
Bridget [109096], 298
Bridget [110211], 510
Catherine [107508], 511
Catherine [92169], 77
Catherine [93063], 407, 411
Catherine [97736], 272
Catherine 'Kate' [92142], 45
Catherine S. [102087], 198
Charles [106473], 234
Child [99426], 348
Cornelius J [102089], 199
Daniel [107493], 511, 567
Daniel F. [92157], 42, 76
Dennis (Keen) [96392], 262, 269
Dennis [107507], 510
Dennis [95130], 54
Dorothy [106475], 234
Elizabeth [92170], 77
Ellen [109194], 1, 7
Ellen L. [101574], 494
Florence F. [92138], 44
Florence Joseph [92166], 76
Hannah [92181], 44
Hannah [97189], 418, 466
Hannah [99427], 349
Hannah wife of Thomas [105302], 411
Hanora 'Nora' M. [102106], 198
Helen W. F. [102086], 198
James [102794], 199
James [109098], 298
James [92134], 11, 42
James [92178], 77
James Francis [92165], 76
James Henry [92143], 45
Jeremiah [109199], 7
Jeremiah [110097], 269
Johanna [107494], 511
Johanna [108112], 26, 57
Johanna [109099], 298
John [107514], 567
John [108064], 299
John [109221], 510
John [92139], 44
John [96941], 423, 510
John [97211], 466
John Anthony [102085], 142, 198
John Francis [102105], 198
John T. [104774], 234
Julia [92140], 44
Julia [95129], 21, 54
Julia Ann [109095], 298
Leo [106474], 234
Leonard, [106471], 234

MALLARKEY
Mary J. [93204], 358
MALONE
Ellen [108727], 375
MALONEY
Annie [83870], 66
John Francis [83874], 66
John T. [101071], 564
John T. [101072], 564
Mary [99481], 420, 486
Matilda [106635], 490, 550
Thomas [99484], 486
MANCHESTER
Betsey wife of Ezek [99561], 36
Ezek [99560], 36
Harriett M. [99562], 37
Ida E. [99563], 37
John W. [99559], 8, 36
MANSFIELD
John M. [103801], 47
Joseph [93751], 14, 47
Loretta [103800], 47
Thomas [93756], 47
MANVILLE
Eliza [105984], 287
MARION
Mr. [108568], 404
MAYES
Dora [92030], 481
MAYMON
Eliza [101519], 91
MCAVINNE
Cornelius [96267], 461
MCAVINUE
Thomas [96266], 461
MCBRIDE
Ellen [105849], 373
MCCABE
Mary J. [94981], 486, 548
Michael [94984], 548
MCCANN
Jane F. [97424], 226
Mary [97270], 384
MCCARTHY
Andrew [93782], 342
Catherine [97674], 96, 107
Catherine L. [96630], 553
Daniel [102406], 338
Dennis Francis [102405], 338
Diarmuid "Nafeithe" [105125], 12
Ellen [106600], 439
Ellen 'Nellie' [109959], 496, 551
Ellen wife of John [95180], 61
Francis J. [95181], 61
George [95183], 61
Hannah F. [96631], 553

Helen [96633], 553
James [109960], 421, 496
James [109967], 496
Jeremiah [109970], 496
Johanna [92237], 3, 18
John [109968], 496
John [95178], 28, 61
John [95179], 61
John F. [95184], 61
John F. [96632], 553
Julia [108743], 324
Julia A. [96627], 553
Margaret [109964], 496
Margaret [93775], 283, 342
Margaret G. [96629], 553
Mary [109966], 496
Mary E. [95182], 61
Mary F. [96634], 553
Mary wife of John [109969], 496
Timothy [109965], 496
Timothy [96624], 497, 551
William S. [96628], 553
MCCARTY
Alexander 'Sandy' [98305], 551
Catherine [93370], 346
Catherine [93408], 263, 272
Child [103256], 551
Eliza [96139], 206
James [103249], 492, 551
Jeremiah or Mortimer [97661], 111
John Vincent [103255], 551
Mary [103258], 551
Mary [108583], 200
Mary [109102], 297
Mary [93242], 96, 111
Mary A. [95561], 55
Mary wife [97662], 111
Michael [95559], 55
Michael H. [95558], 25, 55
Patrick [103257], 551
MCCOLLERAN
Ellen [101826], 225
MCCOMBS
Mary [109226], 554
MCCONNELL
Abbie [105678], 381
Anna [105681], 382
James [105673], 381
James [105676], 381
James W. [105672], 329, 381
John [105679], 381
Margaret [105675], 381
Mary [105677], 381
Robert F. [105682], 382
William [105680], 382
MCCRYSTLE

Sarah [106642], 587
MCCUE
Ellen wife of Jeremiah [95066], 519
Jeremiah [95065], 519
Mary [95064], 431, 519
MCDERMOTT
Alice wife of Michael [101391], 72
Mary [97691], 488
Mary A. [101389], 34, 72
Michael [101390], 72
MCDONALD
Catherine 'Katie' [93349], 292, 345
John [101307], 86
Patrick [101306], 70, 86
Patrick [93350], 345
Raymond [101310], 86
Susie [101309], 86
Thomas F. [95564], 347
MCDONOUGH
Mary [93359], 346
MCENHILL
Hugh [105848], 373
Margaret E. [105846], 323, 373
MCFADDEN
Allen [103860], 398
Elizabeth R. 'Lizzie' [103865], 385, 398
MCGAN
Ellen [93872], 513
MCGRADY
Hannah Wife Of James [83670], 474
James [83669], 474
Joseph [79262], 474
MCGRATH
John [97583], 455
Mary [97573], 416, 455
MCGRAW
Sarah [92419], 541
MCGUIRE
Ann Marie [92300], 261
John James [92299], 253, 261
MCHUGH
Catherine 'Kate' [97774], 159
MCINTIRE
Bridget [93173], 514
MCKEARNAN
Susan [96268], 461
MCKENNA
Lena [99499], 523
William [99500], 523
MCLEAN
Helen [92296], 253
MCMAHON

Hannah [109628], 433
Hannah [95732], 468
Hannah [97944], 515, 567
Hannah F. 'Anna' [93188], 272, 312
Hannah wife of Jeremiah [109011], 502
Hanora 'Annie or Nora' [99406], 588
James [104356], 516
James [95736], 468
James C. [96984], 415, 447
James Edward [105139], 78
James H. (Rev.) [96993], 447
James H. [109632], 433
James H. [99502], 522
Jane A. [98862], 172
Jennie P. [92277], 210, 251
Jeremiah [105435], 95, 101
Jeremiah [109010], 502
Jeremiah [98051], 421, 494
Jeremiah [98053], 494
Jeremiah [98874], 171
Joanna [98596], 274
Johanna [106581], 214
John [100499], 290, 345
John [104353], 516
John [104359], 515
John [109623], 432
John [109627], 432
John [93064], 436
John [93978], 174
John [94023], 282
John [95067], 569
John [98061], 495
John [98934], 360
John H. [105137], 77
John H. [105143], 77
John Henry [102602], 228
John J. [98242], 410, 432
John O. [93197], 312
John T. [96994], 447
Joseph V. [98062], 495
Julia [109631], 433
Julia [92176], 42, 77
Julia [98815], 422, 499
Julia Veronica [98000], 459, 525
Julia wife of Bartholomew [107747], 18
Maggie Jane [105135], 78
Margaret [109625], 433
Margaret [92870], 23, 504
Margaret [93737], 13, 408, 420
Margaret [94008], 265, 282
Margaret [94105], 1, 5
Margaret [95542], 444, 524
Margaret [98856], 172

Margaret Eleanor [93206], 358
Margaret J. [93057], 411, 436
Margaret wife of Jeremiah [98875], 171
Maria [101807], 257
Martin [104383], 516
Mary [105424], 101, 147
Mary [107745], 3, 18
Mary [108424], 94, 99
Mary [108609], 11, 42
Mary [109006], 422, 502
Mary [93974], 110, 174
Mary [96990], 447
Mary [98854], 171
Mary A. [104355], 516
Mary Ann [95058], 517, 569
Mary Elizabeth [105138], 77
Mary 'Mamie' [98055], 494
Mary wife of Cornelius [102595], 228
Mary wife of Cornelius [97065], 560
Mary wife of Cornelius D. [100501], 345
Mary wife of Daniel [103571], 144
Mary wife of John [93065], 436
Matthew [104358], 516
Maybel Ceclia [105145], 78
Michael [104381], 516
Michael [95749], 468
Michael J. [93203], 358
Michael J. [98829], 499
Nell [107983], 353
Owen [95730], 418, 468
Patrick [100566], 251
Patrick [99503], 522
Patrick H. [98057], 494
Patrick J. [98852], 108, 171
Peter [104382], 516
Raymond [93207], 358
Sarah [98859], 173
Sarah A. [102603], 229
Sarah Jane [96985], 447
Stephen [98059], 494
Susan Jane [105141], 78
Theresa [104384], 516
Thomas [92658], 335
Thomas [96089], 216
Timothy [102517], 77
Timothy E. [95737], 469
Walter Joseph [105142], 78
William [102604], 229
MURRAY
Catherine [93437], 105, 157
Joanna [98010], 408, 417

Mary wife of Thomas [100513], 157
Thomas [100512], 157
MUSTER
Joseph [96294], 528
Joseph [96295], 528
NALLY
Michael [101158], 339
NAVIN
Ellen [95010], 317
NAWROCKI
Margaret Mary [108571], 246
NEALGES
Margaret [98012], 459
NEARY
Mary [110030], 287, 343
Thomas [105981], 343
NEFF
George [95742], 469
Lewis G. [95741], 469
NEWMAN
Agnes [103567], 145
John [103568], 145
NEWTON
Ann [98493], 355
NOON
Mary E. [93827], 182
Mary wife of Thomas [93823], 182
Thomas [93818], 118, 182
Thomas [93822], 182
William P. [94837], 182
NOONAN
Johanna [93198], 312
NORMANDIN
Edward [98438], 357
Francois K. [98439], 357
OBRIEN
Annie M. [92866], 505, 557
Bridget wife of Patrick [92868], 557
Catherine Clifford [98505], 268, 301
Elizabeth [97037], 566
Ellen [105014], 79
Ellen [92344], 358
Ellen [94210], 276, 322
Jeremiah [94608], 322
Johanna [108787], 326
John J. [92343], 316, 358
Margaret [97041], 566
Mary wife of Jeremiah [94609], 322
Michael [104949], 358
Michael [98527], 301
Patrick [92867], 557
Stephen J. [96868], 351

William [106624], 366
William E. [105345], 366
PURCELL
Catherine [95171], 60
PYEATT
Lorene Willamina 'Willie'
[101265], 530
QUILL
Margaret [95533], 524
QUINN
Margaret E. [94393], 214, 254
Mary [93757], 47
Michael [94394], 254
RAIDY
Helena 'Lena' [99496], 523
Patrick [99497], 523
RAPOSA
Mr. [89258], 92
RAY
Andrew C. [96485], 166, 231
Maude Edith [96486], 231
REAGAN
Dennis [94950], 272
Hanora [93409], 272
Joanna [103855], 158, 222
Julia [95594], 337
Margaret [96146], 249
Mary [93761], 421, 490
Mary [95883], 97, 124
Mary L. [95592], 337
Michael [95593], 337
Mortimer [95887], 124
Thomas [103856], 222
REARDON
Johanna [97228], 419, 475
RECORD
Mary E. [95295], 36
REDDY
James [109641], 433
Walter [109640], 433
REED
Cora wife of Herbert [99341],
254
Herbert W. [99340], 254
Marion L. [99338], 219, 254
REEVE
Henry Francis Sr. [93456], 223
REILLY
Catherine G. wife of James
[101387], 70
James [101386], 70
James Francis [101385], 70
REYNOLDS
Alfred H. [94482], 233
Edward J. [101070], 564
Eleanor [94483], 233
Peter A. [94476], 171, 233

William H. [94477], 233
RICE
Catherine [110014], 286
Geoge H. [110209], 240
George J. [102281], 240
RICHMOND
Annie P. wife of Leander
[103738], 203
Frederick E. [103736], 203
Leander P. [103737], 203
RIGNEY
Bridget [83640], 65
RILEY
Anna [108464], 40
Anna [98260], 54
Bridget [97781], 159
Dennis [95128], 21, 54
Eugene [95132], 21
Joanna [98259], 54
Mary [100384], 54
Mary [95133], 21
Mary [98258], 54
Morgan [94124], 5, 21
Patrick [95127], 21
William [100383], 54
William [95134], 21
ROBERTS
Adeline [106819], 233
Flavie [96465], 232
Mary E. [58546], 583
ROBINSON
Cornelia May ' Nellie' [105958],
322
Grace M. wife of William
[109731], 401
Helen [97403], 387, 401
Mr. [102760], 553
William L. [101358], 401
ROGERS
Sarah A. [100067], 74
ROLAND
Hannah [94015], 341
RONAYNE
Bridget Marie [94742], 396
ROONEY
Catherine [94019], 282, 340
Catherine wife of Thomas
[94021], 340
Thomas [94020], 340
ROSE
Annie [98488], 355
Charles W. [98459], 308, 355
Francis [98489], 355
ROSS
Alexander [96480], 231
Catherine [96482], 231
James W. [96479], 166, 231

Mercedes Helen [96484], 231
Wallace [96483], 231
ROWAN
Michael [96860], 353
Roseanne A. [96859], 303, 353
ROY
Lydia [106763], 81
RUANE
Winnefred [99554], 523
RUSSELL
Bartholomew [107484], 279,
332
Ellen wife of James [107489],
332
Hanora C. [100756], 49
Hanora wife of Michael
[100754], 49
James [107488], 332
Mary A. [108128], 26, 57
Mary A. [108820], 26
Mary E. [100757], 49
Michael [100753], 49
Patrick F. [94145], 17, 49
Thomas F. [100755], 49
RYAN
John T. [101549], 545
Maggie [101551], 545
Mary F. [100070], 74
Michael Henry [101548], 480,
545
SAMPSON
Melzar B. [109934], 244
Melzar Pierce [99515], 192, 244
Virginia [109933], 244
SANDERS
Catherine [103587], 19
John [103590], 19
John [103594], 19
Matilda [103595], 20
SAUNDERS
Catherine [100774], 53
Cathleen N. [108480], 91
Ellen [100783], 53
James [103597], 20
James E. [100776], 54
John H. [100781], 54
Margaret [108479], 91
Mary E. [100775], 53
Mary E. [108481], 91
Matilda P. 'Mattie' [100777], 54
Michael P. [108477], 91
Patricia A. [110159], 91
Patrick [100772], 4, 19
Paul G. [108478], 91
Peter [100771], 20, 52
Peter F. [108474], 81, 91
Peter Francis [100782], 54, 81

Raymond M. [108476], 91
Sarah E. wife of Peter [103591],
54, 81
Stephen [103596], 20
William [103593], 81
SAVOIE
Elizabeth [108635], 92
SCHIRP
Emma Veronica [41079], 586
SCHOENTZELER
John [101133], 193
John Philip [109524], 136, 193
Mary C. [101134], 193, 246
SCHULTZ
Mary [96296], 528
SCULLY
Daniel F. [94557], 370
Edward H. [94543], 321, 370
Joseph G. [94556], 370
Patrick [94544], 370
SERVANT
Mary [93346], 291
Pierre [93347], 291
SHANAHAN
Catherine wife of John [94804],
115
John [94803], 115
Julia [94161], 38, 96, 115
SHANLEY
Joseph Thomas [102628], 577
SHANNON
Mary [98608], 239
Mary Ellen [103711], 147, 202
Thomas [103713], 202
SHAUGHNESSY
Annie [83875], 66
SHAY
Abbie [95056], 518
Catherine [95048], 518
Dennis [95055], 518
Elizabeth [95059], 569
John [95049], 517
John T. [95047], 429, 517
Margaret [95054], 518
Mark [97725], 458
Mary A. [95050], 517
Mary A. [95060], 569
Quinlan [95052], 517
Timothy [99214], 517
William Desmond [92294], 253
SHEA
Annie [108846], 325
Annie F. [105448], 204
Bridget [101406], 457
Bridget [95044], 517
Bridget wife of Daniel [100529],
194

Catherine [100909], 197
Catherine [108214], 295
Catherine [92285], 253
Catherine [93067], 411, 435
Catherine F. [100520], 224, 257
Catherine wife of Daniel
[100894], 197
Catherine wife of Daniel
[98487], 307
Charles [97730], 457
Daniel [100528], 194
Daniel [100893], 197
Daniel [102202], 11
Daniel [92172], 76
Daniel [98486], 307
Daniel F. [100898], 198
Dennis [100891], 141, 197
Dennis [101413], 457
Dennis [108215], 295
Dennis [110102], 325
Dennis [94806], 116
Dennis D. [109626], 433
Dennis J. [108850], 325
Edward F. [109340], 390
Eileen [109062], 379
Elizabeth [100900], 198
Elizabeth [97733], 457
Ellen [108845], 325
Ellen G. [100897], 197
Ellen wife of Dennis [108216],
295
Ellen wife of John [100762], 229
Eugene [97732], 457
Gertrude [109065], 379
Hannah [92163], 42, 76
Hannah [98485], 307
Hanora [105684], 329
Hanora [108218], 296
Hanora [96965], 418, 464
Helen [100910], 197
Jeremiah [109056], 378
Johanna wife of Dennis
[101414], 457
John [100760], 163, 229
John [100761], 229
John [100763], 229
John [100905], 197
John [93068], 435
John [97724], 416, 457
John [97731], 457
John H. [108848], 325
John J. [100904], 197
John L. [109060], 378
Julia [101010], 353
Julia [108844], 325
Julia [110012], 262, 266
Julia A. [108849], 325

Katherine M. [109063], 379
Margaret [107345], 113, 168
Margaret [108843], 325
Margaret [109059], 378
Margaret [98468], 391
Margaret G. 'Maggie' [97729],
458
Margaret wife of Dennis
[94807], 116
Mary [100527], 139, 194
Mary [100899], 197
Mary [101410], 457
Mary [105122], 2, 12
Mary [107989], 354
Mary [94607], 263, 276
Mary [98501], 349
Mary A. [109061], 378
Mary E. [100764], 230
Mary Jane [92283], 210, 253
Mary wife of Daniel [92173], 76
Mary wife of John [93069], 435
Mary wife of Patrick [96969],
464
Michael [108847], 325
Michael W. [94805], 116
Patrick [108842], 277, 325
Patrick [96968], 464
Patrick [97728], 457
Patrick H. [95053], 517
Theresa Elizabeth [109064],
379
Timothy [92284], 253
Timothy F. [105449], 204
Timothy Francis [95051], 517,
569
Timothy J. [109055], 327, 378
Timothy Joseph [109058], 379
William [100765], 230
SHEEHAN
Daniel [101432], 194
David J. [101435], 195
Dennis [101431], 140, 194
Ellen [110094], 195
Hannah [96621], 407, 415
Hannah B. [96610], 553
Johanna [93158], 274
Johanna 'Siobhan' [105003], 12,
45
Margaret [92929], 1, 4
Margaret wife of Daniel
[101433], 194
Mary [95131], 54
Mary Ann [101434], 195
Michael [107981], 353
Michael [98595], 274
Patrick [107982], 353
SHEEKEY

Eleanor Teresa [94740], 396, 402
Francis S. [94743], 396
James Francis [94739], 380, 396
James Francis [94741], 396
James Francis III. [94745], 396
Thomas J. [94744], 396
SHERMAN
Elizabeth [95435], 576
SHIELS
James [108617], 75
James Joseph [108616], 75
SIMCOCK
Matilda [99752], 85
SISSON
Dorothy 'Dot' [102126], 399, 403
SKIFF
Henry W. [110021], 286
James T. [110022], 286
Mary A. wife of James [110023], 286
SLATTERY
Catherine [102796], 95, 100
SLOAN
John [102214], 72
Margaret F. [102213], 34, 72
Mary wife of John [102215], 72
SMITH
Andrew [95685], 120, 188
Anna L. [102124], 385, 399
Barbara wife of William J. [102664], 188
Elizabeth A. [104350], 568
Julia Etta [95687], 188
Mary A. wife of Walter A. [102143], 399
Mary B. [95688], 188
Walter A. [102142], 399
William J. [102663], 188
SMYTH
Ellen [102687], 263, 270, 314
SOMMER
Anna T. [88992], 85
Edward J. [88991], 67, 85
Martin [91856], 85
SPOHN
Clara Alice [102291], 260
STANDISH
Elizabeth 'Lizzie' [97081], 509, 565
John H. [97082], 565
STANTON
Angela [97108], 567
John [97105], 509, 567
Lucy M. [97109], 567
Luke [97106], 567

STAUNTON
Bridget Isabelle [99543], 443, 523
Patrick J. [99553], 523
STOCK
Christine [102092], 199
STONE
Lydia [98440], 357
SULLIVAN
Abbie [93307], 186
Abbie [95018], 409, 429
Abbie [97719], 114
Abbie F. [105671], 329, 381
Abby (Suonish) [102404], 264, 280
Abby [102414], 337
Abby [92676], 43, 98, 127
Abby [93397], 276
Abby [96959], 291
Agnes [108740], 324
Agnes [98543], 349
Agnes A. [101822], 221
Agnes C. [96469], 233
Agnes F. [93352], 345
Alberta wife of Richard [110024], 287, 343
Alexis J. [97824], 102
Alfred A. [96347], 531
Alice [104466], 242
Alice [94562], 372
Andrew [102795], 94, 100
Andrew [93231], 95, 101
Andrew C. [94398], 213
Andy [108094], 278, 327
Angela [107795], 399
Ann [94876], 24
Ann wife of Cornelius [96365], 408, 418
Anna [103467], 588
Anna [106144], 362
Anna [96478], 166, 231
Anna [98508], 349
Anna E. [102627], 577
Anna L. [108622], 88
Anna Louise [92298], 253
Anna M. [102146], 400, 404
Anna M. [107182], 378
Anna Maria [108465], 40
Anne [104456], 244
Anne M. [92861], 505
Annie [100536], 139
Annie [101257], 463, 529
Annie [105331], 366
Annie [105404], 323, 374
Annie [93345], 292, 345
Annie [93452], 160
Annie [93490], 239

Annie [95038], 520
Annie [97263], 384
Annie [97371], 52
Annie A. [95075], 326, 376
Annie A. [95289], 36
Annie C. 'Nancy' [102801], 207
Annie F. [93058], 437
Annie G. [92269], 211
Annie L. [97027], 509, 566
Annie M. [94152], 547
Annie T. [93353], 345
Annie T. [97940], 568
Annie Theresa [101382], 70
Annis wife of William [99624], 96, 108
Anster wife of John [107339], 95, 103
Arthur [101817], 221
Arthur [99495], 523
Arthur F. [100068], 75
Arthur F. John [94541], 39, 74
Arthur M. [106052], 559
Arthur Stephen [97071], 561
Austin [93463], 224, 257
Bartholomew [109090], 10
Bartholomew [95061], 429
Bartholomew [97230], 475, 541
Bartholomew Patrick [102149], 330, 382
Bertha [99492], 522
Bertha M. [98522], 393
Bettina 'Betty' [106643], 587
Betty [109710], 261
Boetius [99891], 93
Brenda [100521], 257
Bridget [100098], 163
Bridget [101155], 280, 338
Bridget [101315], 34
Bridget [103250], 492, 551
Bridget [103705], 146
Bridget [108121], 57
Bridget [108458], 10
Bridget [92879], 453
Bridget [96452], 106, 166
Bridget [97022], 423, 508
Bridget [97023], 508, 562
Bridget [98503], 301, 349
Bridget Loretta [98517], 350
Bridget wife of William [103731], 95, 101
Caroline Cecilia [101802], 221, 255
Catherine [100035], 319
Catherine [100903], 198
Catherine [101154], 339
Catherine [101305], 70, 86
Catherine [102201], 11

Catherine [102518], 77
Catherine [103677], 340
Catherine [104347], 429, 514
Catherine [105325], 365
Catherine [105510], 222
Catherine [105670], 329, 380
Catherine [105854], 324
Catherine [107368], 445
Catherine [108459], 10
Catherine [108584], 200
Catherine [108613], 42
Catherine [108615], 75
Catherine [108652], 89
Catherine [108779], 378
Catherine [108833], 336
Catherine [109200], 7
Catherine [109361], 126
Catherine [109963], 409, 421
Catherine [110213], 510
Catherine [83685], 480
Catherine [92510], 376
Catherine [93309], 145
Catherine [93898], 6, 31, 185
Catherine [93901], 33, 67, 118, 185
Catherine [93971], 435
Catherine [94025], 283
Catherine [94163], 116
Catherine [94831], 118
Catherine [95158], 28, 59
Catherine [95692], 186
Catherine [95978], 425
Catherine [96153], 414, 440
Catherine [96250], 128
Catherine [96396], 305
Catherine [96419], 511
Catherine [96444], 106, 165
Catherine [96473], 166
Catherine [96619], 415, 446
Catherine [96961], 418, 464
Catherine [97060], 423, 507
Catherine [97066], 507, 560
Catherine [97192], 466
Catherine [97212], 540
Catherine [97574], 453
Catherine [97782], 226, 258
Catherine [98013], 417
Catherine [98052], 421, 494
Catherine [98229], 407, 410
Catherine [98231], 410, 432
Catherine [98514], 350, 392
Catherine [98827], 501
Catherine [99537], 407, 414
Catherine [99558], 9
Catherine A. [93355], 292, 346
Catherine A. 'Katie' [100951], 196, 246

Catherine A. 'Katie' [93244], 112
Catherine Agnes [100912], 198
Catherine D. [97067], 561
Catherine F. [103706], 147, 202
Catherine Gertrude [93455], 223
Catherine Gertrude 'Katie' [99629], 171, 233
Catherine Irene [94539], 39, 73
Catherine 'Kate' (Uonhi) [105439], 247
Catherine 'Kate' [108206], 297
Catherine 'Kate' [108469], 40
Catherine 'Kate' [92603], 190, 280, 332
Catherine 'Kate' [92606], 335
Catherine 'Kate' [93060], 437
Catherine 'Kate' [94473], 170
Catherine 'Kate' L. [103260], 493
Catherine 'Kate' wife of John [109428], 392
Catherine 'Katie' [107980], 353
Catherine L. [102216], 72
Catherine L. [96617], 497, 553
Catherine Linus [92293], 253
Catherine M. [106045], 558
Catherine M. [96254], 129
Catherine M. 'Katie' [97084], 565
Catherine Marie [99749], 84
Catherine R. [107977], 394
Catherine Stella 'Kay' [104455], 243
Catherine T. [102080], 142, 199
Catherine T. [102606], 161
Catherine V. [103716], 202
Catherine wife of Dennis [95164], 1, 6
Catherine wife of Eugene [96563], 96, 109
Catherine wife of Francis [81218], 408, 419
Catherine wife of James [93306], 120, 186
Catherine wife of Michael [98949], 413
Catherine wife of Timothy [103573], 95, 100
Cecilia [102523], 542
Cecilia A. 'Celia' [93458], 223
Charles [96368], 539
Charles B. [93461], 224
Charles E. [99867], 351
Charles H. [93193], 313
Charles H. [97669], 168
Charles L. [99494], 523
Charles M. [106147], 362

Child [100174], 520
Child [100970], 488
Child [102183], 383
Child [103028], 539
Child [103678], 340
Child [105980], 287
Child [106051], 558
Child [93592], 136
Child [94994], 360
Child [95156], 241
Child [95194], 293
Child [96136], 491
Child [96142], 206
Child [98004], 526
Child [99523], 520
Christina V. [107793], 222
Clara [108468], 40
Cornelius [102076], 100, 141
Cornelius [102592], 105, 160
Cornelius [103263], 408, 421
Cornelius [104783], 96, 113
Cornelius [109456], 268
Cornelius [110011], 262, 266
Cornelius [110026], 287
Cornelius [93432], 95, 104
Cornelius [93752], 14
Cornelius [94196], 150
Cornelius [95917], 104
Cornelius [96175], 416
Cornelius [96243], 98
Cornelius [96364], 408, 418
Cornelius [96966], 464
Cornelius [96970], 408, 418
Cornelius [97726], 408, 416
Cornelius [99405], 588
Cornelius [99770], 31
Cornelius A. [93234], 102
Cornelius B. ' Cornie' [96611], 553
Cornelius D. [95828], 152, 216
Cornelius D. Jr. [95837], 219, 254
Cornelius J. [108614], 75, 87
Cornelius J. [95188], 293
Cornelius J. [96339], 463, 530
Cornelius J. [99947], 93
Cornelius Joseph [99931], 90, 93
Cornelius S. [97663], 107, 113, 168
Cornelius S. [97675], 169
Cornelius V. [95185], 267, 292
Dale Anne [102134], 403, 406
Dan [107967], 353
Daniel (Barrule) [108191], 294
Daniel (Cohu) [105002], 12, 45
Daniel [100531], 194

Elizabeth [104465], 242
Elizabeth [105330], 365
Elizabeth [106512], 391
Elizabeth [109337], 402
Elizabeth [109520], 136
Elizabeth [92337], 263, 275
Elizabeth [93061], 437
Elizabeth [93486], 238
Elizabeth [93769], 284
Elizabeth [94009], 283
Elizabeth [94110], 24
Elizabeth [96256], 129
Elizabeth [96893], 352
Elizabeth [97301], 174
Elizabeth [99517], 192
Elizabeth A. 'Eliza and Lizzie"
[93501], 177, 241
Elizabeth 'Eliza' [100769], 53
Elizabeth 'Eliza' [95297], 1, 8,
181, 487
Elizabeth 'Eliza' [97025], 509,
565
Elizabeth 'Eliza' [99556], 8, 36
Elizabeth G. 'Lizzie' [96285],
462, 527
Elizabeth H. [105321], 275, 317
Elizabeth I. [107372], 446
Elizabeth I. [97417], 155
Elizabeth 'Lizzie' [73819], 483
Elizabeth 'Lizzie' [95288], 35
Elizabeth 'Lizzie' [95826], 121
Elizabeth S. [102168], 404
Ella [109462], 302
Ella [109521], 136
Ellen [100770], 20, 53
Ellen [100773], 4, 19
Ellen [102014], 454
Ellen [103698], 147, 201
Ellen [105436], 95, 101
Ellen [105524], 497, 553
Ellen [106625], 366
Ellen [107371], 446
Ellen [107968], 353
Ellen [109195], 7
Ellen [83620], 419, 475
Ellen [92034], 479
Ellen [92258], 101, 151
Ellen [93243], 112
Ellen [93403], 276
Ellen [93873], 427, 512
Ellen [94006], 436
Ellen [94011], 283
Ellen [94103], 5, 25
Ellen [94682], 380
Ellen [94879], 24
Ellen [95151], 177
Ellen [95186], 267, 293

Ellen [95745], 408, 418
Ellen [96027], 423, 511
Ellen [96942], 423, 509
Ellen [97720], 114
Ellen [98416], 309, 356
Ellen [98515], 350
Ellen [9983], 480, 542
Ellen A. 'Ella' [93191], 313, 357
Ellen A. 'Nellie' [95014], 316,
362, 520, 569
Ellen C. [98332], 25, 55
Ellen E. [93811], 118
Ellen F. [100093], 163
Ellen F. 'Nellie' [98824], 501
Ellen M. [97945], 568
Ellen M. 'Nellie' [96460], 167
Ellen 'Nellie' [103261], 492
Ellen 'Nellie' [93750], 14, 47
Ellen 'Nellie' [98458], 308, 356
Ellen 'Nellie' M. [93765], 25, 55
Ellen T. [108430], 137
Ellen Theresa [94988], 316, 362
Ellen U. [108514], 249
Ellen wife of Daniel [94118], 25
Ellen wife of Jeremiah [96449],
165
Ellen wife of Michael [96722],
98, 130
Ellenor [96471], 165
Emma [97077], 561
Emma F. [100949], 196
Emmett [98560], 393
Esther M. [97072], 561
Eugene (Brohill) [98500], 349
Eugene [100945], 141
Eugene [107969], 353
Eugene [108460], 10
Eugene [108466], 40
Eugene [92339], 275
Eugene [93404], 276
Eugene [93502], 241
Eugene [93736], 13, 408, 420
Eugene [95744], 408, 418
Eugene [96562], 96, 108
Eugene Francis (Dr.), Jr.
[107438], 573
Eugene Francis [98502], 302,
349
Eugene Francis DDS [95037],
520, 572
Eugene J. [98761], 549
Eugene Jr. [96394], 305
Eugene 'Owen' (Uonhi)
[105438], 247
Eugene 'Owen' [95043], 430
Eugene R. [96386], 269, 304
Eugene S. [96996], 344, 391

Eugene Sylvester [98516], 350,
393
Eva F. wife of Timothy [102626],
537
Eva M. [94982], 548
Fanny [101378], 70
First wife of Robert [108642], 2,
11
Florance M. [96375], 539
Florence [102186], 59
Florence [93062], 407, 411
Florence [95914], 95, 103
Florence [96178], 408, 417
Florence [98417], 270, 309
Florence Eva [97075], 562
Florence Fletcher 'Laurance'
[93245], 112, 174
Florence 'Flor' [107987], 354
Florence G. [93992], 412
Florence H. [92877], 452
Florence M. [104053], 557
Florence M. [96359], 463, 538
Florence V. wife of Leo D.
[102177], 387
Frances C. (Sister Paula Maria)
[106639], 550
Francis [101380], 70
Francis [92032], 408, 419
Francis [94155], 547
Francis [94170], 179
Francis [97363], 52
Francis A. [93462], 224
Francis H. [107978], 394
Francis Joseph [102280], 241
Francis Michael [96147], 206
Francis P. 'Frank' [94925], 514
Frank [96093], 216
Frank [98398], 341
Frank R. [99490], 522
Fredereick V. 'Fred' [94154],
547
Frederick [97785], 227
Frederick [99946], 542
Fredrick A. [94542], 38
Fredrick W. [96261], 129
Genevieve [106333], 48
Genevieve [99514], 192
George [95263], 133
George [96373], 539
George Edward [101803], 221,
255
George Edward Jr. [93460], 224
George Edward Sr. [93445],
158, 223
George Francis [96343], 532
George Ignatius [104052], 557,
589

John [98335], 55
John [99535], 265
John A. [100950], 196
John A. [105337], 366
John A. [92862], 505, 556
John A. [93233], 102
John Aloysius (Rev.) [92267], 211
John C. [102104], 142
John C. [98228], 407, 410
John Charles [93435], 105, 156
John Charles Jr. [101798], 157, 220
John D. [107181], 378
John D. [83619], 419, 474
John D. [94471], 107, 169
John D. [96034], 423, 511
John D. [99024], 227
John E. [102219], 72
John E. [103206], 190
John E. [105979], 286
John E. [107974], 394
John E. [110025], 343
John E. [92654], 132, 189, 334, 388
John E. [94474], 170
John E. [97114], 259
John E. [97951], 568
John Ed [106582], 214
John Edward [97668], 168
John F. [106588], 521
John F. [107794], 222
John F. [94162], 115, 178
John F. [95287], 35
John F. [97026], 509
John F. [97193], 467, 540
John F. [97415], 155, 219
John F. Jr. [97206], 540
John G. [93774], 415, 441
John G. [95282], 8, 35, 420, 486
John H. [102150], 331, 385
John H. [102605], 162
John H. [98826], 500
John Henry [105845], 373
John J. [102145], 400, 403
John J. [106510], 391
John Joseph [109688], 588
John L. [103710], 147, 202
John L. [97943], 516, 568
John L. [98454], 308
John Lawrence [101381], 70
John M. [108624], 88
John M. [98558], 350, 392
John P. [93744], 48
John P. [95011], 360
John P. [98542], 392
John R. [93813], 118, 182

John 'Sean' [105128], 45
John U. [96103], 31, 61
John U. Jr. [96106], 63, 83
John V. [92858], 422, 503
John V. [95189], 293
John W. [92260], 152, 215
Joseph [102218], 72
Joseph [107485], 279, 331
Joseph [109519], 136
Joseph A. [92270], 211
Joseph A. [92864], 505
Joseph A. [99541], 443
Joseph C. [96252], 128
Joseph Damascus [94529], 38
Joseph Edgar [97671], 169
Joseph F. [96466], 232
Joseph Henry [101383], 70
Joseph J. [109508], 554
Joseph L [94156], 547
Joseph Leo [108579], 201
Josephine [108650], 89
Josephine O. [105001], 46, 78
Joyce [102129], 403
Juila [104613], 500
Juila wife of Giles [100960], 94, 100
Juila wife of John [103195], 507
Juila wife of John [96242], 94, 98
Julia (Shearhig) [95080], 278, 325
Julia [100094], 163, 230
Julia [103721], 147, 202
Julia [104950], 358
Julia [105403], 374
Julia [107979], 353
Julia [107994], 354
Julia [108065], 299
Julia [108114], 5, 25
Julia [108429], 137
Julia [108637], 76
Julia [108841], 277, 324
Julia [109461], 302
Julia [92422], 419
Julia [92930], 4
Julia [93091], 411
Julia [93401], 276
Julia [93742], 48
Julia [93763], 490, 548
Julia [93771], 284
Julia [93899], 32
Julia [94018], 282
Julia [94109], 24
Julia [94840], 183
Julia [94872], 24
Julia [95368], 133
Julia [95919], 104

Julia [95948], 456, 525
Julia [96476], 166
Julia [97575], 453
Julia [97666], 107, 168
Julia [97835], 32
Julia [98545], 349
Julia [99769], 1, 6
Julia A. [103259], 493
Julia A. [95682], 120, 187
Julia C. [93780], 342, 391
Julia C. [96983], 415, 447
Julia E. [95161], 28
Julia F. [109008], 503
Julia Frances [106912], 339, 388
Julia Georgiana [108581], 200
Julia Josephine [108732], 324, 375
Julia 'Judy' [105944], 277, 322
Julia L. [94475], 171, 233
Julia T. [102084], 142, 198
Julia V. [106900], 319, 367
Julia V. [107369], 445
Julia V. [97418], 156
Julia wife of Daniel [109013], 409, 422
Julia wife of Dennis [92416], 408, 419
Julia wife of Dennis [96023], 409, 423
Julia wife of John [105778], 95, 105
Julia wife of John [97043], 508
Julia wife of John [97174], 94, 99
Julia wife of Timothy [100533], 94, 100
Katherine [94216], 192
Katherine M. [94560], 372
Katherine R. 'Katie [93739], 15
Katherine W. wife of Henry [109259], 532
Katheryn [99948], 93
Kathleen [96467], 233
Kathleen L. [106053], 559
Kathryn Ann [109339], 390
Kerry P. [100523], 257
Kevin [100522], 257
Laura [101377], 71
Laura Edna [98520], 393
Laureen A. [109336], 402
Lauretta [92672], 190
Lauretta [93781], 343
Lena [97074], 561
Leo D. [102156], 387
Leo T. [95042], 572

Mary [106146], 362
Mary [106335], 48
Mary [106584], 439
Mary [106754], 256
Mary [107183], 378
Mary [107487], 332
Mary [107964], 330
Mary [107970], 353, 393
Mary [108194], 262, 267
Mary [108263], 280
Mary [108425], 100, 137
Mary [108432], 1, 9
Mary [108449], 519
Mary [108610], 42
Mary [108639], 76
Mary [108773], 277
Mary [109094], 10
Mary [109104], 262, 267
Mary [109197], 7
Mary [109360], 126
Mary [1511], 419, 469
Mary [92031], 479
Mary [92159], 2, 11
Mary [92207], 262, 266, 283
Mary [92653], 132, 190, 334, 387
Mary [92875], 451
Mary [92967], 518
Mary [93308], 186
Mary [93338], 42, 77
Mary [93365], 271, 310
Mary [93402], 276
Mary [93595], 136, 192
Mary [93767], 265, 266, 283, 288
Mary [93995], 411, 437
Mary [94217], 192
Mary [94871], 23
Mary [95012], 360
Mary [95046], 429, 517
Mary [95148], 177, 239
Mary [95283], 8, 34, 420, 487
Mary [95290], 36
Mary [95689], 120
Mary [95748], 468
Mary [96360], 463
Mary [96397], 305
Mary [96457], 167
Mary [96477], 166
Mary [97191], 466
Mary [97203], 540
Mary [97504], 444
Mary [97670], 169
Mary [97994], 525
Mary [98014], 417
Mary [98065], 495
Mary [98071], 493

Mary [98506], 349
Mary [98526], 302
Mary [98598], 263, 273, 306
Mary [98853], 108, 171
Mary [98901], 407, 413
Mary [99545], 523
Mary [99771], 31
Mary A. [100091], 106, 163
Mary A. [100493], 290, 344
Mary A. [100896], 100, 140
Mary A. [101056], 509, 563
Mary A. [102220], 72
Mary A. [106352], 363
Mary A. [107976], 394
Mary A. [93247], 175, 235
Mary A. [93253], 112
Mary A. [93482], 238
Mary A. [94151], 546
Mary A. [95261], 133
Mary A. [95980], 425
Mary A. [96154], 440
Mary A. [96265], 461
Mary A. [97414], 154
Mary A. [97488], 416, 447
Mary A. [98008], 459
Mary A. [98456], 308, 354
Mary Agnes [102148], 401, 405
Mary Agnes [102284], 240, 260
Mary Ann [103720], 147
Mary Ann [93146], 28, 59
Mary Anne [105127], 45, 77
Mary Catherine [92279], 252
Mary D. [92297], 253, 261
Mary E. [100952], 196
Mary E. [103715], 202
Mary E. [104967], 189, 244
Mary E. [105327], 365
Mary E. [106589], 521
Mary E. [108647], 89
Mary E. [92266], 211
Mary E. [93046], 215
Mary E. [93189], 313
Mary E. [93354], 345, 391
Mary E. [93459], 223
Mary E. [94291], 321, 369
Mary E. [94396], 213
Mary E. [94832], 118, 183
Mary E. [96092], 216
Mary E. [96845], 352
Mary E. [97197], 467
Mary E. [98825], 500
Mary E. [99868], 351
Mary Ellen [102591], 161, 228
Mary Ellen [108089], 379
Mary Ellen [94537], 39, 72
Mary F. [102013], 450
Mary F. [106511], 391

Mary F. [4928], 18, 50
Mary F. [96143], 206
Mary F. [98233], 410, 432
Mary F. [99746], 84, 91
Mary Geneveive [95835], 218
Mary H. [92273], 210
Mary H. wife of Thomas [107996], 354, 394
Mary J. [110020], 286
Mary J. [83623], 476
Mary J. [93993], 413
Mary J. [95155], 241
Mary J. [96105], 63
Mary J. [98072], 511
Mary K. [108623], 88
Mary Kerr [109342], 391
Mary Louise [99337], 219
Mary Louise [99339], 254
Mary M. [99540], 443
Mary 'Mamie' [93776], 342, 389
Mary mother of Timothy [95227], 96, 113
Mary Sandra [102128], 403
Mary T. [102342], 337
Mary T. [98764], 549
Mary V. [95412], 536, 575
Mary V. [96370], 539
Mary W. [102407], 338
Mary wife of Cornellius [96971], 408, 418
Mary wife of Daniel [92872], 409, 422
Mary wife of Daniel [97030], 409, 423
Mary wife of Daniel [97360], 3, 19
Mary wife of Daniel J. [94487], 98, 126
Mary wife of Dennis [104349], 568
Mary wife of Florence [102187], 59
Mary wife of Florence [95915], 95, 104
Mary wife of James [100101], 95, 105
Mary wife of Jeremiah [92675], 94, 97
Mary wife of Jeremiah [96051], 511
Mary wife of Jeremiah [97285], 409, 421
Mary wife of Jeremiah [97503], 407, 415
Mary wife of Jeremiah [98484], 263, 270

Patrick P. [93735], 3, 13, 420, 489
Patrick 'Paddy Malachy' [107973], 394
Patrick 'Patsy' [93119], 32
Patrick R. [86000], 3, 15
Paul [109687], 588
Paul [109712], 261
Paul F. [104059], 590
Pauline [98005], 526
Peig [108775], 278
Peter (Seer) [108742], 324
Peter [93895], 31
Phadraig [107958], 269, 303
Philip [102433], 262, 269
Philip [107985], 353
Philip [92272], 210
Philip [92336], 263, 274
Philip [93770], 284
Philip [94993], 360
Philip [95882], 97, 123
Philip J. [100943], 140, 195
Phillip [92340], 315
Phillip [98019], 417
Quinlan (Rev.) [92235], 18
Quinlan [98451], 307
Raymond [103872], 398
Raymond F. [97784], 226
Richard (Dr.) [93738], 15, 47
Richard [109193], 1, 6
Richard [110018], 287, 343
Richard [96158], 441
Richard [97059], 423, 506
Richard [97585], 453
Richard [98007], 526
Richard P. [93743], 48
Rita May [105355], 368
Rita P. [101524], 81, 91
Robert [108641], 2, 11
Robert D. [94563], 372
Robert E. [107440], 574
Robert F. [94538], 38
Robert J. [104056], 590
Roger (Seer) [98467], 391
Roger [92655], 132
Ronald S. [109732], 401
Rosa [108470], 40
Rose A. [105326], 365
Roseanna [92345], 360
Rosella L. [96345], 532, 575
Rowena [106638], 550
Ruth Ann [97204], 541
Ruth Madeline [106054], 559
Sarah [96372], 539
Sarah [97672], 169
Sarah A. [93192], 313
Sarah Ann [95265], 132

Sarah J. [100092], 164
Sarah J. [95819], 123
Sarah J. [97416], 155
Sarah L. 'Sadie' [94157], 546
Sarah M. [107772], 437
Sarah 'Sadie' [94983], 548
Sarah T. [107370], 445
Sarah wife of Timothy [95824], 94, 97
Sheila M. [109338], 402
Son [95746], 418, 467
Stephen [108598], 75
Stephen Christopher [93457], 223
Stephen H. [99542], 443, 523
Stephen H. Jr. [99544], 523
Stephen Patrick [93444], 158
Stephen S. [97061], 507, 559
Susan M. [101384], 71
Sylvester [95152], 176
Sylvester [98002], 417, 458
Theresa [108654], 89
Theresa [96769], 352
Theresa Darlene [98523], 393
Theresa F. [95425], 538
Theresa 'Tracy' [96462], 167
Thomas (Cohu) [105126], 12
Thomas [93434], 105, 153
Thomas [93447], 159
Thomas [93488], 238
Thomas [94169], 179
Thomas [94924], 514
Thomas [97581], 407, 416
Thomas [98009], 408, 416
Thomas [98399], 341
Thomas A. [107975], 394
Thomas F. [109650], 224
Thomas F. [93170], 427, 513
Thomas Francis [93439], 157
Thomas M. [103858], 222
Thomas M. [93446], 158, 224
Thomas P. [99747], 84
Thomas Patrick [107995], 354, 394
Thomas Patrick [95415], 536
Thomas S. [98006], 526
Thomas Sylvester [98001], 459, 525
Timothy (Drummond) [94549], 6, 26
Timothy (Keach) [105527], 554
Timothy (Suonish) [93513], 321, 348
Timothy [100507], 413
Timothy [100524], 100, 138
Timothy [100532], 94, 100
Timothy [100581], 407, 413

Timothy [100967], 488
Timothy [103265], 492
Timothy [103572], 95, 100
Timothy [103575], 144
Timothy [106585], 439
Timothy [107580], 268
Timothy [107608], 334
Timothy [107971], 353, 394
Timothy [108457], 9
Timothy [92604], 190, 280, 334
Timothy [93339], 267, 271, 288, 310
Timothy [93343], 291
Timothy [93367], 271
Timothy [93487], 238
Timothy [93864], 427
Timothy [94171], 179
Timothy [94552], 114, 175
Timothy [94606], 263, 276
Timothy [94681], 380
Timothy [95286], 35
Timothy [95296], 1, 7, 181, 487
Timothy [95532], 524
Timothy [95747], 467
Timothy [95817], 121
Timothy [95823], 94, 97
Timothy [96020], 428
Timothy [96173], 127
Timothy [96366], 463
Timothy [96425], 94, 98
Timothy [96620], 407, 415
Timothy [96903], 59
Timothy [97576], 452
Timothy [99768], 1, 6
Timothy Anthony [104453], 185, 243
Timothy C. [94017], 282, 340
Timothy C. [94102], 5, 21
Timothy C. [95686], 120
Timothy D. [94977], 420, 484
Timothy D. [98759], 490, 549
Timothy Daniel [108651], 89
Timothy F. [94834], 183, 242
Timothy F. [94986], 316, 358
Timothy Francis [98763], 549
Timothy H. [105352], 319
Timothy J. [95410], 463, 534
Timothy James Jr. [95416], 537
Timothy O. [96337], 418, 462
Timothy R. [109341], 390
Timothy R. [92206], 262, 266, 283
Timothy R. [93760], 421, 489
Timothy R. [93773], 283, 341
Timothy R. [93809], 68, 97, 117
Timothy R. [93815], 33, 68, 118, 185

Timothy R. [94531], 321
Timothy R. [99757], 68
Timothy Robert Jr. [93764], 490, 549
Timothy S. [93406], 272
Timothy Sylvester [98509], 350, 392
Veronica M. [97783], 226
Veronica 'Vera' [95418], 537
Virginia [107445], 571
Virginia 'Virgie' [106636], 550
Walter A. (Rev.) [102144], 400
wife of Philip [102456], 262, 269
William [103730], 95, 101
William [105332], 365
William [108472], 40
William [109509], 554, 588
William [109513], 589
William [93443], 158
William [95162], 28
William [96905], 59
William [96964], 464
William [97202], 541
William [97369], 81
William [97870], 414, 438
William [99623], 96, 108
William C. [106049], 505, 558
William David [96140], 206, 248
William E. [95041], 572
William Edward [102155], 386
William F. (Rev.) [94197], 150
William F. [106148], 362
William F. [95017], 520
William F. [97364], 52, 80
William H. [106583], 439, 521
William H. [95264], 132
William J. [106587], 521
William Joseph [104732], 245
William R. [97357], 19, 50
William S. [94220], 192, 244
SUNDERS
Peter F. [108475], 91
SUTCLIFFE
Dorothy E. [101812], 257
Enoch Charles [101805], 221, 257
Enoch F. [101806], 257
Harold [101814], 257
Kenneth E. [101813], 257
Leonard [101815], 257
Louisa [106187], 257
Marion [101808], 257
Mary [101811], 257
Raymond [101809], 257
Veronica C. [101810], 257
SWEENEY
Julia [85204], 544

Julia mother of Margaret [94554], 28
Margaret [94550], 6, 28
Martha A. B. [97825], 103
Mary C. wife of Terence [97828], 103
Terence [97827], 103
SWEET
Mary E. [94928], 514
SWINSON
Florence [105147], 78
SYNAN
Catherine F. [92847], 134, 192
William [92848], 192
TABER
Olive [94926], 514
Thomas [94927], 514
TATTERSALL
Emma [108790], 77
TAYLOR
Adeline [97070], 561
Annie [106866], 87
THACKERY
Charles T. [97494], 448
George E. [97496], 448
John [97490], 448
John R. [97492], 448
Louis [97495], 448
Mary wife of John [97491], 448
William [97489], 416, 448
William Henry [97493], 448
THIEL
Sarah M. [107190], 235
THIVIERGE
Ursula [93348], 291
THOMAS
Harriet [95424], 578
THURSTON
Alton H. [98463], 308, 356
Daniel [97127], 525
Edward H. [97124], 456, 525
Gardner [97125], 525
Nathaniel [98464], 356
Randall A. [98466], 356
TIMMAN
Mary A. [109244], 578
TIMMONS
John F. [109243], 578
Joseph Arthur [109242], 539, 578
TOBIN
Anne [97033], 566
Jane [97032], 566
John F. [97034], 566
Thomas [97110], 566
Thomas A. [97035], 566
Walter J. [97031], 509, 566

TOOLIN
Annie N. [95008], 317
James [95009], 317
TOOMEY
Agnes [95539], 524
Dennis [92466], 415, 443
Ellen [93169], 409, 426
Frank [109127], 524
John [95537], 444
Lena [109129], 525
Mabel [109130], 525
Margaret [109128], 524
Margaret wife of Timothy [94923], 426
Mary [92465], 443
Michael [95536], 443, 523
Nora [95541], 524
Timothy [94922], 426
William [95540], 524
TRACY
Anne Louise [92160], 45
John [92184], 45
TRANFAGLIAS
Celeste [108737], 375
TREMBLAY
August [97069], 561
Joseph Alcide [97068], 561
TURNER
Catherine [105509], 222
Elizabeth (Dr.) [102166], 400, 403
VANASSE
Charles [97232], 542
Victoria [97231], 475, 542
WALKER
Catherine E. [96381], 534
Catherine wife of George [96383], 533
George [96378], 534
George [96382], 533
George E. [96377], 463, 533
Henry Leo [96380], 534
Isabella [96385], 533
Joseph Aloysius [96379], 534
William T. [96384], 534
WALL
Mary [110027], 343
WALLACE
Catherine 'Kate' [92182], 45
Nora A. [95738], 469
William [95739], 469
WALSH
Bridget [107180], 378
Francis A. 'Franky' [29102], 581
James Aloysius [81207], 581
Mary [100184], 211
WARD

Volume III
Descendants of Immigrants born 1805 – 1810
Name Index

Child [99328], 253
James [99325], 253
John [99327], 253
Mary J. [99329], 253
Thomas F. [99324], 174, 253
Thomas F. [99330], 253
BROADBENT
Ellen [97309], 474
Ellen wife of Joseph [97305], 474
James [97302], 440, 474
John [97308], 474
Joseph [97304], 474
BROUGH
George W. [98623], 59
Ida G. [98622], 19, 59
BROWN
Catherine [98576], 192
Eleanor [98030], 328
BUCKLEY
Abina [104799], 430, 441
BURGESS
James [98137], 335
John [98136], 335
BURKE
Maria [100687], 398
Mary [96657], 32
BURNS
Henry [92617], 518
Mary E. [100519], 230
Mary E. [92616], 518
BUTLER
Lillian C. [96323], 155, 240
Nicholas [96324], 240
CAHILL
Edward [104417], 50
Edward J. [102366], 133
Mary Anne [104416], 12, 50
CALLAHAN
Catherine F. 'Katie' [107411], 8, 35
Daniel [102984], 436
Daniel [94242], 354
Daniel [98243], 473
Dennis [98245], 439, 473
Ellen wife of Wiliam [107413], 35
Hannah [94223], 304, 354
Joanna [102983], 436
Mary [98247], 473
Mary wife of Daniel [102985], 436
Patrick [105338], 210
William [107412], 35

William H. [107467], 473
Winifred T. [105334], 135, 210
CALLERY
John [107075], 88
Rita V. [107069], 79, 88
CAMPBELL
John Arthur [100726], 397
Mary E. [98088], 323
CANALES
Joseph [102501], 281
Mr. [102500], 234, 281
Robert [102502], 281
CARDOZA
George [105578], 268
CAREY
Catherine [101675], 505
Edward [101669], 472, 505
Ellen [101676], 505
Erinna C. [104512], 322, 381
Hanora [101673], 505
Jennie [101674], 506
John [101670], 505
John [107416], 34
Margaret Bridget [101679], 506
Mary [101672], 505
Mary [107415], 8, 34
Michael W. [108521], 381
CARR
Andrew [101630], 40
Bridget wife of Andrew [101631], 40
Margaret A. [101629], 40
CASEY
Bridget [101350], 302, 349
Joanna [107387], 319
John [101369], 349
CASSIDY
Mary A. [107315], 396
CAULFIELD
Agnes [97484], 264
Estella V. [97483], 264
James Joseph [97480], 184, 264
John J. [97481], 264
Mary F [97485], 264
CAWLEY
Bridget Ann [105353], 136, 212
Patrick [100038], 212
CHARETTE
Leona Marie [100699], 397, 425

CHEW
Harriet B. [93022], 149, 234
Thomas [102506], 234
CHRISTMAS
Annie [99048], 226
CLARK
Catherine [101702], 303, 351
Charles [99393], 412
Mary J. [99392], 366, 412
Mary wife of Patrick [101759], 351
Patrick [101758], 351
Philip James III. [102566], 533
CLORITE
Eda A. [98897], 245
COFFEY
Anna [95088], 388
Catherine [97246], 515
Child [95105], 388
Dennis [95078], 333, 388
John Dennis [95089], 388
Michael [95079], 388
COLBERT
Margaret [99995], 259
COLBY
Ellen E. [97833], 125
COLEMAN
Catherine wife of Thomas [100709], 395
Ellen [96680], 88
Julia M. [100707], 348, 395
Thomas [100708], 395
COLLERAN
Maria [102110], 479, 512
Thomas [102111], 512
COMHANE
James [108145], 140
CONANT
Ella E. [98932], 426
CONNELL
Hannah [100392], 29
Margaret [97857], 27
Mary T. [109893], 278
CONNELLY
Ann [97402], 400
Elizabeth [107201], 83
Emma T. [98313], 176, 255
Thomas [98314], 255
CONNOLLY
Cornelius D. 'Neil' [99334], 254
Paul [99335], 254
Peter F. [99331], 174, 254

Peter F. [99332], 254
CONNOR
Bridget wife of James
[104321], 466
Elizabeth G. [97137], 151,
236
James [104320], 466
Martha [97138], 236
Thomas J. [104318], 438,
466
CONNORS
Agnes T. [97921], 353
CONROY
Child [103908], 53
Constance wife of Gabriel
[102041], 202
Ellen wife of John [100363],
324
Gabriel [102038], 202
Hannah [93165], 293, 324
James [102040], 202
James F. [102035], 123,
202
James P. [102036], 202
John [100362], 324
John [103902], 53
John [103907], 53
Margaret [96754], 434, 458
Mary [102039], 202
Michael [103901], 14, 53
Philip [96839], 458
CONSEICAO
Maria C. [100479], 250
CONSIDINE
Mary [94954], 413
COOK
Clarinda [105514], 263
COOKLEY
Margaret [108386], 224
CORCORAN
Mary A. [97376], 45, 75,
484, 516
Michael [110184], 45
Stephen S. [107763], 46
Timothy [107764], 45
CORKERRY
Michael [97377], 11, 45,
516
CORREIA
Alban A. [102497], 234
CORRIGAN
Frank [95779], 159
Hanora E. J. [95778], 159
Josephine F. [95774], 158
Owen J. [95963], 43, 158

Sarah [99218], 43
COSGROVE
Ann [98076], 301
COSTELLO
Eva G. [98906], 364, 408
John [98909], 408
COTTER
Joanna [93894], 24
COUGHLIN
Catherine C. [99039], 220
Elizabeth G. [99671], 322,
380
James [94325], 220
James H. [103240], 221
John H. [99038], 141, 220
John H. [99043], 221
Patrick [99679], 380
COURTNEY
Daniel [100697], 346
Mary [100689], 301, 346
COVELL
George [103023], 514
Laura [103022], 479, 514
COX
Catherine [94818], 367
COYNE
Ella [105579], 188
CRAIG
Jane [97822], 437, 464
Mary wife of Robert
[103586], 464
Robert [103585], 464
CRANDEL
Selina [109767], 278
CREIGHTON
Edward J. [103387], 462
Rosa wife of Edward J.
[103388], 462
Rose [103374], 437, 462
CROSSON
Ellen [100467], 250
CROWLEY
Ann [97790], 440
Anna [109579], 338
Catherine [103066], 430,
441
Margaret [94071], 449
Michael [97793], 440
CULLIGAN
John W. [107239], 425
Patrick [107235], 424
Patrick William [107234],
396, 424
CULLINANE
Catherine [102539], 18

CULP
Herbert Joseph [98524],
277
CUMMANE
James [93968], 106
CUMMINGS
Catherine [79192], 140, 220
Dennis [110228], 164
Edward Bernard [102398],
134
Eugene [110218], 164
Eugene J. [83936], 21, 67,
140, 219
Eugene R. [108244], 67
Hannah [97135], 91, 106
Hannah 'Annie' A. [108247],
67
James Lawrence [108248],
67
John A. [108246], 67
Leontine 'Lee' [108243], 67
Lillie T. [108249], 67
Lucy B. [98130], 336
Mary V. [108245], 67
Patrick [98131], 336
CUMMINS
James 'Comhane' [83933],
67, 102, 140
Mary [83935], 140
CUNNINGHAM
Catherine [106030], 4, 15
Ellen [106960], 523
CURRAN
James [108574], 85
Mary Etta [104248], 65, 85
CURRY
Margaret [93027], 150, 235
CURT
Noreen [108573], 85
CUSICK
Andrew [104028], 417
Bridget wife of Andrew
[104029], 417
Florence M. [104032], 417
George D. [104031], 418
James H. [104033], 417
John E. [104030], 418
Matthew [104024], 372, 417
CYR
Angelus E. [95401], 249
Catherine E. [95402], 249
George [95381], 164, 248
Gilbert [95397], 248
Gilbert [95399], 248
Julia M. [95396], 248

Julienne [95400], 248
Louis L. [95403], 249
DAILEY
Benjamin [102226], 473
Robert J. [107465], 473
DAILY
Daniel H. [97960], 477
Ellen [97959], 477
John [97928], 477, 478
John F. [97970], 477
Julia E. [97964], 477
Mary [97925], 441, 478
Mary [97958], 477
William [97956], 441, 477
DALEY
Catherine wife of Thomas
[104405], 49
Charles [104403], 12, 49
Charles [104429], 49
Daniel Francis [104438], 49
Edward [104430], 49
Lizzie [104437], 49
Martha Cecelia [104431],
49, 76
Mary F. [104436], 49
Michael [105692], 153
Thomas [104404], 49
William J. [105691], 153
DALTON
Elizabeth wife of Martin
[97881], 26
James F. [97868], 26
Martin [97880], 26
DAVIDSON
Mary [105697], 153
DAVIS
Arthur [100273], 494
Bertha [100271], 494
Catherine M. [100268], 494,
526
Daniel C. [100276], 494
Daniel H. [100264], 444,
494
Daniel H. [100266], 494
Earnest A. [96681], 87
Frank [100270], 494
George [100272], 494
Mabel [100282], 494
Susanna wife of Daniel
[100267], 494
DECOSTA
Maria [104266], 84
DEEGAN
John [95405], 247
Timothy J. [95409], 248

Vernon F. [95407], 247
William A. [95408], 247
William H. [95404], 163, 247
DELAHANTY
Margaret wife of Michael
[104243], 65
Mary E. [104241], 21, 65
Michael [104242], 65
DELANEY
Elizabeth [98089], 322
Thomas [98100], 322
DELEE
Annie [106541], 420
DEPLITCH
Helen [106549], 377
DESMOND
Patrick [97856], 27
Timothy [97855], 27
DEVER
Nora [98142], 335
DIAMOND
Catherine Ann [108167],
288
DOHERTY
Delia [99869], 434, 459
DOLAN
Bridget [103012], 511
DONAHUE
Daniel [101881], 62
Hannah wife of Daniel
[101882], 62
Joanna [101880], 20, 62
DONEGAN
Margaret [110081], 92, 112
DONNELLY
Agnes V. [96390], 66
Catherine wife of Cornelius
[104327], 466
Cornelius [104326], 466
Dennis [104325], 437, 466
Dennis. [104328], 466
Dorothy H. [108770], 274
Ellen F. [104331], 466
Joseph [104330], 466
Joseph [108767], 189, 274
Joseph F. [108769], 274
Joseph F. [109277], 66
Julie Jeanne [108772], 274
Margaret [104329], 466
Mary [104332], 466
Mary [99385], 410
Muriel S. [108771], 274
Rose M. [108768], 274
DONOVAN
Catherine [93881], 5, 24

Cornelius [93931], 24, 335
Daniel [103614], 310
Daniel [93933], 297, 335
Daniel [98139], 335
Ellen [79133], 246
John E. [98129], 335
Julia A. [98135], 335
Mary [103608], 291, 310
Mary [108038], 181
Mary [98083], 322
Mary Louisa [98134], 336
Mary wife of Daniel
[103615], 310
Michael [98133], 335
Ruth E. [110064], 257, 285
DORCY
Julia [104740], 429, 438
DOUGAN
Janet [102507], 234
DOWNEY
Julia [95848], 173
DOWNING
Margaret 'Peig' [108035],
92, 114
DOYLE
Bridget wife of Henry
[100370], 325
Ellen 'Helena' [105568], 269
Henry [100369], 325
Jeremiah H. [99040], 221
Johanna [100368], 293, 325
Kathryn M. [103561], 509,
530
Thomas [99041], 221
DREFKE
Evelyn Emma [107755], 187
Robert [107756], 187
DRISCOLL
Dennis [107687], 313
Hannah [105759], 143, 148
James [97545], 10
Joanna [94186], 313
Johanna [105581], 189, 271
John [99653], 377
John Minihane [105588],
271
Julia wife of Dennis
[107688], 313
Julia wife of Timothy
[97547], 10
Mary J. [99652], 321, 377
Mary wife of Michael
[106950], 522
Michael [106942], 488, 522
Michael [106949], 522

Volume III Name Index

Patrick [106951], 523
Timothy [97546], 10
William [106945], 523
DROHAN
Catherine [98003], 405
Daniel [103618], 370
Johanna wife of Daniel [103619], 370
Patrick [103617], 370
DRURY
Mary A. [109278], 66
DUDLEY
Matilda [108258], 91, 107, 169
DUFFY
Andrew [107153], 46
Elizabeth [98101], 322
Ellen Agnes [107148], 11, 46
DUGAN
Mary [98315], 255
DUNN
Francis [100832], 77
John [100833], 78
John [92740], 77
John F. [92739], 52, 77
Margaret [100835], 78
Mr. [106607], 386
Owen T. [100836], 78
Paul R. [100831], 77
DWYER
Catherine [110177], 110
Catherine A. [105537], 139, 216
Daniel [108142], 92, 110, 155
Dorothy [110163], 110
Honora [110178], 110
John [110179], 110
Julia A. [100449], 166
Mary [107972], 107, 110, 155, 169
Mary [110180], 110
Quinlan [110181], 110
Richard [100448], 166
Richard [105540], 216
Richard [92722], 109, 166
Richard [92724], 166
EAGAN
Joanna [92741], 77
EBBITTS
Anna M. [96679], 87
ECELES
Lucy A. [104751], 469
ENOS

Mr. [108482], 231
ENRIGHT
Katherine [98538], 193
EVANS
Andrew J. Jr. [106904], 211
Andrew Johnson [106897], 136, 211
George E. [106898], 211
Mary [106903], 211
EVERETT
Warren [99991], 178
William [99986], 178
EYLWARD
Ellen [108575], 85
FADDEN
Bridget [106893], 210
FARRAGHER
Mary [101687], 508
FARRAR
Susan [107071], 88, 89
FARRELL
Bernard [107359], 394
Edward [100828], 435
Elizabeth E. [107358], 347, 394
Mary Ann [95062], 495
Mary wife of Bernard [107360], 394
Rosa wife of William [100830], 435
William [100829], 435
FEARNLEY
Hannah [98569], 275
FEENEY
Mary E. [92997], 105, 145
Mary T. [103002], 441, 479
Timothy [103019], 479
FELTON
Harry King [104426], 50
William S. [104427], 50
FERREIRA
Adelaide [104263], 64, 84
Jose [104265], 84
FINNAN
Mary E. [93915], 71
FINNEAN
Mary [92758], 237
FINNEGAN
Mary [107478], 476
FIRTH
Arthur [98567], 192, 275
Sarah [98574], 275
Thomas [98568], 275
FITZGERALD

Catherine E. 'Katie' [96162], 158, 245
Daniel [96163], 245
Ellen M. [93555], 478, 510
Mary [105745], 485
Robert [97968], 510
FITZPATRICK
Edward [99510], 401
Edward J. [93537], 350, 401
Ethel May [99509], 401
Joseph [99511], 401
Leo [99512], 402
FLAHERTY
Elizabeth [95365], 213
Hannah M. [95350], 213
Johanna [98883], 416
John [95366], 213
John Joseph [95354], 213
John W. [95349], 137, 213
Joseph P. [104590], 213
Mary E. [95364], 213
FLEMING
James H. [100278], 494
Lillie M. [100277], 494
FLYNN
Frank A. [100465], 168, 250
Frank A. Jr. [100476], 250
George T. [100475], 250
Helen M. [100474], 250
John [94774], 144
Margaret wife of Patrick [94775], 144
Mary [105592], 374
Michael [98075], 301
Patrick [94773], 144
Patrick [98074], 301
Thomas [100466], 250
FOGARTY
Catherine [100652], 389
FOLEY
Angela [99692], 422
Catherine 'Katie' [79186], 279
Honora [96636], 90, 101, 140
Mary [96325], 240
Stephen [83760], 422
Timothy Peter [99691], 383, 422
FORAND
Ezabel wife of Francis [106928], 230
Francis [106927], 230
Georgiann P. 'Georgie' [94760], 148, 230

Volume III Name Index

FORD
Bartholomew [101941], 224
Catherine Louise [99857], 224
Daniel [99855], 141, 224
John Daniel [99856], 224
FORISTEL
Katherine [108523], 382
FOX
Alice [107400], 35
Anna Mildred [107407], 35
Ellen Elizabeth [107404], 35
Irene [107406], 35
Margaret [107403], 36
Michael [107392], 9, 35
Robert [107401], 35
Thomas [107398], 35
Thomas [107402], 36
William [107405], 35
FRANCO
William [107789], 16
FRANEY
Bridget [108074], 182
Margaret G. [96534], 322, 383
Michael [96535], 383
FREEMAN
Rose A. [105324], 209
FRIEDRICH
Lucy Clair [102557], 531, 536
Nicholas Theodore [102558], 536
GAGNON
Margaret [105788], 258
GALLAGHER
Agnes [109497], 171, 253
Catherine [109502], 253
Hugh [109498], 253
Teresa [108760], 189, 273
GALLIGAN
Catherine wife of John C. [101845], 80
John C. [101844], 80
John E. [101846], 80
John H. [93506], 54, 80
Lillian D. [101848], 81
Theresa H. [101847], 81
GALLIVAN
Annie [106957], 488, 523
Ellen [96083], 488, 521
Joanna [106939], 488, 522
Joanna wife of John [106948], 487
John [106947], 487

John [96084], 443, 487
Margaret [106943], 488, 521
Mary [106940], 487, 520
Patrick [106938], 488
GALVIN
Elizabeth Gertrude [104439], 49
John J. [92906], 369
John J. [92907], 369
GAMMON
John [93534], 350
Mary [93533], 303, 350
Mary wife of John [93535], 350
GARDELLA
Angela wife of Stephen [95353], 213
Stephen [95352], 213
Stephen A. [95351], 213
GARDNER
Lililan G. [100004], 286
GARRITY
Mary [106342], 524
GARVEY
Andrew [93013], 149
Mary Jane [93012], 106, 149, 238
GAVIN
Annie T. [94228], 354, 404
Thomas [94229], 404
GAYARD
Mary [100275], 527
GERAN
Mary A. [100837], 78
GILL
Mary [95406], 247
GILLESPIE
Elizabeth [102045], 201
Elizabeth wife of Lawrence [102033], 201
Francis [102047], 201
Gabriel G. [102046], 201
Hanora [102049], 201
Irene [102044], 201
Lawrence [102032], 201
Lawrence [102048], 201
Lawrence [98338], 255
Lawrence F. [102031], 123, 201
Margaret V. [102051], 201
Mary [102043], 201
Ruth [98340], 255
William [102050], 201
William F. [98337], 176, 255

GILMURRY
Ellen [102380], 133
GLEASON
Catherine [103624], 370
Dennis L. [93920], 275
GOERL
Kunigunde Lucy [102559], 536
GOFF
John J. [102979], 227
Lillian M. [99049], 227
GOFFE
Charlotte R. [103384], 462
John P. [103385], 462
GOODREAU
Hermime A. [95002], 534
GOODROW
Alice [107367], 423
GOOLEY
Thomas Joseph [106047], 237
GORMAN
Catherine [102392], 134
Ellen [99680], 380
Thomas [102393], 134
GORMLEY
Mary Jane [99258], 132
GOTHAM
Annie M. [107470], 440, 476
GRACE
Catherine [107399], 35
Catherine [98090], 322
Catherine [98093], 384
Daniel [98082], 322
Daniel [98091], 322
Daniel [98095], 384
David [98096], 384
David F. [98084], 322, 383
Eugene [98097], 384
Francis [98098], 384
John H. [98086], 322
Mary [98092], 384
Michael [98081], 293, 322
Michael [98094], 384
William F. [98087], 323
GRAHAM
Ellen Margaert [93041], 438, 470
John [102762], 470
Margaret wife of John [102770], 470
GRANDALL
Carmeleto [103386], 462
GRANFIELD
Catherine [100486], 251

Irene [101893], 83
James [101897], 83
John [101895], 83
John H. [101888], 83
Mary [101891], 83
Rita [101894], 83
Veronica [101892], 83
William J. [101887], 62, 83
HATHAWAY
Ann wife of Dennis [97223], 490
Daniel L. [97221], 444, 490
Dennis [97222], 490
Ella [97225], 491
Emma [97226], 491
Mary [97224], 490
HAYES
Catherine [94214], 481
HAYS
Ernest [108152], 182
HEAD
Frederick B. [97227], 444, 490
William [109921], 490
HEALEY
Catherine J. [95780], 159
HEALY
Catherine 'Cait' [107016], 142
Daniel [108297], 103, 142
Dennis [108298], 91, 103
Denny [107017], 142
Jeremiah [107018], 142
HEAP
Clara Ellen [99391], 411
HEFFEREN
James [97850], 26
HEFFERNAN
Bridget T. [97867], 26
Bridget Theresa [97874], 72
Edward [103893], 467
Edward [93892], 24
Ellen [97869], 27
Hannah C. 'Anna' [97854], 27
James [97852], 27
James [97865], 27
John Joseph [97853], 27, 71
Mary [100202], 26
Michael [93893], 24
Michael [97848], 5, 26
Michael [97861], 27
HENABERRY
Margaret [92908], 369

HENNEHAN
Bridget [102968], 376
HENRY
John [94771], 144
Mary H. [94770], 144
Mr. [108672], 207
HENSHAY
Elizabeth A. [103548], 227
HERBERT
Katherine [98132], 336
HERLIHY
Dennis J. [106353], 489, 525
Irene Margaret [106355], 526
Mary [106354], 525
William [106366], 525
HERRING
Elizabeth [104390], 12, 48
James [104401], 48
Mary wife of James [104402], 48
HICKEY
Mary [98512], 276
HIGGINS
Annie [95526], 496
HILL
Alice Maxine [100002], 259, 286
Arthur G. [100003], 286
HOGAN
Bridget 'Delia' [106340], 489, 524
Francis [106341], 524
HOLLAND
Cornelius [97536], 40
Daniel [97530], 10, 40
Daniel [97537], 40
Dennis [97534], 40
Edward [101638], 41
Eliza [101637], 41
Ellen [103903], 53
Ellen [105526], 252
Ellen wife of Michael [97532], 40
James E. [97535], 40
Mary [105971], 271
Mary [92424], 434, 455
Mary E. wife of James [101636], 40
Mary wife of Timothy [94412], 455
Michael [97531], 40
Morris F. [97543], 41
Nora [108059], 182

Patrick [97533], 40
Thomas J. [97542], 42
Timothy [94411], 455
Timothy F. [97538], 40
HORAN
Ann wife of Michael [94949], 373
Margaret E. [94947], 315, 373
Michael [94948], 373
HOUGHTON
Frances [93426], 496
HOWARD
Hannah M. [97140], 151, 235
Timothy J. [97143], 235
HOWE
Hanora [105706], 203
HUDNER
Genevieve F. [100007], 179, 260
William [100011], 260
HUGHES
Francis [97863], 27
Julia C. [97862], 27
HUMPHREY
Martha J. [95990], 146
HUNT
William F. [106547], 377
William F. [106548], 377
HURLEY
Alice [95868], 176
Ellen [97129], 106, 150
Ellen wife of Jeremiah [107694], 150
Jeremiah [107693], 150
Jeremiah [97962], 477
John [99433], 37
Margaret [99430], 9, 37
Mary [100656], 390
Mary [97996], 291, 304
Nancy [95348], 137
Nellie [97961], 477
HURST
Agnes [103627], 236
Annie [103005], 511
Barbara [107110], 426
Elizabeth [103008], 511
Elizabeth wife of Michael [103000], 511
Elizabeth wife of Michael [92952], 236
James H. [107111], 426
James H. [92950], 152, 236
James H. [98931], 426

Lucy [103006], 511
Maggie [103004], 511
Margaret [107108], 426
Mary J. [103007], 511
Mary J. [103626], 236
Michael [102999], 511
Michael [92951], 236
Nicholas [103003], 511
Nicholas A. [102997], 479, 511
Rosie [103009], 511
Samuel E. [107109], 426
Samuel E. [98930], 406, 426

HUTT
James L. [109540], 339
Lewis [109541], 339

IVERS
Catherine wife of Michael [97942], 375
Eugene [97950], 375
John E. [97939], 316, 375
John E. [97946], 375
Louise [97949], 375
Michael [97941], 375
Raymond C. [97947], 375
Ruth [97948], 375

JOLLS
Everett W. [109758], 424

JONES
Patricia Suzanne [103654], 244

JORDAN
Elizabeth [99394], 412

KANE
Bridget [105693], 153

KEANE
Hannah S. [101166], 330
Michael [101167], 330

KEATING
Dennis [108385], 224
Dennis Joseph [108384], 224
Eleanor [101660], 505
Mary [101659], 505
Mary wife of Patrick [101656], 504
Maurice [101654], 472, 504
Patrick [101655], 504

KEATON
Alice wife of James [107426], 8
James [107425], 8
Johanna [107397], 1, 8

KEAVY

John Savage [93947], 86
Mary E. [94211], 481
Michael J. [94779], 86
Patrick [94213], 481
William Blair [93946], 86
William Corr [93945], 70, 86

KEEFE
Elizabeth A. [93682], 19, 57
Elizabeth wife of Michael [93684], 57
Michael [93683], 57

KEELEY
Mary [105868], 405

KEITH
Eaden Joseph [98642], 44

KELLY
Catherine [95694], 6, 28
Catherine [99032], 225
Catherine V. 'Katie' [92904], 369
Catherine wife of Thomas [95697], 28
Cornelius [92900], 368
Cornelius L. [92883], 306, 368
Cornelius L. Jr. [92896], 369
Daniel [94146], 358
Daughter [92902], 369
Elizabeth J. [98922], 363, 406
Ellen [98785], 116
Ellen M. [92882], 368, 415
Ellen wife of Cornelius [92901], 368
Grace Julia [105973], 272
Hanora [100469], 168
Hanora [107683], 430, 442
Honora [104757], 519
Irene M. [105972], 271
Jack [105974], 272
James C. [105969], 189, 271
Jane Ann 'Jennie' [92895], 368
Jeremiah [92894], 368
Jeremiah H. [95847], 173
Johanna [109480], 98
John [104129], 406
John [92893], 368
John C. [92905], 369
John G. [105970], 271
Julia [92936], 304, 358
Julia [98039], 343
Julia F. [95840], 112, 173
Margaret [104418], 50

Margaret [110090], 177
Margaret [93380], 403
Margaret [94941], 13, 51
Margaret wife of Daniel [94147], 358
Mary [102198], 206
Mary [105018], 114, 180
Mary [94772], 144
Mary Isadore [92892], 368
Peter [105019], 180
Sarah J. [107471], 440, 476
Thomas [107477], 476
Thomas [95696], 28
Timothy [92903], 369

KENDRICK
Mary [97144], 235

KENNEALLY
Anna [95761], 242, 282
William J. [104002], 282

KENNEDY
Francis Edward 'Frank' [101345], 400
Joseph E. [94089], 450
Louise [94087], 450
Margaret [110231], 446
Margaret [94072], 449
Mary Frances [94088], 450, 495
Sarah G. [101328], 187, 267
Thomas [94070], 449
Thomas [95863], 176
Thomas [95867], 176
Thomas D. [101329], 267, 400
Timothy F. [94069], 433, 449

KENNEY
Bridget [102037], 202

KENNY
Catherine [97891], 352
Delia F. [94080], 432, 446
Edward [108886], 353
Elizabeth Ann [97911], 352
James [97923], 352
John T. [108885], 352
Joseph [108889], 353
Louise [108888], 353
Mary E. [106091], 352
Mary wife of Thomas [97908], 352
Patrick [94081], 446
Stephen [97912], 353
Thomas [97889], 304, 352
Thomas [97907], 352

William H. [97920], 353
KENYON
Doris [107185], 232
John [107186], 232
John [93087], 232
John F. [93095], 148, 232
Rita [107184], 232, 281
KERCY
Joanna [93932], 24, 335
KIELY
Ellen M. 'Nellie or Helen'
[101639], 42
Patrick [101640], 42
KILORAN
Annie [106367], 525
KING
Eliza wife of Thomas
[94778], 144
James [94776], 144
Marjorie L. [100727], 397
Thomas [94777], 144
KINNEVAN
Mary W. [106550], 238
Patrick J. [92757], 237
William P. [92756], 152, 237
KIRBY
Abraham [95989], 146
Mary [100279], 494
Sarah J. [95988], 146
KIRKMAN
Angela [94825], 415
Joseph [94821], 415
Mildred A. [94823], 415
William J. [94820], 367, 415
William J. Jr. [94824], 415
KYLE
Eleanor [92425], 428, 456,
499
LACEY
Catherine [107334], 531
LAHEY
James G. [97965], 477
Margaret wife of Patrick
[97967], 477
Patrick [97966], 477
LAMBERT
Mr. [94241], 405
LANE
Margaret [103020], 479
LANGAN
Ellen [99333], 254
LAW
Alice L. [107332], 513, 531
Richard T. [107333], 531
LAWTON

Benjamin H. [96659], 32
Sarah Teresa [96658], 32
LEARY
Abbie E. [79357], 143
Agnes G. [96718], 501
Catherine [93008], 144
Catherine [97797], 111
Catherine 'Kate' [110170],
165
Daniel F. [92157], 14, 53
Dennis [100655], 390
Dennis [94765], 143
Dennis F. [93011], 145
Dennis P. [107686], 313,
371
Ellen [107691], 372
Ellen [93680], 56
Francis B. [96721], 501
Hannah [105151], 73
Hannah [93007], 144
James [92134], 53, 160
Jeremiah [92540], 102, 310
Jeremiah [96715], 501
Jeremiah F. [93009], 144
Johanna [108146], 140
John [92598], 102, 291, 310
John E. [94785], 143
John T. [94408], 456, 501
Julia [94767], 144
Loretta M. [96717], 501
Margaret [94769], 144
Margaret E. [96719], 501
Margaret wife of Dennis
[94766], 143
Mary [100286], 444, 492
Mary [110216], 164
Mary [93005], 144
Mary [93010], 145
Mary [98804], 182
Mary A. [92174], 160
Mary E. [94184], 371, 416
Michael [110162], 109, 164
Sara G. [100654], 390
Timothy (Reen) [97799], 92,
111
Timothy [100287], 492
Timothy [110168], 164
Timothy [93004], 105, 143
Walter C. [96720], 501
LEDDY
Eliza [101352], 349, 400
James [92526], 400
LEE
Kyong Sook [108169], 288
Maria [109325], 290, 300

LEMMERMAN
Dorothy [100151], 533
LEYDEN
Ellen [97844], 341
LONERGAN
Margaret [101641], 42
LONG
Hannah [95993], 228
LOWNEY
Bridget [109422], 199
Catherine [99758], 305
Cecilia [106901], 200
Cornelius [91858], 305
Ellen M. 'Helen' [97842],
341
Ellen 'Nellie' [109416], 199
Francis [106902], 200
Genevieve 'Jennie'
[109417], 199
Gertrude [109418], 199
Hannah [109424], 199
James [109423], 199
Jeremiah [107015], 142
John [109419], 199
John [97843], 341
Margaret [109452], 191,
199, 274, 277
Mark [98540], 119, 199, 274
Mary [109420], 199
Mary [98529], 119, 193
Mary wife of Cornelius
[91859], 305
Michael [109415], 199
William [107002], 142
LUFKIN
Clara A. [98275], 33
LUMAN
Annie Viola [104423], 50
John F. [104424], 50
LUNDY
James A. [108520], 381,
421
James F. [108526], 421
Janet [108529], 421
Karen [108528], 421
Lisa A. [108527], 421
Peter [109914], 421
LYDEN
John [107063], 301
LYNCH
Alice [93677], 58
Alice [98800], 183
Bridget [105576], 268
Catherine [92544], 102, 311
Catherine A. [93687], 58

Cornelius [98630], 58
Cornelius L. [93675], 19, 58
Daniel [98799], 182
Daniel C. [98793], 116, 182
Daniel F. [109548], 336
Daniel J. [98631], 58
Elizabeth [98801], 183
Eugene P. [104793], 535
George W. [98802], 183
Hannah wife of John [109558], 336
Helena S. [93689], 58
James W. [104792], 519, 535
Jeremiah [92600], 91, 101, 311
Johanna wife of Timothy [93003], 105
John [102421], 535
John [109554], 336
John [109557], 336
John [98797], 182
Julia [92609], 142
Julia [92972], 91, 105
Julia Ann [109555], 336
Katherine [110056], 257
Lawrence [93676], 58
Lawrence Edward [93690], 58
Lois G. [93688], 58
Margaret [96663], 72
Margeret 'Maggie' [109556], 336
Mary [109610], 475
Mary [95335], 100, 137, 261
Mary [98798], 182
Michael [109547], 298, 336
Michael [98803], 182
Timothy [93002], 105
Timothy [95347], 137

LYONS
Josephine [92618], 518
Margaret [93322], 1, 3

LYTLE
Alice R. [98273], 33
Felton M. [98274], 33

MACDONALD
Martin [95809], 385

MACK
Ellen wife of Michael [107429], 8
Michael [107428], 8
Patrick [107427], 8

MACOMBER
Milton [99670], 419

MADDEN
Alice V. [101008], 185, 265
Mary [102112], 512
Patrick [101011], 265

MAHER
Bridget [94822], 415
Julia [107466], 473

MAHON
Agnes E. [104149], 237

MAHONEY
Catherine [92899], 369
Catherine [94243], 354
Mary [97929], 477, 478
Mr. [105349], 211

MAKIN
James William [102504], 234
Wilfred [102503], 234

MALEADY
James [93890], 68
Mary [93889], 24, 68
Mary wife of James [93891], 68

MALLOY
Catherine [99598], 294
Martin [99599], 294

MANGAN
Joseph [106961], 523
Mark [106958], 488, 523
Mark [106962], 523
Patrick [106959], 523

MANNING
Catherine [93678], 18, 56
Patrick [93679], 56

MANNION
Ellen wife of William [105807], 251
Matthew William [105804], 170, 251
William [105806], 251
William O. [105810], 251

MANSFIELD
Joseph Francis [94076], 495
Maurice [94075], 449, 495
Patrick [101627], 495

MARINO
Antonio [100283], 494
Guiseppe [100284], 494

MARK
Mandel [95996], 228
Samuel [95995], 228

MARTEL
Mary [102555], 531, 533

MARTIN

Eliza [106651], 207
Eliza [109542], 339
Mary E. [96004], 147, 230
Richard Alden [93950], 86
Thomas B. [100518], 230
Thomas Henry [93949], 70, 86

MARY
Annie wife of Mandel [95997], 228

MATLEY
John [107145], 47
John Charles [107143], 47

MATTHEWS
Cora M. [97539], 41
Lucious [97540], 41

MATTIMORE
Leonard [102123], 513

MAXAM
Annie [103024], 514

MAYMON
Eliza [101519], 148, 231, 536
John [108395], 231

MCBRIDE
Charles J. [98032], 328
Edward C. [98033], 328
Eugene [98025], 294, 328
Mary E. [98034], 328
Patrick [98029], 328
Thomas Winslow [98035], 328
William H. [98031], 328

MCCANN
John Joseph [102368], 133
Thomas [102379], 133

MCCARRON
Ellen [95701], 29

MCCARTHY
Anne E. [101754], 403
Bridget [99255], 132
Catherine [97674], 124
Catherine J. [105703], 96, 126
Dennis [104807], 485
Dennis [99251], 132
Dennis [99257], 132
Eugene [99250], 99, 132
Eugene [99262], 132
Florence [96706], 126
Hanora [99263], 132
Jack [108000], 156
Jeremiah Henry [99264], 132
John [99260], 132

Mary [107999], 156
Mary [99261], 132
Timothy [99256], 132
MCCARTY
Achibald [98306], 344
Alexander 'Sandy' [98305], 300, 344
Bridget [107417], 34
Catherine [93408], 313
Ellen [98244], 473
Ellen J. [93905], 5, 25
Jeremiah [93906], 25
Kate wife of Archibald [98307], 344
Margaret wife of Jeremiah [93907], 25
Mary [93242], 125
MCCOMB
Sarah [96319], 239
MCCONVILLE
Catharine [93919], 70
MCCORMICK
Mary [94493], 180, 261, 283
Thomas [94494], 261
MCCUE
Catherine [107753], 187
MCDONALD
Genevieve [107329], 82
James [107297], 506
Katherine [95810], 385
Margaret wife of James [107298], 506
Mary [95808], 324, 385
Mary Elizabeth [107056], 390
Priscilla E. 'Percie' [107296], 472, 506
MCDONOUGH
Elizabeth A. [104796], 535
Julia [100012], 260
Mary M. [104797], 535
Thomas [104795], 535
Thomas Joseph [104794], 520, 535
MCFARLIN
Mary [109568], 338
MCGAST
Nancy [94235], 290, 304
MCGINN
Mary [95964], 43, 158
MCGOWAN
Bridget E. [97873], 72
MCGRAW
Mary [93929], 1, 5
MCGREAVY

Margaret 'Martha' [92631], 99, 128
Margaret wife of Michael [92652], 128
Michael [92651], 128
MCHUGH
Margaret [97963], 477
Mary [99326], 253
MCKENDRICK
Margaret [99993], 178, 259
Michael [99994], 259
MCKENNA
Sarah [101889], 83
MCKENNEY
Felix [101750], 403
Felix E. [93914], 71
Felix H. [101749], 351, 403
George [101753], 403
Helena H. 'Elena or Lena' [93913], 25, 71
Henry Joseph [101752], 403
Mary wife of Felix [101751], 403
MCLOUGHLIN
Barbara [98140], 335
John [98141], 335
MCMANMON
Mary J. [99400], 413
MCMANUS
Agnes [109549], 337
George [109550], 337
Mary E. [105322], 135, 209
Patrick [105323], 209
Sarah wife of George [109551], 337
MCNERNEY
Agnes K. [95107], 388
Bridget wife of Martin [95083], 388
Louisa B. [95106], 388
Martin [95082], 388
Thomas F. [95081], 333, 388
MCVAY
Alice [109577], 338
Alice G. [95763], 338
James H. [109578], 338
James H. [109652], 338
MCVEY
Henry [103652], 244
Sarah Gertrude [103645], 158, 244
MEADE
Mary [96660], 32
MEEHAN

Daniel J. [103317], 497
Margaret Ann [94409], 456, 497
MEISTRELL
Mary Laura [98519], 199, 277
MERCER
Thomas [106089], 341
Thomas J. [97838], 341
MERNIN
Mary E. [105696], 153
MILEY
Chester Houghton James [93423], 496
John F. [93421], 452, 496
May F. [93422], 496
Patrick [93425], 496
MINEHAN
Ellen [109572], 298, 337
Hannah [100288], 492
MITCHELL
Anne [107292], 150
Lucy A. [104259], 63
MONAHAN
Peter F. [95699], 29
Thomas [95700], 29
MONKOUSKI
John J. [108337], 499
MORAN
Katherine [100696], 347
MORGAN
Elizabeth [101760], 352
John [101761], 352
Permelia Elizabeth 'Lizzie' [109358], 181
MORLEY
Elizabeth Anne [108165], 279, 288
Lewis Richard [108166], 288
MORRISON
Eleanor Rose [99854], 279
MORRISSEY
Ellen [107236], 424
Frank J. [99681], 381
MOSHER
Edna Allen [105516], 263
Harold Cook [105515], 263
Linden P. [105512], 184, 263
Sherman [105513], 263
MOSS
Alfred [99390], 411
Isabella [99389], 366, 411
Mary A. [104352], 376

Volume III Name Index

MULHOLLAND
John [103889], 466
MULLEN
Bernard [97512], 292, 317
Catherine P. [97515], 317
Daniel [97513], 317
David B. [109486], 318
Emmogene [109518], 317
George Henry [109516], 318
Lauretta [109517], 317
Mary E. [109487], 318
Minnie Ida [109515], 318
Winnefred wife of Daniel [97514], 317
MURLEY
Mary [110227], 164
MURPHY
Anna G. [103582], 504
Anne [103864], 467
Annie J. [107468], 473
Bartholomew [99585], 326
Bartholomew 'Batt' [110171], 165
Bridget [105550], 268
Catherine [108670], 130
Catherine [96705], 90, 96
Catherine A. [103377], 501
Charles [103379], 502
Clara [99992], 178
Cornelius [103554], 509
Cornelius [104346], 316
Cornelius [110214], 165
Cornelius C. Jr. [103553], 478, 509
Daniel [97993], 304, 355
Daniel A. [103371], 462, 501
Daniel S. [103605], 310, 371
Dennis [98200], 486
Dennis P. [97999], 355
Edward [103579], 504
Edward T. [103558], 509, 530
Ellen wife of Bartholomew [99586], 326
Eugene [103584], 504
Eugene [99835], 223, 504
Genevieve [103580], 504
Hannah [97944], 292, 316
Hannah [97998], 355
Hannah wife of Timothy [100538], 39

Hanora C. 'Nora" [99659], 321, 376
James [93903], 371
Jean M. [103562], 530
Jeremiah [98184], 442, 486
Jeremiah [98185], 430, 442
Jeremiah 'Darb' [100468], 168
Joanna [105303], 117
Joanna B. [99582], 293, 326
Joanna wife of John [103376], 501
John [103375], 501
John [110217], 164
John Edward [103378], 501
Julia [110200], 111
Julia [95136], 291, 308
Julia Veronica [98000], 355, 405
Katherine [100694], 347
Lauretta V. [103559], 509
Leo J. [103581], 504
Louis [103583], 504
Margaret [100462], 109, 168
Margaret [110215], 165
Margaret [98149], 476
Margaret [98199], 486
Margaret wife of Timothy [105239], 355
Marguerite [103560], 509
Mary [101712], 402, 407
Mary [110079], 113, 177
Mary [97997], 355
Mary A. C. [103557], 509
Mary A. wife of Cornelius [103555], 509
Mary J. [99834], 141, 223
Mary J.. [98910], 408
Patrick [102967], 376
Patrick [95146], 308
Rose C. [103556], 509
Thomas [100695], 347
Thomas [99840], 464, 504
Timothy [100537], 39
Timothy [100539], 39
Timothy [106466], 355
Timothy [95519], 355
MURRAY
Catherine A. [102965], 419
Hannah [97851], 26
MYERS
Richard P. [102364], 133
MYLES
Edward [100961], 344

Edward P. [98043], 344
NALLY
Michael [101158], 330
NANNERY
Joseph [103011], 511
Patrick Henry [103010], 511
NASH
Edward [99265], 132
NAVIN
Mary [97969], 510
NELSON
Margaret [94082], 446
NEWMAN
Alicia F. [98042], 344
Child [98044], 343
Christopher [98047], 343
John [98037], 300, 343
John [98048], 344
Mary J. [98046], 343
Peter [98045], 344
Robert [98038], 343
William [97798], 111
William [97802], 111
NICHOLSON
Rachel A. [98138], 335
NOLAN
James Francis [96011], 228
James P. [96008], 147, 228
James Patrick [96009], 228
Thomas A. [96010], 228
NOON
Sarah [103653], 244
NOONAN
Catherine [98640], 44
Dennis [98635], 10, 43
Hannah [98637], 44
Julia [98638], 44
Margaret [98641], 43
Mary [98639], 44
NORTON
Dennis J. [92753], 79
Elizabeth wife of William [99363], 365
Jane G. 'Jennie' [92749], 52, 79
Margaret W. [93997], 305, 365
William [99362], 365
NOYES
Charles P. [95992], 228
Eva M. [95991], 146, 228
NUTTALL
Joshua [107314], 396
Ruth [107313], 396
OBRIEN

Annie E. [99028], 141, 225
Catherine [101671], 505
Catherine [93668], 4, 17
Catherine [97310], 474
Catherine Clifford [98505],
198
Catherine wife of Dennis
[97312], 474
Catherine wife of James
[99844], 221
Dennis [93691], 17
Dennis [97311], 474
Elizabeth [104444], 76
Helen [98292], 289, 292
James [99843], 221
John [99031], 225
John A. [104442], 49, 76
Julia [98128], 289, 296
Mary [110204], 170
Mary E. [99842], 141, 221
Mary J. [110202], 170
Mary wife of Dennis
[93692], 17
Stephen [110203], 170
Teresa [104445], 76
William R. [104443], 76
O'BRIEN
Mary [107765], 45
OCONNELL
Mary [100962], 344
ODONNELL
Catherine [107154], 46
John [107200], 83
Mary [99600], 294
Mary E. [107199], 62, 83
O'DWYER
Mary [102382], 90, 99
OGRADY
Irene E. [99665], 419
O'GRADY
John P. [99669], 419
Moncia [99668], 419
Patrick Joseph [99662],
376, 419
Rita M. [99666], 419
Thomas [99663], 419
Thomas [99667], 419
OLDING
Alice Loretta [107301], 507
Cumminger [107302], 507
OLIVERIA
John S. [99690], 383
OLLERENSHAW
Ada [104037], 418
OMELIA

Michael J. [107290], 150
Patrick [107291], 150
ONEIL
Catherine [100485], 251
Catherine [108001], 156
Catherine [97919], 90, 97
Corneilius [5205], 449
Ellen [105784], 113, 177
Hannah [95085], 289, 296
Hanora 'Annie' [79386],
433, 449
James [95775], 158
John [110193], 438
Margaret [94143], 429, 438
Margaret wife of John
[110194], 438
Mary [96171], 157
Mary E. [95773], 158
ORPEN
Abbie [102521], 246
Batt [100942], 139
Cornelius [102526], 246
Edward [102524], 246
John [109030], 160
John J. [102519], 160, 246
John J. [102522], 246
Julia [102528], 246
Margaret [102527], 246
Margaret wife of John
[102520], 160, 246
Mary [107664], 101, 139
Michael [102508], 108, 160
Michael [92175], 160
Robert [102525], 246
PACHECO
Marianna [98903], 281
PAINE
Adeline M. [106899], 211
PATE
Helen P. 'Ellen' [104257],
21, 63
Richard [104258], 63
PELOQUIN
Daniel [103891], 467
PERKINS
John [92898], 369
Susan A. [92897], 369
PETERSON
Louise [97541], 41
PHELAN
Mary Ann [101628], 495
PHENEY
Thomas [92998], 145
PICKEL
Albert Marvin [109425], 200

PILLING
Edmund Leo [106356], 526
James F. [95026], 526
PINEAU
George [102554], 531, 533
Helen 'Lena' [100145], 515,
533
Loretta [102553], 515, 531
POLLACK
Charles Henry [99859], 224
POLLOCK
Charles Harold [99858], 224
PONTES
Charles [99880], 460
Isabella Marie [99879], 460
PONTIFF
Eugene Jackson [100477],
168, 250
PONTIFICE
Antoine J. [100478], 250
Eugene [100480], 251
POWER
Ann [92729], 91, 109, 169
POWERS
Christine [105344], 211
Edward [105340], 135, 210
Ellen [105346], 211
Joanna [107076], 88
Johanna 'Liah' [5217], 449
John Joseph [105348], 211
Julia [105343], 211
Mary [93886], 25, 69
Mary E. [105347], 211
Nicholas [93887], 69
William [106624], 210
William E. [105345], 210
PRICE
Margaret [94230], 404
QUINLAN
Amanda [103611], 370
Catherine Frances 'Kate'
[103612], 370
Christpher [103613], 371
John [103623], 370
John Edward [103625], 370
Mary Catherine [109009],
249, 262, 283, 287
Mary wife of Thomas
[101182], 331
Nellie [101180], 331
Patrick [103609], 310, 370
Thomas [101181], 331
William Henry [103610], 370
Winnie [103616], 370
QUINLIVAN

Edward [95392], 250
Elizabeth [95394], 250
Gertrude [95391], 249
Helen [95395], 250
John [95389], 250
Margaret F. [95393], 250
Michael F. [95388], 164, 249, 287
Thomas [105718], 249
QUINN
Elizabeth wife of Michael [104392], 76
Joseph [104387], 48, 76
Joseph [104394], 76
Mary [104393], 76
Michael [104391], 76
William Christopher [104395], 76
RAISH
Blanch L. wife of Edward [99183], 279
Edward Lester [99182], 279
Marian Josephine [99179], 228, 279
RAPOSA
Mr. [108519], 88
READ
Charles E. [95553], 414
Mary [95552], 367, 414
REAGAN
Catherine [107690], 313
Catherine F. [105704], 126, 203
Daniel [94185], 313
Dennis [107689], 313
Dennis [94950], 291, 312
Ellen [101012], 265
Hanora [93409], 313
John [107692], 313
John [94808], 306, 368
Julia [97927], 430, 441
Margaret [104223], 20, 60
Margaret [98183], 442, 486
Mary A. [97887], 313, 371
Mortimer [98180], 486
Patrick [92444], 368
Quinlan [104224], 60
Quinlan [105705], 203
Rosanna [94809], 368
REARDON
Catherine [104434], 76
REDDY
Honora V. wife of John [103393], 502
John F. [103392], 502

Mary Adelaide [103391], 502
REGAN
Mary [106361], 526
REYNOLDS
Annie F. [99044], 142, 226
Patrick [99045], 226
RICHARDS
Armese [100269], 494, 527
Bertha [100280], 527
Pascal [100274], 527
RICHEY
Frederick [103898], 467
George [103900], 466
Hannah 'Annie' [103890], 467
Harriet wife of John [103885], 466
Harriett [103888], 466
John [103884], 466
John [103894], 467
Joseph [103881], 438, 466
Josephine [103897], 467
Julia Ann [103892], 467
Mary [103883], 466
William [103899], 467
RICHIE
Joseph [103880], 467
RILEY
Abbie [102945], 480
Mary [96164], 245
RIORDAN
Johanna [106338], 443, 489
ROBERTS
Jesse M. [110206], 170
ROBINSON
Catherine [106046], 237
Lillian A. [104150], 237
William J. [104148], 237
William J. [104151], 237
William T. [92948], 152, 237
ROHRBACH
Mary Hellen [94077], 495
ROONEY
Elizabeth [98339], 255
ROSTON
James [104036], 418
ROSTRON
William Edward [104035], 418
ROUSE
Annie D. [95704], 6, 29
James B. [100391], 29
RUSSELL
Mary A. [99388], 366

RYAN
Elmer E. [94240], 405
James [105867], 405
James F. [94237], 355, 405
James F. Jr. [94238], 405
Mary G. [94239], 405
SALMON
Ellen [104415], 47
James [104412], 12, 47
James [104413], 47
Mary A. [104414], 47
SARGENT
Elizabeth [92641], 205
Genevieve [92636], 205
Irene [92640], 205
James [92635], 129, 205
John [102194], 205
John [92639], 205
Martha [92637], 205
Sarah E. wife of James [102195], 205
SAUNDERS
Bridget [100648], 301, 344
Catherine [100774], 503
Cathleen N. [108480], 281
Ellen [100783], 503
James E. [100776], 503
John [107060], 290, 300
John H. [100781], 503
Margaret [108479], 281
Mary [107062], 301
Mary E. [100775], 503
Mary E. [108481], 281
Matilda P. 'Mattie' [100777], 503
Michael P. [108477], 280
Patricia A. [110159], 280
Patrick [100772], 502
Paul G. [108478], 280
Peter [100771], 463, 502
Peter F. [108474], 232, 280, 529, 536
Peter Francis [100782], 280, 503, 529
Raymond M. [108476], 280
Sarah E. wife of Peter [103591], 280, 503, 529
William [103593], 529
SAVAGE
Margaret A. [94780], 86
SCHALLER
Florence May [108884], 75
SCHEPIS
Anthony J. [108336], 500
SCHNELL

Elizabeth [107146], 47
SCHWENKE
Anton [109421], 191
Anton [109426], 191
SCULLY
Elizabeth [107303], 507
SHANAHAN
Margaret [110169], 164
SHAW
Hannah [97482], 264
SHEA
Bartholomew [101698], 351, 402
Bartholomew [101700], 402, 407
Bridget [102394], 134
Catherine [96539], 321
Catherine 'Cait' [108296], 103, 142
Catherine wife of Cornelius [97518], 318
Catherine wife of Daniel [98103], 163
Cornelius [100979], 113
Cornelius [94943], 315, 373
Cornelius [97517], 318
Cornelius H. [101706], 363, 407
Daniel [100977], 113
Daniel [108445], 20
Daniel [98102], 163
Dennis [109014], 249
Dennis [94944], 373
Dennis [94946], 373
Dennis [96538], 321
Ellen [109468], 97, 126
Elsie Mae [97619], 446
Elusdere [101703], 402
Francis A. [101709], 407
Hannah wife of Cornelius [100980], 113
John [100905], 249
John [105758], 143, 148
John [110230], 446
Julia [101010], 184
Julia [98766], 262
Katheine 'Kate' [101704], 402
Margaret [107345], 90, 95
Margaret [94758], 106, 143, 148
Margaret [96532], 293, 321
Margaret [97801], 111
Mary [101710], 408
Mary [104240], 4, 20, 220

Mary [107989], 156
Mary [108043], 115
Mary [95377], 109, 163
Mary [96531], 289, 293
Mary [98501], 93, 119
Mary E. [101705], 402
Mary wife of Cornelius [94945], 373
Mary wife of Daniel [108446], 20
Patrick [92608], 142
Patrick E. [101708], 408
Patrick M. [97516], 318
William [107187], 232, 281
William Jr. [107188], 281
SHEEDY
Ellen [92999], 145
SHEEHAN
Annie F. [103640], 157, 242
Catherine [98772], 182, 262
Catherine wife of John [109566], 298
Daniel [103641], 242
Daniel [98773], 116, 182
Denis [110196], 111, 170
Elizabeth Mary [102400], 134
Ellen [110205], 170
Ellen [98792], 182
Hanora 'Annie' [98780], 182
Honora [110198], 92, 111, 170
Honora [97528], 1, 9
John [109565], 298
Margaret [95776], 158
Margaret [98778], 182
Mary [98779], 182
Nancy J. 'Mary' [109538], 290, 298
Patrick H. [98781], 182
Tade [108058], 182
Timothy [110199], 111
William [110201], 170
SHERMAN
Geroge [100667], 390, 422
Noreen K. [100668], 422
SIDLEY
Agnes B. [105148], 33, 73
Edward [98271], 33
Ella [98269], 33
Ellen [108751], 93, 118
George [98268], 33
John [93038], 91, 101, 139
John P. [98261], 7, 33
John T. [98267], 33

Margaret [102296], 101, 139, 140
Patrick [98263], 33
Rebecca [98270], 33
William H. [98272], 33
SILVA
Frank Machado [98896], 245
Louisa Cappura [98895], 245
SILVIA
Antoine [105787], 258
Mary [105786], 177, 258
SIMARD
George [107331], 82
George Joseph [107327], 61, 82
John [107330], 82
Thomas [107328], 82
SIMPSON
Betsy [96322], 239
SISSON
Maria [95554], 414
SKAIN
Joanna wife of Richard [103622], 371
Richard [103621], 371
Sarah E. [103620], 371
SLATTERY
Anna M. [102961], 377, 419
Michael J. [102964], 419
SMITH
Catherine V. [92754], 79
Elizabeth [95230], 452
Elizabeth A. [104350], 317, 376
Florence [97706], 275
George [97707], 275
Hannah Louisa [94810], 306, 367
Isaac [97703], 275
John C. [104351], 376
Mary wife of Morris [94814], 367
Morris [94813], 367
Nicholas [93664], 374
Patrick [105591], 374
Walter [97702], 192, 275
Walter D. [97705], 275
SMYTH
Elizabeth Agnes [96686], 86
SNYDER
David [108662], 206
Ernestine [108661], 206
Harry [108660], 206

Eugene [97136], 151
Eugene [97807], 429, 437
Eugene [97821], 437, 464
Eugene Anthony [102960], 378
Eugene Daniel [101667], 472, 507
Eugene E. [99658], 321, 379
Eugene F. [108393], 495
Eugene Francis [98502], 119, 195, 276
Eugene H. [99673], 381, 420
Eugene J. [98532], 193
Eugene Joseph [93916], 25, 70
Eugene Joseph Jr. [93943], 70
Eugene Michael [103203], 517
Eugene P. [93416], 452
Eugene R. [92974], 105, 145
Eugene R. [96000], 228
Eugene S. [89002], 495
Eugene Sylvester [98516], 198, 276
Eugene William [95341], 137
Evelyn 'Eva' [100473], 168, 251
Everett [99519], 411
Father [106653], 130, 207
Father of child [107243], 396, 424
Fay wife of Edward [95715], 69, 85
Florence [100714], 396, 423
Florence [106027], 4, 15
Florence [107779], 16
Florence [108788], 140
Florence [95086], 332
Florence [95869], 175
Florence [96078], 522
Florence [96653], 1, 6
Florence [99862], 92, 113
Florence F. [96649], 32
Florence K. [100651], 389
Florence M. [96670], 73, 86
Florence Matthew Jr. [96675], 87
Florence T. [104025], 372, 417

Frances Brigid [110060], 256
Frances M. [95717], 85
Frances Mae [95994], 228
Francis [106343], 525
Francis [93029], 235
Francis [95703], 29
Francis Bernard 'Frank' [107754], 187
Francis H. [107978], 241
Francis J. [94284], 56
Francis Joseph [100725], 425
Francis Joseph [106339], 489, 524
Francis Michael 'Frank' [99997], 259
Francis P. [99397], 413
Francis T. [94421], 498
Francis Timothy [101626], 449
Frank [100715], 397
Frank A. [94084], 446
Frank C. [92890], 416
Frank Henry [104221], 392
Frank P. [108522], 382
Frederick [101357], 401
Frederick [94086], 52
Frederick [95713], 68
Frederick Daniel [102767], 470
Frederick J. [100720], 397
Frederick J. 'Fred' D.D.S. [93908], 25, 70
Frederick J. Jr. [93954], 71
Frederick Joseph [100294], 493
Gabriel (Fune) [97347], 94, 121
Gabriel [97351], 123
Genevieve Frances [100010], 260
George E. [101755], 351
George Edward [99999], 259, 286
George F. [97379], 75
George Francis [96676], 87
George H. Jr. [96005], 230
George Henry [96002], 147, 228
George Jr. [100005], 286
George N. [92748], 446
George Washington [99877], 459

George William [97667], 125
Gerald Vincent [92752], 79
Geraldine [98894], 283
Gertrude [104228], 61
Gertrude [104441], 49, 76
Gertrude C. [99688], 383
Gertrude G. [93911], 25
Gertrude M. [99874], 459
Giles [105525], 252
Grace [107335], 531
Grace M. [99870], 459
Grace V. [106035], 393
Gwenilin [106362], 443
Hannah (Suonish) [97348], 94, 121
Hannah [100827], 434
Hannah [101001], 302
Hannah [101330], 267, 400
Hannah [101795], 243
Hannah [101942], 224
Hannah [102297], 139, 216
Hannah [105689], 107, 152, 233
Hannah [107349], 95
Hannah [107469], 439
Hannah [93503], 14, 54
Hannah [94553], 80
Hannah [96117], 10, 45
Hannah [96174], 91, 108
Hannah [96771], 429, 434
Hannah [97217], 444, 490
Hannah [97794], 440
Hannah [98908], 305, 361
Hannah [98921], 363
Hannah [99223], 296
Hannah 'Ann' [104744], 468
Hannah 'Anna' A. [99833], 141, 224
Hannah 'Annie' [101661], 438, 472
Hannah 'Annie' [103063], 481
Hannah 'Annie' [95337], 137, 213
Hannah Louisa [94811], 367, 413
Hannah M. wife of Mark [98892], 245, 283
Hannah wife of Cornelius [98079], 290, 301
Hannah wife of Daniel [101005], 302
Hannah wife of Timothy [93035], 291, 315

John D. [99024], 103, 140
John D. [99029], 225
John Dermot [108761], 273
John E. [102958], 377, 419
John E. [107974], 241
John E. [109575], 338
John E. [93670], 17
John E. [97951], 317, 375
John E. [98628], 59
John E. [98933], 407
John E. [99651], 321, 376
John E. J. [95987], 147
John Edward [104234], 60
John Edward [105582], 271
John Edward [95712], 68
John Edward [97668], 124
John F. [100008], 260
John F. [102531], 452
John F. [103204], 518
John F. [103207], 484, 516
John F. [107661], 139, 216
John F. [95557], 374
John F. [96697], 86
John F. [97131], 151, 235
John F. [98533], 193
John F. [98905], 363, 408
John F. [99593], 327
John F. [99847], 222
John F. Jr. [98917], 408
John Florence [99990], 179, 260
John Francis [96669], 72, 86
John H. [105801], 259
John H. [107348], 95
John H. [109469], 126
John H. [96648], 31, 73
John H. [98775], 262
John H. [99831], 141, 222
John H. Jr. [100691], 347, 391
John Harold [102295], 219
John Henry [106034], 15
John Henry [109656], 73
John J. [101347], 349, 399
John J. [101354], 401
John J. [102115], 513
John J. [105707], 204
John J. [106647], 130
John J. [108669], 130
John J. [109930], 282
John J. [93884], 24, 68
John J. [94490], 180, 261, 283
John J. [94759], 148, 230

John 'Jack' (Barrule) [105586], 118, 188
John Jr. [102963], 420
John L. [106659], 492
John L. [92629], 129
John L. [97943], 292, 316
John L. [98882], 416
John M. [98558], 194, 198, 275, 276
John P. [102563], 532
John P. [98542], 119, 193, 276
John Peter [110068], 257
John R. [109467], 97, 126
John R. [92887], 416
John R. [93033], 315, 373
John R. [94757], 106, 147
John S. [95750], 282
John T. ' Johnson' [103064], 481
John T. [100711], 396, 422
John T. [95861], 176
John Thomas [98144], 29
John V. [101879], 20, 61
John William [99838], 223
John X [101684], 508
John X. [92208], 434, 453
Joseph (Rev.) [109427], 274
Joseph [101793], 243
Joseph [104396], 48
Joseph [106348], 525
Joseph [93731], 130
Joseph A. [95705], 29
Joseph Christopher [107778], 16
Joseph D. [92750], 79, 88
Joseph D. Jr. [107070], 88, 89
Joseph E. [93419], 453
Joseph Edgar [97671], 125
Joseph F. [96541], 383
Joseph Francis [99307], 417, 426, 529
Joseph H. [92886], 416
Joseph H. [99878], 460
Joseph J. [109508], 252
Joseph P. [108335], 428
Josie [107419], 34
Julia (Shearhig) [93039], 91, 101, 139
Julia (Shearhig) [95080], 388
Julia (Suonish) [98179], 486
Julia [102192], 342

Julia [102225], 439
Julia [103380], 462
Julia [104800], 484
Julia [105546], 118, 187
Julia [107388], 320
Julia [108046], 115
Julia [109223], 15
Julia [109431], 195
Julia [109563], 299
Julia [110084], 177
Julia [110235], 291, 313
Julia [94064], 433
Julia [94829], 296
Julia [95147], 308
Julia [96079], 522
Julia [97218], 444
Julia [97666], 95, 124
Julia [97835], 299, 339
Julia [98036], 300, 343
Julia [98264], 33
Julia [98545], 191, 198
Julia [99985], 178
Julia A. [103606], 310, 369
Julia A. [108766], 189, 274
Julia A. [92721], 109, 110, 165, 169
Julia A. [92937], 359
Julia A. [92946], 152
Julia A. [93505], 54, 80
Julia A. [98913], 363
Julia A. [99595], 328
Julia Ann [101716], 351, 402
Julia B. [108673], 131
Julia E. [100367], 325
Julia E. [100723], 425
Julia E. [92745], 52
Julia E. [95142], 309
Julia E. [96003], 147
Julia E. [98262], 7, 32
Julia F. [100464], 168, 250
Julia F. [94815], 367
Julia Frances [106912], 330, 387
Julia G. [97701], 192, 275
Julia V. [106900], 136, 211
Julia V. [99336], 174
Julia wife of Jeremiah [99983], 178
Julia wife of John [107783], 1, 3
Julia wife of Timothy [94827], 289, 295
Justin [104026], 313, 372
Kate [92944], 359

Margaret wife of Timothy [97350], 90, 94
Margaritta [95711], 68
Margorie B. [106926], 230
Maria [109327], 300
Marian B. [100724], 425
Marion P. [109757], 424
Marjorie [107338], 531
Marjorie [98513], 276
Mark [101791], 243
Mark [99217], 9, 38
Mark A. [96166], 245, 283
Mark A. Jr. [100147], 533
Mark Anthony [97254], 515, 532
Mark Augustus [95770], 158, 244
Mark E. [101327], 187, 267
Mark P. [92509], 296, 332
Martha [92633], 130
Martha M. [104435], 76
Mary (Croumhane) [110088], 113, 177
Mary (Cumba) [94951], 291, 312
Mary (Fune) [94061], 52, 429, 432
Mary (Leigh) [109507], 92, 112
Mary (Mor) [99036], 91, 102
Mary (Shearhig) [108789], 140
Mary (Vallig) [83934], 67, 102, 140
Mary [100171], 319
Mary [100352], 37
Mary [100366], 325
Mary [100540], 39
Mary [100650], 345, 389
Mary [100698], 347, 390
Mary [100717], 397
Mary [100778], 463
Mary [100906], 249
Mary [101657], 472, 504
Mary [102008], 108
Mary [102024], 342
Mary [102386], 100
Mary [103208], 484, 516
Mary [103882], 438, 466
Mary [104193], 215
Mary [104230], 60
Mary [104420], 50
Mary [104479], 140
Mary [105020], 180
Mary [105339], 135, 210

Mary [105710], 204
Mary [105722], 520
Mary [105748], 486
Mary [106032], 15
Mary [107365], 423
Mary [107418], 34
Mary [107970], 155, 240
Mary [108037], 114
Mary [108144], 91, 102
Mary [108255], 20
Mary [108257], 20
Mary [108295], 106
Mary [108299], 91, 103
Mary [109444], 191
Mary [109446], 119, 191, 277
Mary [109471], 127
Mary [109611], 475
Mary [110083], 177
Mary [110187], 107
Mary [83880], 422
Mary [92511], 333
Mary [92599], 102, 291, 310
Mary [92967], 220
Mary [93034], 315
Mary [93073], 232
Mary [93338], 14, 52
Mary [94062], 432
Mary [94506], 261
Mary [94649], 306
Mary [94828], 295
Mary [95383], 91, 108
Mary [95462], 460
Mary [96168], 245
Mary [96772], 434, 456
Mary [97141], 235
Mary [97219], 444, 490
Mary [97670], 125
Mary [97994], 304, 355
Mary [98080], 293, 322
Mary [98186], 430, 442
Mary [98290], 292
Mary [98506], 198
Mary [98911], 361
Mary [99216], 9, 37
Mary [99374], 409
Mary [99589], 327
Mary [99980], 113, 178
Mary A. [101364], 400
Mary A. [104742], 438, 468
Mary A. [106345], 525
Mary A. [106352], 489, 525
Mary A. [107685], 487
Mary A. [107976], 241
Mary A. [92949], 152, 236

Mary A. [93289], 435, 460
Mary A. [93415], 452, 495
Mary A. [93669], 18
Mary A. [94283], 56
Mary A. [94407], 456, 500
Mary A. [96540], 383, 422
Mary A. [96646], 31, 72
Mary A. [97248], 482, 515
Mary A. [97932], 478, 509
Mary Ann [108657], 130, 206
Mary Ann [96315], 154
Mary Barbara [93944], 70, 85
Mary C. [107758], 187
Mary C. [96193], 291, 312
Mary C. [96194], 312
Mary D. [93529], 303
Mary Denista (Sister) [106602], 386
Mary E. [101699], 351, 402
Mary E. [101872], 373
Mary E. [102765], 470
Mary E. [102998], 479, 510
Mary E. [105327], 209
Mary E. [105768], 520
Mary E. [107665], 139
Mary E. [109535], 299, 338
Mary E. [109573], 337
Mary E. [92973], 105, 142
Mary E. [94415], 497
Mary E. [95986], 147
Mary E. [98126], 297, 334
Mary E. [99364], 365
Mary E. [99868], 458
Mary E. wife of Edward J. [104060], 57
Mary Elizabeth [96698], 86
Mary Elizabeth 'Lizzie' [103071], 482
Mary Ellen [104388], 48, 75
Mary Ellen [105968], 189, 271
Mary Ellen [107144], 46
Mary Estelle [98923], 406, 426
Mary Etta [107431], 35
Mary F. [103372], 462, 501
Mary F. [105511], 184, 262
Mary F. [97849], 5, 26
Mary G. wife of Jeremiah [109403], 262
Mary Gertrude [98530], 193
Mary H. [92624], 499
Mary H. [95841], 174, 253

Theresa 'Eleanor T.' M. [94416], 498

Therese L. [101685], 508

Thomas [104389], 12, 47

Thomas [106347], 525

Thomas [107410], 9

Thomas [109324], 290, 299

Thomas [109326], 300

Thomas [109989], 139

Thomas [93025], 234

Thomas [94491], 180

Thomas [95710], 68

Thomas A. [107975], 241

Thomas A. [95984], 146

Thomas D. [94233], 404

Thomas D. [95771], 158

Thomas E. [93952], 70

Thomas F. [94504], 261

Thomas F. [95143], 310

Thomas H. [106351], 489

Thomas Jefferson [93912], 25

Thomas M. [94500], 215

Thomas S. [98006], 405

Thomas Sylvester [98001], 355, 405

Timothy (Keach) [105527], 112, 171

Timothy (Keach) [109506], 92, 111

Timothy (Og) [96635], 90, 101, 140

Timothy (Shearhig) [110054], 112, 176

Timothy (Shearhig) [110080], 92, 112

Timothy (Shearhig) [96504], 90, 95

Timothy [100169], 289, 292

Timothy [100290], 492

Timothy [100545], 10

Timothy [101321], 92, 117

Timothy [101325], 186

Timothy [101794], 243

Timothy [102030], 122

Timothy [102114], 513

Timothy [103389], 429, 436

Timothy [104743], 468

Timothy [104791], 520

Timothy [107391], 320

Timothy [107971], 155, 240

Timothy [108256], 91, 107, 169

Timothy [108671], 131

Timothy [109279], 289, 297

Timothy [109281], 297

Timothy [109429], 195

Timothy [109449], 191

Timothy [109472], 127

Timothy [110086], 177

Timothy [110189], 107

Timothy [93333], 14

Timothy [93336], 14, 51

Timothy [93431], 429, 434

Timothy [93939], 6

Timothy [93998], 291, 305

Timothy [94060], 52, 429, 431

Timothy [94552], 80

Timothy [94646], 291, 305

Timothy [94940], 13

Timothy [94960], 45

Timothy [95340], 137

Timothy [95386], 163

Timothy [95600], 293, 318

Timothy [95777], 157

Timothy [96173], 91, 107

Timothy [96506], 162

Timothy [96530], 289, 293

Timothy [96664], 32

Timothy [96776], 457

Timothy [97147], 151

Timothy [97349], 90, 94

Timothy [97913], 367

Timothy [98291], 289, 292

Timothy [98765], 262

Timothy B. [99830], 141, 221

Timothy C. [94406], 455, 496

Timothy C. [94418], 498

Timothy Christopher [110055], 256

Timothy D. [93323], 3

Timothy D. [99655], 321, 376

Timothy Dionysius (Rev.) [104803], 484

Timothy F. [109445], 119, 189, 277

Timothy H. [104253], 20, 62

Timothy H. [105352], 135

Timothy J. [102293], 140, 218

Timothy J. [92742], 52, 78

Timothy J. [94066], 433, 447

Timothy J. [95376], 108, 162

Timothy P. [94826], 289, 295

Timothy R. [93030], 291, 314

Timothy R. [93413], 434, 450

Timothy R. Jr. [93420], 452

Timothy S. [93406], 313

Timothy Sylvester [98509], 198, 276

Walter [109657], 73

Walter E. Jr. [104249], 85

Walter Edward [104244], 65, 84

Walter J. [95864], 176, 254

Webster B. [104745], 469

Wife of Timothy D. [95332], 3

William [100292], 493

William [101527], 232

William [101790], 243

William [102966], 420

William [103651], 283

William [104322], 429, 437

William [105332], 209

William [106149], 123

William [109509], 252, 283

William [109513], 284

William [92942], 359

William [93902], 25

William E. [100700], 348, 394

William E. [100712], 396

William E. [101353], 400

William E. [94509], 262

William E. [99030], 226

William E. [99033], 141

William F. S. [98927], 406

William H. [101361], 399

William H. [102957], 377

William H. [96533], 322, 382

William H. Jr. [99689], 383

William H. 'Willie' [95768], 157

William Henry [107433], 35

William J. [106655], 131

William Joseph [96650], 32

William Michael [96169], 245

William P. [102199], 206

William S. [106546], 379

William S. [92638], 129, 205

William Taft 'T'homas' [99872], 460

Williiam P. [110051], 285

Volume IV
Descendants of Immigrants born 1815 – 1820
Name Index

Patrick [99829], 265
BRAHMSTEDT
Joseph [99852], 445
William F. [99851], 445
William Joseph [99850], 432, 445
BRAZELTON
Velma Lorene [106401], 442
BROOKS
Margaret T. [92794], 101, 154
William J. [92796], 154
BROWN
Nora [101096], 348
BUCHLER
Augustus Edward [102976], 214, 273
BUCKLEY
Bridget T. [95634], 408
Catherine [103512], 173
Emanuel [109897], 173
Herbert [103513], 173
Herbert William [103510], 160, 173
Mary [103511], 173
Mary [99903], 476
BULGER
Eva [100033], 87
Florence May [100025], 87, 139
George [100024], 87
John [100017], 86
John J. [100032], 87
Joseph W. [100013], 28, 86
Lillian J. 'Lilly' [100019], 86
BULHOES
Manuel Correia [108686], 179
BURKE
Edward F. [104078], 409
Edward P. [103117], 412
Ellen 'Nellie' [103122], 413
Francis M. [104077], 409
James [95000], 409
James H. [103120], 412
James H. [104075], 409
James Henry [104074], 364, 409
Jane C. wife of Matthew [103130], 413
John [103296], 279
Mary L. [103119], 412
Matthew [103112], 412
Matthew Joseph [103121], 412

Patrick [103111], 371, 412
Rose [94999], 409
Thomas H. [103297], 279
William F. [103118], 412
BURNS
Christopher [100450], 25
Godfried [100452], 25
BURR
Bronson S. [103124], 412
Maryetta [103123], 412
BUTKUS
Carl J. Sr.. [99976], 404
BUTLER
Mr. [99417], 380
BUTT
Joseph V. [99928], 401
BYRNE
Bridget [106422], 152
BYRON
Edward [102941], 289
Mary Elizabeth [102940], 289
CADEN
Catherine [106122], 422
Hannah [106121], 422
James [106120], 422
Jeremiah J. [106117], 421
John [106118], 422
Mary [106119], 422
Patrick [106075], 421
Patrick [106123], 422
Thomas P. [106116], 421
Thomas Patrick [106074], 376, 421
CALDEN
Dennis [109916], 219
Dennis [96505], 187, 219
Jeremiah [109032], 219
John [109033], 219
Julia [109034], 219
CALLAHAN
Ellen [93179], 1, 9
John [95635], 408
John P. [95632], 359, 408
Patrick J. [95633], 408
CALVEY
Ellen [106419], 30, 95
CARLEY
Margaret [93140], 507
CARMAN
Sarah A. [106560], 249
William [106563], 249
CARRAGHER
Anna K. [95242], 274
Bertha M. wife of Hugh [95248], 274

Catherine wife of Hugh [95241], 273
Daniel H. [95246], 274, 305
Elizabeth [95244], 274
Henry N. [95239], 214, 273
Hugh [95240], 273
Hugh John [95247], 273
Lillian Sarah [95243], 274
Mabel Mary [95245], 273
Robert Z. [95250], 305
CARROLL
Catherine F. [104022], 280
Johanna [104503], 94
Joseph A. [104021], 222, 280
Peter [96756], 280
Theresa J. [108983], 271
CASEY
Daniel [95313], 61
Hannah wife of Daniel [95314], 61
Mary [95298], 18, 61
CHAMBERLAIN
Amelia M. [102071], 144
Mr. [99419], 381
CHILES
Anna 'Nancy' wife of Thomas [106574], 194
Caroline [106566], 183, 194
Thomas [106573], 194
CHIPMAN
Hannah [106571], 249
CHRISTMAS
Annie [99048], 437
CLARK
Charles M. [102065], 144
Charles M. [97876], 89, 144
Ester V. [102069], 144
Frank [102070], 144
Mary E. wife of Peter [104094], 474
Mary J. [104092], 454, 474
Peter H. [104093], 474
Philip James III. [102566], 309
Sadie K. [97877], 145
CLIFFORD
Bridget [95638], 407
COFFEY
Catherine [97246], 282
COLBERT
Margaret [99995], 138
COLE
Edatha [107318], 177
COLEMAN
Eileen [101786], 170

Volume IV Name Index

George [101785], 132, 170
George William (The Most Reverend) [101787], 170
COLLINS
Annie [102714], 120
Johanna [104726], 366
Julia [109917], 219
Mary [95531], 201
COLLORAN
Sabina [99972], 443
CONNELLY
Bridget [93522], 1, 8
Dennis [91303], 373
Mary [104485], 324, 373
Sarah M. [106303], 124
CONNIFF
Mary [105030], 482
CONNOLLY
Mary [106678], 501
William Frances [99929], 401
CONNORS
Bridget [105656], 222
CONROY
Catherine M. [104857], 124
Child [104858], 124
Felix [93640], 123
John E. [93639], 52, 123
Margaret [104859], 124, 169
Mary V. [104856], 124
CONWAY
Daniel [100119], 457
Elizabeth [105028], 482
Jane [100118], 457
Margaret wife of Daniel [100120], 457
Patrick [105029], 482
COOK
Mary [100072], 283
COOKLEY
Margaret [108386], 435
COONAN
Dora [95609], 406
COONEY
Hannah [109984], 505
Sarah [93098], 132
COPPINGER
Eileen [103495], 166, 180
CORAY
John [108679], 179
CORBETT
Ann wife of William [99899], 475
Carmelita [99908], 403

John W. [99893], 344, 403, 476, 500
John W. Jr. [99907], 403
Joseph A. [99894], 403, 458, 475
Joseph Anthony [99906], 476
Mary E. [99900], 476
William [99898], 475
William J. [99904], 476
CORCORAN
Mary [102951], 289
Mary wife of Michael [102938], 288
Michael [102937], 288
Michael F. [102939], 288
Sarah [93134], 492
Timothy [102933], 241, 288
COSGROVE
Anne E. [103456], 310
COUGHLIN
Catherine C. [99039], 431
Ellen wife of Patrick [94905], 265
Henry [99828], 266
James [94325], 430
James [94900], 200, 265
James [94902], 265
James H. [103240], 431
John H. [99038], 394, 430
John H. [99043], 431
John J. [94903], 265
Julia O. [99825], 265
Lillian wife of John [99821], 265
Margaret [99826], 265
Mary F. [99820], 265
Patrick [94904], 265
Richard [99827], 266
COURTNEY
Alice [105734], 4, 29
COWEN
Ada A. [100856], 229
CROFTON
Mary [108979], 209
CRONIN
Mary [99738], 292
CROTEAU
Russell [108685], 179
CROWLEY
Catherine [103066], 231
Catherine [94192], 12
Catherine 'Katie' V. [105036], 482
Charles [105033], 482
Child [101086], 348

Cornelius [105858], 67
Daniel [105843], 22, 66
Daniel P. [105027], 482
Ida Louise [102715], 120
James [101080], 319, 348
James [101097], 348
Jeremiah [105026], 482
Jeremiah [105859], 67
Johanna [105855], 66
John (Ceohane) [108714], 66
John [102713], 120
John [105021], 460, 482
John [105032], 482
John [92664], 315, 335
John Henry [105856], 66
John J. [101087], 348
John T. [106302], 124
Joseph Michael [102712], 46, 120
Margaret [100424], 17
Margaret [101085], 348
Margaret [106304], 124
Mary (Ceohane) [105406], 127
Mary [105842], 66, 127
Mary Jane [92663], 335
Michael [101083], 348
Michael [101088], 348
Michael [106701], 17
Michael [108717], 67
Miriam [102716], 120
Nora [101084], 348
Patrick [105022], 482
Patrick [105034], 482
Patrick [105857], 67
Thomas N. [101089], 348
Timothy [105031], 482
William M. [106298], 52, 124
CUCICK
Fannie [101578], 457
Jennah wife of Thomas [101582], 457
Thomas [101581], 457
CUMMINGS
Adeline [95639], 407
Ellen [104697], 335
John J. [95637], 407
Thomas [95636], 407
Thomas F. [95628], 358, 407
CURRAN
Jane Elizabeth [97697], 56
CURRY
Catherine [109331], 445

DALEY
Catherine [95237], 273
DALTON
Edward [99579], 469
DECHER
Mary [97385], 44
DEMORANVILLE
Luther K. [100855], 229
Maurice A. [100854], 229
DENNIS
Catherine [93143], 493
DESMOND
Abby [98347], 10, 48
Abby wife of John [98351], 48
John [98350], 48
DEVITT
Bartholomew [106734], 427
John [106749], 428
Patrick Joseph [93791], 385, 427
Timothy [106750], 428
Wiliam [106733], 428
DILLON
Daniel [109111], 333
Edward [109112], 333
DINUCCI
Roger [103451], 284
Thomas Francis [103450], 284
DION
Cecelia V. [99956], 345, 404
Cecilia V. [99924], 345, 404
Joseph [99977], 404
DIVELBISS
Marvin Leroy [100248], 149, 172
DOHERTY
Frances J. 'Fannie' [95309], 126
Frederick J. [100208], 351
DOLAN
Catherine [103481], 160
Eliza [106127], 420
John [95645], 355
Martin [95643], 355
Mary Ellen [103476], 106, 165
Michael [103477], 165
DONAHUE
Daniel [99797], 20
Mary E. [99472], 118
Michael [99798], 20
DONOVAN
Edward [105654], 222

Jeremiah [98955], 463, 489
John [98961], 489
Margaret wife of Timothy [98957], 489
Mary [108038], 313, 320
Michael [105655], 222
Timothy [98956], 489
DOWD
John [106677], 501
Susannah Celia [106676], 478, 501
DOWNEY
Catherine [94545], 300
John P. [101091], 348
John P. [98808], 277
John R. [101090], 348
John Raymond [98807], 277
DOWNING
Margaret 'Peig' [108035], 353
DOYLE
Catherine [109895], 510
Ellen 'Nellie' [103452], 284
Jeremiah H. [99040], 431
Thomas [99041], 431
DRISCOLL
Catherine [103292], 279, 306
Catherine [94559], 302
Cecilia A. [103303], 279, 306
Cornelius L [103295], 279
Daniel A. [103284], 279
Daniel F. [103281], 222, 278
Edmund [103282], 278
Edward Francis [103288], 278
Francis Raymond [103285], 279
John L. [103287], 279
Laureta M. [103286], 279
Margaret [106388], 396
Margaret [106683], 478
Margaret [93145], 492
Mildred wife of Francis [103302], 279
DROGUE
Clara [102468], 415, 444
DUFFEY
Bridget [103363], 82
William [97382], 43
DUFFY
Gertrude A. [92813], 153
John [106421], 152

John Henry [92811], 97, 153
Margaret T. [92812], 153
Marie Agnes [106420], 95, 152
DUGAN
Mary [95219], 285
DUNN
Joanna [94912], 199
DUNNEGAN
Julia [98364], 23, 72
DUNNIGON
Cornelius [98365], 72
DURANT
Eliza [101784], 70
DWYER
Elizabeth [100455], 143
Hanora [94158], 2, 12
Jeremiah [109975], 511
Mary Jane [99930], 344, 401
Mary Loretta [108516], 503, 511
William [94191], 12
William [99932], 401
DYER
James [101094], 348
Jennie [101093], 348
Mary [95306], 127
EAGAN
Ann [98172], 166
Mary E. [93551], 306
Mary wife of Owen [93550], 275, 306
Owen [93543], 275
Owen Louis (Dr.) [93545], 275, 305
Patrick F. [93542], 214, 275
ENWRIGHT
Marion [95235], 273
Thoams H. [95236], 273
EVERETT
Warren [99991], 85
William [99986], 85
FALEY
Hannah [99312], 23, 72
Margaret wife of Thomas [99314], 72
Thomas [99313], 72
FALLON
Edward [106672], 136
Ellen C. 'Helen' [103411], 82, 136
FANNING
Annie wife of Patrick [105232], 39

John Francis [99451], 39
Patrick [105231], 39
FARRELL
Annie [104184], 190
Ellen [108792], 443
Ellen O. [95805], 376
Thomas [104185], 190
FAY
John E. [103458], 177
FEELEY
Margaret [97375], 43
FELIES
Augustus [104097], 455
Catherine wife of Pierre
[104098], 455
Pierre [104099], 455
FENNELLY
Catherine [95238], 273
Daniel John [95234], 272
Francis J. [95231], 214, 272
Thomas [95232], 272
FITZGERALD
Catherine [106719], 503
Margaret [96927], 490
Mary J. [99905], 476
FLAHERTY
Johanna [98883], 3, 26
John L. [98886], 26
Mary A. [106155], 303
FLEMMING
Bridget wife of Patrick
[100738], 363
Catherine [100734], 363
Catherine wife of Peter
[100732], 362
Genevieve L. [100736], 363
Mary [100735], 363
Patrick J. [100733], 363
Peter [100731], 362
Thomas [100730], 323, 362
Thomas J. [100737], 363
FLYNN
Bridget [100672], 368
Catherine [95006], 371, 414
James D. [95007], 414
Mary [104102], 454
FOGARTY
Andrew [106663], 50, 121
Catherine [100652], 313,
322
Gerald A. [106664], 121
John [106665], 121
John [106667], 121
Margaret [106668], 121
Margaret wife of John
[106666], 121

FOLEY
Daniel [83688], 54
Esther [91994], 55
Hanora [83765], 55
John [79272], 54
John 'Derrycreeveen'
[3851], 54
Mary A. [83689], 55
Michael F. [79276], 12, 54
FORAN
James [93142], 493
Margaret A. [93141], 493
FORD
Bartholomew [101941], 435
Catherine Louise [99857],
435
Daniel [99855], 394, 435
John Daniel [99856], 435
FORREST
Edwin Raymond [100456],
143
Edwin Raymond [109689],
143
FRANKLIN
Mary Ellen [107352], 240
FRAWLEY
Bridget [106735], 427
FREEBORN
Edward William [103535],
174
Mary Catherine [103515],
173
Samuel [103517], 174
Samuel Simpson [103514],
160, 173
FRIEDRICH
Lucy Clair [102557], 307,
312
Nicholas Theodore
[102558], 312
FURZE
Charles [107583], 337
John [92481], 337
GAGE
Sarah Prescott [106578],
249
GALE
Carl Custer [106576], 249
Nathaniel Smith [106577],
249
GALLAGHER
John Joseph [99455], 7
Margaret wife of Michael
[99457], 7
Michael [99456], 7
GALLIVAN

Ellen [96083], 466, 495
John [96084], 495
GARDNER
Emma [99923], 344, 400
Lililan G. [100004], 171
GARRITY
Margaret [110147], 388
GEREGHTY
Winnefred [93563], 254
GIBBONS
Bridget [103361], 27, 82
Edward [103362], 82
Margaret [103425], 234
GOERL
Kunigunde Lucy [102559],
312
GOFF
John J. [102979], 438
Lillian M. [99049], 438
GRADY
Mary [104829], 130
GRAY
Mary A. [105965], 389
GREADY
Austin [98614], 458
Mary wife of Austin [98615],
458
Michael [98610], 458
GREEN
Catherine [106266], 287
Joanna [101112], 25, 75
Joanna [96595], 149
John (Uohni) [108113], 480
Margaret [99435], 6, 38
Mary [95793], 377
Mary A. wife of Charles
[94354], 481
Mary wife of Philp [101115],
75
Matthew (Uohni) [99436],
38
Philip [101114], 75
GREENE
Charles E. [108132], 480
Cora [108131], 480
Eileen 'Della' [108130], 480
Harry J. [94353], 481
John [98331], 459, 480
Mary E. [98336], 480, 505
Matthew Richard [108137],
481
GRIMSHAW
Mr. [100788], 63
GRONAN
Francis J. [99468], 40
Lenora [99467], 40

Volume IV Name Index

HACKETT
Mary [93582], 295
HADFIELD
Grace W. [108680], 179
Pauline [108681], 179
Rita [108684], 179
Thomas [108682], 179
Thomas Joseph [103525],
165, 179
HANEHAN
Mary A. [106076], 421
HANGHLING
Joanna [104138], 130
HANLEY
Abbie [98476], 320, 351
Cornelius [79108], 328
Jeremiah [98477], 351
Margaret [79098], 314, 328
Mary [83636], 450, 465
HARDING
Charles [95374], 469
Ellen wife of Charles
[95375], 469
Jennie I. [95370], 228, 469
Loretta [99580], 469
Mary E. [99578], 469
William H. [95371], 228,
452, 469
HARNLEY
Ellen [95318], 18, 60
Mary wife of Michael
[95320], 60
Michael [95319], 60
HARRIGAN
Bridget [100307], 414
HARRINGTON
Anna [108785], 2, 19
Annie [106113], 391
Bridget (Caobach) [79110],
328
Bridget (Causkey) [99863],
85
Bridget [100658], 362
Bridget [105017], 481
Catherine [100839], 188,
227, 469
Catherine [92926], 223
Catherine [99025], 334, 394
Catherine 'Kate' [95788],
378
Catherine 'Katie' [96589],
219
Catherine wife of Timothy
[107557], 36
Cornelius (Tokirre) [94911],
199

Cornelius (Trokirre)
[109003], 320
Cornelius [106929], 486
Cornelius [108716], 66
Daniel [100840], 227
Daniel [106917], 168
Daniel [107677], 198
Daniel [92197], 461, 485
Daniel [94299], 58
Daniel [95785], 377
Daniel [95792], 377
Daniel [99035], 394
Daniel H. [101162], 111,
168
Daniel P. [100659], 362
Dennis [104000], 223
Dennis [108966], 209
Dennis [108968], 209
Dennis [98070], 449, 461
Ellen [100239], 92
Ellen [107563], 5, 36
Ellen [107843], 373
Ellen [93086], 69
Ellen [95604], 321, 356
Ellen wife of Cornelius
[106930], 486
Emma V. [95790], 378
Florence [100663], 361
Frances [106916], 168
Francis H. [108978], 271
Francis H. [109330], 445
Frank [100657], 362
Frank [108969], 210
Frederick Joseph [100661],
362
Hannah (Caobach) [95765],
422
Hannah [109105], 331
Hannah [93181], 9, 47
Hannah [96583], 218
Hannah [98266], 44
Hannah 'Annie' [95621],
321, 358
Hannah 'Nancy Ann'
[97883], 187, 221
Hanora [101322], 390
Helena [100660], 362, 408
James [109315], 225
James [109319], 182, 188
James [96546], 188, 224
Jeremiah [100240], 92
Jeremiah [100647], 361
Jeremiah J. [92196], 485
Joannah J. [96545], 225,
280
Johanna [92924], 223

Johanna [95791], 378
Johanna 'Ann' [86004], 219
Johanna wife of Dennis
[104001], 223
John [101152], 168
John [109316], 225
John [92202], 485
John [92215], 22
John [96582], 219
John [96585], 218
John D. [108965], 185, 209
John D. [95901], 387
John F. [100653], 361
John J. [108973], 209, 270
John J. [108975], 271
Julia [109314], 225
Julia [98069], 461, 483
Julia wife of Patrick
[102320], 111
Louisa J. [108970], 209
Mabel Mary [108977], 271
Margaret (Trokirre) [93514],
184, 199
Margaret [102316], 33, 111
Margaret [106236], 28, 90
Margaret [106914], 461,
486
Margaret [108976], 271
Margaret [95900], 1, 6, 83
Margaret J. [95781], 377,
422
Margaret 'Maggie' [96587],
219
Mark H. [108971], 210
Mary (Trokirre) [102339],
370
Mary (Trokirre) [108998],
313, 320
Mary [100576], 259
Mary [106934], 449, 461
Mary [107674], 198
Mary [109107], 331
Mary [86003], 219
Mary [92446], 486
Mary [94298], 18, 58
Mary [95787], 377
Mary [96096], 223
Mary [97886], 221
Mary [99042], 431
Mary A. [108972], 210
Mary A. [95898], 331, 387
Mary C. [92804], 30, 97
Mary E. [100664], 361
Mary Elizabeth [109332],
427, 445

Volume IV Name Index

Kathleen [107839], 420
Margaret [94187], 26, 78
Margaret T. [92785], 101
Margaret wife of Dennis
[94189], 78
Theresa [107836], 420
William [105724], 151
LYTLE
Alice R. [98273], 45
Felton M. [98274], 45
MACK
Peter [99016], 459
MADIGAN
Hannah F. [106379], 397,
441
John [106412], 441
MAGEE
Hannah J. [107841], 419
MAHER
Edward [92614], 214
Ellen [92216], 22
Nellie L. [92611], 214
MAHONEY
Catherine [95607], 357, 406
Catherine C. 'Katie' [94294],
2, 16
Dennis [94302], 16
Hannah F. [92800], 157,
409
James [95608], 406
Leonora Philomena
'Margaret Fitzgerald'
[76866], 158
Nancy wife of Dennis
[94303], 16
MALEY
Ann wife of Thomas
[101132], 20
Thomas [101130], 20
Thomas [101131], 20
MALLOY
Margaret [100016], 4, 28
MALONEY
Mary E. [93580], 253, 295
Thomas [93581], 295
MANCHESTER
Margaret [107123], 14
MANNING
Catherine wife of Maurice
[104693], 397
James M. [104691], 335,
397
Katherine F. [93135], 493,
508
Maurice [104692], 397
Thomas F. [93136], 508

Thomas Francis [104694],
397
Timothy Francis [104695],
397
MARTEL
Mary [102555], 307, 308
MARTIN
Eliza [106651], 399
MARTINS
Edward C. [108494], 146
MAY
Dennis F. [100193], 167
John [100194], 167
John J. [100192], 110, 167
MAYO
Frank [93568], 253, 294
Frank [97448], 295
Frederick L. [97446], 294
John [97444], 294
John [97447], 295
MCCAFFERTY
Alice [93641], 123
MCCALLUM
Catherine Theresa [97695],
15, 56
William [97696], 56
MCCARTHY
Abbie [93795], 329
Alice [97693], 2, 14
Andrew [93782], 314, 329
Catherine [93798], 330
Charles [93797], 330
Daniel [102056], 142
Daniel [102406], 323, 369
Daniel [108831], 370
Daniel D. [93792], 329
Dennis (Rohane) [108828],
369
Dennis Francis [102405],
369
Earl Robert [95257], 274
Elizabeth [108936], 391
Ellen J. [93793], 329
Ellen 'Nellie' [109959], 381
Jeremiah [107114], 14
John [93796], 330
Margaret [93775], 329, 384
Margaret wife of Jeremiah
[107115], 14
Maria G. [102055], 89, 142
Mary [101416], 5, 35
Mary [108830], 370
Michael [108832], 370
Timothy [93794], 329
MCCARTY
Annie L. [109978], 511

Catherine [95272], 117
Charles [95271], 117
Ellen [95267], 117
Grace Wallace [106392],
396, 439
Jeremiah [95266], 37, 116
John F. [95268], 117
Julia [95269], 117
Margaret [98478], 351
Martin [94589], 297
Mary E. [95680], 291
Mary Frances [95270], 117
Mary wife of Martin [94590],
297
Michael [95273], 117
Michael [95274], 116
Rosanna [94588], 259, 297
Terrance [106393], 439
MCCLELLAND
Amelia [93586], 296
MCCONNELL
Abbie [105678], 122
Anna [105681], 122
James [105673], 122
James [105676], 122
James W. [105672], 51, 122
John [105679], 122
Margaret [105675], 122
Mary [105677], 122
Robert F. [105682], 122
William [105680], 122
MCCONVILLE
James [106382], 441
Jean Marie [106384], 442
Thomas Francis [106378],
397, 441
Thomas Paul [106383], 442
MCCORMICK
Brigid [108839], 314, 330,
340
Mildred Rita [106398], 440
MCCOY
Daniel F. [99318], 53, 125
Daniel F. [99319], 125
Daniel F. [99322], 125
James H. [99321], 125
MCDERMOTT
Sarah [106400], 441
MCDONALD
John [100022], 87
Mary Elizabeth [107056],
362
Patrick [100020], 87
MCDONOUGH
Ellen wife of Patrick
[107121], 14

Volume IV Name Index

Julia [100012], 139
Patrick [107120], 14
Patrick Joseph [107116], 14
MCGOWAN
Bridget E. [97873], 28, 88
William [102063], 88
MCGRATH
Margaret [99437], 38
Mary Veronica [103412], 82, 137
MCGREAVY
Andrew [100803], 497, 510
Edward J. [109894], 510
John E. [100804], 510
MCGUINESS
Jane [100439], 473
MCGUIRE
Charles E. [102067], 145
Chester Joseph [102066], 145
MCHUGH
James [105652], 222
William H. [98751], 222
MCKAY
Ann [101137], 318
MCKENDRICK
Margaret [99993], 85, 138
Michael [99994], 138
MCLAUGHLIN
Mary wife of Michael [107611], 290
Michael [107610], 290
Rosanna [107609], 245, 290
MCMAHON
Catherine [99621], 84
MCMULLEN
George [102655], 318
Sydney 'Sinney' [101138], 318
MCNAMARA
Nancy [102064], 88
MCNERNEY
James C. [94907], 303
James Christopher [94906], 267, 303
Timothy W. [106154], 303
MEEHAN
Catherine A. [103448], 310
MILLER
John [99453], 39
John Francis [99452], 39
Mary wife of John [99454], 39
Susan [92954], 169
MILLS

James [94558], 302
Mary Alice [94555], 263, 302
MITCHELL
Alfred Francis [95668], 247, 292
Charles [95669], 292
Charles H. [95671], 292
Edmond J. [95673], 293
Mary A. [105674], 122
Raymond F. [95672], 292
MOFFITT
Hannah [99408], 380
MONAHAN
Michael [110146], 388
Peter Michael [95913], 388
MOORE
Rita L. [99968], 404, 443
William Michael [99971], 443
MORGAN
Mary A. [103298], 279
MORIARITY
Mary [108781], 64
MORIARTY
Hannah [103283], 278
MORISSETTE
Hilaire [107170], 133
Matilda [107169], 73, 133
MORLEY
Anne Beatrice [104147], 131
MORRIS
Catherine [95233], 272
Gertrude [93584], 254, 296
John [93585], 296
MORRISON
Eleanor Rose [99854], 445
Mary Louise Josephine [99243], 128, 169
MORRISSEY
Margaret [101105], 134
MULCAHEY
John [101695], 457
MULCHY
Daniel [101696], 457
MULLANEY
Dorothy Bridget [107131], 156
MULLINS
John [99823], 266
John F. [99822], 266
MUNHALL
Bridget [97373], 43
John [97374], 43
MURHIL

John [106387], 396
MURPHY
Agnes [97750], 255
Anna [94864], 268, 304
Annie R. [104076], 409
Catherine [103603], 113, 185, 208
Catherine [108670], 313, 316
Catherine [109350], 509
Catherine [97749], 255
Catherine B. [92522], 465, 492
Catherine wife of Jeremiah [98410], 475
Child [94755], 133
Clara [99992], 85
Cornelius [97743], 196, 255
Cornelius [97751], 255
Daniel [103600], 5, 33, 270
Daniel [97744], 255
Daniel [97752], 255
Daniel [98413], 475
Daniel D. [103598], 33, 111, 208, 270
Daniel R. [108919], 112
Edward [93131], 506
Ellen [97885], 182, 187
Eugene [99835], 434
Eveline [108915], 113
Hannah [95665], 183, 192, 460, 468
Hanora 'Annie or Nora' [99406], 314, 326
Herbert Ambrose [108914], 112
Honora wife of Daniel [97745], 255
James [95666], 247, 447, 451
Jeremiah [98409], 475
Johanna [108895], 17
Johanna [93132], 506
John [98407], 456, 475
Julia [92806], 97
Julia E. [106707], 459, 479
Julia F. [99888], 317, 343, 500
Katherine [104186], 190
Lillian C. [108911], 112
Margaret [100841], 227
Margaret [103527], 105
Margaret [103604], 113
Margaret [92747], 449, 464
Margaret [93512], 258
Margaret [95277], 5, 37

Margaret [95651], 192, 247, 451, 468
Margaret [98149], 100, 108
Margaret Anne [109348], 493, 509
Margaret L. [93128], 493, 506
Mary [102763], 255
Mary [108711], 67
Mary [92012], 158
Mary [95205], 285
Mary [98414], 475
Mary E. [108920], 113
Mary J. [99834], 394, 434
Michael [109349], 509
Michael [93144], 492
Patrick [93097], 132
Patrick J. [93096], 70, 132
Thomas [92658], 335
Thomas Henry [92662], 335
Timothy [106710], 479
Timothy [97753], 255
Timothy [99889], 343
William J. [108910], 112
MURRAY
John [99478], 119
William John [99479], 119
MYERS
Mary [92615], 214
NABB
Thomas [109971], 283
William H. [103438], 283
NADEAU
Joseph [95562], 153
NAVIN
Ellen [105025], 482
NEGUS
Carlton B. [99006], 378
Henry L. [99007], 378
NOLAN
Annie Martha [99237], 68, 127
Bridget wife of Thomas [99233], 68
Ella [99236], 68
Maria [104482], 419
Thomas [99230], 22, 68
Thomas [99234], 68
NORMYLE
Annie [103420], 105, 163, 309
Michael [103462], 163
OBRIEN
Annie E. [99028], 395, 436
Catherine wife of James [99844], 432

Catherine wife of Peter [103134], 123
Dennis [95799], 375
Ellen [101092], 348
Ellen [106671], 136
Francis [103137], 123
Hannah wife of Dennis [95800], 375
James [103242], 123
James [99843], 432
Jeremiah F. [103136], 123
John [99031], 436
Joseph W. [103132], 52, 123
Madeline Mary [95910], 387, 428
Mary [95797], 325, 375
Mary E. [99842], 394, 432
Mary L. [103138], 123
Nellie [98809], 277
Peter [103133], 123
Thomas Edward [109721], 428
OCONNELL
Catherine [95275], 116
Ellen [108394], 429
Jane [101095], 348
Mary [99890], 343
O'CONNELL
Mary A. [103289], 279
Timothy [103290], 279
ODONNELL
Edward J. [106715], 480, 505
Helen J. [109981], 505
John [109983], 505
OGARA
Charles E. [106923], 167
Charles Edward [106919], 111, 167
Mary E. [106922], 167
Patrick H. [106920], 167
OHARA
Bridget [92698], 497
OHARE
Angela [103503], 178
Helen [103504], 178
Mary [103501], 178
Rosanna [104062], 323, 364
Virginia [103502], 178
William [103500], 165, 178
William [103505], 178
O'HARE
Patrick [104065], 364
OLEARY

Catherine [96547], 188, 225
Dennis [109317], 225
O'LEARY
Bridget [102453], 414
OLOUGHLIN
Bridget A. [109722], 428
O'LOUGHLIN
Susan A. [105039], 483
OMALLEY
Anthony [93562], 254
Charles F. [93561], 254
OMARA
Catherine [101108], 134
Daniel [101104], 134
Donald [101111], 134
James [101110], 134
James J. [101103], 75, 134
Mabel [101109], 134
ONEAL
Bridget [94585], 199, 259
Daniel [98753], 276
Jeremiah [100575], 259
Mary wife of Daniel [98754], 276
ONEIL
Annie [108777], 65
Catherine [92854], 196, 253
Catherine [97919], 71
Catherine wife of James [98588], 49
Child [100818], 468
Cornelius [100812], 451, 468
Cornelius [100813], 468
Cornelius [98255], 191, 240
Dennis [93552], 212, 253
Ellen [107346], 240
Ellen [98592], 50
Ellen wife of John [98257], 240
Hanna [98589], 49
Hannah [107351], 240
Henry F. [104860], 124, 169
James [98587], 49
James [98590], 49
Joanna [107350], 240
Joanna [92613], 185, 212
John [98256], 240
John F. [108780], 64
John H. [97665], 240
Julia wife of Cornelius [100814], 468
Kathleen M. [104861], 169
Margaret [106921], 167
Margaret [109113], 333
Margaret [95950], 280

Michael [106112], 391
Stephen [106109], 334, 390
SCANLON
Mary [108683], 179
SCARAMUZZI
Frank [97700], 56
SCHENE
Jeremiah [92529], 9
John [98277], 9
Mary wife of Jeremiah [92530], 9
SCULLY
Daniel F. [94557], 300
Edward H. [94543], 263, 300
Joseph G. [94556], 300
Patrick [94544], 300
SENAY
Charles [107434], 166
Helen M. [99527], 166
James [99529], 166
Leo C. [99526], 109, 166
Leo C. Jr. [99528], 166
SHAY
Dennis [96121], 250
Jeremiah [96118], 195, 250
John [96120], 250
Mary [96122], 250
Patrick [96126], 250
William [96125], 250
SHEA
Abbie [100191], 110, 166
Beatrice C. [93083], 132, 170
Bridget [92480], 337
Catherine [101401], 460
Catherine [93080], 132
Catherine [99933], 401
Cornelius [109025], 383
Daniel [103305], 306
Daniel [109029], 382
Daniel [95120], 382
Daniel H. [103304], 279, 306
Dennis [100203], 111
Dennis [100891], 383
Dennis [109014], 383
Dennis [92473], 337
Dennis [93079], 132
Dennis [96014], 183, 191
Edward F. [109340], 427
Elizabeth [107586], 290
Ellen [79109], 328
Ellen Hannah [94579], 199, 261

Ellen wife of John [101405], 460
Frances Louise [108981], 271
Hanora [105684], 1, 11
Helena M. [107588], 290
James [109028], 383
Jeremiah [109023], 383
Jeremiah [92474], 337
Jeremiah [95648], 354
Joanna [98254], 191, 239
Johanna [95191], 190, 235
John [100905], 328, 382
John [101404], 460
John [107594], 289
John [107821], 475
John [108783], 64
John [92471], 316, 336
John [92472], 336
John [95201], 235
John [95641], 321, 354
John F. [108982], 271
John J. [100904], 383
Julia [105035], 482
Julia [107678], 198
Julia [93183], 47
Marcella [107585], 289
Margaret [103072], 191, 240
Margaret [107587], 290
Margaret [107604], 183, 191
Margaret [94758], 170
Margaret [98468], 313, 319
Margaret E. [93081], 132
Margaret M. O. [95803], 376
Margaret 'Maggie' [95646], 354
Margaret wife of Patrick [96127], 250
Mary [100899], 383
Mary [106725], 1, 10, 459
Mary [107820], 456, 475
Mary [79106], 328, 384
Mary [92482], 337
Mary [93084], 132
Mary [93553], 212, 253
Mary [94607], 262
Mary [98253], 215
Mary A. [95642], 355
Mary L. [106690], 502
Mary wife of John [107822], 475
Mary wife of Patrick [100188], 110
Michael [100186], 33, 110

Michael [109027], 382
Michael [92475], 337
Michael [95121], 384
Michael O. [95804], 376
Nora [95647], 355
Patrick [100187], 110
Patrick [92476], 337
Patrick F. [93078], 70, 132
Timothy [109026], 383
Timothy Clinton [92478], 244, 289
William [107187], 170, 181
William [109024], 383
William Francis [93082], 132
William Jr. [107188], 181
SHEEHAN
Ann [100233], 92
Anne [100236], 92
Daniel [100242], 92
Daniel F. [100230], 92
Hanora [92700], 447, 454
Johanna [100231], 92
John F. [100235], 92
Josephine T. 'Josie' [96609], 92, 148
Mary [100234], 92
Matthew [100228], 29, 92
Matthew [100232], 92
SHERMAN
Geroge [100667], 362, 408
Noreen K. [100668], 408
SHINE
Annie V. [106238], 90, 147
Mary [92670], 335
Patrick [106239], 147
SHURTCLIFFE
Mr. [100802], 376
SIDLEY
Agnes B. [105148], 45, 119
Edward [98271], 45
Ella [98269], 45
George [98268], 45
John P. [98261], 8, 44
John T. [98267], 44
Margaret [109318], 225
Mary [98276], 9
Patrick [98263], 1, 8
Rebecca [98270], 45
William H. [98272], 45
SILVIA
Charles J. [105037], 483
John [105038], 483
SLOAN
Annie H. [100262], 116
Eugene F. [100263], 116

John E. [100256], 116
John M. [100254], 116
John Martin [100253], 34, 116
Joseph [100260], 116
Leo [100258], 116
Mary [100257], 116
Mary wife of John [100255], 116
Matilda [100261], 116
Mortimer [100259], 116
SMALLEY
Jane [95670], 292
SMITH
Honora [107606], 244
Mary [103463], 163
Mary [107584], 337
SMITHSON
Elizabeth [103228], 224
George [103229], 224
SNYDER
David [108662], 398
Ernestine [108661], 398
Harry [108660], 398
Roy Lee [108658], 338, 398
Sophie May [108659], 398
SPERLING
Adrian [99418], 380, 424
David M. [99425], 424
Harry [110157], 424
Michelle [99422], 425
Paul A. [99420], 424
SPILLANE
Catherine [106646], 316, 338
Jeremiah [108664], 338
STACK
Johanna [105740], 150
SULLIVAN
Abbie [107770], 241
Abbie [97896], 223
Abbie Angela [92781], 101, 157
Abbie F. [105671], 51, 121
Abby [102437], 372, 417
Abby [102700], 9, 45
Abby [97746], 196, 255
Abby J. [102706], 46
Agnes [104069], 365, 409
Agnes Catherine [106691], 502
Agnes Marion [106654], 399
Agnes T. [103070], 233
Agnes V. [103475], 107
Alfred J. [99939], 402
Alfred James [99979], 346

Alfred Joseph [108836], 340
Algernon Deneal [92798], 101, 157
Alice [106259], 148
Alice [94562], 303
Alice [99996], 138
Alice A. [92626], 135, 171
Alice wife of Thomas [106258], 90, 148
Andrew P. [101418], 36
Ann [100229], 29, 91
Ann [106271], 239
Ann [97895], 221
Ann E. [100103], 29, 91
Ann M. wife of Paul [109697], 410
Ann Marilyn [99248], 169
Ann wife of Daniel [98349], 1, 10
Ann wife of John [99897], 448, 458
Anna [100001], 138
Anna [100451], 24
Anna [103467], 382
Anna [94575], 259
Anna B. [99837], 434
Anna Frances 'Nana' [99926], 400
Anna 'Hannah' F. [95652], 247, 291
Anna L. [106305], 52
Anna M. [107615], 291
Anne C. [106416], 441
Anne Gertrude [100246], 149, 171
Anne Marie [100570], 410
Anne Marie [103439], 176
Anne Marie [106426], 153
Anne Mary [104690], 335, 397
Annie [106251], 90
Annie [109302], 256
Annie [95323], 60
Annie [98756], 277
Annie [99922], 317
Annie A. 'Hannah' [104136], 70, 130
Annie D. [105685], 507
Annie Elizabeth [100252], 34, 115
Annie F. [103465], 163, 177
Annie F. [99921], 344
Annie L. [104723], 323, 365
Annie T. [97875], 89, 143
Arthur [103441], 177
Arthur [105153], 120

Arthur A. [99464], 40
Arthur Francis [106698], 503
Arthur J. (Dr.) [100435], 473
Arthur J. [103418], 163, 175, 284, 309
Bartholomew [94448], 2, 18
Bartholomew F. [105720], 93, 149
Bartolomew 'Bart' [94565], 199, 260
Bertha A. [105154], 119
Boetius [99891], 344, 401
Boetius M. [99936], 402
Boetius Patrick [108840], 340
Bridget [100014], 28, 86
Bridget [100729], 322, 362
Bridget [101081], 319, 347
Bridget [101155], 168
Bridget [103114], 371, 411
Bridget [104115], 326
Bridget [105728], 93
Bridget [109320], 182, 188
Bridget [95317], 18, 60, 463
Bridget [95667], 247, 447, 451
Bridget [99306], 79
Bridget Elizabeth [95655], 247, 292
Bridget wife of Eugene [92984], 2, 12
Bridget wife of John [101403], 448, 460
Bridget wife of John G. [99534], 192, 449, 460
Bridget wife of Thomas [99795], 2, 19
Caleb Knowles Chiles [106561], 194, 248
Caroline Amelia [106572], 194
Catherine (Suonish) [109004], 320
Catherine [100673], 368
Catherine [100801], 376
Catherine [101417], 35
Catherine [101781], 70
Catherine [103061], 232
Catherine [103601], 5, 33, 270
Catherine [104499], 4, 29
Catherine [105534], 373
Catherine [105670], 50, 121
Catherine [105769], 150
Catherine [106252], 90

Volume IV Name Index

Catherine [106648], 338, 398
Catherine [106686], 479
Catherine [106712], 480
Catherine [106935], 495
Catherine [107565], 36
Catherine [107595], 289
Catherine [107596], 245
Catherine [108665], 338
Catherine [108779], 19, 64
Catherine [86002], 186, 218
Catherine [92470], 316, 336
Catherine [94685], 69, 128
Catherine [94798], 453, 469
Catherine [94851], 203
Catherine [94901], 200, 264
Catherine [95662], 247
Catherine [96396], 206
Catherine [96419], 196, 251
Catherine [96422], 183, 195
Catherine [96503], 187
Catherine [97893], 222, 279
Catherine [98371], 23, 70
Catherine [98408], 456, 475
Catherine [98571], 57
Catherine [99046], 438
Catherine [99848], 432
Catherine A. [99037], 394, 430
Catherine A. 'Katie' [93540], 214, 273
Catherine Aloysius [107112], 14
Catherine C. [104071], 365
Catherine D. [94440], 19, 63
Catherine E. [105732], 94
Catherine F. [101045], 21, 65
Catherine F. [95616], 356, 404
Catherine F. [95627], 358, 407
Catherine F. [96550], 280
Catherine F. [99441], 6, 27, 40, 83
Catherine G. [108025], 353
Catherine H. [95905], 387
Catherine J. [102457], 416
Catherine 'Kate' [102934], 241, 287
Catherine 'Kate' [95783], 325, 376
Catherine 'Kate' L. [103260], 483
Catherine 'Katie' [93567], 253, 294

Catherine 'Katie' [99643], 256
Catherine 'Kit' [106115], 391
Catherine L. [94304], 58
Catherine L. [94582], 262
Catherine M. [92707], 497, 510
Catherine M. 'Kay' [108493], 146
Catherine Mary [99475], 118
Catherine 'Rena' [103482], 160, 173
Catherine V. [93637], 52, 123
Catherine wife of Dennis [98406], 3, 23
Catherine wife of James [97748], 184, 196
Catherine wife of James [99635], 184, 196
Catherine wife of Michael [98161], 5, 32
Catherine wife of Patrick [98363], 3, 23
Catherine wife of Philip [102336], 3, 21
Charles [101797], 423
Charles [97251], 282
Charles A. [94571], 258
Charles A. [94910], 298
Charles A. [99476], 119
Charles Arthur [99474], 119
Charles J. [106272], 238
Charles R. [102465], 417
Child [105726], 151
Child [106695], 502
Child [106726], 478
Child [97253], 282
Child [98878], 77
Child [99845], 432
Child [99987], 85
Claire [103440], 176
Clare D. [99413], 380
Clare P. [103271], 499
Clarence Gray [94592], 298
Clarence Patrick D.D.S. [100436], 473, 498
Cornelius (Suonish) [101907], 478
Cornelius (Suonish) [108021], 320, 352
Cornelius (Suonish) [79097], 314, 327
Cornelius [100816], 447, 451

Cornelius [101792], 423
Cornelius [103263], 483
Cornelius [104180], 183, 189
Cornelius [106565], 183, 193
Cornelius [106702], 478
Cornelius [108052], 353
Cornelius [108495], 145
Cornelius [79103], 328
Cornelius [93558], 254
Cornelius [94890], 200, 266
Cornelius [95211], 236
Cornelius [97892], 221, 275
Cornelius [98159], 33, 108
Cornelius [99405], 314, 325
Cornelius [99885], 317, 341, 500
Cornelius A. [98165], 109
Cornelius B. [94439], 19, 61
Cornelius George [102556], 307, 312
Cornelius J. [109907], 344
Cornelius J. [99947], 443
Cornelius John [100149], 309
Cornelius John [97255], 282, 306
Cornelius Joseph [99931], 401, 443
Cornelius M. [103062], 232
Cornelius M. [99967], 404, 443
Cornelius S. [106237], 90, 146
Cornelius S. [94443], 63
Cornelius T. 'Conn' [95764], 422
Corrine [102562], 307
Daniel (Suonish) [108033], 313, 320
Daniel (Suonish) [110118], 332
Daniel [100015], 4, 28
Daniel [100117], 456
Daniel [100409], 3, 25, 488
Daniel [100823], 447, 451, 453
Daniel [101420], 37
Daniel [102053], 89
Daniel [102322], 447, 451
Daniel [102704], 1, 9
Daniel [102709], 9
Daniel [103065], 231
Daniel [104091], 454, 474
Daniel [105739], 150

Daniel [106309], 52
Daniel [106661], 50
Daniel [106724], 1, 10, 459
Daniel [107603], 183, 191
Daniel [108049], 353
Daniel [108500], 146
Daniel [108712], 3, 22
Daniel [109000], 319
Daniel [110236], 324
Daniel [83635], 450, 465
Daniel [95217], 237
Daniel [95373], 447, 452
Daniel [95674], 192
Daniel [96920], 449, 464
Daniel [97476], 450, 466
Daniel [97692], 2, 13
Daniel [98148], 100, 108
Daniel [98169], 108
Daniel [98348], 1, 9
Daniel [98353], 48
Daniel A. [93123], 492
Daniel Augustine [97694], 15, 55
Daniel Austin [93790], 427
Daniel B. [97872], 28, 87
Daniel C. [94532], 263, 300
Daniel C. [94598], 303
Daniel Edmund [93778], 384, 426
Daniel F. [109335], 445
Daniel F. [92680], 453, 469
Daniel F. [92809], 97
Daniel F. [93129], 506
Daniel F. [94212], 231
Daniel J. [102461], 417, 444
Daniel J. [106377], 397, 440
Daniel J. [106931], 486
Daniel J. [107598], 245, 290
Daniel J. [92612], 185, 210
Daniel J. [92681], 454, 470
Daniel J. [92704], 497
Daniel J. [96917], 140
Daniel J. [99027], 395, 435
Daniel J. [99981], 28, 84
Daniel J. [99988], 85
Daniel O. [100857], 228
Daniel P. [98757], 277
Daniel R. [92799], 157, 409
Daniel R. [93766], 384
Daniel R. [94764], 455
Daniel S. [92008], 30, 97
Daniel S. Jr. [92780], 101
David [109392], 447, 452
David [93521], 1, 8
David [97698], 56

David Cornelius [94581], 261
David D. [109334], 445
David T. [109333], 427, 444
Dennis (Barrule) [105405], 127
Dennis [100417], 73
Dennis [100440], 447, 454
Dennis [100821], 447, 451, 452
Dennis [106432], 95
Dennis [107492], 328
Dennis [108827], 313, 323
Dennis [109114], 333
Dennis [92699], 447, 453
Dennis [92701], 471
Dennis [92922], 182, 187
Dennis [94159], 2, 11
Dennis [94173], 1, 7
Dennis [94799], 447, 453
Dennis [95311], 2, 18, 448, 456, 463
Dennis [96022], 216
Dennis [96557], 2, 20
Dennis [96975], 254
Dennis [98354], 49
Dennis [98367], 72
Dennis [98403], 3, 23
Dennis F. [106692], 478
Dennis J. [106674], 459, 476
Dennis J. [94295], 17
Dennis Jerome [107113], 14
Dennis Joseph [94597], 302
Dennis O. [100838], 188, 225, 469
Dennis P. [105015], 460, 481
Dennis P. [107177], 65
Dennis T. [94289], 200, 262
Donald [102560], 307
Donna Elizabeth [99970], 443, 446
Dora [100892], 383
Doris [100146], 308
Doris wife of Richard [102567], 308
Dorothea G. [106243], 147
Dorothy [103415], 136
Dorothy G. [102459], 417
E. [92918], 447, 455
Edward [100678], 369
Edward [101788], 423
Edward [104072], 365
Edward [105687], 507
Edward [106956], 495

Edward [95206], 286
Edward [95207], 286
Edward [95210], 237
Edward A. [94445], 63
Edward A. [99846], 432
Edward A. Jr. [100571], 409
Edward Aloysius [100845], 228
Edward Aloysius [103407], 82, 137
Edward Anthony [94055], 366, 409
Edward F. [100244], 149
Edward F. [94577], 259, 297
Edward J. [92628], 135, 171
Edward J. [94908], 298
Edward John [99238], 68, 127
Edward John III [99244], 169
Edward John Jr. [99240], 128, 169
Edward L. [103272], 499
Edward M. [93124], 493, 506
Edward M. [98168], 110
Edward R. [103487], 161
Edward R. [99047], 438
Edward W. [93779], 384
Eileen [100150], 309
Eileen [107173], 133
Eileen [108497], 145
Eileen P. [99411], 380
Elaine [103523], 174
Eleanor [103466], 163
Elizabeth [102058], 142
Elizabeth [105730], 93
Elizabeth [106512], 352
Elizabeth [109337], 445
Elizabeth [94708], 129
Elizabeth [95629], 359
Elizabeth A. [94849], 203
Elizabeth A. [97871], 88, 140
Elizabeth Ann [102568], 312
Elizabeth Bernadette [99449], 39
Elizabeth C. [99317], 53, 125
Elizabeth E. [95303], 61, 126
Elizabeth E. wife of Francis [95911], 387
Elizabeth 'Lizzie' [104117], 327

Elizabeth 'Lizzie' [98473], 350
Ellen [100105], 4, 29
Ellen [102010], 186, 219
Ellen [102439], 313, 324
Ellen [104100], 454
Ellen [104483], 373, 418
Ellen [107554], 429
Ellen [107607], 245
Ellen [110140], 313, 323
Ellen [92448], 449, 461
Ellen [92981], 195
Ellen [93076], 70, 132
Ellen [94682], 128
Ellen [95312], 2, 18, 448, 455, 463
Ellen [95623], 358
Ellen [95631], 358
Ellen [96027], 186, 216
Ellen [96217], 455
Ellen [96560], 21
Ellen [96942], 251
Ellen [97465], 450, 467
Ellen [97888], 222, 278
Ellen [98123], 47
Ellen [98482], 320
Ellen [99298], 77
Ellen C. [98332], 459, 480
Ellen F. 'Lena' [94706], 128, 169
Ellen G. [99231], 22, 67
Ellen M. [103472], 106
Ellen 'Nellie' [106713], 480
Ellen 'Nellie' [99315], 52
Ellen T. [95617], 357
Ellen V. [93556], 253
Ellen V. [94756], 130, 170
Ellen V. 'Nellie' [95302], 61, 125
Ellen wife of Cornelius [100817], 447, 451
Ellen wife of Daniel [102323], 447, 451
Ellen wife of Daniel [102705], 1, 9
Ellen wife of David [109393], 447, 452
Ellen wife of Jeremiah [101580], 448, 457
Ellen wife of Jeremiah [108436], 315
Ellen wife of Jeremiah [93962], 2, 20
Ellen wife of John [109037], 182, 186

Ellen wife of Michael [99799], 20
Ellen wife of Patrick [100454], 3, 24
Emma G. [92801], 102
Esther Rita [99241], 128
Eugene [100842], 182, 188
Eugene [102893], 16
Eugene [105532], 313, 324
Eugene [105660], 372
Eugene [107818], 448, 456
Eugene [86056], 182, 186
Eugene [92983], 2, 12
Eugene [93072], 69, 128
Eugene [94707], 129
Eugene [96571], 186, 218
Eugene [96773], 18, 58
Eugene [96774], 2, 18
Eugene [96777], 59
Eugene [98481], 351
Eugene E. [95369], 227, 469
Eugene F. [106722], 11, 458
Eugene F. [107833], 373
Eugene Francis [99247], 169
Eugene Henry [106684], 478, 502
Eugene Henry [106699], 502
Eugene J. [98761], 115
Eugene Jr. [96394], 206
Eugene 'Owen' [108935], 391
Eugene R. [96386], 184, 203
Eugene S. [96996], 320, 351
Eunice E. [99925], 404
Fannie [99465], 41
Father [106653], 338, 399
Florence [103489], 165
Florence [106390], 314, 334
Florence [108788], 314, 334
Florence [110149], 334
Florence [93062], 462
Florence [95677], 193
Florence [96078], 450, 465
Florence [99862], 85
Florence Francis [106386], 396, 438
Florence G. [93992], 462
Florence K. [100651], 313, 321

Florence M. [103460], 32, 102
Florence M. Jr. [103470], 106
Florence W. [103484], 160, 174
Francis ' Frank' [105731], 94, 151
Francis [104068], 365
Francis [99443], 7
Francis A. [94859], 268
Francis E. [102462], 417
Francis 'Frank' [96128], 31
Francis 'Frank' [99448], 39
Francis Michael 'Frank' [99997], 138
Francis P. [95906], 387
Francis Walsh [103488], 160, 172
Frank [106260], 90
Frank [97894], 222
Frank A. [92782], 101
Frank Henry [106274], 239
Franklin [94595], 298
Franklyn G. [105766], 151
Frederick Thomas [94863], 269
Gary Joseph [99969], 443
Genevieve Frances [100010], 139
George A. [109313], 280
George Edward [99999], 138, 171
George F. [93125], 493, 507
George F. [98479], 351
George F. Jr. [105781], 508
George Henry (Dr.) [99461], 40
George Jr. [100005], 171
George W. [103521], 161
George W. [94446], 64
Gerald [105967], 389
Gertrude Annie [103483], 160, 174
Giles [104484], 324, 372
Grace L [94591], 298
Hannah [100820], 451, 453
Hannah [101330], 430
Hannah [101795], 423
Hannah [101942], 435
Hannah [102332], 21
Hannah [102707], 9
Hannah [106301], 11, 52
Hannah [106721], 503
Hannah [106723], 10, 459
Hannah [92432], 31

Volume IV Name Index

Hannah [92692], 471
Hannah [92703], 471
Hannah [94889], 200, 263
Hannah [96081], 466
Hannah [96119], 195, 250
Hannah [96174], 469
Hannah [96771], 59
Hannah [98352], 49
Hannah [98585], 10, 49
Hannah [98958], 463, 489
Hannah [99207], 464, 489
Hannah 'Anna' A. [99833], 394, 434
Hannah 'Annie' [103063], 232
Hannah 'Annie' [106696], 479, 503
Hannah 'Annie' [99442], 7
Hannah E. 'Annie' [101027], 205
Hannah V. 'Annie' [107599], 245
Hannah wife of Bartholomew [94449], 2, 19
Hannah wife of Michael [98594], 1, 10
Hannah wife of Patrick [102318], 5, 33
Hanora [92198], 461, 484
Hanora [99887], 313, 317, 385
Hanora wife of John [99019], 448, 459
Hanora wife of Patrick [101003], 452
Hanora wife of Timothy [109262], 4, 31
Harold Anthony [106694], 503, 510
Helen [103417], 136
Helen D. [106424], 152, 172
Helena [100498], 352
Helena 'Lena' [94561], 303
Helena R. 'Lena' [106714], 480, 504
Helene 'Lena' V. [94530], 263, 299
Henry [101796], 423
Henry Aloysious [98167], 109
Henry E. [107613], 290
Henry F. [99477], 119
Henry Francis [107124], 156
Henry Francis [92778], 101, 155

Henry Patrick [93557], 254
Herbert [97433], 297
Herbert Ashley [106559], 249
Honora (Suonish) [108023], 320, 353
Humphrey [100305], 324, 371
Humphrey [102438], 313, 323
Humphrey [109260], 31
Humphrey [96770], 59
Ida [95630], 359, 407
Ida A. [100310], 414
Ida Bernard [102702], 46, 120
Ignatius L [95853], 344
Infant [109955], 502
Isabella [109311], 280
Isabella [92706], 497
Isabella 'Bella' [94852], 203, 268
Isabelle E. 'Bella' [94858], 268
Jack (Suonish) [108034], 353
Jack (Suonish) [109109], 332
Jake [92979], 194
James [100407], 25, 72, 461, 488
James [100419], 73
James [101106], 75
James [102564], 308
James [104070], 365
James [104178], 189
James [106306], 52
James [106307], 1, 11
James [107673], 197
James [108674], 339
James [94846], 202
James [95954], 225, 280
James [96573], 218
James [97747], 183, 196
James [98411], 448, 456
James [99634], 184, 196
James [99645], 256
James A. [94857], 268, 303
James E. [95663], 248
James Edward [92784], 101, 153
James Eugene [96594], 149
James F. [95202], 236, 285
James F. [95208], 286
James Florence [106673], 478, 501

James Francis [107612], 291
James H. [105156], 119
James J. [104118], 327, 381
James J. [95767], 377, 422
James J. [99901], 476
James J. Jr. [98563], 382
James K. [100433], 454, 472
James K. [103270], 499
James L. [92524], 493, 508
James L. [95907], 387
James L. Jr. [109351], 509
James M. [100309], 414
James M. [93546], 215
James P. [109115], 333
James P. [94177], 26, 78
James Q. [94580], 261
James R. [92971], 455
James Roger [103453], 284, 310
James Roger Jr. [103457], 311
James T. [109312], 280
Jeffery S. [109724], 445
Jennie Helena [100437], 473
Jennie K. [103437], 283
Jennie M. [100676], 369
Jennie V. [92779], 101
Jeremiah (Buaig) [99886], 313, 317, 385
Jeremiah (Fune) [95613], 313, 320
Jeremiah [100006], 171
Jeremiah [100115], 448, 456
Jeremiah [100418], 74
Jeremiah [101098], 25, 74
Jeremiah [101579], 448, 457
Jeremiah [101697], 448, 457
Jeremiah [105664], 11, 50
Jeremiah [105683], 1, 11
Jeremiah [106247], 4, 28
Jeremiah [106256], 90
Jeremiah [106374], 335, 395
Jeremiah [107564], 5, 36
Jeremiah [108435], 315
Jeremiah [108784], 2, 19
Jeremiah [109376], 184, 206
Jeremiah [109382], 207

Volume IV Name Index

John J. [103360], 27, 80
John J. [106510], 352
John J. [106647], 338
John J. [106716], 480
John J. [108669], 313, 316
John J. [108922], 375
John J. [93126], 492, 505
John J. [94297], 18, 57
John J. [95620], 321, 357
John J. III. [103416], 136
John J. Jr. [103406], 82, 135
John J. Jr. [85892], 506
John J. Jr. [95626], 358
John Joseph (Dr.) [98573], 14
John Joseph [106249], 90, 145
John Joseph [106700], 503
John Joseph [109303], 256
John Joseph [109688], 382
John Jr. [109684], 178
John L. [102442], 372, 415
John L. [106685], 479, 503
John L. [98877], 77
John L. [98882], 3, 25
John Lawrence Jr. [102458], 416
John Louis (Rev.) [93554], 214
John M. [96974], 294
John Normyle [94442], 163, 177
John P. [102563], 308
John R. [102694], 9, 46
John R. [94757], 170
John Richard [105767], 151
John S. [106048], 319
John T. ' Johnson' [103064], 232
John T. [93515], 199, 257
John V. [97882], 187, 220
John W. [100414], 73
John W. [109378], 207
John W. [98174], 109
John Walter [109947], 304
John William [99838], 434
John X. [106415], 441
Joseph [101116], 75
Joseph [101793], 422
Joseph [104067], 365
Joseph [104095], 474
Joseph [106275], 239
Joseph [106425], 153
Joseph [106430], 4, 30
Joseph [107616], 290

Joseph C. [98401], 24
Joseph Calvey [106417], 95, 151
Joseph F. [100574], 259
Joseph F. [98879], 26, 75
Joseph Francis [99307], 79, 134
Joseph L. [100679], 369
Joseph Mattew [99450], 39
Joseph P. [108335], 171
Joseph V, [92525], 494
Joseph William [94860], 269
Juila A. [101129], 20
Julia [105531], 373
Julia [108026], 353
Julia [108114], 480
Julia [108720], 67
Julia [92921], 187, 223
Julia [92978], 194
Julia [93763], 34, 115
Julia [95262], 37, 116
Julia [96079], 450, 466
Julia [98264], 1, 8
Julia [98611], 458
Julia [99985], 85
Julia A. [102443], 371
Julia A. [103079], 321, 359
Julia A. [103259], 483
Julia A. [103599], 33, 113, 208, 270
Julia A. [106376], 397, 441
Julia A. [99895], 403, 458, 475
Julia B. [108673], 339
Julia C. [93780], 385, 427
Julia E. [94584], 262
Julia E. [98262], 8, 44
Julia Frances [106912], 111, 167
Julia G. [106697], 479
Julia L. [106397], 439
Julia M. [94566], 199
Julia V. [93539], 214, 272
Julia wife Dennis [92923], 182, 187
Julia wife of Daniel [100824], 447, 451, 453
Julia wife of Dennis [94174], 1, 7
Julia wife of Dennis [96023], 216
Julia wife of Dennis [96558], 3, 21
Julia wife of Frank [96129], 31

Julia wife of Jeremiah [99983], 4, 27
Julia wife of John [100190], 5, 33
Julia wife of John [96435], 182, 185
Kate [94578], 259
Kate [94801], 470
Katherine C. [105686], 507
Katherine D. [94444], 63
Katherine M. [94560], 302
Katheryn [99948], 443
Kathleen [103519], 173
Kathryn [103436], 309
Kathryn Ann [109339], 426
Kenneth L. [100572], 409
Laureen A. [109336], 445
Lauretta [93781], 385
Lauretta Theresa [103485], 160, 173
Lawrence [98360], 10
Lawrence J. [94861], 269
Lena F. [94594], 298
Leo [107172], 133
Leo F. [98375], 277
Leroy Daniel [100245], 149
Letitia [97699], 56
Letitia A. [99410], 380, 423
Lillian [102441], 418
Lillian [95209], 286
Lillian F. [98570], 57
Lillian M. [102463], 417
Lizzie M. [102701], 46
Lois [109686], 382
Louise C. [98166], 109, 166
Louise M. [103273], 500
Lucy Theresa [99444], 39
Mabel [100680], 369
Mabel E. wife of Francis [103518], 160, 173
Mabel R. [107614], 291
Maggie M. [95654], 247, 291
Margaert wife of Eugene [96584], 182, 186
Margaret (Ukirre) [99439], 314, 331
Margaret [100226], 34
Margaret [100408], 25, 73, 461, 487
Margaret [100815], 451, 468
Margaret [100873], 462, 488
Margaret [101320], 333, 389

Margaret [101419], 36
Margaret [101904], 459, 478
Margaret [102009], 470
Margaret [103067], 232
Margaret [104096], 455
Margaret [104112], 326
Margaret [104181], 183, 189
Margaret [105665], 11, 50
Margaret [105668], 50
Margaret [105729], 93
Margaret [105770], 150
Margaret [105844], 22, 66
Margaret [106244], 147
Margaret [106253], 90
Margaret [108496], 145
Margaret [108678], 107
Margaret [109002], 319
Margaret [109110], 333
Margaret [109383], 207
Margaret [79102], 328
Margaret [85893], 506
Margaret [92479], 244, 289
Margaret [92737], 464
Margaret [92987], 13
Margaret [93523], 8, 42
Margaret [93565], 293
Margaret [94290], 200, 262
Margaret [94292], 263
Margaret [94574], 258
Margaret [95213], 236, 285
Margaret [96388], 205
Margaret [96393], 205
Margaret [98373], 71
Margaret [98562], 381
Margaret [98805], 278
Margaret [99647], 18
Margaret 'Aggie' V. [99026], 394
Margaret Agnes [99998], 138
Margaret E. [93074], 70, 131
Margaret G. [94895], 267
Margaret G. [95387], 383
Margaret I. [102460], 416
Margaret J. [106299], 52, 124
Margaret J. [94848], 202
Margaret J. [96013], 188, 229
Margaret J. [98162], 108, 166
Margaret K. [93777], 384, 425

Margaret L. [81208], 101, 157
Margaret M. [107125], 156
Margaret M. [94447], 64
Margaret M. [98480], 351
Margaret 'Maggie' [94436], 253
Margaret 'Maggie' J. [96551], 280
Margaret Maud [99446], 39
Margaret or Nancy wife of Matthew [102062], 4, 28
Margaret P. [95908], 387
Margaret T. [100847], 229
Margaret wife of Dennis [100822], 447, 451, 453
Margaret wife of Dennis [94800], 447, 453
Margaret wife of James [106308], 1, 11
Margaret wife of Jeremiah [95649], 354
Margaret wife of John [92430], 4, 30
Margaret wife of John [97307], 216
Margaret wife of Timothy [100508], 449, 462
Margaret wife of Timothy [106277], 183, 190
Margaret wife of Timothy [94451], 63
Margaret wife of Timothy [95322], 60, 449, 463
Marguerite R. [94056], 157
Maria wife of John [99235], 3, 22
Marie [102060], 142
Marion [100677], 369
Mark [101791], 423
Mark [93509], 258
Mark [94586], 259
Mark A. Jr. [100147], 309
Mark Anthony [97254], 282, 308
Mark E. [101327], 390, 429
Mary (Barrule) [108715], 66
Mary (Ceartan) [95122], 384
Mary (Mor) [99036], 394
Mary (Shearhig) [108789], 314, 334
Mary [100185], 33, 110
Mary [100650], 322, 360
Mary [100906], 328, 382
Mary [102436], 371
Mary [102710], 9

Mary [103408], 82
Mary [103413], 137
Mary [103474], 5, 32
Mary [104496], 30, 94
Mary [105020], 449, 460
Mary [105666], 50
Mary [105722], 29, 93
Mary [106250], 90
Mary [106255], 145
Mary [106675], 459, 478
Mary [107582], 191, 244
Mary [107597], 245
Mary [107819], 448, 456
Mary [108024], 353
Mary [108718], 67
Mary [108835], 317, 330, 340, 385
Mary [108943], 314, 333
Mary [108964], 185, 208
Mary [108974], 209, 271
Mary [108999], 319
Mary [109108], 332
Mary [109611], 216
Mary [79271], 12, 53
Mary [92010], 4, 30
Mary [92807], 97, 153
Mary [92967], 430
Mary [92985], 12
Mary [93073], 70, 129
Mary [93525], 8, 41
Mary [93767], 384
Mary [93964], 20
Mary [94112], 429
Mary [94564], 199
Mary [95193], 183, 190
Mary [95300], 61
Mary [95612], 406
Mary [95614], 313, 321
Mary [95615], 357
Mary [95619], 321, 353
Mary [95656], 247
Mary [96080], 466
Mary [96397], 206
Mary [96772], 18, 59
Mary [96922], 465, 490
Mary [98071], 449, 461
Mary [98370], 23
Mary [99480], 119
Mary [99644], 256
Mary [99980], 28, 85
Mary A. [100493], 352
Mary A. [101694], 457
Mary A. [103135], 52, 122
Mary A. [103469], 105
Mary A. [103491], 165, 178
Mary A. [106100], 334, 391

Mary A. [106264], 190, 237
Mary A. [107834], 373, 419
Mary A. [93538], 214
Mary A. [94176], 8
Mary A. [95372], 228, 452, 468
Mary A. [95798], 375, 420
Mary A. [97248], 233, 282
Mary A. [99463], 40
Mary Ann [108657], 338, 398
Mary Ann [95212], 235
Mary Ann [99440], 6
Mary C. [103464], 163
Mary C. [94896], 267, 303
Mary Carmel [99927], 401
Mary Catherine [103449], 284
Mary D. wife of Joseph [108383], 260
Mary E. [100308], 414
Mary E. [101102], 75, 134
Mary E. [105768], 150
Mary E. [106414], 441
Mary E. [92684], 472, 497
Mary E. [92856], 253, 293
Mary E. [93559], 254
Mary E. [94291], 263, 298
Mary E. [94705], 128
Mary E. [95849], 344
Mary E. [96549], 280
Mary E. [98163], 108
Mary E. [98475], 350
Mary E. [98758], 278
Mary Elizabeth [106373], 396, 440
Mary Elizabeth 'Lizzie' [103071], 233
Mary Ellen [102711], 46
Mary Emma [94583], 261
Mary F. [106262], 239, 286
Mary F. [106511], 352
Mary F. [94909], 298
Mary F. [97849], 140
Mary F. [99017], 459
Mary Frances [99447], 39
Mary G. [106693], 502
Mary J. [92705], 497
Mary J. [93993], 462
Mary J. [98072], 217
Mary J. [98884], 26
Mary J. [99832], 394
Mary Jane [103486], 161, 175
Mary Jane [94573], 258
Mary Jane [98881], 77

Mary Julia Mamie [100000], 138
Mary Kerr [109342], 427
Mary L [95912], 387
Mary L. [102321], 451
Mary L. [109485], 84
Mary L. [94847], 202
Mary L. [94856], 268
Mary L. [99409], 380
Mary Louise [106687], 502
Mary M. [93516], 199, 258
Mary M. [97252], 282
Mary M. wife of John N. [102179], 163, 178
Mary 'Mamie' [93776], 384, 425
Mary 'Mamie' [95625], 358
Mary Margaret Kathryn [99849], 432, 445
Mary Margret [106918], 111, 167
Mary Martha [99239], 127
Mary Matilda [106567], 249
Mary P. [102466], 417
Mary R. [97435], 296
Mary Rose [105152], 120
Mary S. Leona [106242], 147
Mary T. [102342], 370
Mary T. [104073], 364, 408
Mary T. [98764], 115
Mary Teresa [107174], 133
Mary Theresa [108518], 511
Mary V. [94435], 253, 294
Mary W. [102407], 323, 369
Mary W. [106394], 439
Mary wife of Daniel [100410], 3, 25, 488
Mary wife of Daniel [106310], 52
Mary wife of Daniel [99577], 447, 452
Mary wife of E. [92919], 447, 455
Mary wife of Eugene [100843], 182, 188
Mary wife of Eugene [96775], 2, 18
Mary wife of Jeremiah [100116], 448, 456
Mary wife of Jeremiah [96051], 182, 186
Mary wife of John [101324], 314, 333
Mary wife of John [95279], 37

Mary wife of John [95479], 127
Mary wife of John [98613], 448, 457
Mary wife of John [99211], 449, 464
Mary wife of John [99617], 4, 27
Mary wife of Michael [99460], 3, 27, 40
Mary wife of Patrick [100412], 73, 449, 461
Mary wife of Patrick [92977], 183, 194
Mary wife of Roger [103427], 183, 188
Mary wife of Timothy [100875], 449, 462
Mary wife of Timothy [96124], 183, 195
Mary wife of Timothy [96973], 183, 196
Mary wife of Timothy [98960], 449, 463
Matilda [100251], 5, 34
Matilda C. 'Millie' [99892], 344, 403, 476, 500
Matilda V. [98760], 115
Matthew [102059], 142
Matthew [102061], 4, 28
Matthew W. [102052], 89
Michael [101415], 5, 34
Michael [106933], 449, 461
Michael [109484], 84
Michael [109608], 185, 215
Michael [109912], 444
Michael [79104], 328
Michael [92447], 449, 461
Michael [93077], 3, 22
Michael [94802], 469
Michael [96561], 21
Michael [96574], 218
Michael [97245], 282
Michael [97898], 222
Michael [97917], 23, 71
Michael [98160], 5, 32
Michael [98372], 71
Michael [98584], 1, 10
Michael [99459], 3, 27, 40
Michael E. [106385], 396
Michael E. [106932], 487
Michael F. [103468], 105, 159
Michael F. [92610], 212
Michael F. [93070], 23, 68

Volume IV Name Index

Michael Francis [98164], 109

Michael H. [100416], 73, 133

Michael Henry [95904], 387, 428

Michael Henry [99403], 327, 378

Michael J. (a Chaird) [102338], 370

Michael J. [104061], 323, 363

Michael J. [95005], 371, 413

Michael J. [95949], 280

Michael J. [97250], 233, 281

Michael P. [104131], 332

Michael P. [105727], 93

Michael T. [92808], 97

Michael U. [107817], 456, 474

Mildred Ann [99242], 128

Mortimer [100250], 5, 33

Mortimer [103473], 5, 32

Mortimer [105016], 481

Mortimer [107581], 191, 243

Mortimer James [98762], 115

Mortimer Steven [107760], 242

Murtaugh 'Murtie' [99989], 86

Nancy [109911], 444

Nancy [98355], 49

Nancy M. [103414], 137

Nancy or Catherine wife of James [98412], 448, 456

Nancy Thomas [106575], 194

Nora [105669], 50

Patricia A. [108556], 310

Patrick (Sean Rua - Suonish) [108719], 67

Patrick [100411], 73, 449, 461

Patrick [100413], 73

Patrick [100453], 3, 24

Patrick [100819], 451, 453

Patrick [101002], 452

Patrick [101100], 3, 25

Patrick [101400], 460

Patrick [101577], 457

Patrick [102317], 5, 33

Patrick [103253], 461, 483

Patrick [105661], 372

Patrick [105733], 4, 29

Patrick [107605], 244

Patrick [108050], 353

Patrick [92976], 183, 194

Patrick [93180], 9, 46

Patrick [93564], 293

Patrick [95611], 406

Patrick [96391], 206

Patrick [96421], 183, 195

Patrick [97884], 182, 187

Patrick [98265], 44

Patrick [98362], 3, 23

Patrick [98368], 72

Patrick [99618], 27, 83

Patrick E. [100669], 323, 367

Patrick H. [103419], 105, 161, 309

Patrick H. [105149], 45, 119

Patrick H. [105721], 29, 92

Patrick H. [105741], 150

Patrick H. [94413], 171

Patrick H. [95802], 375

Patrick H. [99034], 395, 437

Patrick J. [106706], 459, 479

Patrick P. [95897], 331, 385

Paul [109687], 382

Paul Brendan [100573], 410

Paul E. [109719], 428, 445

Paul Edward [100148], 309

Pauline [109720], 428

Pauline G. [94711], 169

Peter (Shearhig) [99438], 314, 330

Peter [103116], 331

Peter [104688], 315, 335

Peter [108517], 511

Peter [95899], 1, 6, 83

Peter F. [95903], 387, 428

Peter 'Suonish' [97918], 71

Philip [102335], 3, 21

Philip [99633], 196, 256

Philip Aloyisius [109301], 257

Phillip [98885], 26

Quinlan [106235], 28, 89

Quinlan A. [98469], 319, 349

Raymond W. [98806], 278

Rebecca Thomas [106568], 249

Richard [101000], 452

Richard E. [102561], 307

Rita M. [99412], 380, 424

Robert C. [106246], 148

Robert D. [94563], 302

Robert Kevin [99249], 169

Robert T. [94888], 200

Robert Vincent [94862], 269

Roger (Seer) [98467], 313, 318

Roger [103422], 188, 234

Roger [103426], 182, 188

Roger [108838], 314, 330, 340

Roger Francis [99940], 402

Rose A. [92683], 471

Rosetta W. [104079], 365

Ruth Elizabeth [99466], 41

Ruth Marie [99245], 169

Ruth Patricia [106245], 148

Sarah [93566], 254

Sarah C. [103364], 82

Sarah G. [103421], 163, 176, 284, 309

Sarah L. [96548], 280

Sarah R. [93541], 214, 274

Sarah 'Sadie' [102703], 46

Sarah W. [103492], 165

Sheila M. [109338], 445

Sheila R. [100009], 139

Silvester [96082], 466, 494

Simon [103443], 284

Simon Stephen [103428], 176, 234, 282

Stephen [100846], 228

Sylvester Jr. [106936], 495

Teresa [103496], 180

Terrance [106395], 439

Thomas [108499], 145

Thomas [92702], 471

Thomas [94853], 268

Thomas [99794], 2, 19

Thomas F. [92953], 169

Thomas James [103445], 284, 309

Thomas M. [105782], 508

Thomas Quinlan [106257], 90, 148

Timothy (Buaig) [108834], 317, 330, 339, 385

Timothy (Suonish) [93513], 184, 198

Timothy [100104], 4, 29

Timothy [100112], 29

Timothy [100507], 449, 461

Timothy [100874], 449, 462

Timothy [101321], 390

Timothy [101325], 390

Timothy [101794], 422

Timothy [103602], 113, 185, 208

Timothy [104498], 4, 29

Timothy [106276], 183, 190
Timothy [108671], 338
Timothy [108921], 27
Timothy [109261], 4, 31
Timothy [110117], 323
Timothy [92477], 313, 316
Timothy [92746], 449, 463
Timothy [92980], 195
Timothy [92986], 13
Timothy [93963], 20
Timothy [94450], 63
Timothy [94567], 200
Timothy [94587], 259
Timothy [94606], 262
Timothy [94681], 128
Timothy [94843], 184, 200
Timothy [95190], 190, 234
Timothy [95216], 236
Timothy [95321], 60, 449,
463
Timothy [95605], 357
Timothy [95610], 406
Timothy [96123], 183, 195
Timothy [96173], 469
Timothy [96506], 470
Timothy [96776], 59
Timothy [96972], 183, 196
Timothy [97468], 467
Timothy [98959], 449, 463
Timothy [99616], 3, 27
Timothy B. [99830], 394,
431
Timothy C. [92803], 30, 95
Timothy D. [93297], 452
Timothy D. [95603], 321,
355
Timothy D. [98759], 34, 113
Timothy F. [95624], 358
Timothy Francis [98763],
115
Timothy J. [95301], 61
Timothy J. [99434], 6, 38
Timothy J. Jr. [94845], 201
Timothy Joseph [99920],
344, 399
Timothy L. [94441], 63
Timothy P. D.D.S. [105963],
333, 388
Timothy R. [109341], 426
Timothy R. [93583], 254,
296
Timothy R. [93760], 115
Timothy R. [93773], 329,
384
Timothy R. [94531], 263

Timothy S. [95650], 192,
245, 451, 468
Veronica [100674], 368
Wallace Francis [106396],
439
Walter Edward 'Eddie'
[103493], 165
Walter Green (Dr.) [99445],
39
wife of Paul [109723], 428,
445
William [101790], 423
William [106241], 147
William [95618], 407
William [98876], 77
William [99246], 169
William [99622], 84
William Ambrose [94710],
128, 169
William E. [92795], 154
William E. [94894], 267
William E. [99030], 437
William E. [99033], 395
William F. [100026], 140
William H. [95215], 236
William Henry [108837], 340
William J. [103432], 283,
309
William J. [106655], 338
William M. [99937], 402
William Matthew [95851],
345
William P. [95606], 357, 406
William Stephen [107126],
156
William W. [103520], 161
William 'Willie' [94437], 254
Winifred [94178], 27, 79
Winifred Veronica [103490],
165, 178
SUTCLIFFE
Charles A. [108980], 272
SWEENEY
Edward F. [92814], 153
Maria F. [109904], 499
SYLVESTER
Horace [100021], 87
SYNDER
Sophia wife of David
[108663], 398
TAVARES
Maria [108687], 179
TOLAN
Mr. [103524], 174
TOOLIN
James [105024], 482

Katherine [105023], 482
TOOMEY
John [103080], 321, 360
Mary E. [103084], 360
Nora [103083], 360
Patrick [103081], 360
TRAVERS
Joseph [106428], 172
Joseph H. [106427], 152,
172
Marie [106429], 172
TREMBLAY
Edward [99310], 135
Emily wife of Edward
[99311], 135
Irma [99308], 79, 135
TURNER
Arthur J. [107058], 362
TWOMEY
Johanna [96085], 495
VACCHI
Mr. [108557], 310
VAUGHAN
Grace Margaret [103454],
285, 310
Michael Curley [103455],
310
VERA
Sarah E. [103499], 165
WADE
Annie [104492], 419
WALLACE
Anna [104145], 131
Arthur A. [104140], 131
Charles Lester [104139],
131
Francis [104141], 131
George Francis [104135],
70, 130
Jennie [104143], 131
Lizzie V. [104142], 131
Mabel A. [104144], 131
Margaret E. [104146], 131
Richard D. [104137], 130
WALSH
Annie Agnes [103479], 105,
160
Catherine wife of David
[103435], 309
Daniel J. [81210], 158
David [103434], 309
Francis A. 'Franky' [29102],
158
James Aloysius [81207],
101, 158
James E. [81209], 158

Volume V
Descendants of Immigrants born 1825 – 1840
Name Index

Lena [104599], 362
Lillian [104606], 362
Mary A. [104605], 362
William [104602], 362
BROWN
Mary [103176], 139, 165
BRUNENGRABER
Julia [107273], 271
BURGESS
Daniel Mason [110151], 402
Wiliam Noble [105757], 402
BURKE
Edward P. [103117], 346
Ellen 'Nellie' [103122], 347
James H. [103120], 346
Jane C. wife of Matthew [103130], 347
Mary L. [103119], 346
Matthew [103112], 346
Matthew Joseph [103121], 346
Patrick [103111], 333, 346
Rebecca E. [83815], 207
William F. [103118], 346
BURNS
Abby [100616], 378, 399
Catherine wife of Timothy [100646], 399
Hugh A. [101912], 18, 60
Katie [101915], 60
Mary [107280], 457
Matthew [101913], 60
Matthew Sullivan [101916], 60
Timothy [100645], 399
BURR
Bronson S. [103124], 346
Maryetta [103123], 346
BYRNE
Margaret [102161], 108
BYRON
Edward [102941], 317
Mary Elizabeth [102940], 317
CAHILL
Johanna [106984], 377, 393
Louisa [99733], 27, 70
Thomas [99734], 70
CALLAHAN
Anna Josephina [103793], 216, 273
Ellen [101595], 24
CAMPBELL
Anne [100489], 205
Mary A. [97158], 262
CAREY

Angeline L. [106282], 264
Bartholomew J. [106279], 264
Bridget [106969], 394, 434
Edward A. [106283], 264
Edward J. [106278], 184, 264
John [101670], 164, 243
John [101832], 243
John [101834], 164
Michael [101828], 163, 243
Michael [101831], 243
CARROL
John [101508], 196
CARROLL
Agnes [103032], 383, 406
Bridget [98980], 31
Daniel D. [104642], 386, 416
James [101290], 313
John P. [104643], 416
Margaret [101538], 237
Mary Louise [101289], 313
Michael [103033], 406
Sarah wife of Michael [103034], 406
CASEY
Edward J. [103747], 220
Honora 'Nora' [103748], 220
John [103740], 155, 220
Margaret [103746], 220
Mary [105102], 302
Timothy [103741], 220
William [103749], 220
CAULFIELD
Agnes [97484], 120
Estella V. [97483], 120
James Joseph [97480], 102, 120
John J. [97481], 120
Mary F [97485], 120
CAVANAUGH
Ann [107255], 272
CERNERE
Bridget [103110], 217
CHARETTE
Marceline [102487], 193
CHARTERS
Catherine [97142], 274
CHEFETZ
Goldie Katherine [101917], 60
Nelson [101921], 60
CHURCH
Edwin Wilbur [101339], 46
CLARK

Dale Frank [102328], 465
Minor Frank [102329], 465
Philip James III. [102566], 289
CLARKE
Mary Aloysius [109886], 456
CLEVENGER
Rebecca Elizabeth [110160], 402
CLIFFORD
Jane [107287], 439
CLYNER
Margaret [100212], 184
COFFEY
Catherine [97246], 160, 228
Patrick [102542], 228
COLBERT
Mary J. wife of Thomas [96712], 176
Thomas [96711], 176
Thomas P. [96709], 176
COLE
Arnold F. [97627], 19, 65
Charles F. [97638], 65
Harriet [97637], 65
John [97636], 66
Joseph [97628], 65
Mary Elizabeth [97635], 65
COLEMAN
Ellen [96680], 79
Margaret [99053], 141
COLLINS
Anne M. [102175], 133
Annie [102714], 79
Elizabeth V. [102176], 133
Henry [103050], 219
James Joseph [102172], 133
Joseph M. [102174], 133
Margaret M. [102173], 133
Patricia [102170], 133
Shirley A. [102169], 133
William J. [102171], 133
William J. Sr. [102165], 128, 133
CONDON
James [103788], 413
Mary [103770], 385, 413
CONLON
Andrew [97160], 261
Harold Avery [97162], 261
Henry Elmer [97153], 176, 261
CONNELLY
Johannah [96177], 191

Mary [94663], 139, 169
CONNORS
Bridget wife of Michael
[108125], 383
Donald [105249], 455
Jeremiah [102669], 320
Johanna [105623], 375, 381
John [102668], 305, 320
Mary [103771], 413
Mary J. [102671], 320
Michael [108124], 383
Michael Jr. [108123], 383
Mr. [105248], 424, 455
CONROY
Catherine [104703], 418
Hannah [96837], 94, 114
Mary [107192], 312
Philip [96839], 114
CONSIDINE
Annie Laurie [107278], 434,
457
John [107279], 457
CONWAY
Bridget [104677], 446
COOK
Clarinda [105514], 74
COOKE
Elizabeth [85894], 394, 440
CORBETT
Joseph [109371], 405
CORCORAN
David [100989], 165, 245
David [100990], 246
Elizabeth [100996], 246
Elizabeth wife of Thomas
[100994], 245
Ella M. [100992], 246
Fannie [100997], 246
Ida [100991], 246
Katherine A. [100999], 246
Margaret M. [100998], 246
Mary [102951], 317
Mary wife of Michael
[102938], 316
Michael [102937], 316
Michael F. [102939], 316
Thomas [100993], 245
Timothy [102933], 303, 316
CORRIVEAU
Alfred [109178], 461
Jeanette [109177], 448, 461
COSGROVE
Mary [105045], 423
COSTELLO
Patrick [102233], 255
Sarah [102232], 255

COULEY
Bridget [105908], 232
CRANE
Mary [103875], 430
CRAWFORD
John Robert [100627], 464
Marjorie Sylvania [100629],
464
Thomas A. [100624], 452,
464
Thomas A. [100625], 464
CREAMER
John F. [97164], 261
Katherine T. [97163], 261
Mary E. [98943], 253
CREEDAN
Anna E. [104644], 416
Cornelius [104645], 416
CRISHAM
Bridget [105203], 448
CRISTIE
John [103180], 248
Sarah [103179], 248
CROSSLEY
Joan [109946], 276
CROSSON
Hazel wife of James
[101609], 69
James [101607], 69
James D. [101604], 69
James Daniel V. [101603],
24, 69
Marguerite [101608], 69
Mary 'Mamie' [101606], 69
CROWLEY
Bridget wife of John
[104014], 408
Ellen [96844], 84, 93
Helen [104016], 409
Ida Louise [102715], 79
John [102713], 79
John [104013], 408
John [107008], 325
John Thomas [104018], 408
Joseph Michael [102712],
57, 79
Julia [94263], 166
Margaret [107567], 440
Margaret [94071], 310
Margaret F. [104015], 409
Margaret G. [104020], 409
Mary [104017], 408
Mary [104699], 376, 387
Mary or Ellen [101248], 42
Michael [104009], 384, 408
Miriam [102716], 79

Timothy [107009], 325
William J. [104019], 408
CROWTHER
Daniel [108341], 263
Daniel L. [109929], 251
Joseph [108338], 263
Joseph Henry [101076],
167, 250
Margaret [109927], 251
Philip C. [109928], 251
Sarah A. [109926], 251
Sarah wife of Thomas
[101075], 250
Thomas [101074], 250
Walter [109924], 251
William E. Jr. [108340], 263
William Edward [99309],
181, 263
William H. [109925], 251
CUMMINS
Catherine [108948], 111
CUNNEEN
Annie L. [99962], 17, 58
Martin [99963], 58
CURLEY
Catherine Emma [106285],
398, 450
Patrick [106288], 450
CURRAN
Annie [105103], 302
Child [103100], 359
Patrick [105104], 302
Peter Francis [96826], 339,
359
Peter Sr. [96827], 359
CURT
Louis [105617], 116
CURTIN
Andre [100610], 462
Charles [100612], 463
Charles E. [100609], 452,
462
Irene C. [100613], 462
DACEY
Julia [91836], 207
DALEY
Louise V. [107884], 225,
276
DALTON
Bridget [110093], 318
DANAHAY
John [100587], 54
DAVIS
Bella E. [105057], 363
Earnest A. [96681], 78
DAVISON

Letitia E. [104109], 410
ESTENTELOCKKEN
May [108868], 230
Ola [108869], 230
FAHEY
Bertha Catherine [96811], 309
Ellen F. [96809], 308
Martin [96807], 308
Mary E. [96810], 308
Thomas B. [96806], 297, 308
FALVEY
Cecilia [107252], 272
John [107249], 214, 272
John Vincent [107251], 272
Mary Sullivan [107250], 272
Patrick [107254], 272
FARRELL
Ellen [97593], 64
FAULKNER
Olivia [103186], 247
FERGUSON
Catherine [103862], 429
FERRY
Anne wife of Manuel [103846], 403
Annie [103850], 403
Augustus [109580], 404
Edward [103852], 403
John T. [103849], 403
Lena [103854], 404
Lillian [103851], 403
Manuel [103843], 380, 403
Manuel [103845], 403
Mary [103853], 404
FINNEGAN
Ellen [101291], 313
FINSTAD
Gunhild [108870], 230
FITZGERALD
Mary [100078], 209
FITZGIBBONS
Margaret E. [98941], 253
William [98942], 253
William [98979], 31
William T. [98978], 31
FLANNAGAN
Mary A. [107875], 225
FLEMMING
James [92678], 147, 191
Lawrence [96176], 191
FLYNN
Catherine [95006], 334, 348
James D. [95007], 348
FOGARTY

Anastasia [104997], 368
Edward [100929], 213
Edward C. [100928], 213
FOLEY
Catherine [97646], 65
Edward F. [79200], 207
Ellen [97642], 65
Hannah [97645], 65
Honora wife of John [97632], 65
James [97631], 65
James [97641], 65
James A. [83707], 207
Jerome Dennis [83662], 207
John [83702], 207
John [97630], 19, 65
John [97644], 65
John M. [79195], 207
Julia [97643], 65
Martin [108955], 112
Nellie [79194], 207
Raymond [83663], 207
William W. [4284], 153, 207
William W. Jr. [4162], 207
FRANCIS
Jeffrey Scott [102137], 135
Jennifer Lynn [102136], 135
Ronald R [102135], 132, 135
Stephanie Michelle [102138], 135
FRANEY
Agnes [100081], 210
Ann Rita [100935], 214, 271
Catherine A. [100082], 210
James [100084], 209
Mary [100085], 209
Michael [107992], 271
Patrick [100076], 153, 209
Richard [100077], 209
William [100083], 210
FREDERICKS
Frank [105246], 424
FRIEDRICH
Lucy Clair [102557], 287, 291
Nicholas Theodore [102558], 291
FULLER
Fred (Dr.) [103974], 261
GAFFNEY
Ellen [102151], 89, 109
Partrick [102152], 109
GALIVAN
Johanna [94668], 169, 256
GALLAGHER

Lena [107284], 458
GALLIGAN
Catherine wife of John C. [101845], 35
John C. [101844], 35
John E. [101846], 35
John H. [93506], 9, 35
Lillian D. [101848], 35
Theresa H. [101847], 35
GALLIVAN
Ellen [96083], 380, 402
John [96084], 402
GARLAND
Bernard L. [104108], 410
John [104107], 385, 410
GARRITY
Elizabeth 'Lizzie' [100914], 154, 212
Ellen wife of John [100920], 212
John [100919], 212
GAUDETTE
Mary Adeline [103188], 283
GEARY
Margaret [101277], 292, 299
GILES
Catherine [103667], 218, 274
John [97145], 274
GILLIGAN
Mary [96828], 359
GILLIS
Archibald 'Archie' [104177], 224
GOERL
Kunigunde Lucy [102559], 291
GOLDING
Delia [102234], 255
GORDON
Elizabeth [100055], 66
John W. [100047], 20, 66
John W. [100053], 67
Margaret wife of Thomas [100049], 66
Thomas [100048], 66
Thomas Francis [106894], 67
GORE
Ellen [97591], 19, 63
James [97596], 63
GRACE
Catherine [98093], 365
Daniel [98095], 366
David [98096], 366

David F. [98084], 340, 365
Eugene [98097], 366
Francis [98098], 366
Mary [98092], 365
Michael [98081], 365
Michael [98094], 365
GRADY
Mary [96947], 150
GRAY
Ida [94678], 169
Joseph [97010], 235
Mary A. [97009], 235
GREEN
Catherine (Uonhi) [103099], 324, 338
Catherine [106266], 259
Catherine [108115], 406, 454
Cornelius J. (Sullivan) [108111], 382, 406
Joanna [96595], 136, 143
John (Uohni) [108113], 406
Julia [96600], 143
Margaret Mary [101534], 138, 162
Mary (Uohni) [105541], 436
Mary [96789], 292, 297
Philip [96804], 297
GREGSON
Marion [103958], 455
GRINNELL
Bernice May [105076], 364
HACKEY
Katherine [100611], 462
HAMILTON
Edna H. [108867], 230
Fred [100984], 245
HANLEY
Hanora [99914], 84, 93
HANLON
James F. [107293], 268
Louis F. [103369], 203, 268
Mary [103370], 268
HANNIFY
Catherine [101509], 197
Edward [101514], 197
John [101504], 196
Joseph E. [101511], 197
Julia [101507], 196
Maria [101506], 196
Michael [101503], 150, 196
HANSON
Charles H. [105075], 363
Cora B. [105073], 363
David H. [105056], 363
David W. H. [105064], 363

Edith [105068], 364
Edward Charles [105070], 364
George E. [105067], 363
Grace [105069], 363
Irene M. [105062], 363
John L. [105072], 363
Lena M. [105066], 363
Mabel [105065], 363
Marion [105063], 363
Minnie B. [105074], 363
William [105071], 363
William H. [105058], 340, 363
HARRIGAN
Bridget [100307], 348
HARRINGTON
Abbie E. [103307], 407
Anna [101250], 42
Annie [106113], 111, 338
Bridget [101252], 42
Bridget [92243], 163, 240
Bridget G. [103308], 407
Catherine (Caupey) [108795], 366
Catherine [102638], 152, 204
Catherine [104831], 352, 376, 387
Catherine [110071], 338
Catherine [98774], 76
Catherine E. [83634], 387, 420
Cornelius [107799], 49
Cornelius 'Con' [110074], 338
Daniel [101395], 28
Daniel [104900], 12
Daniel [79121], 407
Daniel H. [106611], 344
Daniel J. [101243], 11, 42
Daniel J. [101255], 43
Elizabeth [96684], 54, 77
Elizabeth C. [104922], 12
Elizabeth 'Eliza' [100740], 163, 239
Ellen 'Lena' [101251], 42
Ellen T. [101394], 7, 28
Francis X. [101727], 75
Gertrude A. [95487], 198, 267
Gertrude Bridget [103310], 407
Hannah (Caobach) [96836], 170
Hanora [101322], 52

Hanora Wife Of Daniel [79122], 407
Honora [106206], 382
Honora [110053], 338, 355
James F. [95488], 267
James P. [99059], 147
Jeremiah (Greasai) [106609], 344
Joanna wife of John [98999], 33
Johanna (Caobach) [107741], 19
Johanna [102178], 89, 104
Johanna [104646], 416
Johanna [110145], 109
Johanna wife of Timothy [100329], 55
John [101247], 42
John [110073], 338
John [98998], 33
John Francis [101725], 75
John J. [98997], 9, 33
John Joseph [103796], 272
Julia [110075], 338
Julia M. [92305], 321
Margaret [108793], 366
Margaret [110070], 337
Margaret [99001], 34
Margaret 'Maggie' [101253], 42
Margaret wife of Patrick [102182], 104
Mary [101254], 42
Mary [104652], 443
Mary [105754], 401
Mary [110057], 337
Mary [96274], 292, 304
Mary [96645], 54
Mary A. [101348], 46
Mary A. [102227], 168, 255
Mary A. [104648], 396, 443
Mary A. [107798], 14, 49
Mary A. wife of Cornelius [107811], 49
Mary E. [107569], 395, 440
Mary P. [100327], 16, 55
Mary T. [99000], 33
Mary wife of Daniel [101396], 28
Mary wife of Timothy [102229], 255
Michael [107275], 204
Michael [108794], 366
Michael 'Mick' [106114], 111, 324, 337
Michael 'Mick' [110072], 338

Nora [103309], 407
Patrick [102181], 104
Paul [101719], 74
Philip [94262], 166
Philip [94264], 166
Philip [99058], 147
Philip F. [96685], 77
Phillip H. [92230], 239, 240
Quinlan (Trokirre) [93966], 339
Samuel Francis [101723], 47, 74
Sylvester [104651], 443
Theresa [103306], 407
Timothy [100328], 55
Timothy [102228], 255
Timothy [107570], 377, 395
Timothy [99002], 33
Timothy D. [79130], 384, 407
William F. [101249], 43
HARRISON
Elizabeth [104668], 444
John H. [105883], 201
Rose A. [105882], 151, 201
HART
Nora [103168], 67, 282
HAYES
John Thomas [105107], 302
HEALY
Ann Jane [101529], 162, 236
Bridget wife of Ann [101531], 236
Catherine 'Cait' [107016], 326
Daniel [107022], 326
Daniel [108297], 326
Johanna [104953], 377, 395, 446
Patrick [101530], 236
HEARN
Mary A. [103955], 414, 455
Thomas [103962], 455
HEBERT
Adaline [103173], 283
Caroline [103158], 283
George L. [103172], 283
Henry E. [103174], 283
Joseph [103157], 249, 283
Joseph [103187], 283
Michael J. [103171], 283
HEFFERNAN
Ellen [100930], 213
HERLIHY
Dennis [104269], 5

HICKEY
Bartholomew [102258], 10
Joanna [102255], 10
Mary [102546], 138, 160
Mary wife of Bartholomew [102259], 10
HINCH
Mary [97258], 280
HINCKLEY
Charles [104312], 428
Charles W. [104308], 390, 427
Daniel [104309], 427
Dorothy [104315], 428
John [104316], 428
Margaret [104310], 428
Mary [104311], 428
Raymond [104314], 428
William [104313], 428
HODGSON
Alice [104063], 97
Frederick [110045], 252
Jennie [110044], 252
HODNETT
John [108027], 420
Peter F. [104781], 420
HOLLAND
Benjamin [95004], 97
Giles [96835], 170
Hannah [96834], 139, 170
James H. [95003], 97
Mary [103656], 155, 218
Mary [105287], 426
Mary [92424], 353
Timothy [103659], 218
HOLMAN
Doris [101726], 75
HOLMES
Annette wife of Chester [103975], 261
Chester H. [103972], 261
Esther A. [103970], 261
Hanora [104637], 376, 385
Herbert [103973], 260
Herbert G. [103967], 176, 260
Hiram [103968], 260
Mary E. wife of Hiram [103969], 260
Roy F. [103971], 261
HOLT
Ann E. [102449], 350
HOPKINS
Bridget Beatrice [93384], 74
Charles L. [106268], 259
Frank S. [106267], 259

George [106261], 174, 259
George William [106269], 259
Joseph D. [106270], 259
Rhodes [106265], 259
HOSFORD
Charles W. [106626], 343
HOULIHAN
Julia 'Jude' [108946], 90, 111
Margaret [108022], 420
Mary [105874], 323, 336
Maurice [108947], 111
HOUSTON
Catherine [100394], 14, 47
John [100395], 47
Mary wife of John [100396], 47
HOWARD
Charles F. [95214], 97, 117
Charles W. [95218], 117
Mary [101625], 376, 388
Michael [105251], 388
Mr. [101197], 187
William [95221], 117
HOWE
Minnie [101288], 314
HURLEY
Denis [86026], 27
Mary [86032], 6, 27
Timothy [104270], 5
IRVING
James F. [105906], 162, 232
James H. [105907], 232
Mary E. L. [105909], 233
JANERIO
Augustus [109582], 403
Celia [109581], 403
JENKINS
Jennifer J. [100626], 464
JETTE
Mary [99735], 70
JOHNSON
Augusta wife of Patrick [102325], 465
Dorothy M. [102326], 465
Lillian Pearl [102327], 465
Patrick [102324], 465
Rudolph Waldemar [100630], 452, 465
JOHNSTON
Benjamin [100601], 463
Evelyn Louise [100622], 464

Irene Margaret [100619], 463

Ritta Agnes [100620], 463

Robert [100623], 464

William Benjamin [100621], 463

William Minot [100600], 452, 463

JONES

Bridget [103431], 425

KANE

Bridget [103113], 346

KEITHAN

Anthony 'Tony' [107876], 225, 276

Antoine [94129], 158, 224

Antoine [94130], 224

Frank [107878], 225

George E. [107880], 225

Gladys [107888], 276

Hannah M. [107883], 225

Margaret [107877], 225

Margaret wife of William [107885], 225

Mary F. [94132], 225

Matthew [107879], 225

Rosa wife of Antoine [94131], 224

William [107882], 225

KELLEHER

Andrew J. [102452], 348

Andrew J. Jr. [110049], 368

Andrew Joseph Francis [102467], 348, 368

Francis J. [102451], 334, 348

Margaret [96283], 322

KELLY

Catherine [96437], 84, 94

Cornelius L. [92883], 36

Ellen [106815], 221

Ellen M. [92882], 10, 36

Ellen 'Nellie' [94274], 165

Eva M. 'Geneva' [97099], 29, 71

Jeremiah [107739], 22

Johanna [110048], 139, 168

John [96641], 94

Julia [107728], 4, 22

Margaret [103153], 165, 247

Mary [102153], 109

Mary wife of John [96642], 94

Michael [108941], 90

Peter [107455], 139, 165

Richard [103185], 247

Rose [92659], 93

Thomas [97100], 71

KENNEALLY

Anna [95761], 408, 454

Bridget wife of James [104007], 408

James [104006], 408

James A. [104008], 408

William J. [104002], 384, 408

KENNEDY

Abigail Helen [101337], 46

Charles Francis [101343], 46

Edward [103167], 67, 282

Francis Edward 'Frank' [101345], 46

George Henry [101341], 46

Margaret [98749], 310

Mary [107572], 440

Mary Ellen [101336], 46

Mary G. [98748], 311

Mary wife of Michael [101335], 46

Michael [101334], 46

Michael A. [107568], 395, 440

Nora [103166], 67, 248, 282

Sarah G. [101328], 46, 74

Thomas [107566], 440

Thomas [94070], 310

Thomas D. [101329], 12, 46

Thomas E. [98737], 298, 310

Thomas E. Jr. [98750], 311

Thomas Stephen [101340], 46

KENNEY

Elizabeth [107294], 268

Hugh [97616], 81

John [105813], 73

Mabel [105819], 73

Margaert [105815], 73

Mary E. 'Minnie' [97615], 63, 81

Mildred [105817], 73

Raymond [105818], 73

Regina [105820], 73

William [105812], 33, 73

William [105816], 73

KILEY

Catherine [108339], 263

Daniel Francis [109956], 131

Loretta [102127], 127, 131

Nora Francis [105240], 389, 424

Thomas C. [105241], 424

KILMARTIN

Catherine [106558], 431

John [106557], 392, 430

KING

Mary T. [106656], 312

Patrick [107191], 312

KINNANE

Charles [105224], 437

David [105221], 437

Francis [105225], 437

Frederick [105229], 438

George J. [105223], 437

Henry [105226], 437

John J. [105214], 394, 437

Mabel wife of George [105230], 437

Margaret A. [105222], 438

Mary E. [105228], 438

Michael [105218], 437

Michael J. [105220], 437

William [105227], 438

KIRKMAN

Joseph [103367], 268

Joseph [99089], 203, 267

Margaret M. [103368], 268

Thomas [99090], 267

Thomas H. [108117], 454

William H. [108116], 406, 454

William Henry [108119], 454

KNIGHT

Mary E. [97101], 71

KRESS

Julia [106211], 391

LACHAPELLE

Nancy [102164], 134

Roger N. [102162], 129, 134

Steven T. [102163], 134

LAHAIE

Amanda [109179], 461

LAHEY

Daniel [98991], 8

Joanna wife of Daniel [98992], 8

Mary [98990], 8

LAMOUREUX

Ralph George [110161], 402

LARDNER

John [110092], 318

William Joseph [110091], 318

LARKIN
Julia [105891], 199
LAROSA
Frank [96802], 297
LAROSE
Joseph B. [96801], 297
LAVACEK
Stanley William Jr.
[102977], 186, 264
LEARY
Abbey [108269], 335
Agnes G. [96718], 354
Annie [98975], 30
Annie C. 'Nans' [106620],
343
Annie E. [102483], 192
Arthur [96579], 47
Child [102479], 192
Cornelius [102476], 192
Daniel [98970], 30
Daniel [98984], 31
Dennis [106615], 324, 342,
393
Dennis [108275], 335
Edward F. [101998], 234
Ellen [107276], 204
Ellen [96604], 188
Ellen T. [106614], 344
Esther [102478], 192
Francis B. [96721], 354
Genevieve [102477], 192
Hannah [105151], 292, 294
Hannah J. [109671], 13, 39,
47
James [108271], 335
Jeremiah [105160], 294
Jeremiah [96715], 323, 336
Johanna [108112], 382, 406
John [101991], 233
John [102471], 192
John [102480], 192
John [108267], 335
John H. [98976], 30
John J. [101989], 162, 233
John T. [94408], 336, 353
Julia [102481], 192
Julia wife of John [102472],
192
Loretta M. [96717], 353
Margaret [102942], 317
Margaret [108122], 382
Margaret [95720], 323, 327
Margaret E. [96719], 354
Margaret Ellen [98974], 30
Margaret F. [106621], 343
Mary [102482], 192

Mary [106553], 430
Mary [108274], 335
Mary A. [98977], 30
Mary A. [98982], 30
Mary E. [106622], 343
Michael [102470], 149, 192
Michael [108270], 335
Michael [98969], 7, 30
Michael D. [106617], 342,
393
Michael Francis [102475],
192
Michael 'Micil' (Dana)
[108265], 323, 335
Patrick [108120], 375, 382
Patrick 'Patsy' [108268],
335
Peter [108276], 335
Stephen [108273], 335
Tady [108272], 335
Timothy [108261], 327
Walter C. [96720], 353
LEDUC
Mary [96803], 297
LEE
Jane [104594], 361
John Joseph [94676], 258
Mary Agnes [94675], 258
Mary E. [108118], 454
Mary E. [99091], 267
Michael T. [94674], 169,
258
LEFEBVRE
Marshall [100925], 213
Virginia P. 'Jennie'
[100924], 213
LEMMERMAN
Dorothy [100151], 290
LEWIS
Pauline [100628], 464
LOFTUS
Claire [109700], 372, 373
LOMAS
Mary Winifred [109945], 275
LOWNEY
Bridget [107019], 326
Ellen [107021], 326
Jeremiah [107015], 326
Jeremiah [96191], 109
Johanna [107023], 326
Julia [106608], 344
Margaret [107966], 88, 91,
330
Margaret 'Maggie' [108949],
90, 99, 109
Mary [107007], 325

Michael H. [107001], 325
William [107002], 323, 325
William [107020], 327
LUNDY
Agnes [97011], 235
LUTH
Anna [102551], 281
Christian Thorkid [102548],
281
Lawson Henry [102547],
229, 281
Lawson Jr. [102550], 281
LYNCH
Elizabeth [102427], 315
Ellen T. 'Nellie' [102435],
314, 321
Eugene P. [104793], 321
James W. [104792], 314,
321
Johanna wife of John
[102426], 314
John [102421], 300, 314
John [102425], 314
Julia [92609], 87
Katherine [110056], 357
Margaret [96663], 3, 15
Margaret J. [102429], 315
Mary [102434], 314
Mary A. [101621], 389, 425
Sarah [102428], 315
Thomas J. [103430], 425
LYNE
Christopher [105870], 336,
354
Mary [105875], 354
Patrick [105871], 354
LYONS
Ellen [101854], 244
Jeremiah [101849], 244
Jeremiah [101851], 165,
244
Mary [110098], 62
Mary wife of Jeremiah
[101850], 244
MADDEN
Alice V. [101008], 102, 121
Patrick [101011], 121
MAHER
Mary [106106], 117
MAHONEY
Cornelius [103916], 72
Jeremiah [103911], 72
John [103913], 72
Margaret wife of Jeremiah
[103912], 72
Mary A. [103914], 72

Mr. [105349], 432
Thomas [102513], 191
Timothy [103909], 32, 72
Timothy Jr. [103915], 72
MALONEY
James F. [102512], 191
Jeremiah [96281], 318, 322
John [96282], 322
Mary Gertude [105893], 322
MANETTA
Dorothy [107807], 76
Emilio [107804], 76
Lillian L. [107805], 76
Tomaso [107803], 49, 76
Vera [107806], 76
MANNION
Ellen wife of William
[102007], 234
William [102000], 234
William [102006], 234
MARCILLE
Cyril [105272], 426, 456
Francis M. [105274], 456
Joseph [105273], 456
Joseph Leopold [109885],
456
Paul [105275], 456
MARION
Mr. [108568], 132
MARTEL
Mary [102555], 287, 289
MATHER
Frank [105237], 389
Sadie E. [105236], 389
MATTHEWS
Catherine [101513], 197
MAXWELL
Lisa [98987], 30
MCALISTER
James [104156], 223
Mary Ann [104155], 156,
223
MCALLISTER
Anne wife of James
[104157], 223
Francis P. [104172], 157
Partick [104173], 157
MCBRIDE
Hellen T. 'Nellie' [101344],
46
MCCANN
Mary [97270], 106
MCCARDLE
Katherine [104174], 157
MCCARTHY
Abbie [106623], 343

Annie [107734], 68
Charles [105618], 381
Christopher [108260], 343
Elizabeth [108936], 84, 89,
96
Ellen [107264], 269
Eugene [107735], 68
Eugene F. [107732], 22, 68
Francis P. 'Frank' [107736],
68
Michael Edward [101338],
46
Owen [105619], 381
William Henry [107733], 68
MCCARTY
Barbara [105042], 376, 387
MCCLOSKEY
Cecelia [100931], 154, 214
Ceciley wife of John
[100938], 214
John [100939], 214
MCCUE
Catherine [107753], 3, 15
MCDERMOTT
Margaret [101605], 69
Mary [97691], 208
MCDONALD
John [106513], 364
John [106515], 364
Marion [106516], 364
Michael V. [106507], 340,
364
MCELROY
Sophia [110046], 252
MCFADDEN
Allen [103860], 126, 391,
429
Catherine [103869], 429
Charles [103861], 429
Charles [103866], 429
Elizabeth R. 'Lizzie'
[103865], 106, 126, 429,
456
John C. [103867], 429
Mary [103868], 429
MCGEE
Florence A. [109698], 361,
372
MCHUGH
Mary [99060], 147
MCKAY
Ann [101137], 241
MCKEAN
George V. [105050], 423
MCKENNEY
Mary [97169], 260

MCKEON
Mary [106289], 450
MCLINDEN
Alexander [103940], 227
Hugh [103937], 227
James [103939], 227
John [103936], 160, 227
Mary [103938], 227
MCMAHON
James [92694], 168, 252
James S. [109586], 252
Thomas [109585], 252
William [110043], 252
MCMANUS
Ann [99087], 152, 203
Anne [108909], 141, 177
Margaret [99097], 203
MCMULLEN
Catherine [101145], 241
Child [101146], 242
Child [101147], 242
Concord wife of George
[101149], 242
Eleanor M. 'Lena' [101150],
242
George Grover [101148],
242
Grace [101140], 241
Samuel [101141], 241
Sydney 'Sinney' [101138],
241
William [101139], 241
William [101144], 241
William Young [101135],
163, 241
MCNAMARA
Ellen [102695], 17, 58
Ellen wife of James
[102699], 58
James [102698], 58
MCNEIL
Anne [104612], 168
MCTAGUE
Peter [101600], 25
Peter A. [101599], 25
MELVILLE
Margaret [103963], 455
MERRILL
Charlotte Snow [104999],
260
Jarvis [97168], 260
John H. [97154], 176, 260
MILES
Edward [98740], 310
MOFFITT
George [101510], 197

Volume V Name Index

Nelson T. [101512], 197

MOONEY

Bridget wife of Michael [103762], 215

Delia Bridget [103759], 154, 215

Michael [103761], 215

MORAN

Johanna wife of William [103184], 248

Placid E. [103182], 248

William [103183], 248

MORIARTY

Edward [103877], 430, 456

John [103878], 457

MORRIS

George E. [102430], 315

Patrick [102431], 315

MORRISSEY

Ann wife of Thomas [104192], 146

Jennie E. [104190], 146

Thomas [104191], 146

MOSHER

Edna Allen [105516], 74

Harold Cook [105515], 74

Linden P. [105512], 41, 74

Sherman [105513], 74

MURPHY

Anne [103864], 377, 391

Bartholomew [106814], 221

Bartholomew [107697], 169

Bridget [101038], 299, 311

Cornelius [110110], 62

Cornelius [85073], 86

Cornelius J. [103840], 62

Daniel (Maheesh) [110058], 337

Daniel F. [108871], 230

Dennis [101039], 311

Edward [99915], 113

Elizabeth M. [103826], 62

Ellen [110125], 62

Ellen F. [106806], 155, 221

Etta F. [110124], 62

Frank J. [92657], 93

Hannay [92239], 239, 240

Hanora [104111], 376, 384

Hanora [107696], 139, 169

Jeremiah [110123], 62

Jeremiah [94127], 156

Joanna [98596], 304

John [103806], 148

John C. [103824], 18, 62

John W. [110126], 62

Josephine [110120], 62

Julia [104610], 139, 167

Julia [104901], 12

Margaret [103839], 62

Margaret [104154], 138, 156

Margaret [105886], 136, 151

Margaret [85072], 86

Margaret [96276], 304, 317

Margaret M. [103805], 148

Margaret wife of Dennis [101040], 311

Margaret wife of John [103807], 148

Margaret wife of John [85074], 86

Mary [110079], 356

Mary [94128], 156

Mary A. [107004], 326

Mary E. [106280], 264

Nell [107983], 98

Patrick [103234], 230

Patrick C. [105878], 337

Thomas [92658], 93

Timothy [105279], 426

Timothy [107005], 326

Timothy [99889], 113

Timothy E. Jr. [99911], 93, 113

William H. [105286], 426

MYERS

Henry T. [106210], 391

Sarah [100643], 453

Theo [105474], 391

MYLES

Margaret 'Maggie' [98739], 298, 310

NAYLOR

Bridget [97617], 81

NEESON

James [104995], 367

NORBOY

Mary wife of Thomas [103948], 404

NORBURY

Elizabeth [103949], 404

John J. [103944], 380, 404

John R. [103950], 404

Thomas [103947], 404

NORTON

James [104638], 417

Mary J. [104635], 386, 417

Michael [105761], 161

Thomas A. [105760], 161

Winefred wife of Michael [105762], 161

OBRIEN

Alice C. [95497], 195

Catherine [101671], 164, 243

Ellen [105990], 445

James C. [94666], 257

Mary Ann [103792], 272

Michael [94665], 169, 256

Patrick [101518], 196

Patrick [95496], 150, 195

Thomas [95501], 196

OCARROLL

Kathleen Theresa [109191], 378, 399

OCONNELL

Catherine 'Kate' [103046], 219

John [103040], 155, 219

John Thomas [103047], 219

Julia [103049], 219

Julia wife of Thomas [103042], 219

Margaret [103048], 219

Mary [99890], 113

Thomas [103041], 219

ODONNELL

Margaret M. [99084], 178

Mary wife of Patrick [99066], 178

Patrick [99065], 178

William J. [99064], 141, 178

William J. [99085], 178

OLEARY

Catherine A. [101995], 235

Ellen wife of John [101992], 233

Emma F. [101997], 233

John J. [101996], 233

M. L. [101999], 234

Mary Margaret [104994], 323, 330

Timothy [108851], 330

O'LEARY

Bridget [102453], 348

ONEAL

Joanna wife of William [98900], 253

John J. [98940], 253

Mary [102574], 189

Mary [98944], 253

William [98898], 168, 253

William [98899], 253

William [98945], 253

ONEIL

Catherine 'Katie' [105752], 379, 401

Volume V Name Index

Catherine [104639], 417
James [106105], 117
Mary J. [106104], 97, 117
RUSSEL
Elizabeth [102541], 278
RUSSELL
Catherine [103926], 159, 226
Catherine A. [94116], 381, 405
David [103927], 226
Ellen [96808], 308
James [109373], 405
Mary wife of David [103928], 226
RYAN
Abbie [104341], 411
Annie [104339], 410
Benjamin F. [104340], 410
Beverly Ann [106139], 460
Catherine 'Katie' [104336], 410
Charles F. [104344], 411
Donald [106136], 446, 460
Dorothy wife of Donald [106138], 446, 460
Henry [104345], 411
Irene [106137], 446
James E. [104343], 411
Jeremiah D. [104337], 410
Mabel [104342], 411
Martin [104675], 396, 446
Martin A. [106140], 446
Mary [104338], 410
Mary L. [106135], 446
Michael E. [102723], 385, 410
Patrick [102725], 410
Patrick [104676], 446
RYDER
Frank T. [104704], 418
Hannah H. [104705], 418
James Edward [104707], 418
John [103109], 217
John William [104709], 418
Margaret [104706], 418
Margaret [104708], 418
Mary C. [104710], 418
Michael [104702], 418
Thomas [104701], 387, 418
Thomas J. [103108], 217
SALINSKY
Evelyn T. [106297], 451
Mary wife of William [110192], 451

William [110191], 451
SANTOS
John [100089], 209
SAUNDERS
Anna W. [102549], 281
James [108942], 110
John [106111], 110
Mary A. [106110], 111
Michael [106112], 110, 338
Stephen [106109], 90, 110, 338
SCHOFIELD
Margaret [100602], 463
SELLECK
Mary A. [96602], 144, 188
William [96603], 188
SEMPLE
Ellen Mae [109587], 252
SEXTON
Mary [107085], 359
SHANAHAN
Bridget [100591], 55
SHAW
Hannah [97482], 120
SHEA
Anna L. [100983], 245
Catherine 'Cait' [108296], 326
Cornelius [100979], 245
Cornelius [94787], 40
Cornelius [97426], 103
Daniel [100977], 165, 245
Daniel [100988], 245
Daniel [103105], 216
Daniel [97425], 88, 103
Dennis [106551], 392, 430
Dennis [96014], 302
Elizabeth A. [101566], 26
Ellen wife of Timothy [101562], 26
Frank William [105616], 116
Hannah wife of Cornelius [100980], 245
Hanora [103660], 218
Helen C. [101569], 26
James [106552], 430
Jeremiah [92546], 166, 249
Johanna [92593], 249
Johanna wife of Patrick [92589], 249
John F. [101564], 26
John H. [100985], 245
John M. [100351], 41
Julia [101010], 84, 87
Julia [98738], 292, 297
Julia [98766], 15, 52

Julia M. [106775], 275
Julia W. [101565], 26
Lillian A. [101568], 26
Louise [100350], 41
Margaret [100349], 41
Margaret [103072], 292, 302
Margaret [106556], 377, 392
Margaret [107767], 2, 13
Margaret [95198], 1, 7
Mary [100742], 138, 162
Mary [100986], 245
Mary [104188], 136, 145
Mary [107989], 99
Mary E. [101567], 26
Mary S. [103102], 154, 216
Mary wife of Daniel [103106], 216
Michael [92594], 250
Michael [94790], 11, 40
Michael [97592], 64
Michael P. [106205], 382
Patrick [92588], 249
Patrick [92608], 87
Patrick E. [100987], 245
Ruth M. [101563], 26
Theresa [100348], 41
Thomas [97588], 64
Timothy [101558], 6, 26
Timothy [101561], 26
Timothy [106201], 382
Timothy [98769], 52
Timothy A. [92597], 249
SHEEHAN
Annie F. [103640], 454
Catherine [98772], 52, 76
Daniel [98773], 76
Delia [101536], 237
Johanna [93158], 293, 304
John [101537], 237
Josephine T. 'Josie' [96609], 144, 185
Mary [101614], 137, 153
Mary [96805], 297
Matthew [100228], 185
Michael [107981], 98
Michael [98595], 304
Norah [104957], 377, 397, 441
Patrick [107982], 98
SHIELDS
Alice [109389], 206
Ann [109390], 206
Hannah [109384], 206
James [100488], 205

Bridget wife of John [104012], 376, 384
Carol [109707], 372
Catherine (Cromhane) [96716], 323, 336
Catherine [100399], 47
Catherine [100585], 16, 54
Catherine [101014], 122
Catherine [101827], 163, 242
Catherine [101911], 17, 59
Catherine [102654], 381
Catherine [103245], 375, 379
Catherine [103933], 160, 227
Catherine [104640], 418
Catherine [105055], 388
Catherine [105269], 426, 456
Catherine [105877], 337
Catherine [106554], 392, 430
Catherine [106616], 324, 340, 393
Catherine [107571], 377, 395
Catherine [107738], 22
Catherine [108940], 90
Catherine [108953], 111, 129
Catherine [110062], 357
Catherine [92592], 139, 166
Catherine [95384], 15, 50
Catherine [95757], 439
Catherine [95944], 168, 252
Catherine [96710], 175
Catherine [96796], 297, 308
Catherine [97478], 88, 100
Catherine [97634], 19
Catherine [98085], 340, 365
Catherine [99004], 32
Catherine A. [104763], 420
Catherine A. [105204], 448
Catherine A. [108345], 383
Catherine Agnes [101346], 46
Catherine C. V. [92888], 37
Catherine E. [107751], 15, 52
Catherine F. [107801], 49, 75
Catherine F. [99960], 58, 79
Catherine G. [106103], 97
Catherine Grace [102238], 256

Catherine J. [102457], 350
Catherine 'Kate' [100429], 44
Catherine 'Kate' [102934], 303, 315
Catherine 'Kate' [92603], 84, 91
Catherine 'Kate' [92606], 92
Catherine 'Katie' [104955], 395, 397, 441, 446
Catherine 'Katie' [107980], 98
Catherine 'Kit' [106115], 111, 323, 337
Catherine M. [106281], 184, 263
Catherine M. [97260], 281
Catherine R. [107977], 118
Catherine T. [100631], 399, 452
Catherine T. [107265], 270
Catherine Theresa [103664], 218
Catherine V. [92884], 36
Catherine wife of Daniel [100982], 138, 165
Catherine wife of Dennis [99724], 1, 6
Catherine wife of Eugene [98994], 7, 32
Catherine wife of John [107491], 84, 86
Catherine wife of Michael [107810], 3, 14
Catherine wife of Patrick [98105], 3, 14
Catherine wife of Timothy [100584], 3, 16
Cecilia [100940], 214
Charles [97251], 280
Charles J. [106272], 173
Charles Norman [103961], 455, 466
Charles R. [102465], 351
Child [100227], 188
Child [101041], 311
Child [101399], 29
Child [102183], 104
Child [105544], 436
Child [95156], 35
Child [97253], 279
Child [97601], 63
Child [98742], 310
Child [98744], 310
Child [99737], 70
Christopher [100748], 240

Claire [109704], 374
Clara [100428], 44
Clarence [100431], 45
Cornelius [101276], 292, 298
Cornelius [101298], 311
Cornelius [103863], 377, 391
Cornelius [104110], 376, 384
Cornelius [104273], 1, 5
Cornelius [105216], 377, 394
Cornelius [105538], 377, 394
Cornelius [95195], 8, 32
Cornelius [96601], 144
Cornelius A. [98952], 168, 254
Cornelius F. [96644], 54
Cornelius George [102556], 287, 291
Cornelius J. [102022], 39, 47
Cornelius J. [103665], 218
Cornelius J. [103671], 274
Cornelius J. [105233], 388
Cornelius John [100149], 290
Cornelius John [97255], 279, 287
Corrine [102562], 288
Dale Anne [102134], 132, 135
Dan [107967], 98
Daniel (Rua) [108951], 90
Daniel (Seer) [103098], 324, 338
Daniel [100981], 138, 165
Daniel [101078], 139, 167
Daniel [101528], 154, 214
Daniel [101560], 1, 5
Daniel [101591], 1, 5
Daniel [102516], 136, 147
Daniel [102704], 57
Daniel [103044], 137, 155
Daniel [103847], 375, 380
Daniel [104334], 376, 385
Daniel [104958], 442
Daniel [104965], 395
Daniel [104986], 330, 345
Daniel [105199], 377, 397
Daniel [105205], 448
Daniel [105207], 448
Daniel [106295], 450
Daniel [106555], 377, 392

Volume V Name Index

Daniel [106812], 138, 155
Daniel [107354], 13
Daniel [107743], 21
Daniel [107955], 88
Daniel [108855], 148
Daniel [110047], 139, 168
Daniel [92671], 113
Daniel [93922], 286
Daniel [96639], 329
Daniel [96788], 292, 296
Daniel A. [99722], 6, 26
Daniel B. [99961], 17, 58
Daniel D. [103244], 375, 379
Daniel E. [102653], 381, 404
Daniel E. [106807], 221
Daniel E. [92602], 91
Daniel F. [101532], 162, 235
Daniel F. [103101], 154, 216
Daniel F. [106296], 398
Daniel F. [106986], 434, 458
Daniel F. [93500], 9, 34
Daniel F. [99054], 142, 178
Daniel F. Jr. [106993], 458
Daniel H. [100213], 184
Daniel J. [102461], 351, 368
Daniel J. [102569], 147, 189
Daniel J. [104587], 180
Daniel J. [107267], 270, 286
Daniel J. [96672], 54
Daniel Michael [103765], 215, 272
Daniel P. [102637], 152, 204
Daughter [105506], 361
David [103957], 455
David [104004], 376, 384
David D. [103775], 414, 454
David Daniel [103769], 385, 411
David Russell [103929], 226, 277
Dennis [100739], 163, 238
Dennis [101292], 299
Dennis [101397], 1, 6
Dennis [101877], 1, 6
Dennis [102473], 136, 148
Dennis [103192], 257
Dennis [103803], 136, 148
Dennis [104187], 136, 145
Dennis [107490], 331
Dennis [108342], 375, 383

Dennis [108857], 161, 229
Dennis [108944], 84, 86, 111
Dennis [108945], 97
Dennis [109305], 153
Dennis [79105], 86
Dennis [94466], 292, 300
Dennis [95759], 440
Dennis [99723], 1, 6
Dennis [99913], 84, 93
Dennis D. [104649], 377, 395
Dennis E. [101393], 7, 27
Dennis Edward [101392], 29
Dennis J. [102139], 127
Dennis J. [102158], 109, 129
Dennis J. [103871], 106, 123, 429, 456
Dennis J. [104654], 443
Dennis J. [109670], 13, 39, 46
Dennis J. Jr. [109733], 129
Dennis Jeremiah [97261], 89, 105, 456
Dennis Patrick [101543], 237
Dolores [95504], 267
Donald [102560], 288
Doris [100146], 289
Doris [97623], 82
Doris wife of Richard [102567], 288
Dorothy G. [102459], 351
Earnest J. [106294], 450
Edmund [103786], 376, 385
Edmund C. [102245], 285
Edna Francis [103797], 273
Edward [103036], 406
Edward [103782], 414
Edward [104963], 442
Edward [107870], 444
Edward [96032], 145
Edward A. [105503], 361, 372
Edward 'Eddie' [94654], 257
Edward F. [100244], 185
Edward F. [106991], 458
Edward F. [95927], 144, 186
Edward J. [106976], 435
Edward J. [106982], 434
Edward J. [98777], 77
Eileen [100150], 290
Eilene [97622], 81, 83

Elaine [93921], 286
Eleanor [103799], 273
Eliza C. [100422], 12, 44
Elizabeth [103666], 218
Elizabeth [104632], 417
Elizabeth [104641], 386, 416
Elizabeth [94661], 258
Elizabeth A. [103781], 414
Elizabeth A. 'Eliza and Lizzie" [93501], 9, 34
Elizabeth Ann [102568], 291
Elizabeth C. [109534], 277
Elizabeth G. 'Lizzie' [92889], 37
Elizabeth H. [105321], 431
Elizabeth J. [105159], 294
Elizabeth 'Lizzie' [100918], 213
Elizabeth 'Lizzie' [108957], 112
Elizabeth M. [104160], 224
Elizabeth M. [95755], 439
Elizabeth S. [102168], 132
Ellen [101559], 5, 25
Ellen [101833], 164
Ellen [102422], 300, 314
Ellen [102439], 333
Ellen [102764], 153
Ellen [103043], 155, 219
Ellen [103155], 249
Ellen [103214], 149, 194
Ellen [104272], 5
Ellen [104274], 1, 5
Ellen [104748], 161
Ellen [105217], 377, 394
Ellen [105467], 390
Ellen [106204], 375, 382
Ellen [106625], 343, 377, 392
Ellen [107003], 323, 325
Ellen [107698], 169
Ellen [107814], 171
Ellen [107968], 98
Ellen [108950], 90
Ellen [110067], 358
Ellen [95196], 8, 32
Ellen [97614], 44
Ellen [98995], 32
Ellen McCarthy [107731], 22, 68
Ellen 'Nell' (Seer) [108266], 323, 335
Ellen 'Nellie' [100430], 45
Ellen 'Nellie' [103844], 380, 403

Volume V Name Index

Ida Bernard [102702], 57, 79

Inez [105889], 200

Irene [98743], 310

Irene F. [105604], 116

Irene R. [104161], 224, 275

Isabelle 'Belle' [97151], 176, 261

Jackie [110121], 130

James [100400], 47

James [100425], 44

James [101293], 299

James [101613], 137, 153

James [102254], 9

James [102256], 1, 9

James [102564], 288

James [103243], 379, 402

James [103365], 203

James [104162], 223

James [105158], 294

James [105622], 375, 381

James [106203], 375, 381

James [106977], 434

James [107098], 250, 283

James [109660], 136, 151

James [83666], 137, 152

James [92881], 2, 10

James [95382], 50

James [95385], 50

James [96838], 93, 114

James [96846], 114

James [97621], 82

James C. [92891], 37

James E. [97595], 64

James Eugene [96594], 136, 142

James F. [103774], 413

James Francis [102235], 255

James H. [102125], 127, 131

James H. [105156], 307

James H. [97265], 106, 126

James J. [101542], 237

James Jr. [107102], 284

James Jr. [96597], 143

James M. [100309], 348

James P. [103246], 402

James P. [105206], 448

James P. [93924], 12, 43

James T. [105962], 266

James Vernon [103959], 455

Jane 'Jennie' [102074], 426

Jane M. 'Jennie' [99076], 180

Jane Marie [109187], 399

Jean [107997], 119

Jean Ann [96699], 77

Jennie [102484], 149, 192

Jennie E. [104661], 444

Jeremiah   H. [105320], 431

Jeremiah (Brohill) [101009], 84, 87

Jeremiah [100121], 139, 167

Jeremiah [100161], 2, 10, 45

Jeremiah [100490], 137, 152

Jeremiah [100746], 240

Jeremiah [101853], 138, 164

Jeremiah [102017], 2, 10, 50

Jeremiah [102644], 205

Jeremiah [102652], 381

Jeremiah [103945], 375, 380

Jeremiah [104153], 138, 156

Jeremiah [104166], 223

Jeremiah [104607], 167

Jeremiah [104609], 139, 167

Jeremiah [107816], 171

Jeremiah [107952], 102

Jeremiah [107984], 98

Jeremiah [107988], 99

Jeremiah [94470], 145

Jeremiah [94792], 2, 11

Jeremiah [95760], 440

Jeremiah [96661], 15, 53

Jeremiah [98599], 293, 304

Jeremiah [99095], 203

Jeremiah [99295], 2, 11

Jeremiah D. [104647], 396, 442

Jeremiah D. [83631], 376, 387

Jeremiah E. [107871], 158

Jeremiah F. [104634], 386, 416

Jeremiah F. [104636], 376, 385

Jeremiah Francis [104762], 420

Jeremiah Gerald [107660], 436

Jeremiah J. [104663], 444

Jeremiah J. [104672], 445

Jeremiah J. [105989], 445

Jeremiah J. [83633], 387, 419

Jeremiah 'Jer' [107954], 88, 98, 109

Jeremiah P. [106774], 275

Jeremiah S. [106799], 221, 274

Joan Grace [109734], 129

Joanna (Rochtirre) [107962], 84, 88

Joanna [100306], 323, 333

Joanna [103930], 226

Joanna [95494], 150, 195

Joanna [97626], 19, 64

Joanna [98968], 7, 29

Joanna [99294], 41, 102

Joanna M. [104333], 385, 410

Joanna wife of Daniel [103848], 375, 380

Joanna wife of James [109661], 137, 152

Joanna wife of Michael [103658], 137, 154

Joanna wife of Patrick [103031], 375, 383

Johanna [101007], 102

Johanna [103879], 392

Johanna [105200], 377, 397

Johanna [105539], 377, 394

Johanna [107456], 139, 165

Johanna [108853], 148

Johanna [96015], 302

Johanna Josephine [92693], 168, 251

Johannah [102450], 334, 348

Johannah [99092], 203, 268

Johannah wife of Patrick [102020], 3, 14, 39

John (Dorohy) 'Jack' [108960], 130

John (Rocktirre) [107965], 88, 91, 330

John [100164], 2, 12, 40

John [100393], 14, 47

John [100443], 2, 11

John [100615], 378, 398

John [100749], 240

John [100921], 137, 154

John [101142], 138, 163

John [101245], 2, 11

John [101332], 2, 12

John [101533], 138, 162

John [102423], 292, 300

John [102440], 335, 352

John [102639], 137, 152
John [103103], 137, 154
John [104011], 376, 384
John [104189], 146
John [104698], 376, 386
John [104830], 352, 376, 387
John [104924], 2, 12
John [104959], 442
John [105150], 292, 294
John [105155], 307
John [105535], 386
John [105885], 136, 151
John [107288], 377, 394
John [107766], 2, 13
John [107797], 14, 48
John [107942], 269
John [107990], 99, 109
John [108866], 230
John [108879], 162
John [109192], 378, 399
John [109672], 2, 13
John [92133], 136, 147
John [92205], 84, 86
John [92517], 440
John [92880], 10, 35
John [93504], 9
John [93507], 9
John [93965], 339
John [94468], 301
John [94496], 292
John [95258], 112
John [96275], 304, 317
John [96440], 94
John [96662], 3, 15
John [96794], 298
John [96843], 84, 93
John [97624], 19
John [97633], 19
John [99062], 136, 146
John [99293], 41, 102
John Arthur [103766], 215
John B. [101319], 15, 52, 74
John B. [101331], 74
John B. [105198], 397, 447
John C. [105536], 394, 435
John C. [106263], 140, 172
John C. [106273], 173
John C. [95766], 454
John C. III. [103650], 454
John C. Jr. [103644], 408, 454
John Charles [92445], 439, 459
John D. [100805], 59
John D. [104659], 396, 444

John D. [96012], 279
John D. [99965], 3, 16
John E. [100426], 44
John E. [100913], 154, 210
John E. [100923], 213
John E. [103206], 113
John E. [104176], 223
John E. [105756], 402
John E. [107974], 118
John E. [109674], 14
John E. [92654], 91, 112
John E. [97102], 71
John E. [97235], 228, 277
John E. Jr. [97238], 278
John Edward [104779], 420
John F. [101296], 300
John F. [103073], 292, 302
John F. [104662], 444
John F. [105494], 340, 359
John F. [105602], 96, 115
John F. [106108], 97
John F. [95483], 198, 266
John F. [96697], 77
John F. [99093], 203
John F. Jr. [95506], 267
John Francis [101535], 237
John Francis [103662], 218, 273
John Francis [96669], 54, 77
John Francis Jr. [103670], 274
John H. [102150], 89, 106
John H. [102464], 351
John H. [107355], 13
John H. [107701], 169
John H. [98775], 77
John Henry [102231], 255
John Henry [96608], 144, 184
John J. [100059], 20
John J. [101347], 46
John J. [101590], 5, 23
John J. [102015], 10, 14, 38, 47, 50
John J. [102145], 128, 132
John J. [103366], 203
John J. [104152], 156, 222
John J. [104966], 397
John J. [105504], 361
John J. [107277], 434, 457
John J. [107802], 49
John J. [109175], 461
John J. [109180], 448, 460
John J. [109930], 459
John J. [99086], 152, 201

John Joseph [107281], 458
John L. [102442], 334, 349
John L. [103925], 159, 225
John L. [105543], 436
John L. [97098], 29, 70
John Lawrence Jr. [102458], 350
John M. [104956], 377, 396, 441
John M. [95721], 329
John Michael [107260], 204, 268
John P. [102563], 288
John P. [109699], 372, 373
John P. [97600], 63, 80
John P. Jr. [97618], 82
John Peter [110068], 358
John R. [102694], 17, 56
John R. [108896], 141, 177
John R. [92887], 38
John R. [99050], 136, 141
John Richard [103177], 248
John Russell C. [100937], 214
John S. [95750], 394, 438
John T. [109951], 284
John V. [104673], 445
John W. [97159], 175
John X. [92208], 353
Joseph [102237], 256
Joseph [103780], 414
Joseph [106275], 174
Joseph [107485], 323, 330
Joseph [97242], 279
Joseph A. [106801], 275
Joseph A. [96599], 144, 187
Joseph F. [106292], 450
Joseph H. [92886], 37
Joseph H. [99736], 70
Joseph L. [104158], 223
Joseph P. [104964], 442
Joseph R. [106985], 435
Josephine Johanna [103661], 218, 273
Josephine L. [97589], 64
Joyce [102129], 131
Juila [96640], 329
Julia [102209], 16
Julia [103237], 230
Julia [105811], 33, 72
Julia [107979], 98
Julia [107994], 99
Julia [108114], 406
Julia [109201], 27
Julia [97625], 19, 65
Julia [99005], 32

Julia [99055], 141, 177
Julia A. [100138], 9
Julia A. [102443], 334
Julia A. [93505], 9, 35
Julia E. [98262], 307
Julia E. [99061], 147
Julia L. [100210], 143, 182
Julia M. [104747], 162, 232
Julia Monica [106784], 221, 275
Julia W. [99070], 180
Julia wife of Dennis [94467], 292, 301
Julia wife of Jeremiah [103946], 375, 380
Julia wife of John [100165], 2, 12, 40
Kate [96284], 318
Katherine [103931], 226
Katherine [105048], 423
Kenneth J. [109701], 373
Kenneth J. [95505], 267
Lauretta [92672], 113
Lauretta C. [100934], 214, 271
Lawrence Daniel [99083], 182
Lena [104592], 340, 361
Lena H. [101602], 24
Leo D. [102156], 108
Leo F. [100932], 214
Leonard [101300], 300
Leonora [104760], 421
Leonora [104788], 314, 321
Leroy Daniel [100245], 185
Leslie B. [109620], 189
Lillian [102441], 352
Lillian C. [105607], 115
Lillian H. [102544], 229, 281
Lillian M. [102463], 351
Lillian Mae [100603], 452
Lizzie M. [102701], 57
Louis E. [102240], 256
Louis J. [99075], 180
Louisa [101540], 237
Madeline [95806], 405
Madeline wife of Charles [103964], 455, 466
Mairead 'Margaret' [107959], 98
Margaret (Ukirre) [96840], 114
Margaret [100050], 19, 66
Margaret [101320], 74
Margaret [101539], 237

Margaret [103097], 339, 358
Margaret [103156], 248, 282
Margaret [103941], 159
Margaret [104307], 390, 427
Margaret [104758], 420
Margaret [104987], 330, 345
Margaret [105093], 292, 302
Margaret [105098], 302
Margaret [107010], 325
Margaret [107353], 13
Margaret [107815], 170
Margaret [107872], 157
Margaret [108952], 90
Margaret [110061], 356
Margaret [83632], 376, 387
Margaret [94791], 11, 40
Margaret [95502], 151
Margaret [96671], 54
Margaret [97183], 112
Margaret [98747], 310
Margaret [99003], 32
Margaret [99094], 203
Margaret [99292], 11, 41
Margaret [99602], 385, 414
Margaret A. [101612], 153, 208
Margaret A. [95220], 97, 117
Margaret A. [99072], 181
Margaret A. [99731], 27
Margaret C. [105270], 426
Margaret E. [99912], 93, 113
Margaret F. [105157], 295
Margaret I. [102460], 350
Margaret J. [101294], 300
Margaret J. [104670], 396, 445
Margaret J. [105606], 115
Margaret J. [96013], 279
Margaret L. [106803], 275
Margaret L. [106811], 222
Margaret M. [102130], 128
Margaret M. [102157], 109
Margaret M. [102230], 256
Margaret M. [104671], 445
Margaret M. [109735], 129
Margaret M. [97266], 106
Margaret 'Maggie' [96792], 298
Margaret T. [102147], 129

Margaret T. [96278], 318, 321
Margaret V. [101596], 24, 69
Margaret wife of Daniel [101592], 1, 5
Margaret wife of Daniel [103045], 137, 155
Margaret wife of Daniel [106813], 138, 155
Margaret wife of Florence [98973], 1, 7
Margaret wife of Jeremiah [100491], 137, 152
Margaret wife of Jeremiah [94793], 2, 11
Margaret wife of John [101246], 2, 11
Margaret wife of John [99063], 136, 147
Margaret wife of Patrick [101994], 138, 162
Margaret wife of Patrick [98768], 3, 15
Margaret wife of Timothy [106277], 172
Margaret wife of Timothy [95596], 115
Margaret wife of William [100080], 137, 153
Marguerite [103768], 413
Marie wife of Francois [100131], 1, 9
Marion A. [95440], 190
Marion E. [103668], 274
Mark [104923], 12
Mark [105271], 426
Mark A. Jr. [100147], 289
Mark Anthony [97254], 280, 289
Mark E. [101327], 46, 74
Mark E. [109703], 373
Martin Carlton [105243], 424
Martin F. [105234], 389, 423
Mary (Ukirre) [108262], 327
Mary (Ukirre) [108852], 330
Mary [100123], 167, 251
Mary [100745], 239
Mary [101623], 426
Mary [101852], 165, 244
Mary [101874], 6
Mary [102180], 104
Mary [102436], 333
Mary [102469], 149, 191
Mary [103742], 220

Mary [103743], 155, 219
Mary [103773], 413
Mary [103859], 126, 391, 428
Mary [103882], 392
Mary [103934], 160
Mary [104167], 156
Mary [104832], 336, 352, 387, 421
Mary [104835], 323, 336, 422
Mary [105054], 388
Mary [105244], 424
Mary [105339], 393, 431
Mary [105869], 336, 354
Mary [107082], 339, 359
Mary [107487], 331
Mary [107668], 436
Mary [107961], 88
Mary [107964], 89
Mary [107970], 98, 118
Mary [108864], 230
Mary [108943], 110
Mary [79131], 384, 407
Mary [92653], 91, 112
Mary [92677], 147, 190
Mary [95383], 50
Mary [95484], 198
Mary [96607], 187
Mary [96790], 298
Mary [97599], 4, 19
Mary [98080], 365
Mary [98745], 310
Mary [98996], 8, 33
Mary [99057], 177
Mary A. [101136], 163, 240
Mary A. [101273], 299, 312
Mary A. [101541], 237
Mary A. [101990], 162, 233
Mary A. [102246], 255
Mary A. [102667], 305, 318
Mary A. [103825], 18, 61
Mary A. [104742], 161, 230
Mary A. [105235], 389
Mary A. [106100], 86, 90, 96, 109, 338
Mary A. [106264], 140, 172
Mary A. [107737], 22
Mary A. [107800], 49
Mary A. [107976], 118
Mary A. [94407], 336, 353
Mary A. [94659], 257
Mary A. [95126], 190
Mary A. [95930], 186
Mary A. [96646], 15, 54
Mary A. [97248], 229, 279

Mary A. [97602], 64
Mary A. [99073], 181, 263
Mary Agnes [102148], 129, 134
Mary Ann [92590], 166, 249
Mary Ann [96438], 94
Mary Anne [103876], 430, 456
Mary B. [103178], 247
Mary C. [102021], 39
Mary C. [105215], 394, 437
Mary C. [106978], 434
Mary C. [107758], 53
Mary D. [104764], 420
Mary E. [100308], 348
Mary E. [100917], 212
Mary E. [101597], 24
Mary E. [104633], 417
Mary E. [105047], 423
Mary E. [105059], 340, 362
Mary E. [106202], 382
Mary E. [106809], 222
Mary E. [107204], 278, 287
Mary E. [109370], 405
Mary E. [96596], 145
Mary E. [96845], 114
Mary E. [97152], 176, 260
Mary E. [99071], 180
Mary E. 'Mae' [97104], 29
Mary Elizabeth [105884], 201
Mary Elizabeth [96698], 77
Mary Ellen [102711], 57
Mary Ellen [103663], 218
Mary Ellen [95752], 439
Mary F. [103035], 406
Mary F. [105511], 41, 73
Mary F. [106262], 173, 259
Mary Gertrude [105542], 436
Mary H. wife of Thomas [107996], 99, 119
Mary J. [101244], 11, 42
Mary J. [103943], 380, 404
Mary J. [104653], 444
Mary J. [106816], 117
Mary J. [110059], 356
Mary J. [95155], 35
Mary J. wife of John F. [109708], 340, 361
Mary L [109676], 47
Mary L. [104746], 231
Mary Louise [103795], 272
Mary Louise [96277], 318
Mary M. [97252], 279

Mary Margaret [106800], 275
Mary O. [102643], 204
Mary P. [102466], 351
Mary R. [104666], 444
Mary R. [109533], 277
Mary Rose [105152], 308
Mary S. [105473], 391
Mary Sandra [102128], 131
Mary V. [105500], 361
Mary wife of Alexander [103924], 138, 159
Mary wife of Daniel [101079], 139, 167
Mary wife of Daniel [104335], 376, 385
Mary wife of Dennis [103804], 136, 148
Mary wife of Edmund [103787], 376, 385
Mary wife of Jeremiah [100162], 2, 10, 45
Mary wife of Jeremiah [101855], 138, 164
Mary wife of Jeremiah [99296], 2, 11
Mary wife of John [100444], 2, 11
Mary wife of John [101143], 138, 163
Mary wife of John [107289], 377, 394
Mary wife of John [93508], 9
Mary wife of John [94497], 293
Mary wife of John [95124], 136, 147
Mary wife of Michael [103763], 137, 154
Mary wife of Michael [110127], 4, 18
Mary wife of Michael [98951], 139, 168
Mary wife of Patrick [100398], 3, 14
Mary wife of Patrick [101830], 138, 163
Mary Wife Of Patrick [83658], 375, 383
Matilda A. 'Mattie' [92605], 93
Maud or Mary wife of James [92885], 2, 10
Maureen [104658], 460
Maureen [109706], 372

Sarah 'Sadie' [102703], 57
Shirley A. [103960], 455
Stephen [104165], 224
Stephen Francis [105097], 302
Steven [94658], 257
Sylvester [101624], 376, 388
Sylvester L. [101620], 389, 425
Teresa [105502], 361
Teresa [97237], 278
Teresa Elizabeth [105755], 401
Thomas [102075], 426
Thomas [103767], 216
Thomas [103777], 414
Thomas [95490], 136, 149
Thomas [95495], 150
Thomas A. [107975], 118
Thomas E. [104664], 444
Thomas H. [97594], 64
Thomas Kiley [105250], 424
Thomas N. [95468], 198, 264
Thomas Patrick [107995], 99, 118
Timothy (Shearhig) [110054], 356
Timothy [100051], 4, 19
Timothy [100326], 16, 55
Timothy [100330], 3, 16
Timothy [100583], 3, 16
Timothy [100741], 138, 162
Timothy [100743], 239
Timothy [101321], 52
Timothy [102208], 3, 15
Timothy [102545], 138, 160
Timothy [102651], 375, 380
Timothy [103870], 392, 429
Timothy [104743], 138, 160
Timothy [105092], 292, 301
Timothy [105860], 93
Timothy [106276], 172
Timothy [107080], 339
Timothy [107608], 91
Timothy [107742], 20
Timothy [107971], 98, 118
Timothy [92591], 139, 166
Timothy [92604], 84, 91
Timothy [94125], 157
Timothy [94552], 34
Timothy [94651], 169, 257
Timothy [94655], 257
Timothy [95386], 50
Timothy [95723], 189

Timothy [98765], 15, 51
Timothy A. [105881], 151, 198
Timothy Christopher [110055], 357
Timothy D. [108863], 230
Timothy E. [104164], 224
Timothy F. [98989], 8
Timothy J. [95376], 15, 50
Timothy T. [94886], 84, 85
Timothy T. [95595], 115
Veronica [92520], 440
Vincent Anthony [100933], 214, 271
Vincent Anthony Jr. [100936], 271
Vincent Curley [106293], 450
Walter A. (Rev.) [102144], 128
Walter Francis [97259], 281
Walter Joseph [103764], 216, 273
Walter Joseph Jr. [103794], 273
Webster B. [104745], 231
William [100079], 137, 153
William [103651], 454
William [105046], 423
William [105208], 448
William [95125], 190
William [99096], 203
William E. [103778], 414
William Edward [102155], 108
William Edward [109675], 14
William H. [107096], 166, 250
William H. [97155], 176
William Henry [110000], 139, 166
William J. [97243], 279
William Michael [106979], 434
Williiam P. [110051], 370
Winifred C. [109679], 47
SWAN
Margaret E. [104608], 168
Robert [104611], 168
TAYLOR
Annette S. 'Nettie' [97256], 229, 280
Frederick [97257], 280
George [107285], 439
James [107286], 439

John [99068], 180
Margaret [105219], 437
Mary T. [99067], 142, 180
TEAHAN
Johannah [105609], 116
TEFFT
Grace D. [97639], 65
THOMAS
Alice A. [109999], 284
THOMSON
James H. [96682], 78
Jessie Patterson [96677], 78
THORNTON
Catherine [102726], 410
THUME
Emilia [107757], 53
THURSTON
Mr. [108856], 148
TINSLEY
Jane [107097], 166, 250
TONGE
Ethel [102530], 122
TOOMEY
Mary [105161], 294
TRAVIS
Agnes [99615], 416
Bridget A. [99610], 415
Elizabeth [99611], 416
Henry [99603], 385, 415
Henry [99606], 415
James [99604], 415
James H. [99612], 416
James H. I [99614], 415
Jeremiah F. [99609], 415
John Thomas [99613], 416
Philip [99607], 416
William J. [99608], 416
TUILL
Mary [108343], 375, 383
TUITE
Annie [106514], 364
TURLEY
Mary E. [97165], 261
TURNER
Elizabeth (Dr.) [102166], 128, 132
TWOMEY
Johanna [96085], 402
TWOOMEY
Johanna [86027], 27
TYNAN
Anna [106892], 368
John [104998], 368
Michael [104996], 345, 368
TYSON

Volume V Name Index

Volume V Name Index